William Leete Stone

The Campaign of Lieut. Gen. John Burgoyne

And the expedition of Lieut. Col. Barry St. Leger

William Leete Stone

The Campaign of Lieut. Gen. John Burgoyne
And the expedition of Lieut. Col. Barry St. Leger

ISBN/EAN: 9783337324537

Printed in Europe, USA, Canada, Australia, Japan

Cover: Foto ©ninafisch / pixelio.de

More available books at **www.hansebooks.com**

THE CAMPAIGN

OF

LIEUT. GEN. JOHN BURGOYNE,

AND

THE EXPEDITION

OF

Lieut. Col. Barry St. Leger.

BY

WILLIAM L. STONE,

Author of the Life and Times of Sir William Johnson Bart., Life and Writings of Col. Wm. L. Stone, Reminiscences of Saratoga and Ballston, Translator of the Memoirs and Military Journals of Mrs. and Major General Riedesel, &c., &c.

ALBANY, N. Y.:
JOEL MUNSELL.
1877.

PART I.

THE CAMPAIGN OF LIEUT. GENERAL JOHN BURGOYNE.

INTRODUCTORY.

NINE miles east of Saratoga Springs, and nearly midway between the villages of Schuylerville and Stillwater, is the site of the Battle of Saratoga or Bemis's heights.[1] It is only within a comparatively short period that the historian has been enabled to write of that event with clearness and accuracy. While authentic materials on the American side are abundant, loose and hurried reports of prisoners taken at the time, and the biased testimony of interested parties, have formed, in a large measure, the basis for a narration of the strategic movements of the English and German troops. Fortunately, these impediments are now removed.

There have recently appeared in Germany, two works of surpassing value, viz: a history of the *German Auxiliary Forces in the War of North American Independence*, and the *Memoirs and Military Journals of Major General Riedesel.*[2]

---

[1] These heights were thus named from a man by the name of Bemis, who kept at this time the only tavern of any note on the river road between Albany and Fort Edward.

[2] Both of these works have been translated into English. The translation of *The Memoirs of General Riedesel* has already been published, by J. Munsell, but that of *The Auxiliaries in America* is still in MS., and in the possession of Mr. T. W. Fields, of Brooklyn, N. Y.

These works, which are made up of some sixty manuscript journals and orderly books, written during the Revolution by Brunswick and Hessian officers, who served here during that time, throw a flood of light upon the period of our national history to which they refer, and especially upon the campaign of General Burgoyne; and while the evidence there presented dissipates in a great measure, the halo which remoteness has thrown around the great generals of that period — blinding us to their deficiencies — yet the errors that have hitherto obtained concerning that campaign are of such a serious nature, as to justify an attempt to place before American readers the plain truth in relation to an event, which in its results was the most important of any in our Revolutionary annals.

In Appendix No. XIX. will be found a list of authorities consulted in the preparation of this work. Many of them, for this purpose, are intrinsically valueless, but, nevertheless, have been given for the benefit of the investigating reader.

WILLIAM L. STONE.

Saratoga Springs, Sept. 1st, 1877.

CONTENTS.

Part I. The Campaign of Lieut. Gen. John Burgoyne, - - - 5
Part II. The Expedition of Lieut. Col. Barry St. Leger, - - - 137
Appendices.
No. I.   Anecdotes of Burgoyne's Campaign, personal reminiscences, etc.,
           by the late Charles Neilson, - - - - - - - - 225
No. II.   Force employed under Lieutenant General Burgoyne in the
           Campaign of 1777, - - - - - - - - - - 275
No. III.   Instructions for Lieutenant Colonel Baum, on a secret expedition
           to the Connecticut river. — Narrative of a Participator in the
           Battle of Bennington. — Description of St. Luke's Bridge. —
           Letter from E. W. B. Canning about Bennington, - 277
No. IV.   The Jane McCrea Tragedy, - - - - - - - 302
No. V.   A Visit to the Battle Ground in 1827, - - - - - 314
No. VI.   Fraser's Remains — probable Origin of the Tradition of their
           having been removed, - - - - - - - - 328
No. VII.   Lady Ackland, - - - - - - - - - - - 331
No. VIII. Statement by Sergeant Lamb of the Royal Welsh Fusileers in
           regard to the Burning of General Schuyler's House and Barns.
           Correspondence between Gates and Burgoyne, - - - 333
No. IX.   Sketch of Fort Edward, - - - - - - - - 338
No. X.   Fight at Diamond Island, - - - - - - - - 346
No. XI.   Alexander Bryan, the Scout, - - - - - - - 353
No. XII.   Sketch of Charles de Langlade, and his relations with Burgoyne, - - - - - - - - - - - - 358
No. XIII. Letter of General Ebenezer Mattoon, a participator in the Battle, with notes by the Author. — Letter from the Duć de la
           Rochefoucauld-Liancourt, - - - - - - - 368
No. XIV.   Professor Silliman's Visit to the Battle Ground in 1820, with
           notes by the Author, - - - - - - - - - 384

Contents.

No. XV.   Sergeant Lamb's Account of his Journey through the woods from Fort Miller to Ticonderoga, to expedite supplies for Burgoyne's Army, - - - - - - - - - -   406

No. XVI. The Ballads of Burgoyne's Campaign, - - - - -   413

No. XVII. Description of Ticonderoga and the Forts south of it at the Time of their occupation by the Americans in the year 1777. From the Military Journal of Maj. Gen. Riedesel, -   434

No. XVIII. The Saratoga Monument Association, - - - - -   438

No. XIX. List of Authorities consulted in the preparation of this Work, - - - - - - - - - - - - -   445

ITINERARY OF GEN. BURGOYNE.

THE ADVANCE.

General Burgoyne arrives at Quebec, - - - 6th May, 1777.
Receives the command of the Army from Gen.
   Carleton, at Quebec, - - - - - - - 10th "
Montreal, - - - - - - - - - - - 12th "
Three Rivers, - - - - - - - - - - 15th " —7th June.
Fort Chambly, - - - - - - - - - 10th June — 14th "
Isle Au Noix, - - - - - - - - - - 15th "
Cumberland Head, - - - - - - - - 17th — 20th June.
River Bouquet, - - - - - - - - - 21st — 28th "
Crown Point, - - - - - - - - - 29th — 30th "
Four Mile Point, - - - - - - - - 1st July.
Ticonderoga, - - - - - - - - - 1st — 6th July.
Skenesborough (Whitehall), - - - - - - 7th — 23d "
Fort Anne, - - - - - - - - - - 25th — 28th "
Pitch-Pine Plains, - - - - - - - - 29th July.
Fort Edward, - - - - - - - - - 30th July — 13th Aug.
Duer's House (Fort Miller), - - - - - - 14th Aug. — 10th Sept.
Batten kil, - - - - - - - - - - 11th to 13th Sept.
Schuyler's House (Saratoga), - - - - - - 13th — 15th "
Dovegat, - - - - - - - - - - - 16th "
Sword's House, - - - - - - - - - 17th — 18th "
Freeman's House, on the Field of Battle, - 19th "
Freeman's House, - - - - - - - - 20th "
Camp on Freeman's Farm, - - - - - - 21st Sept. — 7th Oct.

THE RETREAT.

Wilbur's Basin, near the Redoubts at the River, 8th Oct.
Dovegat, - - - - - - - - - - - 9th — 10th Oct.

Saratoga, - - - - - - - - - - 10th — 17th Oct.
Half Moon, - - - - - - - - - - 18th   "
Albany, - - - - - - - - - - - 18th — 20th "
Worcester, Mass., - - - - - - - - 4th Nov.
Marlborough, "   - - - - - - - - - 5th   "
Cambridge,   "   - - - - - - - - - 7th   "
Embarks for England, - - - - - - - 15th April, 1778.

ERRATA.

On page 33, 4th line from top, for *"on* the bridge" read *"beyond* the bridge."
"   "   237 (note), for "*ten* miles" read "*four* miles."
"   "   347, 1st line, for "Col. *Baum's*" read "Col. *Brown's*."

Saratoga, - - - - - - - - - - - 10th — 17th Oct.
Half Moon, - - - - - - - - - - 18th   "
Albany, - - - - - - - - - - - - 18th — 20th "
Worcester, Mass., - - - - - - - - 4th Nov.
Marlborough, "   - - - - - - - - - 5th   "
Cambridge,   "   - - - - - - - - - 7th   "
Embarks for England, - - - - - - - 15th April, 1778.

ERRATA.

On page 33, 4th line from top, for "*on* the bridge" read "*beyond* the bridge."
"   " 237 (note), for "*ten* miles" read "*four* miles."
"   " 347, 1st line, for "Col. *Baum's*" read "Col. *Brown's*."

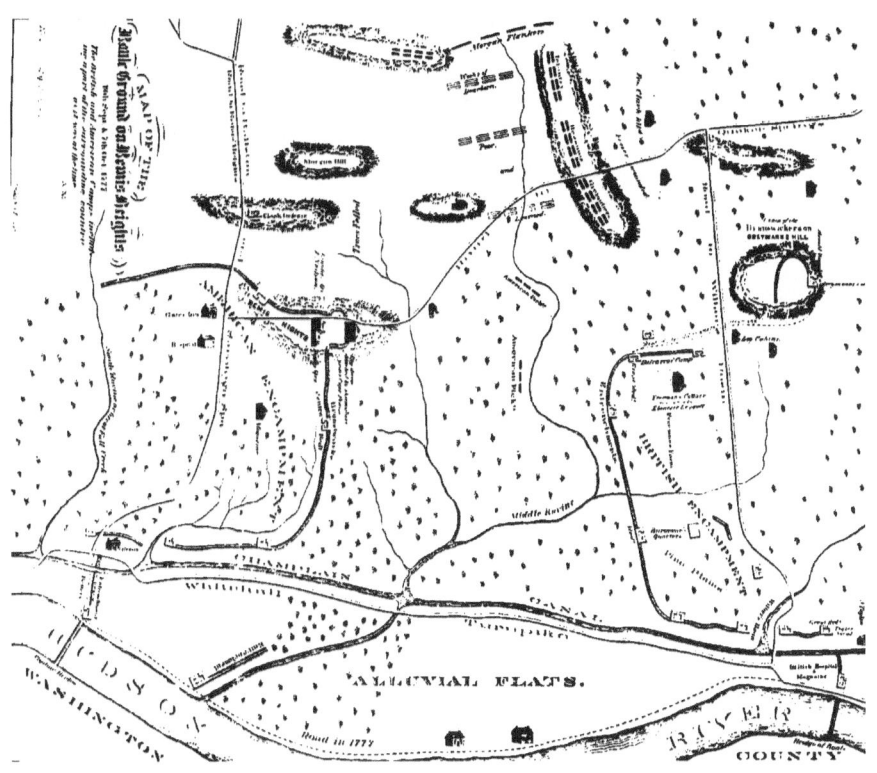

1

S
H
A
W
N
C
E

O
'
'

BURGOYNE'S CAMPAIGN.

I.

THE disastrous result of the campaign of General Burgoyne is to be ascribed more to his own blunders and incompetency than to any special military skill on the part of his conqueror. In December, 1776, Burgoyne, dissatisfied with his subordinate position under Carleton, concocted with the British ministry a plan for the campaign of 1777. A large force under himself was to proceed to Albany by way of Lakes Champlain and George; while another large body, under Sir Henry Clinton, advanced up the Hudson in order to cut off communication between the northern and southern colonies, in the expectation that each section being left to itself would be subdued with little difficulty. At the same time, Colonel Barry St. Leger was to make a diversion on the Mohawk river.

For the accomplishment of the first part of this plan, a powerful force was organized in Canada, the command of which was transferred from Sir Guy Carleton — the ablest British general, by the way, at that time or subsequently in America — and conferred upon General Burgoyne — an army which, for thoroughness of discipline, and completeness of appointment had never been excelled in America.[1] The generals, also, who were to second him in the expedition were trustworthy and able officers. Major General Phillips was not only distinguished as an artillery officer, but had given proof of exceptional strategical skill; Major General Riedesel had been specially selected for his military experience, acquired during a long service, and particularly during the seven years' war, where he had enjoyed the entire confidence of Prince Ferdinand. The English Brigadiers Fraser and Hamilton, and the German ones, Specht, and Gall and Lieut. Col. Breymann, had been appointed to commands solely on the ground of their professional merits. The former had attained a high reputation for judgment and cool daring, and was considered one of the most promising officers in the army. Colonel Kingston, the adjutant-general, had served with distinction in Burgoyne's horse in Portugal, and Majors Lord Balcarras,

---

[1] Burgoyne arrived in Quebec on the 6th of May, 1777, and received the command of the forces from General Carleton on the 10th. General Riedesel, however, with his Brunswick Contingent, had been in Canada for fully a year — during which time, he, with the practical strategy and acuteness of observation which always distinguished him, had employed that time in drilling his troops to meet the customs of the Americans. "Thus," he says in one of his letters, "I perceived that the American riflemen always shot further than our forces — consequently I made my men practice at long range and behind trees that they might at least be enough for them." Speaking of the removal of Carleton at this juncture, Riedesel further says: "a great mistake was undoubtedly here made by the British ministry. Carleton had, hitherto, worked with energy and success; he knew the army thoroughly, and enjoyed the confidence of the officers and men. It was a great risk to remove a man, who was so peculiarly fitted for so important a position, without a better cause."

Campaign of General John Burgoyne. 11

and Ackland, commanding respectively the light infantry and grenadiers, were each, in his own way, considered officers of high professional attainments and brilliant courage.[1]

All things being in readiness, Burgoyne, in the early summer of 1777, sailed up Lake Champlain; and, on the 17th of June encamped on the western shore of that lake at the falls of the little river Bouquet, now Willsborough. At this place he was joined by about four hundred Indians, under the Chevalier St. Luc and Charles De Langlade,[2] whom, in a council and war feast called and given specially for the purpose, he addressed in a speech designedly couched in their own

---

[1] Fonblanque's *Life of Burgoyne*. For the detailed return of the troops (English and German) employed on the expedition (compiled at considerable labor by Mr. Fonblanque), and also for remarks on the question of the employment of Germans by the English government, see Appendix No. II.

[2] Thomas Anburey, an officer in the army of General Burgoyne, wrote in 1777 from the borders of Lake Champlain: "We are expecting the Ottawas. They are led by M. de Saint Luc and M. de Langlade, both great partisans of the French cause in the last war; *the latter is the person who, at the head of the tribe which he now commands planned and executed the defeat of General Braddock.*"

Burgoyne, the unfortunate commander of the aforesaid army, expressed himself in a no less formal manner, in a letter to Lord George Germain, dated Skenesborough, July the eleventh, 1777: "I am informed," says he, "that the Ottawas and other Indian tribes, who are two days' march from us, are brave and faithful, and that they practice war and not pillage. They are under the orders of a M. Saint Luc, a Canadian of merit, and one of the best partisans of the French cause during the last war, and of a M. de Langlade, the very man who with these tribes projected and executed Braddock's defeat. See Appendix XII, for a further account of Langlade's connection with Burgoyne and the latter's relations with his Indian allies.

figurative language, and intended both to excite their ardor in the approaching campaign, and "to inculcate those humane principles of civilized warfare which to them must have been incomprehensible." On the 30th of June, the main army made a still further advance and occupied Crown point[1] (Fort St. Frederick), while General Fraser pushed ahead as far as Putnam's creek, three miles north of Ticonderoga. In the evening the following orders were given : " The army embarks to-morrow to approach the enemy. The services required on this expedition are critical and conspicuous. During our progress occasions may occur in which nor difficulty, nor labor, nor life are to be regarded. This army must not retreat." Then, having issued a grandiloquent proclamation designed to terrify the inhabitants of the sur-

---

[1] Called *Kruyn*, or *Kroon punt* (or *Scalp point*), by the Dutch; and by the French, *Point a la Chevelcure*. The ramparts of this fortress, which are still standing, are of wood and earth riveted with solid masonry. They are twenty-four feet high, twenty-five thick, and inclose an area of fifteen hundred yards square, surrounded by a deep, broad moat, cut into granite. There are, also, a double row of stone barracks; and on the north, a gate with a draw-bridge, together with a subterranean or covered passage leading from one of the bastions to the bank of the lake. The size and extent of these works render their exploration very satisfactory and instructive. The promontory which juts out from the farther shore directly opposite Crown point and on which Gen. Riedesel was encamped for a day or two, is called Chimney point. When Fort Frederick was built, in 1731, a French settlement of considerable size was begun at this place. During the old French war, however, it was destroyed by a party of Mohawk Indians, who burned the wood-work of the houses, leaving the stone chimneys standing. For many years afterwards these stood, like solitary and grim sentinels, watching over the ruins. Hence the name.

Campaign of General John Burgoyne. 13

rounding country into submission, Burgoyne prepared to invest Ticonderoga.

Leaving a detachment of one staff officer and two hundred men at Crown point for the defence of the magazines, the royal army in their bateaux started again at five o'clock in the morning of July 1st, in two divisions. The corps of General Phillips was on the west and that of General Riedesel on the east side of the lake. The Dragoons formed the van of the whole army. The fleet advanced as far as Putnam's creek almost within cannon shot of the Americans. The right wing of the army encamped on the spot recently occupied by the brigade of Fraser (that officer having again gone ahead), and the left wing under Riedesel occupied the eastern shore opposite the right wing. The corps of General Breymann advanced on the same shore as far as the left wing of the fleet, from the flag-ship of which, the Royal George, the American position could easily be seen. The garrison of Ticonderoga was estimated at from four to five thousand men, and consisted of twelve regiments divided into four brigades commanded by General St. Clair. Its position was covered on the right flank by Fort Independence, a star-fort built on a considerable eminence, on the east shore of Lake Champlain and fortified by three successive lines of fortifications. It was separated by water from Ticonderoga which lay on the opposite side and consisted chiefly of the old French works.[1] In the lake between the two forts lay four

---

[1] Ticonderoga (called by the French respectively Fort Vaudreuil — after an early Canadian governor — and Fort Carillon) is situated fifteen miles

armed vessels, and both were connected by a bridge. In front of this bridge there was a strong iron chain hanging across the water, which was intended to break the first assault of the British. To the left of Ticonderoga there was another fortification upon a hill covering the enemy's left toward the saw-mills on the portage between Lake Champlain and Lake George. Ticonderoga was garrisoned by one-half of the American force, or two brigades; the third brigade was at Fort Independence, and the fourth was distributed in the entrenchments outside of the fort. This was the position of the Americans when General Burgoyne arrived in front of Ticonderoga.

At noon of the 2d of July, Fraser moved forward, and taking possession of some high ground which commanded the American line and cut off their communication with Lake George, named it Mount Hope, in

---

south of Crown point and thirty north of Whitehall. It is formed by a sharp angle in the narrow waters of the lake, and an arm of that lake stretching to the westward which receives the waters of Lake George at the foot of a precipitous fall of some twenty feet. The stream which connects these lakes makes a considerable curvature to the west, and in the distance of two miles tumbles over successive layers of rocks about 300 feet — the difference of the level between the surface of Lake George and that of Lake Champlain, furnishing a variety of excellent mill-sites, accessible to the navigable waters of Lake George forty miles, and to those of Lake Champlain and the river Sorel 130 miles. This position was fortified by the French long before the war of 1755. It is rendered famous by the repulse of Abercrombie by Montcalm in 1758 with the loss of 2000 men, although he might, by taking possession of Mt. Defiance (Sugar-loaf hill) have carried the place without hazarding a man.

Campaign of General John Burgoyne. 15

anticipation of victory.[1] At the same time, Phillips moved more to the right and occupied the saw-mills.[1] Riedesel likewise advanced with Breymann's corps and took up a position in front of Fort Independence behind the stream, Petite Marie. Meanwhile, unfortunately for the Americans, their engineers had overlooked the high peak or mountain, called Sugar-loaf hill (Mount Defiance), situated south of the bridge on the point of land at the

---

[1] In the beginning of this skirmish Lord Balcarras, who commanded the light-infantry, had his coat and trousers pierced with thirty balls, and escaped with a slight wound; while at the same time, Lieut. Haggit received a mortal wound in both eyes by a ball, and Lieut. Douglass of the 29th, while being carried wounded off the field, was shot through the heart by a sharp-shooter.

Mount Hope is thus described by Wilkinson: "When the French officer [Montcalm] who commanded at Ticonderoga in 1758, heard of Abercrombie's approach, he found it necessary to take possession of an elevated ridge on the direct route to it from the landing at Lake George, which, at less than half a mile entirely overlooked the works. This ridge is flat on the summit and extends westwardly about half a mile to the saw-mills at the perpendicular fall at the outlet of Lake George where it terminates in still higher ground called Mount Hope. On the south it presents a bold declivity washed by the strait, and on the north it declines until it sinks into a plain which is extended about one hundred rods to the shore of the lake where the bank is ten or twelve feet high." It was here that Abercrombie suffered so disastrous a repulse.

[2] On the approach of Gen. Fraser, the Americans, most unaccountably, immediately abandoned all their works in the direction of Lake George, setting fire to the block-houses and saw-mills; and without sally or other interruption, permitted the enemy under Maj. Gen. Phillips, to take possession of the very advantageous post of Mount Hope, which besides commanding their lines in a dangerous degree, totally cut off their communication with Lake George. The only excuse for such an early abandonment of this important point, was found in the fact that General St. Clair had not force enough to man all the defences."— *Stone's Brant.*

confluence of the waters of Lakes George and Champlain. Originally it had been supposed and taken for granted, that the crest of Sugar-loaf hill was not only inaccessible, but too distant to be of any avail in covering the main fortress. This opinion was an error, to which the attention of the officers had been called the preceding year by Colonel John Trumbull, then adjutant general for the Northern department. When Colonel Trumbull made the suggestion, he was laughed at by the mess; but he soon proved the accuracy of his own vision, by throwing a cannon-shot to the summit; and subsequently clambered up to the top, accompanied by Colonels Stevens, Wayne and Arnold.[1] It was a criminal neglect, on the part of the Americans, that the oversight was not at once corrected, by the construction of a work upon that point, which would have commanded the whole post. It was a neglect,* however, that was soon to cost them dear. While the maneuvers of Fraser and Phillips, above described, were executing, Lieutenant Twiss made a thorough personal examination of Sugar-loaf hill, and reported that the hill " completely commanded the works and buildings both at Ticonderoga and Fort Independence; that it was distant about 1400 yards from the former and 1500 from the latter; that the ground might be levelled so as to receive cannon ; and that a road to convey them, though extremely difficult, might be built in twenty-four hours. Accordingly, as soon as darkness had set in, a

---

[1] Conversations of the author's father with Col. John Trumbull.

Campaign of General John Burgoyne.

winding road was cut to its summit, a battery commenced and cannon to serve it transported thither. In fact, so expeditiously was the work carried forward under Phillips,[1] that the garrison of Ticonderoga, on awaking the next morning found to their amazement and dismay that from the crags seven hundred feet above, the British were coolly looking down upon them, watching their every movement, and only waiting for the completion of their batteries to open fire. In this critical situation, St. Clair at once called a council of war, which unanimously decided on an immediate evacuation. It was also determined that the baggage of the army, with such artillery, stores and provisions as the necessity of the occasion would admit, should be embarked with a strong detachment on board of two hundred bateaux, and dispatched under convoy of five armed galleys, up the lake to Skenesborough (Whitehall), and that the main body of the army should proceed by land, taking its route on the road to Castleton in Vermont, which was about thirty miles south-east of Ticonderoga, and join the boats and galleys at Skenesborough. Absolute secrecy was also enjoined. Accordingly, early in the evening, Colonel Long, with five armed galleys and six hundred men, set out with the sick and wounded for Skenesborough; and a few hours later, about two o'clock in the morning of July 6th, St. Clair with the

---

[1] " General Phillips has as expeditiously conveyed cannon to the summit of this hill [Mount Defiance], as he brought it up in that memorable battle at Minden, where, it is said, such was his anxiousness in expediting the artillery, that he split no less than fifteen canes in beating the horses."—*Anburey's Letters.*

main body of the troops passed over the floating bridge in safety, and probably would have effected his retreat wholly undiscovered, had not the head-quarters of General Roche De Fermoy, who commanded Fort Independence, either through accident or treachery, been set on fire.[1] This unfortunate occurrence threw the Americans into disorder, and informed the British of the retreat. At early daylight, Riedesel embarked his men and took possession of Fort Independence ; at the same time that Fraser occupied Ticonderoga. Eighty large cannon, five thousand tons of flour, a great quantity of meat and provisions, fifteen stands of arms, a large amount of ammunition, and two hundred oxen, besides baggage and tents, were found in the deserted forts.

There would seem to have been no necessity for this stampede. The camps of the Americans were not surrounded — on the contrary the road to Vermont was still open — and the batteries of the assailants were not yet in position. "Great fright and consternation," says General Riedesel in his journal, "must have prevailed in the enemy's camp, otherwise they would have taken time to destroy the stores and save something."[2]

---

[1] It is a somewhat singular fact, says General J. Watts De Peyster, that generally whenever the Americans were unsuccessful a foreigner was mixed up in it. A little thought on the part of the reader will confirm the truth of this observation.

[2] And yet, St. Clair's retreat was by no means so disorderly as some have represented it. Lamb, who was a conscientious and shrewd observer, speaking of this says : "After the enemy retreated we marched down to the works, and were obliged to halt at the bridge of communication which had been broken down. In passing the bridge and possessing ourselves of the

Campaign of General John Burgoyne.

The news of the fall of Ticonderoga was received in England with every demonstration of joy. The king rushed into the queen's apartment, crying "I have beat them, I have beat all the Americans;" and "Lord George Germaine announced the event in parliament as if it had been decisive of the campaign and of the fate of the colonies."

II.

In the retreat from Fort Ticonderoga, Colonel Francis succeeded in bringing off the rear guard in a regular manner. When the troops arrived at Hubbardton, in Vermont, they were halted for nearly two hours, and the rear guard was increased by many who did not at first belong to it, but were picked up on the road, having been unable to keep up with their regiments. The rear guard was here put under the command of Col. Seth Warner, with *strict orders* to follow the army, as soon as the whole came up, and to halt a mile and a half short of the main body. The army under St. Clair, then proceeded to Castleton, about six miles

---

works we found four men lying intoxicated with drinking, who had been left to fire the guns of a large battery on our approach. Had the men obeyed the commands they received, we must have suffered great injury; but they were allured by the opportunity of a cask of madeira to forget their instructions, and drown their cares in wine. It appeared evident they were left for the purpose alluded to, as matches were found lighted, the ground was strewed with powder, and the heads of some powder-casks were knocked off in order, no doubt, to injure our men on their gaining the works. An Indian had like to do some mischief from his curiosity — holding a lighted match near one of the guns, it exploded, but being elevated, it discharged without harm."

further — Col. Warner, with the rear guard and the stragglers, against the express orders of his commanding general, remaining at Hubbardton.[1]

The retreat of the Americans from Ticonderoga and Mount Independence, was no sooner perceived by the British, than Gen. Fraser began an eager pursuit with his brigade, Major-General Riedesel being ordered to follow with the greater part of his Brunswickers. Fraser continued the pursuit through the day, and having received intelligence that the rear-guard of the American army was at no great distance, ordered his men to lie that night upon their arms. On the 7th July, at five o'clock in the morning, he came up with Colonel Warner; who had about one thousand men. The British advanced boldly to the attack, and the two bodies formed within sixty yards of each other. The conflict was fierce and bloody. Colonel Francis fell at the head of his regiment while fighting with great gallantry, and after the action, was buried by the Brunswick troops.[2] Colonel Warner

---

[1] "Col. Warner was a hardy, valiant soldier, but uneducated and a stranger to military discipline; his insubordination at Hubbardton, exemplifies the danger and misfortunes which attend the disobedience of military commands; for, if he had obeyed the orders he received, our corps would have been united, and as the discipline of the enemy could have availed them little in a mountainous country covered with wood, we should infallibly have dismembered, and probably captured, the flower of the British army."— *Wilkinson's Memoirs.*

[2] Speaking of the death of Col. Francis, Lamb says: "The nature of hostilities on the American continent acquired a sort of implacable ardor and revenge, which happily are a good deal unknown in the prosecution of war in general. This remark is justified by the fate of Capt. Shrimpton, of the 62d, after the battle [Hubbardton] just mentioned. Some of our

Campaign of General John Burgoyne. 21

was so well supported by his officers and men, that the assailants broke and gave way. They soon, however, recovered from their disorder, reformed, and charged the Americans with the bayonet, who, in turn, began to waver. The latter, however, again rallied, and returning to the charge, the issue of the battle hung in the balance, when at this critical juncture General Riedesel appeared, with his Brunswickers. He saw at a glance that the Americans were moving more and more to the right with the evident intention of surrounding Fraser's left wing. He therefore resolved to out maneuver them, if possible, and gain their rear. Accordingly, he ordered a company of yägers to advance to the attack, while the rest of the troops were to endeavor to fall upon the rear of the Americans. In order, moreover, to make them believe that their assailants were stronger than they really were, he ordered a band of music to precede the yägers. At this moment, an aid arrived with a message from Fraser to the effect that he feared his left wing would be surrounded. Riedesel sent word back to him to keep up courage for that he was, at that very instant, about to attack the enemy's right wing. Accordingly, at the word, Riedesel's yägers, chaunting their national hymns, advanced courageously upon the Americans, and were met by a brisk fire from four hundred

---

officers stood examining papers taken from the pocket of Col. Francis on the field. As the captain held the papers he leaped and exclaimed that he was badly wounded. The officers heard the whizzing of the ball, and saw the smoke of the fire, but failed to find the man who aimed with such effect, and who escaped without seizure or even being seen."

men. Far, however, from shrinking, the Brunswickers pressed on so vigorously that the Americans seeing themselves almost surrounded, stopped fighting and retreated, leaving behind them twelve pieces of artillery. The victory, however, had not been easily won. General Fraser acknowledged that he would have been in great danger had it not been for Riedesel's timely aid; since if reinforcements had not arrived at the very moment they did, his whole corps would have been surrounded and cut off to a man.

The loss in this action was severe on both sides. Colonel Hale, who, on account of illness, had not brought his regiment into action, fell in with a small party of the British, and, with a number of his men, all raw militia, was captured.[1] In killed, wounded and prisoners, the Americans lost in this action three hundred and twenty-four men, and the British, one hundred and

---

[1] Col. Nathan Hale (the grandfather of Hon. Robert S. Hale, M.C. of Elizabethtown, Essex Co., N. Y.), who was in this battle was charged, at the time, by personal enemies, not only with cowardice, but also with treasonable communication with Burgoyne while a prisoner. The matter was thoroughly investigated, and both charges found without a shadow in evidence to sustain it. Indeed, I have now before me a certificate in Burgoyne's own handwriting (who, although he may not have been a great general, yet certainly was a man of honor), in which he certifies "on his honor as a gentleman and a soldier," that Col. Hale has never communicated to him any improper information, and further, that no conversation, even, has passed between them, "except the ordinary dinner table courtesies between gentlemen." Poor Hale died a prisoner at the age of thirty-seven, and never had the opportunity, which he earnestly sought, to vindicate himself by court martial.

eighty-three — among whom was Maj. Grant, of the grenadiers, a most excellent and brave officer.

While these events were taking place upon the land, General Burgoyne was pursuing the enemy upon the water. In a few hours he destroyed the boom and bridge which had been constructed in front of Ticonderoga, and which had been the work of months to complete; and by a few well directed cannon shots, he broke in two the colossal chain upon which so many hopes had hung. The passage being cleared, the fleet of Burgoyne immediately entered Wood creek, and favored by a brisk wind, came up with the American flotilla at Skenesborough, in the afternoon. Meanwhile, three regiments, which had landed at South bay, crossed a mountain with great celerity, with the object of turning the Americans above Wood creek, and destroying their works at Skenesborough, thus cutting off their retreat to Fort Anne. The Americans, however, eluded this stroke by the rapidity of their flight, but in the meantime the British frigates having now come up, the galleys, already hard pushed by the gun boats, were completely overpowered. Two of them surrendered, and three were blown up. The Americans now despaired, and having set fire to their works, mills and bateaux, and otherwise destroyed what they were unable to burn, the detachment, under Colonel Long, hastily retreated by way of Wood creek to Fort Anne.

Meanwhile, General St. Clair, who had arrived with the van-guard at Castleton, in Vermont, upon learning of the discomfiture at Hubbardton and the disaster at Skenesborough, and apprehensive that he would be interrupted if he proceeded toward Fort Anne, struck into the woods, uncertain whether he should repair to New England or Fort Edward. Being joined, however, two days afterward at Manchester, by the remains of the corps of Colonel Warner, he proceeded to Fort Edward and united with the force of General Schuyler.

As soon as Burgoyne had taken possession of Skenesborough, he detached Lieutenant Colonel Hill, with the 9th regiment, to Fort Anne, with the view both of intercepting such of the enemy as should attempt to retreat to that fort, and of increasing the panic produced by the fall of Ticonderoga. This detachment had not proceeded many miles through the woods, before it overtook some boats laden with baggage, women and invalids belonging to the enemy, moving up Wood creek in order to escape to Fort Anne. These were at once secured. Arriving within a quarter of a mile of the fort, Col. Hill learned through an American deserter (in reality a spy) that it was strongly garrisoned; and although he had with him five hundred and forty-three veterans, he at once halted in a strong position, and sending back a messenger to Burgoyne for reinforcements, lay that night upon his arms.

Meanwhile, Colonels Long and Van Rensselaer, who, by the direction of Schuyler, with five hundred men — many of them convalescents — had taken post at Fort Anne, were not persons to await an attack.[1] Learning

---

[1] When Ticonderoga was abandoned by the Americans, Gen. Schuyler requested Gen. Washington to send Col. Henry Van Rensselaer to the

Campaign of General John Burgoyne. 25

from the spy before mentioned, who had returned, the strength of the British, they determined to force an engagement before Burgoyne should be able to assist Col. Hill. Accordingly, early the following morning (July 8th), Long suddenly issued from the fort and attacked the English in front ; while, at the same time, a strong column under Van Rensselaer crossed the creek, and, taking advantage of a thick wood, passed nearly round the left flank of the British, and, in the language of a participator in the action, "poured down upon them like a mighty torrent." This, accompanied by a tremendous

---

Northern army. The First New York regiment, with a park of brass artillery, was at Fort George. To save it was all-important to the American cause. Col. Van Rensselaer was directed to pick out of the militia then at Fort George four hundred volunteers, and stop the British advance at a defile near Fort Anne at all hazards, until he could remove the stores, etc., from Fort George. How far he executed this order, and the good effect it had in rallying a new army, will be found in *Burgoyne's Trial, Wilkinson's Memoirs*, etc. In this affair he was so grievously wounded, as to disqualify him from taking rank in the line, and he became a cripple for life. The ball, which entered the upper part of the thigh bone, was extracted after his death, quite flattened.

Whatever prejudice afterward existed against the manor influence, in the counties of Albany and Rensselaer, it was fortunate for the American cause that it existed, and was exerted with all its energy at the dawn of the Revolution, to give impulse to its progress. Whilst some other manors held back until after the surrender of Burgoyne, the upper and lower manors of the Van Rensselaers struck at once for American freedom; and by so doing enlisted in its cause all its numerous connections of blood, marriage and dependence; and this produced a counterpoise to the numerous and powerful tory families residing in those frontier counties. The Van Rensselaers, in 1776, consisted of eighteen males. During the struggle every adult except two old men, and all minors except four boys, bore arms at one or more battles, during its progress.

and well directed fire of small arms,[1] compelled Col. Hill, in order to avoid being completely surrounded, to take post on the top of a hill. No sooner, however, had he taken up this position, than the Americans reformed and attacked it so vigorously, in an engagement which lasted for more than two hours, that he must soon have surrendered, had not the ammunition of the Americans given out — a misfortune, moreover, which was increased by the arrival, at this critical time most opportunely for the British, of a party of Indians, under Colonel Money, who with the war-whoop, dashed in, and forced the Americans, in their turn, to give way. Colonel Long, thereupon, not being able to withstand the force of Major General Phillips, who with the 20th regiment consisting of five hundred and twenty men and two pieces of artillery, was pressing forward to the assistance of Hill, fired the fort, and with the remnants of his spartan band fell back on Fort Edward.

General Phillips, learning upon his arrival, that the enemy had retired, immediately marched back to Skenesborough, leaving behind a sergeant and a small guard to take care of the wounded.[2] On the 13th the Americans reoccupied the site of the fort.

---

[1] Deputy Quartermaster-General Money said that the Americans' fire was heavier at Fort Anne than on any other occasion during the campaign, except in the action of the 19th September.

[2] *Journal of Occurrences during the late American war, to the year* 1783, by R. Lamb, sergeant in the Royal Welsh fusileers, Dublin, 1809. Mr. Lamb, who is the one referred to in the text as a "participator in the action," and who was the sergeant left in charge of the wounded, was evidently a man of education and intelligence. He gives a graphic account of the action at Fort Anne, and says:

Campaign of General John Burgoyne. 27

General Burgoyne, in accordance with his usual policy, claimed a victory in this affair, a claim which was not justified by the facts. He certainly did not retain possession of the battlefield; and not only does General Riedesel state, in his journal, "that the English, after a long fight at Fort Anne were forced to retreat," but the British abandoned Captain Montgomery — a brother-in-law of Lord Townshend and a wounded officer of great merit — a surgeon and other prisoners, when — in the language of Burgoyne in describing this action to Lord Germaine — they "changed ground." This scarcely reads like a victory.[1]

"It was a distressing sight to see the wounded men bleeding on the ground, and what made it more so, the rain came pouring down like a deluge upon us; and still to add to the distress of the sufferers, there was nothing to dress their wounds, as the small medicine box which was filled with salve, was left behind with Sergeant Sheily and Captain Montgomery at the time of our movement up the hill. The poor fellows earnestly entreated me to tie up their wounds. Immediately I took off my shirt, tore it up, and with the help of a soldier's wife (the only woman that was with us, and who also kept close by her husband's side during the engagement), made some bandages, stopped the bleeding of their wounds, and conveyed them in blankets to a small hut about two miles in our rear. . . . Our regiment now marched back to Skenesborough, leaving me behind to attend to the wounded with a small guard for our protection. I was directed that, in case I was either surrounded or overpowered by the Americans, to deliver a letter, which General Burgoyne gave me, to their commanding officer. There I remained seven days with the wounded men, expecting every moment to be taken prisoners, but although we heard the enemy cutting trees every night during our stay, in order to block up the passages of the road and the river, we were never molested."

[1] To enable the reader of the present day to have a clear idea of the scene of this action, the following is given from *Neilson*: "On leaving the street of Fort Anne village, there is a bridge over Wood creek, leading to

Up to the time of Burgoyne's occupying Skenesborough, all had gone well. From that point, however, his fortunes began to wane. His true course would have been to return to Ticonderoga, and thence up Lake George to the fort of that name, whence there was a direct road to Fort Edward;[1] instead of which he determined to push on to Fort Anne and Fort Edward, a course which gave Schuyler ample time to gather the yeomanry together, and effectually oppose his progress.

---

its left bank. Immediately beyond the bridge there is a narrow pass, only wide enough for a carriage, and cut in a great measure, out of a rocky ledge, which terminates here exactly at the creek. This ledge is the southern end of a high rocky hill, which converges towards Wood creek, and between the two is a narrow tract of level ground, which terminates at the pass already mentioned. On this ground the battle took place, and the wood on the right bank of the creek, from which the Americans fired upon the left flank of the British, is still there, and it was up this rocky hill that they retreated and took their stand."

[1] The excuse which Burgoyne gives for not going round by Lake George, "that the fort there (Fort George) would have detained him, is not adequate, for it would have offered no opposition whatever; Fort George, as Schuyler very truly replied to Washington as a reason for abandoning it at this time, " was part of an unfinished bastion of an intended fortification. In it was a barrack capable of containing between thirty and fifty men; without ditch, without wall, without cistern, and without any picket to prevent an enemy from running over the wall. So small, as not to contain above one hundred and fifty men, and commanded by ground greatly overlooking it, and within point blank shot; and so situated that five hundred men may lie between the bastion and the lake, without being seen from this *extremely* defensible fortress." Neither, however, do we give credence to the report current at the time that Burgoyne chose the route to Fort Anne in order to oblige his friend Major Skene — a large landholder in that region — by giving him the use of his troops to open for him a road to the river. Burgoyne, whatever else his faults, was an honorable man. He probably simply erred in judgment.

Campaign of General John Burgoyne. 29

The country between Fort Anne and Fort Edward, a distance of about sixteen miles, was extremely rough and savage; the ground unequal and broken up by numerous roads and creeks interspersed by wide and deep swamps. General Schuyler neglected no means of adding by art to the difficulties with which nature seemed to have purposely interdicted this passage. Trenches were opened; the roads and paths obstructed; large rocks thrown into Wood creek, the bridges broken up; and, in the only practicable defiles, immense trees were cut in such a manner on both sides of the road, as to fall across and lengthwise, which with their branches interlocked presented an insurmountable barrier. In fact, this wilderness, in itself so horrible, was rendered almost impenetrable. Burgoyne, consequently, was compelled not only to remove all these obstructions, but to build more than forty bridges — one particularly, over a morass of more than two miles in length. Nor was this all. On his arrival at Fort Anne[1] instead of advancing at once upon Fort Edward and thence to Albany before Schuyler had time to concentrate his forces in his front, he sent a detachment of Brunswickers, under Colonel Baum, to Bennington to surprise and capture some stores which he had heard were at that place, and of which he stood sorely in need. He was also influenced to this step by the advice of his friend Major Skene, who assured him that large numbers of the yoemanry of the

---

[1] It was while Burgoyne was at Fort Anne that the accidental shooting of Jane McCrea by the garrison of Fort Edward occurred. For a true history of this affair see Appendix No. IV.

country would flock to his standard — an expectation which the event proved to be entirely fallacious.

General Riedesel, who commanded the German allies, was totally opposed to this diversion, but being overruled, he proposed that Baum should march in the rear of the enemy, by way of Castleton, toward the Connecticut river. Had this plan been adopted, the probability is, that the Americans would not have had time to prevent Baum from falling unawares upon their rear. Burgoyne however, against the advice of Riedesel and Phillips, insisted obstinately on his plan, which was that Baum should cross the Batten kil opposite Saratoga, move down the Connecticut river in a direct line to Bennington, destroy the magazine at that place, and mount the Brunswick dragoons, who were destined to form part of the expedition.[1] In this latter order a fatal blunder was committed by employing troops, the most awkward and heavy in an enterprise where everything depended on the greatest celerity of movement, while the *rangers* who were lightly equipped, were left behind!

Let us look for a moment at a fully equipped Brunswick dragoon as he appeared at that time. He wore high and heavy jack boots, with large long spurs, stout and stiff leather breeches, gauntlets, reaching high up upon his arms, and a hat with a huge tuft of ornamental feathers. On his side he trailed a tremendous broad sword; a short but clumsy carbine was slung over his shoulder; and down his back like a Chinese mandarin, dangled a long

---

[1] And yet General Riedesel states that 1500 horses had been purchased in Canada as early as the middle of June, for the army. What became of them?

queue. Such were the troops sent out by the British general, on a service requiring the lightest of light skirmishers. The latter however, did not err from ignorance. From the beginning of the campaign the English officers had ridiculed these unwieldy troopers, who strolled about the camp with their heavy sabres dragging on the ground, saying (what was a fact) that the hat and sword of one of them were as heavy as the whole of an English private's equipment. But, as if this was not sufficient, these *light* dragoons were still further cumbered by being obliged to carry flour, and drive a herd of cattle before them for their maintenance on the way.

The result may be easily foreseen. By a rapid movement of the Americans under Stark, at three o'clock of the afternoon of the 16th of August, Baum was cut off from his English allies, who fled and left him to fight alone, with his awkwardly equipped squad, an enemy far superior in numbers. In this maneuver Stark was greatly aided by a ruse practiced on the German colonel. "Toward 9 o'clock on the morning of the 16th," writes General Riedesel, in giving an account of this action, "small bodies of armed men made their appearance from different directions. These men were mostly in their shirt sleeves. They did not act as if they intended to make an attack; and Baum, being told by a provincial who had joined his army on the line of march, that they were all loyalists and would make common cause with him, suffered them to encamp on his sides and rear.[1]

---

[1] This confidence, perhaps, was the first and chief false step which caused the defeat of Bennington, and consequently the failure of Burgoyne. This is an entirely new revelation.

Shortly after another force of the rebels arrived and attacked his rear; but with the aid of artillery, they were repulsed. After a little while a stronger body made their appearance and attacked more vigorously. This was the signal for the seeming loyalists, who had encamped on the sides and rear of the army, to attack the Germans; and the result was that Baum suddenly found himself cut off from all his detached posts." For over two hours he withstood the sallies and fire of the Americans — his dragoons to a man, fighting like heroes — but at last, his ammunition giving out, and the reinforcements which he had sent for not arriving, he was obliged to give way before superior numbers and retreat. "The enemy," says Riedesel, "seemed to spring out of the ground." Twice the dragoons succeeded in breaking a road through the forces of Stark, for, upon their ammunition being used up, Baum ordered that they should sling their carbines over their shoulders, and trust to their swords. But bravery was now in vain; and the heroic leader, himself mortally wounded in the abdomen by a bullet, and having lost three hundred and sixty out of four hundred, was forced to surrender. Meanwhile, the Indians and Provincials had taken flight and sought safety in the forest.

While these events were taking place, Lieutenant Colonel Breymann, who had been sent by Riedesel to the aid of Baum, reached the bridge of St. Luke at three o'clock in the afternoon. Here he was met by Major Skene, who assured him that he was only two miles distant from Lieutenant Colonel Baum. Skene, however, not informing him of the latter's defeat, he continued his

Campaign of General John Burgoyne. 33

march as quickly as possible, although his troops — the day being unusually hot and sultry — were greatly fatigued. Scarcely had he advanced fifteen hundred paces on the bridge, when he descried a strongly armed force on an eminence toward the west. Skene assured him this force were not the enemy; but Breymann, not satisfied with this assurance, sent ahead some scouts who were immediately received with a volley of musketry.[1] Perceiving how the case stood, he at once ordered Major Barner to advance upon the hill, sent his grenadiers to the right, put the guns of both regiments into position, and directed the fire upon a log-house occupied by the Americans. The Germans drove the enemy across three ridges of land, but their ammunition giving out, they were obliged to desist from the pursuit. Thereupon, the Americans, guessing the cause of the halt, in their turn once more advanced; upon which Breymann, relying solely upon the fast gathering darkness to save himself, halted his men opposite the enemy, and remained there until it was perfectly dark. Then under cover of the night, he retreated across the bridge but was forced to leave his cannon. At twelve o'clock that same night, he arrived with his tired troops at Cambridge, and reached the main army at Fort Miller on the 17th. In this

---

[1] Stedman, in his *History of the American War*, part 1, p. 417, states that Baum captured on the first day, an American corps, which was released the following day by Major Skene, under the impression that this act of magnanimity would influence the released Americans to take no farther part against their king. He adds that these very ones fought the hardest against the English at Bennington. No mention, however, of this circumstance is made either in Riedesel's journals or in the report of Baum.

HOUSE IN WHICH COL. BAUM DIED.

action, the Americans captured four brass cannons,[1] besides some hundred stands of arms and brass barrelled drums, several Brunswick swords, and about seven hundred prisoners.[2] "It is true," says Riedesel, in commenting upon this action, "that justice was done to the bravery of Colonel Baum, but the English also said, that he did not possess the least knowledge of the country, its people, or its language. But who selected him for this expedition?"

With the failure of this expedition against Bennington, the first lightning flashed from Burgoyne's hitherto serene sky. The soldiers, as well as their officers, had set out on this campaign with cheerful hearts; for the campaign successfully brought to a close, all must end in the triumph of the royal arms. "Britons never go back,"

---

[1] These beautiful brass pieces of artillery were destined to undergo several of the vicissitudes of war. They are French cast, and were brought from Quebec with the army of Burgoyne. They were afterward inscribed "taken at Bennington, August 16, 1777," and constituted a part of the artillery of General Hull's army, and fell into the enemy's hands at Detroit. When the British officer of the day ordered the evening salutes to be fired from the American cannon, he chanced to read the inscription, "Taken at Bennington, August 16th, 1777," whereupon he observed that he would cause to be added as an additional line to the verse, "Retaken at Detroit, August 16th, 1812." The guns were carried by the British down to Fort George, at the mouth of the Niagara river, where they again fell into the hands of the American army, which captured that fortress. General Dearborn had them transported to Sackett's-Harbor, and with them were fired the salutes in honor of Harrison's victory over Proctor at the river Thames, in Upper Canada. The guns are now in Washington.

[2] For Stark's account of the battle of Bennington in a letter to General Schuyler, and also a narrative of one of the participants in the action, see Appendix, No. III.

Bugoyne exultantly had said, as the flotilla passed down Lake Champlain. Now, however, the Indians deserted by scores, and an almost general consternation and languor took the place of the former confidence and buoyancy.

On his arrival at Fort Edward, which had been evacuated by the Americans on the approach of the British army, the English general was joined by the Mohawk Nation, or, as they were called, Sir William Johnson's Indians. They agreed to fight provided their women and children were sent to Canada and supported, a condition which was faithfully carried out. Beyond this post, the country was peopled with German, Dutch, and English settlers. The latter, pretending to be good royalists, were allowed by Burgoyne, against the strong representations of his officers, not only to carry their arms, but to stroll about the camp at their leisure, and without any restraint. "These men, however," says Riedesel's journal, "were all but royalists. They consequently improved the opportunity to gain intelligence of all the occurrences in the army by appearances, and they forthwith communicated to the commanders of the enemy's forces that which they had seen and heard." Having finally reached the Hudson at the mouth of the Batten kil, those of the German dragoons that were left were horsed. Their number had now diminished to twenty, and this number constituted the entire cavalry force of the invading army.

III.

On the 13th of September, the royal army, with the exception of the German troops composing the left wing, crossed the Hudson by a bridge of boats, with the design of forming a junction with Sir Henry Clinton at Albany.[1] It encamped on the heights and plains of Saratoga near the mouth of Fish creek (the present site of Schuylerville), within a few miles of the northern division of the continentals under Gates — Burgoyne selecting General Schuyler's house as his headquarters.[2] After

---

[1] The Brunswick Journal states, that as early as the 19th of August, Fraser having occupied Fort Miller on the 9th of that month, a bridge was first made *above* the present Saratoga falls or rapids; but upon a better place being found lower down, it was broken up and a new one built *below* the rapids.

While preparations for crossing the river were making, Burgoyne, says Neilson, "encamped on an extensive flat or intervale, about one hundred rod north of Lansing's saw-mill. Here he had quite an extensive slaughter-yard which so enriched the soil that its effects are still visible on the corn crops and other productions." The exact place where the British crossed the Hudson was just below the Saratoga falls, two miles above Schuylerville, some eighty rods northwest of the present residence of Abraham Yates Rogers. The entrenchments which were at that time thrown up to cover the passage of the river, are still to be seen very plainly. They are three hundred feet in length and from four to six feet high, but are overgrown with scrub pines. Mr. Rogers, whose grandfather lived on the farm at the time, informs me that within thirty years the wooden platforms for the cannon were in existence behind the entrenchment." The survey of the railroad from Greenwich to Saratoga Springs was through these entrenchments.

[2] Burgoyne did not cross as soon as he expected, because, finding his provisions short, he was obliged to wait until supplies could be brought up

crossing the bridge [1] the 9th, 20th, 21st and 62d regiments, with the artillery, were stationed on the plain near the river, between the barracks [2] and the Fish kil, the bateaux on the right bank being crossed by six companies of the 47th. The hills around Saratoga were so densely covered with woods and underbrush that it was impossible to place the army in position to withstand an attack from the Americans. Accordingly all of the generals

---

from Ticonderoga. Sergeant Lamb was accordingly sent back alone (as being thus less liable to attract observation) to that post and soon returned with a month's provisions. For an account of his trip, see Appendix No. XV.

[1] The Brunswick Journal, in speaking of the passage of this bridge, says: "The *avant-guarde* under Fraser was the first to march over. At nine o'clock the reserve under Lieut. Col. Breymann followed after them in order to cover Fraser's left flank. The Germans, who formed the left wing of the army went over last of all [two days afterwards]; as soon as the last man had crossed the bridge it was broken up. They had passed the *Rubicon*, and all further communication with Canada was now cut off. The army which, on first setting off from there, was 10,000 strong, had already diminished to 6000 [1000 had been left at Ticonderoga] and even these were provided with provisions not only scant in quantity, but bad in quality.

[2] These barracks were used as a hospital and were located on the north side of the road to Saratoga Springs, directly upon the present site of the red barns of the Hon. Alonzo Welch of Schuylerville, who resides a few rods east of the barns in the main village street. The barracks were standing and occupied by a farmer up to within thirty years. In March, 1867, Mr. Welch, while plowing back of his barns, came across the burying place of the hospital. The bones thus exhumed, he carefully reburied.

Schuyler's house (so say the manusciipt Journals of the Brunswick officers) was *between* the old village of Ticonderoga and the Fish kil. This fact is of great importance in locating the old village, which, by the way, at best consisted of only a few scattered houses.

carefully inspected the high ground nearest the camp, and agreed upon a position to be taken up at a moment's notice, in case of an attack. The situation of the army, moreover, was rendered still more precarious by the fact of its being divided by the river, and thus obliged to be constantly on its guard. New entrenchments were therefore thrown up, especially on the side toward Bennington.

After the evacuation of Fort Edward, Schuyler had fallen down the river, first to Stillwater, and then to Van Schaick's island at the mouth of the Mohawk.[1] On the 19th day of August, however, he was superseded by Gates, who, on the 8th day of September, advanced with six thousand men to Bemis's heights, three miles north of Stillwater. These heights were at once fortified,

---

[1] "The reason," says Neilson, "why Schuyler fortified Van Schaick's island with the expectation of opposing Burgoyne in his march to Albany, was as follows: at that time there were no bridges across either the Hudson or Mohawk, nor were there ferries as plenty as they have been since. The only ferry on the Mohawk, between the Hudson river and Schenectady, was Loudon's, five miles above its mouth, where Arnold was posted with the left wing of the American army, for the purpose of preventing a passage at that place. There was another ferry near Halfmoon point (Waterford), across the Hudson, but that would only have been leading him out of the way on the opposite side of the river. Besides, the conveying so large an army over that stream in a common scow-boat, and at the same time subject to be opposed by the Americans who lay near by, would have rendered such an undertaking impracticable. Those being the facts, his course necessarily lay across the *sprouts*, as they were called, or mouths of the Mohawk, which, except in time of freshets, were fordable, and by four of which that stream enters the Hudson; the second and third forming Van Schaick's island, across which the road passed, and was the usual route at that time."

under the direction of Kosciusko. Along the brow of the river hills he threw up a line of breastworks about three-fourths of a mile in extent, with a strong battery at each end, and one in the centre, in such positions as to sweep the alluvial meadows between them and the river. A line of entrenchments, also, ran from west to east half a mile in length, and terminated on the east end on the west side of the intervale. The right wing occupied a hill nearest the river, and was protected in front by a wide, marshy ravine, and behind this by abattis. From the foot of this hill, across the flats to the river, an entrenchment was opened, at the extremity of which, on the margin of the river, another strong battery was constructed. The left wing commanded by Arnold (who after the defeat of St. Leger at Fort Stanwix, had joined Gates) extended onto a height three quarters of a mile further north, its left flank being also protected on the hillside by felled trees, or *slashings*. Gates's headquarters were in the centre, a little south of what was then, and is now, known as the Neilson farm.

On the 15th, the Germans crossed the river, and Burgoyne, having destroyed the bridge, gave the order to advance in search of the enemy, supposed to be somewhere in the forest; for, strange as it appears, that general had no knowledge of the position of the Americans, nor had he taken any pains to inform himself upon this vital point.[1] The army in gala dress, with its left wing

---

[1] For an account of Alexander Bryan, the scout who gave Gates timely notice of the passage of the Hudson by Burgoyne, see Appendix XI.

Campaign of General John Burgoyne. 41

resting on the Hudson, set off on its march with drums beating, colors flying, and their arms glistening in the sunshine of that lovely autumn day. " It was a superb spectacle," says an eye-witness, "reminding one of a grand parade in the midst of peace." That night they pitched their camp at Dovogat's house (Coveville).[1]

On the following morning, the enemy's drums were

---

[1] This house, which is still (1877) standing in good preservation, on the margin of the Champlain canal, about fifty rods from the Hudson, is situated about forty rods east of the road from Schuylerville to Stillwater, in what is called Van Vechten's cove, at Coveville.

In regard to the origin of this name, Professor Asa Fitch writes as follows:

"*July* 4, 1877—Dear Sir — Having resided six years in Stillwater, eight miles below, and in Ft. Miller over a year, eight miles above *Coveville*, I have often been to and through the place, and am quite familiar with the names it has had. Here is very much the largest of the coves or narrow bays (ancient beds of the river) which occur along the stream between Ft. Miller and Stillwater. In summer, when the river is low, this cove is an immense mud-hole or marsh. Hence it was first named by the Dutch, the *Great Vlie*, or simply the *Vlie*. This was its current name during the Old French war, and the New England troops passing have probably supposed the name alluded to the swarms of musketoes they here encountered, for they wrote it the *Fly*, and the *Great Fly*.

The cove was formerly a noted resort for flocks of wild ducks, attracting hunters hither from all the country around; and from this the place received its next name, *Dovecot*, i.e., dove house or dove place. This is the current statement among the inhabitants of the vicinity, and I doubt not it is correct. This was the prevalent name at the period of the revolution and for many years after. Some writers, unaware of the derivation and meaning of the name spell it differently. Thus in *Wilkinson's Memoirs* it is spelled *Davocote*. No doubt Baron Riedesel, on inquiring the origin or signification of this name, was told it meant *dove's house*, and he, imperfectly acquainted with our language, and supposing it to be the name of a person, and writing it as he understood it to be pronounced, entered it in his journal, *Dovegat's house*."

heard calling the men to arms, but although in such close proximity, the invading army knew not whence the sounds came, nor in what strength he was posted. Indeed, it does not seem that up to this time, Burgoyne had sent off *eclaireurs* or scouting parties to discover the situation of the enemy. Now, however, he mounted his horse to attend to it himself, taking with him, a strong body guard, consisting of the four regiments of Specht and Hesse-Hanau with six heavy pieces of ordnance, and two hundred workmen to construct bridges and roads. This was the party, with which he proposed, "to scout, and if occasion served," these were his words, " to attack the rebels on the spot." This remarkable scouting party moved with such celerity, as to accomplish two and a half miles the first day,[1] when in the evening, the entire army, which had followed on, encamped at Sword's house, within five miles of the American lines.[2]

I am inclined, however, to think that the word is a compound from the Dutch words *doof* or *doove*, dull, and *gat*, *hole*, in other words a kind of *Sleepy* hollow. Riedesel probably gives the name to the house not from a person of that name living in it, but from the place, i.e., the house at *Dovogat.*

[1] A New Hampshire regiment, while endeavoring to head off Clinton and save Albany, marched forty miles from Saratoga (Schuylerville), in fourteen hours and forded the Mohawk below Cohoes falls. *Belknap's New Hampshire.* Col. Otho Williams marched forty miles on the 18th of November, 1781. *Bancroft,* x, 473. Tarleton rode seventy miles in twenty-four hours, destroying public stores on the way. *Idem.* And Cornwallis, in marching order, pursued Greene's lightened retreating troops at the rate of thirty miles in a day.

[2] The site of Sword's house is on the south side of a spring brook, about fifty yards west of the Hudson river, and a few rods north of the south

Campaign of General John Burgoyne. 43

The night of the 18th passed quietly, the scouts that had finally been sent out, having returned without discovering a trace of the enemy. Indeed, it is a noteworthy fact that throughout the entire campaign, Burgoyne was never able to obtain accurate knowledge, either of the position of the Americans or of their movements; whereas, all his own plans were publicly known long before they were officially given out in orders. "I observe," writes Mrs. General Riedesel at this time, "that the wives of the officers are beforehand informed of all the military plans. Thus the Americans anticipate all our movements, and expect us whenever we arrive; and this, of course, injures our affairs."

On the morning of the 19th, a further advance was again ordered, an advance which prudence dictated should be made with the greatest caution. The army was now in the immediate vicinity of an alert and thoroughly aroused enemy, of whose strength they knew as little as of the country.[1] Notwithstanding this, the army not only was divided into three columns, each marching half a mile apart, but at 11 o'clock, a cannon, fired as a

---

line of the town of Saratoga. It may be readily found from being about thirty rods north of a highway leading from the Hudson river road westerly, which highway is the first one north of Wilbur's basin. This highway was nearly the same at the time of General Burgoyne's visit in 1777 as now. All traces of the house are now (1877) obliterated save a few bricks and a slight depression in the soil where was the cellar.

[1] "At this encampment (Sword's house) several of our men having proceeded into a field of potatoes, were surprised by a party of the enemy that killed about thirty of them. They might without difficulty have been surrounded and taken prisoners, but the Americans could not resist the opportunity of shedding blood."—*Lamb's Memoirs.* Dublin, 1811.

ORDER OF MARCH

OF THE BRITISH AND GERMAN TROOPS FROM SWORD'S HOUSE ON THE MORNING OF THE 19TH SEPTEMBER, 1777.

LEFT WING,
LED ON BY
MAJOR GENERALS PHILLIPS
AND
RIEDESEL.
British Artillery commanded by
MAJOR WILLIAMS
sustained by the German Corps.

47th Regiment guarding the bateaux.[1]

[1] Two companies of this regiment were left on Diamond island, in Lake George.

CENTRE,
LED ON BY
LIEUT. GEN. BURGOYNE
AND
BRIG. GEN. HAMILTON.

20th Regiment, Lieut. Col. Lynd
21st " Lieut. Col. Brig.-Gen. Hamilton.
62d " Lieut. Col. Anstruther.

Lord Petersham,[1] Sir James Clerke, aide-de-camps to General Burgoyne.

9th Regiment, Lieut. Col. Hill and Reserve.

[1] Afterwards Earl Harrington, commander-in-chief in Ireland.

RIGHT WING,
LED ON BY
BRIG. GEN. FRASER,
MAJORS ACKLAND
AND
LORD BALCARRAS.
British Light Infantry and Grenadiers,[1] and 24th Regiment sustained by
COLONEL BREYMANN'S
German Riflemen.

Canadians, Provincials and Indians on their flanks and front.

[1] These flank companies belonged to the 9th, 20th, 21st, 24th, 29th, 31st, 34th, 47th, 53d and 62d regiments.

signal for the start, echoed through the still aisles of the primeval forest, informing the Americans of the position and forward movement of the British.

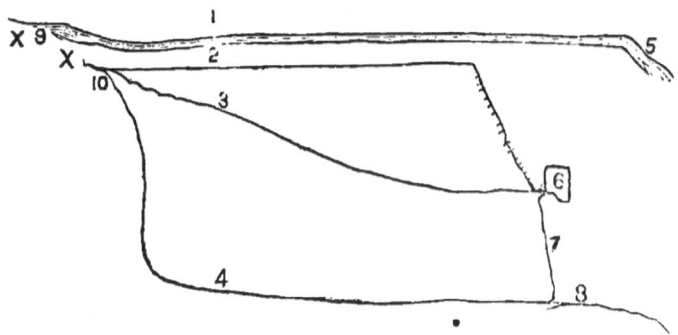

ROUTE OF THE ENGLISH TROOPS TO FREEMAN'S FARM.

1. Hudson River.
2. Left column under Riedesel.
3. Centre column under Burgoyne.
4. Right column under Fraser.
5. Bemis's Heights.
6. Freeman's Farm.
7. Route of Fraser to assist Burgoyne.
8. Road to Quaker Springs.
9. Dovogat.
10. Sword's House.

The left column, which followed the river-road, consisted of four German regiments, and the 47th British, the latter constituting a guard for the bateaux. These troops, together with all the heavy artillery and baggage, were under the command of General Riedesel. The right column, made up of the English Grenadiers and Light Infantry, the 24th Brunswick Grenadiers, and the light battalion, with eight 6 pounders under Lieut. Col. Breymann, was led by General Fraser, and followed the present road from Quaker springs to Stillwater, on the heights. The centre column, also on the heights, and mid-way between the left and right wings, consisted of the 9th, 20th, 21st and 62d regiments, with six 6 pounders, and was led by Burgoyne in person. The front and flanks of the centre and right columns were protected by Canadians, Provincials, and Indians. The march was exceedingly tedious, as frequently new bridges had to be built, and trees cut down and removed.

About one o'clock in the afternoon Colonel Morgan, who with his sharpshooters had been detached to watch the movements of the British and harass them, owing to the dense woods, unexpectedly fell in with the centre column, and sharply attacked it. Whereupon Fraser, on the right, wheeled his troops, and coming up forced Morgan to give way. A regiment being ordered to the assistance of the latter, whose numbers had been sadly scattered by the vigor of the attack, the battle was renewed with spirit. By four o'clock, the action had become general, Arnold, with nine continental regiments and Morgan's corps having completely engaged the whole force of Burgoyne and Fraser. The contest, accidentally begun in the first instance, now assumed the most obstinate and determined character, the soldiers often being engaged hand to hand. The ground being mostly covered with woods embarrassed the British in the use of their field artillery, while it gave a corresponding advantage to Morgan's sharpshooters. The artillery fell into the hands of the Americans at every alternate discharge, but the latter could neither turn the guns upon the enemy, nor bring them off. The wood prevented the last, and the want of a match the first, as the lint-stock was invariably carried away, and the rapidity of the transitions did not allow the Americans time to provide one.

Meanwhile General Riedesel, who had kept abreast

of the other two columns and had reached the present site of Wilbur's basin, hearing the firing, on his own responsibility, and guided only by the sound of the cannon, hastened at five o'clock with two regiments through the woods to the relief of the commander-in-chief. When he arrived on the scene, the Americans were posted on a corner of the woods, having on their right flank a deep muddy ravine, the brink of which had been rendered inaccessible by stones and underbrush. In front of this corner of the forest, and entirely surrounded by dense woods, was a vacant space, on which the English were drawn up in line. The struggle was for the possession of this clearing, known then, as it is to this day, as Freeman's farm. It had already been in possession of both parties, and now served as a support for the left flank of the English right wing, the right flank being covered by the troops of Fraser and Breymann. The Continentals had, for the sixth time, hurled fresh troops against the three British regiments, the 20th, 21st and 62d. The guns on this wing were already silenced, there being no more ammunition; and the artillerymen having been either killed or wounded. These three regiments had lost half their men, and now formed a small band surrounded by heaps of the dead and dying. The timely arrival of the German general alone saved the army of Burgoyne from total rout. Charging on the double-quick with fixed bayonets, he repelled the Americans, and Fraser and Breymann were preparing to follow up the advantage, when they were recalled by Burgoyne and reluctantly forced to retreat. General Schuyler, referring to this in his diary, says: "Had it not been for this order of the British general, the Americans would have been if not defeated, at least held in such check as to have made it a drawn battle, and an opportunity afforded the British to collect much provision of which he [*sic*] stood sorely in need." The British officers also shared the same opinion. Fraser and Riedesel severely criticised the order, telling its author in plain terms that he did not know how to avail himself of his advantages." Nor was this feeling confined to the officers; the privates gave vent to their dissatisfaction against their general in loud expressions of scorn, as he rode down the line. This reaction was the more striking, because they had placed the utmost confidence in his capacity at the beginning of the expedition. They were also still more confirmed in their dislike, by the general belief that he was addicted to drinking. Neither does this seem to have been owing to an unwillingness to fight or a lack of *esprit*; for when, subsequently, the men were reduced to short rations, "they put up," says Riedesel, "with this, as also with all the fatiguing labors, duties and night watches, with the greatest patience and perseverance."

In connection with this battle, the heroism of Lieutenant Hervey, of the 62d regiment, and nephew to the adjutant general of the same name, should not be forgotten. Early in the action he received several wounds, and was repeatedly ordered off the field by Lieutenant Colonel Anstruther; but his enthusiasm would not allow him to leave his brave comrades as long as he could stand. Presently, however, a ball striking one of his legs, his

Campaign of General John Burgoyne.

removal became a necessity, and while he was being borne away, another wounded him mortally. In this situation, the surgeon recommended him to take a powerful dose of opium if he would avoid seven or eight hours of dreadful torture. To this he consented, and when his colonel entered the tent with Major Harnage, who were both wounded, they asked whether he had any affairs they could settle for him? His reply was, that being a minor, every thing was already adjusted; but he had one request, which he retained just life enough to utter; and, with the words, "Tell my uncle I died like a soldier," expired.

Night put an end to the conflict. The Americans withdrew within their lines, and the British and German forces bivouacked on the battle field, the Brunswickers composing in part the right wing. Both parties claimed the victory, yet as the intention of the Americans was not to advance, but to maintain their position, and that of the English, not to maintain theirs, but to gain ground, it is easy to see which had the advantage of the day. The loss of the former was between 300 and 400, including Colonels Adams and Coburn, and of the latter from 600 to 1000 — Captain Jones of the artillery, an officer of great merit, being among the killed. The ground afforded on the following day a scene truly distressing. The bodies of the slain, thrown together into one receptacle, were scarcely covered with the soil; and the only tribute of respect to fallen officers was, to bury them by themselves without throwing them into the common grave. In this battle an unusual number of youthful officers fell on the British side, as their army abounded at this time with young men of high respectability, who after several years of peace anterior to the Revolution, were attracted to the profession of arms. Three subalterns of the 20th regiment on this occasion, the oldest of whom did not exceed the age of seventeen years, were buried together.[1]

It was the intention of General Burgoyne, the morning following this engagement, to attack the Americans on their left with his entire force. His sick and wounded were disposed of at the river; the army was drawn up in order of battle; and he waited only for the dispersion of a heavy fog, when General Fraser observed to him that the grenadiers and light infantry, who were to lead the attack, appeared fatigued by the duty of the preceding day, and that if he would suspend the operation until the next morning (the 21st), he believed they would enter into the combat with greater spirit. Burgoyne yielded

---

[1] "The morning after the action, I visited the wounded prisoners who had not been dressed, and discovered a charming youth not more than sixteen years old lying among them; feeble, faint, pale and stiff in his gore: the delicacy of his aspect and the quality of his clothing attracted my attention, and on enquiry, I found he was an Ensign Phillips. He told me he had fallen by a wound in his leg or thigh, and as he lay on the ground was shot through the body by an army follower, a murderous villain, who owned the deed, but I forget his name. The moans of the hapless youth affected me to tears; I raised him from the straw on which he lay, took him in my arms and removed him to a tent, where every comfort was provided and every attention paid to him; but his wounds were mortal, and he expired on the 21st. When his name was first mentioned to General Gates, he exclaimed 'just heaven! he may be the nephew of my wife,' but the fact was otherwise."—*Wilkinson*.

Campaign of General John Burgoyne. 51

to this suggestion; the orders were countermanded and the troops returned to their quarters.[1] Meanwhile, in the course of the night, a spy reached the British general with a letter from Sir Henry Clinton, advising him of his intended ascent of the Hudson for his relief. Thereupon, he resolved to postpone the meditated attack and await the arrival of Clinton at Albany.[2]

---

[1] "If General Burgoyne," says Wilkinson, "had attacked us on the 20th or 21st of September, as he intended, his force would have enabled him to lead a column of 5000 rank and file against our left, where the ground was most favorable to his approach; whilst a point on our right, by the plain near the river, would have kept every man at his station within our extended lines; and under such advantages on his side, it is highly probable he would have gained a decisive victory, and taken our artillery and baggage; for although our numbers in rank and file exceeded 6000, the sick, casualties, and contingencies of the service, would not have left us more than 5500 men for defence; and from the formation of our camp, by penetrating on the left he would have cut off our right. We were badly fitted to defend works or meet the close encounter; the late hour at which the action closed the day before, the fatigue of officers and men, and the defects of our organization had prevented the left wing from drawing ammunition, and we could not boast of a bayonet for every three muskets. Presumptious as well as blind must be he who presumes to ascribe this critical combination of circumstances to mere accident, or the caprice of fortune!"

[2] That Burgoyne, however, believed that he was *whipped* by the result of the action of the 19th is evident from this fact. In the library of the late John Carter Brown of Providence, R. I., there is a volume of *Stedman* with marginal notes in the handwriting of Sir Henry Clinton, who once owned the book. In that portion of the work where Stedman speaks of the failure of Burgoyne, Clinton writes as follows: "If General Burgoyne had not been sure of a coöperation, 'tis pity he ever passed the Hudson. Sir H. Clinton, thinking General Burgoyne might want some coöperation (though he had not called for it in any of his letters), offered in his of the 12th of September, to make an attempt on the forts as soon as the expected

Accordingly, the day that was to have witnessed a renewal of the action of the 19th, Burgoyne devoted to the laying out of a fortified camp. He made the site of the late battle his extreme right, and extended his intrenchments across the high ground to the river. For the defence of the right wing, a redoubt (known as the Great redoubt), was thrown up in the late battle-field, near the corner of the woods that had been occupied by the Americans during the action, on the eastern edge of the ravine.[1] The defence of this position was intrusted to the corps of Fraser. The reserve corps of Breymann were posted on an eminence on the western side of the ravine for the protection of the right flank of Fraser's division.[2] The right wing of the English (Hamilton's) was placed in close proximity to the left wing of

---

reinforcements should arrive from Europe. General Burgoyne fought the battle of Saratoga on the 19th, and on the 21st tells General Clinton in answer, *that no attempt, or even the menace of an attempt, would be of use.*" This discovery was made by a writer (J. C. S) of Providence, who sent the account to the *N. Y. Tribune*, in Aug., 1875.

[1] This redoubt — destined to be the scene of the hottest part of the engagement of the 7th of October, was three rods south of the present barnyard of Mr. Ebenezer Leggett, whose house — as mentioned in a preceding note — stands on the old clearing of Freeman, the site of the first action of the 19th of September. Balls and skeletons are still, even at this late day, picked up on this spot. I myself, once, while following the plow of a farmer, picked up four grape shot on the site of this redoubt.

[2] The traces of Breymann's entrenchments are yet to be seen very plainly. They lie about twenty rods northwest of Mr. Leggett's house. The place is considerably elevated by nature, and is known among the farmers in the vicinity as *Burgoyne's hill*. Properly, it should be *Breymann's hill*. It was at the northeast corner of this eminence that Arnold was wounded in the action of the 7th of October.

Fraser, thus extending the line on the left to the river bank where were placed the hospital and supply trains. The entire front was protected by a deep muddy ditch, running nine hundred paces in front of the outposts of the left wing. This ditch ran in a curve around the right wing of the English brigade, thereby separating Fraser's corps from the main body.

General Burgoyne made his head-quarters between the English and German troops on the heights at the left wing.[1] This was the new camp at Freeman's farm.

V.

During the period of inaction which now intervened, a part of the army, says the private journal of one of the officers, was so near the Americans that "we could hear his morning and evening guns, his drums, and other noises in his camp very distinctly, but we knew not in the least, where he stood, nor how he was posted, much less how strong he was." "Undoubtedly," *naively* adds the journal, "a rare case in such a situation."

---

[1] The Taylor house (Smith's house), has often been mistaken for the head-quarters of Burgoyne. The Brunswick Journal, however, is very explicit in stating that "Burgoyne camped between the English and German troops of Riedesel on the heights at the left wing." This statement, moreover, receives additional confirmation in the following incident. On one of my visits to the battle-ground, I pointed out to Mr. Wilbur (on whose land we were then standing), the place designated by the Brunswick Journal as Burgoyne's head-quarters. "That," exclaimed Mr. Wilbur, "explains what I have often wondered at." He then stated that when he first plowed up that particular spot, he was accustomed to find great quantities of old gin and wine bottles, and that until now, he had often been puzzled to know "how on earth those bottles came there."—*See Map.*

Meanwhile the work of fortifying the camp was continued. *A place d'armes* was laid out in front of the regiments, and fortified with heavy batteries. During the night of the 21st considerable shouting was heard in the American camp. This, accompanied by the firing of cannon, led the army to believe that some holiday was being celebrated. Again, in the night of the 23d, more noise was heard in the same direction. " This time, however," says the journal of another officer," it may have proceeded from working parties, as the most common noise was the rattling of chains. From the fact also that voices were heard, it is evident that the enemy must have been very near the other side of the ditch. Lamb, also bears testimony to the close proximity of the Americans. " We could," says that writer, " distinctly hear the Americans felling and cutting trees; and they had a piece of ordnance which they used to fire as a morning gun, so near us that the wadding from it struck against our works." On the 28th a captured cornet, who had been allowed by Gates to return to the British camp for five days, gave an explanation of the shouting heard on the night of the 21st. This was, that General Lincoln, with a strong body of militia from New Hampshire and Connecticut, had attempted to surprise Ticonderoga, and though unsuccessful had captured four companies of the 53d, together with an armed brig and one bateau. Thus Burgoyne was indebted to an enemy in his front for information respecting his own posts in his rear.

But the action of the 19th had essentially diminished his strength, and his situation began to grow critical. His dispatches were intercepted, and his communications with Canada cut off by the seizure of the posts at the head of Lake George. The pickets were more and more molested, the army was weakened by the sick and wounded, and the enemy swarmed on its rear and flanks, threatening the strongest positions. In fact the army was as good as cut off from its outposts, while in consequence of its close proximity to the American camp, the soldiers had but little rest. The nights, also, were rendered hideous by the howls of large packs of wolves that were attracted by the partially buried bodies of those slain in the action of the nineteenth.[1] On the 1st of October a few English soldiers who were digging potatoes in a field a short distance in the *rear* of head-quarters within the camp, were surprised by the enemy who suddenly rushed from the woods and carried off the men in the very faces of their comrades.

There were now only sufficient rations for sixteen days; and foraging parties, necessarily composed of a large number of men, were sent out daily. At length Burgoyne was obliged to cut down the ordinary rations to a pound of bread and a pound of meat; and as he had heard nothing from Clinton he became seriously

---

[1] The first two nights this noise was heard, General Fraser thought it to have been the dogs belonging to the officers, and an order was given for the dogs to be confined within the tents. The next night the noise was much greater; when a detachment of Canadians and Provincials were sent out to reconnoitre, and it proved to have arisen from large droves of wolves that came after the dead; they were similar to a pack of hounds; for one setting up a cry, they all joined, and when they approached a corpse, their noise was hideous till they had scratched it up."—*Anburey*.

alarmed. Accordingly, on the evening of the 5th of October, he called a council of war. Riedesel and Faser advised an immediate falling back to their old position, beyond the Batten kil, Phillips declined giving an opinion, and Burgoyne reserved his decision until he had made a reconnaissance in force " to gather forage, and ascertain definitely the position of the enemy, and whether it would be advisable to attack him." Should the latter be the case, he would, on the day following the reconnaissance, advance on the Americans with his entire army; but if not, he would march back to the Batten kil.

VI.

At ten o'clock on the morning of October 7th, liquor and rations having been previously issued to the army, Burgoyne, with fifteen hundred men, eight cannons and two howitzers, started on his reconnaissance, accompanied by Generals Riedesel, Phillips and Fraser. The Canadians, Indians, and three hundred of Breymann's Brunswickers, were sent ahead under Captain Fraser (not the general) to make a diversion in the rear of the Continentals. They succeeded in reaching a point a little in the rear of a log barn which formed the extreme left of the American breastworks; but they were speedily discovered, and after a brisk skirmish of half an hour, were driven back, hotly pursued by the Americans, to within a short distance of the British line of battle which was then forming.[1]

---

[1] A great many balls have since been picked up on both sides of where this breastwork stood, some of them flattened and others misshaped, showing

The British advanced in three columns toward the left wing of the American position, entered a wheat field two hundred rods southwest of the site of the action of the 19th, deployed into line, and began cutting up wheat for forage. The grenadiers under Major Ackland, and the artillery under Major Williams, were stationed on a gentle eminence.[1] The light infantry, skirted by a low ridge of land and under the Earl of Balcarras, were placed in the extreme right. The centre was composed of British and German troops under Phillips and Riedesel. In advance of the right wing, General Fraser had command of a detachment of five hundred picked men. The movement having been seasonably discovered, the centre advanced guard of the Americans beat to arms. Col. Wilkinson, Gates's adjutant general, being at headquarters at the moment, was dispatched to ascertain the cause of the alarm. He proceeded to within sixty rods of the enemy, and returning, informed General Gates that they were foraging, attempting also to reconnoitre the American left, and likewise in his opinion, offering

---

that they had come in contact with opposing obstacles. "And here," says Neilson, "is one circumstance strongly confirming the often repeated assertion, 'that the Americans, in addition to one musket ball, added two buck shot, by which they did so much execution,' viz : the buck shot are frequently found on the side of the breastwork toward which the Americans fired, and not on the other."

[1] This eminence is now (1877), covered by an orchard, about two rods east of the road leading from Quaker springs to Stillwater, and twenty rods southeast of the house now (1877) occupied by Joseph Rogers. Fraser was shot midway between the orchard and Rogers's house. A bass-wood tree now marks the spot. This tree is a shoot out of the stump of the tree that stood at the time when Fraser fell.

battle. In this view, Generals Lincoln and Arnold, who had also reconnoitred the British lines, coincided. "What is the nature of the ground, and what is your opinion?" asked Gates. "Their front is open," Wilkinson replied, "and their flank rests on woods, under cover of which they may be attacked; their right is skirted by a height; I would indulge them." "Well then," rejoined Gates, "order on Morgan to begin the game." At his own suggestion, however, Morgan was allowed to gain the ridge on the enemy's right by a circuitous course, while Poor's and Learned's brigades should attack his left.

The movement was admirably executed. At half past two o'clock in the afternoon, the New York and New Hampshire troops marched steadily up the slope of the knoll on which the British grenadiers and the artillery under Ackland and Williams were stationed. Poor had given them orders not to fire until after the first discharge of the enemy; and for a moment there was an awful stillness, each party seeming to bid defiance to the other. At length the artillerymen and grenadiers began the action by a shower of grape and musket balls, which had no other effect than to break the branches of the trees over the heads of the Americans, who, having thus received the signal, rushed forward firing and opening to the right and left. Then again forming on the flanks of the grenadiers they mowed them down at every shot, until the top of the hill was gained. Here a bloody and hand to hand struggle ensued which lasted about thirty minutes, when Ackland being badly hurt, the grenadiers

Campaign of General John Burgoyne. 59

gave way, leaving the ground thickly strewn with their dead and wounded. In this dreadful conflict one field-piece that had been taken and retaken five times, finally fell into the hands of the Americans; whereupon Col. Cilley of New Hampshire leaped upon the captured cannon, waved his sword, and dedicated it "to the American cause," jumped down and turning its muzzle, fired it on the British with the ammunition they had left behind.[1]

Soon after Poor began the attack on the grenadiers, a flanking party of British was discerned advancing through the woods, upon which Col. Cilley was ordered to intercept them. As he approached near to a brush fence, the enemy rose behind and fired, but so hurriedly that only a few balls took effect. The officer in command then ordered his men to "fix bayonets and charge the damned rebels." Cilley who heard this order, replied, "it takes two to play that game, charge and we'll try it." His regiment charged at the word, and firing a volley in the faces of the British, caused them to flee, leaving many of their number dead, upon the field.

---

[1] "The ground which had been occupied by the British grenadiers presented a scene of complicated horror and exultation. In the square space of twelve or fifteen yards lay eighteen grenadiers in the agonies of death; and three officers were propped up against stumps of trees, two of them mortally wounded, bleeding, and almost speechless. A surgeon, a man of great worth, who was dressing one of the officers, raising his blood-besmeared hands in a frenzy of patriotism, exclaimed, ' Wilkinson, I have dipt my hands in British blood!' He received a sharp rebuke for his brutality, and, with the troops, I pursued the hard pressed flying enemy."— *Wilkinson.*

While pursuing the flying grenadiers, Wilkinson heard a feeble voice exclaim, "Protect me, sir, against that boy." Turning his eyes he saw a lad taking deliberate aim at a wounded British officer, whom he at once knew to be Major Ackland. Wilkinson dismounted, and taking him by the hand expressed the hope that he was not badly wounded. "Not badly," replied the gallant officer, " but very inconveniently, as I am shot through both legs. Will you, sir, have the goodness to have me conveyed to your camp?" Wilkinson at once directed his servant to alight, and lifting the wounded man into the vacant seat, had him conveyed to head-quarters.[1]

As soon as the action began on the British left, Morgan, true to his purpose, poured down like a torrent from the ridge that skirted the flanking party of Fraser, and attacked them so vigorously as to force them back to their lines; then by a rapid movement to the left, he fell upon the flank of the British right with such impetuosity that they wavered, and seemed on the point of giving way. At this critical moment Major Dearborn arrived on the field with two regiments of New

---

[1] Lamb gives a different account of this. Both statements, however, may be substantially correct. He says : "Major Ackland when wounded, observed the British troops were retreating. He requested Capt. Simpson of the 31st regiment, who was an intimate friend, to help him into camp. Upon which, being a stout man, he conveyed the major on his back a considerable way; when the enemy pursuing so rapidly, he was obliged to leave him behind to save himself. As the major lay on the ground, he cried out to the men who were running by him, that he would give fifty guineas to any soldier who would convey him into camp. A stout grenadier instantly took him on his back, and was hastening into camp, when they were overtaken and both made prisoners."

England troops, and delivered so galling a fire into their front that they broke and fled in wild confusion. They were, however, quickly rallied by Balcarras behind a fence in rear of their first position, and led again into action. The Continentals next threw their entire force upon the centre commanded by Lt. Col. Specht with three hundred men. Specht, whose left flank had been exposed by the retreating of the grenadiers, ordered the two regiments of Rhetz and Hesse-Hanau to form a curve, and supported by the artillery thus covered his flank which was in imminent danger. He maintained himself long and bravely in this precarious situation, and would have stood his ground still longer, had he not been separated from Balcarras, in consequence of the latter, through a misunderstanding of Burgoyne's orders, taking up another position with his light infantry. Thus Specht's right flank was as much exposed as his left. The brunt of the action now fell upon the Germans, who alone had to sustain the impetuous onset of the Americans.

Brigadier-General Fraser, who, up to this time, had been stationed on the right, noticed the critical situation of the centre, and hurried to its succor with the 24th regiment. Conspicuously mounted on an iron grey horse, he was all activity and vigilance, riding from one part of the division to another, and animating the troops by his example. Perceiving that the fate of the day rested upon that officer, Morgan, who, with his riflemen, was immediately opposed to Fraser's corps, took a few of his sharpshooters aside, among whom was the celebrated marksman Tim. Murphy, men on whose precision of aim he could rely, and said to them, " That gallant officer yonder is General Fraser ; I admire and respect him, but it is necessary for our good that he should die. Take your station in that cluster of bushes and do your duty."

Within a few moments, a rifle ball cut the crouper of Fraser's horse, and another passed through his horse's mane. Calling his attention to this, Fraser's aid said : " It is evident that you are marked out for particular aim ; would it not be prudent for you to retire from this place ?" Fraser replied, " my duty forbids me to fly from danger." The next moment he fell mortally wounded by a ball from the rifle of Murphy, and was carried off the field by two grenadiers.[1]

Upon the fall of Fraser, dismay seized the British, while a corresponding elation took possession of the Americans, who, being reinforced at this juncture by General Ten Broeck with three thousand New York militia, pressed forward with still greater vehemence. Up to this time Burgoyne had been in the thickest of the fight, and now finding himself in danger of being surrounded, he abandoned his artillery, and ordered a retreat to the Great redoubt. The retreat took place exactly fifty-two minutes after the first shot was fired, the

---

[1] The distance between Fraser and Murphy, when the latter fired, is about one-quarter of a mile. In those days this was considered a great shot. General Mattoon, however, denies that Fraser was shot by Morgan's men, and claims the credit for another. In this connection consult Mattoon's letter in Appendix No. XIII. Mattoon was a lieutenant in the battle.

enemy leaving all the cannon on the field, except the two howitzers, with a loss of more than four hundred men and among them the flower of his officers, viz : Fraser, Ackland, Williams, Captain Money, deputy quarter master general, Sir Francis Clerke,[1] and many others.

The retreating British troops had scarcely entered their lines when Arnold, notwithstanding he had been refused a command by Gates, placed himself at the head of the Continentals, and under a terrific fire of grape and musket balls assaulted their works from right to left. Mounted on a dark brown horse he moved incessantly at a full gallop over the field, giving orders in every direction, sometimes in direct opposition to those of the commander, at others leading a platoon in person, and exposing himself to the hottest fire of the enemy. " He behaved," says Samuel Woodruff, a sergeant in the battle, in a letter to the late Col. William L. Stone,[2] " more like a madman than a cool and discreet officer." But if it were madness, there was " method in it." With a part of Patterson's and Glover's brigades he attacked, with the ferocity of a tiger, the Great redoubt, and encountering the light infantry of Balcarras, drove them

---

[1] Clerke was wounded while in the act of riding on to give an order — an order which Burgoyne (see *State of the Expedition*) claimed would have changed the fortunes of the day had it been delivered. Wilkinson and others spell the name *Clark* — a mistake which probably arose from the fact that the English pronounce the name Clerke as if written *Clark*.

[2] For this letter see Appendix No. V.

at the point of the bayonet from a strong abattis within the redoubt itself.[1] Then, spurring boldly on, exposed to the cross fire of the two armies, he darted to the extreme right of the British camp.

This right flank defence of the enemy was occupied by the Brunswick troops,[2] under Breymann, and consisted of a breast work of rails piled horizontally between perpendicular pickets, and extended two hundred yards across an open field to some high ground on the right,[3] where it was covered by a battery of two guns. The interval from the left of this defence to the Great redoubt was intrusted to the care of the Canadian Provincials. In front of the east breastwork, the ground declined in a gentle slope for one hundred and twenty yards when it sunk abruptly. The Americans had formed a line under this declivity, and covered breast high were warmly engaged with the Germans, when about sunset Learned came up with his brigade in open column, with Col. Jackson's Massachusetts regiment, then in command of Lieut. Gov. Brooks, in front. On his approach, he inquired where he could "*put in* with most advantage." A slack fire was then observed in

---

[1] "So severe was the fighting at this point, that an old soldier who was in the battle once told me that in the low ground in front of the redoubt, the blood and water was knee-deep."— *E. R. Freeman to the author.*

[2] The statement of Mr. Irving that the Hessians bore the brunt of the battles of Freeman's Farm and Saratoga is erroneous. Only one Hessian regiment was in these battles, the rest being in Long Island and the Southern department.

[3] This high ground is now called Burgoyne's (Breymann's) hill. See note, p. 52.

that part of the enemy's line between the Germans and light infantry where were stationed the Provincials, and Learned was accordingly requested to incline to the right and attack that point.

This slack fire was owing to the fact that the larger part of the Canadian companies belonging to the skirmishing expedition of the morning were absent from their posts, part of them being in the Great redoubt and the others not having returned to their position. Had they been in their places, it would have been impossible, Riedesel thinks, for the left flank of Breymann to have been surrounded. Be this as it may, on the approach of Learned, the Canadians fled, leaving the German flank uncovered; and at the same moment Arnold, arriving from his attack on the Great redoubt, took the lead of Learned's brigade, and passing through the opening left by the Canadians, attacked the Brunswickers on their left flank and rear with such success that the chivalric Breymann was killed, and they themselves forced to retreat, leaving the key of the British position in the hands of the Americans. Lieut. Col. Specht, in the Great redoubt, hearing of this disaster, hastily rallied four officers and fifty men and started in the growing dusk to retake the intrenchment. Unacquainted with the road, he met a pretended royalist in the woods, who promised to lead him to Breymann's corps, but his guide treacherously delivered him into the hands of the Americans, by whom he and the four officers were captured. The advantage thus gained was retained by the Americans; and darkness put an end to an action, equally brilliant and important to the Continental arms. Great numbers of the enemy were killed, and two hundred prisoners taken. Burgoyne himself narrowly escaped, one ball having passed through his hat, and another having torn his waistcoat. The loss of the Americans was inconsiderable.[1]

VII.

In their final retreat, the Brunswickers turned and delivered a parting volley, which killed Arnold's horse. Just at this moment, a wounded Brunswicker fired at Arnold and wounded him in the same leg that had been injured by a musket ball at the storming of Quebec, two years previously. A private, by the name of John Redman, seeing his general wounded, at once ran up to bayonet the offender, but was prevented by Arnold, who, with true chivalry, exclaimed, " He's a fine fellow — don't hurt him!"[2] At this instant, while Arnold

---

[1] The British and German troops who were killed in this battle were slightly covered with earth and brush where they fell, apparently unlamented by friend or foe. " It was not an uncommon thing," says Neilson, "after the land was cleared and began to be cultivated, to see five, ten, and even twenty human skulls piled up on different stumps about the field." I have myself, when a boy, seen human bones thickly strewn about on the ground, which had been turned out with the plow. " Near the place where Fraser fell, a hole was dug into which the bodies of forty soldiers were thrown, after being stripped of their clothing by the women of the American camp."

[2] This was told in 1848 to Mr. Jeptha R. Simms by Nicholas Stoner, the celebrated scout, who was an eye witness of the circumstance. The Germans, he says, always continued to fight after they were down, because

Campaign of General John Burgoyne. 67

was striving to extricate himself from his saddle, Major Armstrong rode up and delivered to him an order from Gates to return to camp, fearing he " might do some rash thing." " He indeed," says Mr. Lossing, " did a rash thing in the eyes of military discipline. He led troops to victory without an order from his commander." " It is a curious fact," says Sparks, " that an officer, who had really no command in the army, was the leader in one of the most spirited and important battles of the Revolution. His madness or rashness, or

---

they had been assured by their employers that the Americans would give no quarter.

Nicholas Stoner, one of the most noted trappers of Central New York, was among those who followed Arnold into Breymann's camp. He was wounded in this charge in a singular manner. " A cannon shot," says Simms, who had it from the scout, "from the breastwork killed a soldier near Stoner, named Tyrrell. The ball demolished his head, sending its fragments into the face of Stoner, which was literally covered with brains, hair and fragments of the skull. He fell senseless, with the right of his head about the ear severely cut by portions of the skull bone, which injury still affects [1848] his hearing in that ear. Shortly after, as the young fifer [Stoner was a fifer] was missing, one Sweeny, an Irish soldier, was sent to seek out and bear him from the field; but a cannon shot whizzed so near his own head, that he soon returned without the object of his search. Col. Livingston asked Sweeny where the lad Stoner was? 'Jasus! Colonel,' replied the soldier, ' a goose has laid an egg there, and you don't catch me staying there !' Lieut. Wm. Wallace then proceeded to the spot indicated by the Irishman, and found our hero with his head reclining upon Tyrrell's thigh; and taking him in his arms, bore him to the American camp. When young Stoner was found, a portion of the brim of his hat, say about one-fourth the size of a nine pound-shot, was observed to have been cut off very smoothly; the rest of it was covered with the ruins of the head of Tyrrell, who, to use the words of Stoner, ' *did not know what hurt him.*' "

whatever it may be called, resulted most fortunately for himself. The wounds he received at the moment of rushing into the very arms of danger and death, added fresh lustre to his military glory, and was a new claim to public favor and applause." In the heat of the action, he struck an officer on the head with his sword and wounded him, an indignity which might justly have been retaliated on the spot, and in the most fatal manner. The officer did, indeed, raise his gun to shoot him, but he forebore, and on the next day when he demanded redress, Arnold declared his entire ignorance of the act, and expressed his regret. Wilkinson ascribed his rashness to intoxication, but Major Armstrong, who, with Samuel Woodruff assisted in removing him from the field, was satisfied that this was not the case. Others ascribed it to opium. This, however, is conjecture unsustained by proofs of any kind, and consequently improbable. His vagaries may perhaps be sufficiently explained by the extraordinary circumstances of wounded pride, anger and desperation in which he was placed. But his actions were certainly rash, when compared with "the stately method of the commader-in-chief, who directed by orders from his camp, what his presence should have sanctioned in the field."

Indeed, the conduct of Gates does not compare favorably either with that of his own generals, or of his opponents. While Arnold and Burgoyne were in the hottest of the fight boldly facing danger and almost meeting face to face, Gates, according to the statement of his adjutant general, was discussing the merits of the

Revolution with Sir Francis Clerke, Burgoyne's aid-de-camp, who, wounded and a prisoner, was lying upon the commander's bed seemingly more intent upon winning the verbal than the actual battle. Gates became incensed because Sir Francis would not admit the force of his argument, and calling his aid out of the room, asked him if "he had ever heard so impudent a son of a b—h?" A few days afterward Sir Francis died.[1]

Gates has been suspected of a lack of personal courage.[2]

---

[1] "Sir Francis, who was I think a member of parliament, appeared to be an impetuous, high-minded, frank, fearless fellow, for suddenly changing the conversation he enquired of me, 'whether our surgeons were good for anything, as he did not like the direction of his wound, and was desirous to know whether it was mortal or not?' . . Sir Francis died, I think the 13th; and the day before, questioned Doctor Townshend, who attended him, as to the probable result of his wound. The doctor feeling a reluctance in announcing his doom, he observed it, and remarked, 'Doctor why do you pause? Do you think I am afraid to die?' The doctor then advised him, as an act of prudence, to arrange his private affairs. 'Thank you, doctor,' replied he, 'I understand you. As to my private affairs, my father settled them for me, and I have only a few legacies to bequeath.' Among them he gave twenty guineas to the matron of our hospital, who had paid particular attention to him. Some time after the conversation, the matron presented her claim to Captain Money, the British deputy-quarter-master general, who discharged it *in Continental bills then at a considerable depreciation*. The woman complained of the circumstance, and was recommended to General Burgoyne, who expressed his abhorrence of the act, directed the woman *to hold the Continental bills*, and obliged Money to atone for the imposition, *by paying the legacy in hard guineas of British coinage,' without reference to the sum he had already paid her* — which a due regard to justice and the memory of his much lamented friend would not permit him to consider as the accomplishment of Sir Francis's intention."— *Wilkinson.*

[2] "'I will bring the rascals back with me into line,' exclaimed Gates, as the militia broke and fled at Camden; and, leaving Kalb to bear the brunt

He certainly looked forward to a possible retreat; and, while he cannot be censured for guarding against every emergency, he, to say the least, was not animated by the spirit which led Cortez to burn his ships behind him. At the beginning of the battle Quarter Master General Lewis was directed to take eight men with him to the field to convey to Gates information from time to time concerning the progress of the action. At the same time, the baggage trains were all loaded up ready to move at a moment's notice. The first information that arrived, represented the British troops to exceed the Americans, and the trains were ordered to move on; but by the time they were under motion, more favorable news was received, and the order was countermanded. Thus they continued to move on and halt alternately until the joyful news — "The British have retreated" — rang through the camp, which reaching the attentive guard of the teamsters, they all with one accord swung their hats, and gave three long and loud cheers. The glad tidings were transmitted with such rapidity from one to another that by the time the victorious troops had returned to their quarters, the American camp was thronged with inhabitants from the surrounding country and formed a scene of the greatest exultation.

From the foregoing account it will be seen that the term *Battle of Bemis's Heights*, used to designate the action of October 7th is erroneous, and calculated to

---

of the attack, he spurred after them, not drawing rein till he reached Charlotte, sixty miles from the field of battle!"— *Green's German Element in the War of American Independence.*

mislead. The original maps show that the second engagement began on ground two hundred and twenty-five rods southwest of the site of the first (known as the battle of Freeman's farm) and ended on the same ground on which that action was fought. The only interest, in fact, that attaches to Bemis's heights — fully one mile and a quarter south of the battle ground — is, that they were the head-quarters of Gates during, and a short time previous, to the battle. This is called variously the "Battle of Stillwater, Bemis's Heights, and of Saratoga."

VIII.

On the morning of the 8th, before daybreak, Burgoyne left his position, now utterly untenable, and defiled on to the meadows by the river where were his supply trains, but was obliged to delay his retreat until the evening because his hospital could not be sooner removed. He wished also to avail himself of the darkness. The Americans immediately moved forward and took possession of the abandoned camp. Burgoyne, having condensed his forces upon some heights which were strong by nature, and covered by a ravine running parallel with the entrenchments of his late camp, a random fire of artillery and small arms was kept up through the day, particularly on the part of the German chasseurs and the Provincials. These stationed in coverts of the ravine kept up an annoying fire upon every one crossing their line of vision, and it was by a shot from one of these lurking parties, that General Lincoln received a severe wound in the leg while riding near the line. It was evident from the movements of the British that they were preparing to retreat; but the American troops, having, in the delirium of joy consequent upon their victory, neglected to draw and eat their rations, and being withal not a little fatigued with the two days' exertions, fell back to their camp which had been left standing in the morning. Retreat, was, indeed, the only alternative left to the British commander, since it was now quite certain that he could not cut his way through the American army, and his supplies were reduced to a short allowance for five days.

Meanwhile, in addition to the chagrin of defeat, a deep gloom pervaded the British camp. The gallant and beloved Fraser, the life and soul of the army, lay dying in the little farm-house on the river bank occupied by Mrs. General Riedesel.[1]

General Fraser had been borne off the field supported by two soldiers, one on each side of his horse. "When he arrived in camp," says Lamb, "the officers all anxiously

---

[1] The quarters which Mrs. Riedesel then occupied, and in which General Fraser died — known then as the Taylor house, and since as the Smith house, was situated three miles and a half south of Fish creek, and about one hundred rods north of Wilbur's basin or the old Ensign store. At the time of the battle, it stood by the side of the old road to Stillwater, on the west margin of the intervale at the foot of the hill on which General Fraser was buried. When, some years afterward, the present turnpike was constructed, running twenty rods from the old road, the latter was discontinued, and a Mr. Smith (who had purchased the old house) drew it to the west side of the turnpike and turned it into a tavern. It stood until within four years, when it was torn down. The foundations can yet be seen. In 1820, the late Theodore Dwight visited the spot, and made a drawing of it, which has been engraved and is here given on the opposite page.

SMITH OR TAYLOR HOUSE, IN WHICH GEN. FRASER DIED.

inquired as to his wound; but the downcast look and melancholy that were visible to every one too plainly spoke his situation, and all the answer he could make to the many inquiries, was a shake of his head, expressive that all was over with him. So much was he beloved, that even the women flocked round, solicitous for his fate. When he reached his tent, and was recovered a little from the faintness occasioned by the loss of blood, he told those around him, that he saw the man who shot him; he was a rifleman, and aimed from a tree. After the surgeon had dressed his wound he said to him very composedly, 'Tell me, to the best of your skill and judgment, if you think my wound is mortal?' when he replied, 'I am sorry, sir, to inform you, that it is; and that you cannot possibly live more than twenty-four hours,' the general called for pen, ink, and paper, and after making his will, and distributing a few little tokens to the officers of his suite, desired that he might be removed to the general hospital."

Mrs. Riedesel, whose "charming blue eyes," General Wilkinson says, he has often seen bedewed with tears at the recital of her sufferings — has described the last scene in the life of this unfortunate officer with such unaffected pathos, that we give it in her own words, simply premising that on the previous day she had expected Burgoyne, Phillips and Fraser to dine with her after their return from the reconnaissance of the morning. Mrs. Reidesel says:

"About four o'clock in the afternoon, instead of the guests who were to have dined with us, they brought in to me, upon a litter, poor General Fraser mortally wounded. Our dining table, which was already spread, was taken away, and in its place, they fixed up a bed for the general. I sat in a corner of the room trembling and quaking. The noises grew continually louder. The thought that they might bring my husband in the same manner was to me dreadful, and tormented me incessantly. The general said to the surgeon, 'do not conceal anything from me, must I die?' The ball had gone through his bowels precisely as in the case of Major Harnage. Unfortunately, however, the general had eaten a hearty breakfast, by reason of which the intestines were distended, and the ball had gone through them. I heard him often, amidst his groans exclaim, 'oh fatal ambition! Poor General Burgoyne! My poor wife!'. Prayers were read to him. He then sent a message to General Burgoyne begging that he would have him buried the following day at six o'clock in the evening, on the top of a hill, which was a sort of a redoubt.

"I knew no longer which way to turn. The whole entry was filled with the sick who were suffering with the camp-sickness, a kind of dysentery. I spent the night in this manner, at one time comforting Lady Ackland, whose husband was wounded, and a prisoner, and at another looking upon my children, whom I had put to bed. As for myself, I could not go to sleep, as I had General Fraser, and all the other gentlemen in my room, and was constantly afraid that my children would wake up and cry, and thus disturb the poor dying man, who often sent to beg my pardon for making me so much trouble. About three o'clock in the morning, they told me that he could not last much longer. I had desired to be apprised of the approach of this moment. I accordingly wrapped up the children in the coverings and went with them into the entry. Early in the morning, at eight o'clock, he died."

General Fraser belonged to the house of Lovatt, whose family name was Fraser. The Earl of Lovatt was one of the noblemen who were compromised by the rebellion of the last Stuart pretender, and whose fortunes were reversed at the battle of Culloden in 1795. General Fraser, a scion of the house, of a sanguine temperament, ardent and ambitious, entered the army, and became so distinguished for his military ability, as to be advanced to the rank of brigadier general, and was selected for a command in Burgoyne's expedition. He had received intimations that if the enterprise were successful, the government would revoke the act of attainder, and restore to him the family title and estates. With a knowledge of these facts, it is easy to understand the meaning of the wounded general's exclamations as he lay waiting for death in the little Taylor farm house, the first alluding to the sad extinction of his own cherished hopes of well earned position and renown; the second betraying his anxiety for his commander, whose impending disgrace he clearly foresaw.[1]

---

[1] In this connection, the reader will doubtless recall the last words of the Hessian colonel, Donop, who fell at the battle of Red Bank, N. J., Oct. 22, of the same year, aged 37. He was found by the French officer, Capt. Duplesse, lying helpless on the battle-field among the dead and wounded, and brought to the house of a Quaker, where he lay three days in agony

"After they had washed the corpse," Mrs. Riedesel continues, "they wrapped it in a sheet, and laid it on a bedstead. We then again came into the room, and had this sad sight before us the whole day. At every instant, also, wounded officers of my acquaintance arrived, and the cannonade again began. A retreat was spoken of, but there was not one movement made towards it. About four o'clock in the afternoon I saw the new house which had been built for me in flames; the enemy therefore were not far from us. We learned that General Burgoyne intended to fulfill the last wish of General Fraser and to have him buried at six o'clock, in the place designated by him. This occasioned an unnecessary delay, to which a part of the misfortunes of the army was owing. Precisely at six o'clock the corpse was brought out, and we saw the entire body of generals with their retinues assisting at the obsequies. The English chaplain, Mr. Brudenel, performed the funeral services. The cannon balls flew continually around and over the party.[1] The American general, Gates, afterward said

---

before he expired. Almost his last words to Duplesse, who had tenderly nursed him were: "I die in the arms of honor — a sudden termination for a glorious career; but I die the victim of my ambition, and of the avarice of my prince!"

[1] These shots were fired from the rising ground above the eastern shore, almost opposite the scene of the interment, and not, as some have thought, from Willard's mountain. This last is quite an elevated portion of land about three miles north-east of Wilbur's basin and derives its name from the following fact: "At the time Burgoyne, with his veteran army, was encamped at and near Wilbur's basin, a man by the name of Willard, in company with a few others, took a good spyglass, and went to the top of

that if he had known that it was a burial he would not have allowed any firing in that direction. Many cannon balls also flew not far from me, but I had my eyes fixed upon the hill, where I distinctly saw my husband in the midst of the enemy's fire, and therefore I could not think of my own danger." Certainly, says General Riedesel in his journal, "it was a real military funeral, one that was unique of its kind."

General Burgoyne has himself described this funeral with his usual eloquence and felicity of expression. "The incessant cannonading during the solemnity, the steady attitude and unaltered voice with which the chaplain officiated, though frequently covered with dust, which the shot threw up on all sides of him, the mute but expressive mixture of sensibility and indignation upon the mind of every man who was present, the growing duskiness added to the scenery, and the whole marked a character of that juncture that would make one of the finest subjects for the pencil of a master that the field ever exhibited. To the canvas, and to the

---

this mountain, for the purpose of ascertaining, as near as possible, the number of the British troops, the situation of their camp, and to watch their movements, and made his reports accordingly; which, it was said, were of much benefit to the Americans, and from which circumstance it has ever since retained the appellation of 'Willard's mountain.'"

The *precise* spot where Fraser was buried, is now (1877) marked by two tall pines, which stand like two grim sentinels over the remains of the gallant general. The hills on the top of which the latter was buried, stands some forty rods west of the river-road from Schuylerville to Stillwater, and about two hundred rods north of Wilbur's basin. The Champlain canal passes close to its base. For an incident connected with the tradition of the removal of Fraser's remains see Appendix No. V.

faithful pen of a more important historian, gallant friend! I consign thy memory. There may thy talents, thy manly virtues, their progress and their period find due distinction, and long may they survive, long after the frail record of my pen shall be forgotten!"

IX.

As soon as the funeral services were finished and the grave closed, an order was issued that the army should retreat as soon as darkness had set in; and the commander, who, in the beginning of the campaign, had vauntingly uttered in general orders that memorable sentiment, "Britons never retreat," was now compelled to steal away in the night, leaving his hospital containing four hundred and sixty sick and wounded, to the mercy of a victorious and hitherto despised enemy. Gates in this, as in all other instances, extended to his former companion in arms the greatest humanity.

The army begun its retrograde movement at nine o'clock in the evening of the 8th in the midst of a pouring rain, Riedesel leading the van, and Phillips bringing up the rear with the advanced corps. All deplored the loss of Fraser who had always shown "as great skill in managing a retreat as bravery in leading an attack." Indeed, he used frequently to say that if the army had the misfortune to retreat, he would ensure, with the advanced corps, to bring it off in safety. This was a piece of generalship of which he was not a little vain, having, during the Seven years' war, made good his retreat with five hundred chasseurs in sight of the French army.

In this retreat, the same lack of judgment on the part of Burgoyne is apparent. Had that general, as Riedesel and Phillips advised, fallen immediately back across the Hudson and taken up his former position behind the Batten kil, not only would his communications with Lake George and Canada have been restored, but he could, at his leisure, have awaited the movements of Clinton. Burgoyne, however, having arrived at Dovegat two hours before daybreak on the morning of the 9th, gave the order to halt, greatly to the surprise of his whole army. "Every one," says the journal of Riedesel, "was, notwithstanding, then of the opinion, that the army would make but a short stand, merely for its better concentration, as all saw that haste was of the utmost necessity, if they would get out of a dangerous trap."

At this time the heights of Saratoga, commanding the ford across Fish creek, were not yet occupied by the Americans in force; and up to seven o'clock in the morning, the retreating army might easily have reached that place, and thrown a bridge across the Hudson. General Fellows, who, by the orders of Gates, occupied the heights at Saratoga opposite the ford, was in an extremely critical situation. On the night of the 8th, Lieut. Col. Southerland, who had been sent forward to reconnoitre, crossed Fish creek, and guided by General Fellows's fires, found his camps so entirely unguarded, that he marched round it without being challenged. He then returned and, reporting to Burgoyne, entreated permission to attack Fellows with his regiment, but was refused. "Had not Burgoyne halted at Dovegat," says Wilkinson, "he must

GENERAL RIEDESEL.

have reached Saratoga before day, in which case Fellows would have been cut up and captured or dispersed, and Burgoyne's retreat to Fort George would have been unobstructed. As it was, however, Burgoyne's army reached Saratoga, just as the rear of our militia was ascending the opposite bank of the Hudson, where they took post and prevented its passage." Burgoyne, however, although within half an hour's march of Saratoga, gave the surprising order that "the army should bivouac in two lines, and await the day."

Mr. Bancroft ascribes this delay to the fact that Burgoyne "was still clogged with his artillery and baggage, and that the night was dark, and the roads weakened by rain." But according to the universal testimony of all the manuscript journals extant, the road which up to this time was sufficiently strong for the passage of the baggage and artillery trains, became, during the halt, so bad by the continued rain, that when the army again moved at four o'clock in the afternoon, it was obliged to leave behind the tents and camp equipage, which fell most opportunely into the hands of the Americans. Aside, however, from this, it is a matter of record that the men, through their officers, pleaded with Burgoyne to be allowed to proceed, notwithstanding the storm and darkness ; while the officers themselves pronounced the delay "madness." But whatever were the motives of the English general this delay lost him his army, and perhaps the British crown her American colonies.

During the halt at Dovegats, there occurred one of those incidents which relieve with fairer lights and softer tints the gloomy picture of war. Lady Harriet Ackland had, like the Baroness Riedesel, accompanied her husband to America and gladly shared with him the vicissitudes of campaign life.[1] Major John Dyke Ackland, a son of Sir Thomas Ackland, was a rough, blunt man, but a gallant soldier and devoted husband, and she loved him dearly. She had already been subjected to great inconvenience and distress before the army arrived at Saratoga. She had been distinguished by her devotion and unremitting attention to her husband, when he lay sick at Chamblee in a miserable hut. She was, indeed, not only the idol of her husband but, together with the Baroness Riedesel, shared the admiration of the whole army, continually making little presents to the officers belonging to the major's corps, whenever she had anything among her stores that she thought would gratify

---

[1] "While the British army on their advance were encamped at Dovegat (Coveville), Major Ackland's tent took fire, and Lady Harriet and himself were nearly lost in the flames. The major being with the advance guard, and obliged to be very diligent in attending to his command, in consequence of the difficulty and danger of his position, kept a candle burning in his tent. A Newfoundland dog, of which they were very fond, unfortunately pushed the candle from a table or chair where it was standing; it fell against the side of the tent, and instantly the whole was in a blaze. A soldier who was keeping guard near them, rushed in and dragged Major Ackland from the flames, while Lady Harriet crept out almost unconsciously through the back part of the tent. When she looked round she saw with horror her husband rushing into the flames in search of her. Again the soldier brought him out, though not without considerable injury to both. Everything in the tent was consumed; but the major and his lady were too happy to see each other in safety to regret the loss of their camp equipage." — *Neilson*.

them. In return she received from them every attention which could mitigate the hardships she daily encountered. Again, when her husband was wounded at Hubbardton, she carefully watched over him until he was restored to health. The moment she heard of his wound, she hastened from Montreal, where she had intended to remain, and crossed the lake in opposition to her husband's injunctions, resolved to share his fate and be separated from him no more. And now, ever since he had been wounded and taken prisoner in the action of the 7th, she had been in sore distress, and it had required all the comforting attentions of the baroness to reassure her. As soon as the army halted, by the advice of the latter, she determined to visit the American camp, and implore the permission of its commander to join her husband, and by her presence alleviate his sufferings.

Accordingly, on the 9th, she requested permission of Burgoyne to depart. "Though I was ready to believe," says that general, "that patience and fortitude in a supreme degree were to be found, as well as every other virtue, under the most tender forms, I was astonished at this proposal. After so long an agitation of spirits, exhausted not only for want of rest, but absolutely want of food, drenched in rains for twelve hours together, that a woman should be capable of such an undertaking as delivering herself to an enemy probably in the night, and uncertain of what hands she might fall into, appeared an effort above human nature. The assistance I was enabled to give was small indeed. All I could furnish to her was an open boat, and a few lines, written upon dirty wet paper to General Gates, recommending her to his protection." [1]

In the midst of a driving autumnal storm, and with nothing but a little spirits and water, obtained from the wife of a soldier, to sustain her, Lady Ackland set out at dusk in an open boat for the American camp, accompanied by Mr. Brudenell the chaplain, her waiting maid, and her husband's valet. At ten o'clock, they reached the American advanced guard under the command of Major Henry Dearborn. Lady Ackland, herself, hailed the sentinel, and as soon as the bateau struck the shore, the party were immediately conveyed into the log-cabin of the major, who had been ordered to detain the flag until the morning, the night being exceedingly dark, and the quality of the lady unknown. Major Dearborn gallantly gave up his room to his guest, a fire was kindled, a cup of tea provided, and as soon as Lady Ackland made herself known, her mind was relieved from its anxiety by the assurance of her husband's safety. "I visited," says Adjutant General Wilkinson, "the guard before sunrise. Lady Ackland's boat had put off, and was floating down the stream to our camp, where General Gates, whose gallantry will not be denied, stood ready to receive her with all the tenderness and respect to which

---

[1] Nor was it in the higher walks of life only that female heroism and conjugal devotion were displayed. Lamb relates an instance of the confinement of a serjeant's wife in the woods near Lake George through which she was going in pursuit of her husband then in Burgoyne's army at Fort Miller. For this in detail see Appendix No. XV.

her rank and condition gave her a claim. Indeed, the feminine figure, the benign aspect, and polished manners of the charming woman, were alone sufficient to attract the sympathy of the most obdurate; but if another motive could have been wanting to inspire respect, it was furnished by the peculiar circumstances of Lady Harriet, then in that most delicate situation, which cannot fail to interest the solicitude of every being possessing the form and feelings of a man." The kindness which had been shown to his wife, Major Ackland reciprocated, while in parole in New York, by doing all in his power to mitigate the sufferings of the American prisoners. His end was particularly sad. On his return to England, he was killed in a duel to which he had been challenged for warmly defending American courage against the aspersions of a brother officer. Lady Ackland became insane, and remained so two years, when, having recovered, she married the chaplain, Brudenell.¹

X.

On the evening of the 9th, the main portion of the drenched and weary army forded Fish creek waist deep, and bivouacked in a wretched position in the open air on the opposite bank. Burgoyne remained on the south side of the creek, with Hamilton's brigade as a guard, and passed the night in the mansion of General Schuyler. The officers slept on the ground with no other covering

---

¹ As every thing connected with this devoted wife must be of interest, the reader is referred to Appendix No. VII for some particulars of her after life.

than oilcloth. Nor did their wives fare better. "I was wet," says the Baroness Riedesel, "through and through by the frequent rains, and was obliged to remain in this condition the entire night, as I had no place whatever, where I could change my linen. I therefore seated myself before a good fire and undressed my children, after which we laid down together upon some straw. I asked General Phillips who came up to where we were, why we did not continue our retreat while there was yet time, as my husband had pledged himself to cover it, and bring the army through? 'Poor woman!' answered he, 'I am amazed at you! completely wet through, have you still the courage to wish to go further in this weather! Would that you were our commanding general! He halts because he is tired, and intends to spend the night here and give us a supper.'"

Burgoyne, however, would not think of a further advance that night; and while his army were suffering from cold and hunger, and every one was looking forward to the immediate future with apprehension, "the illuminated mansion of General Schuyler," says the Brunswick Journal, "rang with singing, laughter, and the gingling of glasses. There Burgoyne was sitting with some merry companions, at a dainty supper, while the champagne was flowing. Near him sat the beautiful wife of an English commissary, his mistress.[1] Great as

---

[1] Were this statement made by Mrs. Riedesel only — for she states the same thing — instead of by the Brunswick Journal, it might be necessary to receive it with caution, since her prejudices sometimes unintentionally led her into extremes. Mr. Fonblanque, however, in his admirable *Life*

the calamity was, the frivolous general still kept up his orgies. Some were even of opinion that he had merely made that inexcusable stand for the sake of passing a merry night. Riedesel thought it his duty to remind his general of the danger of the halt, but the latter returned all sorts of evasive answers." This statement is corroborated by Mrs. Riedesel who also adds, "the following day General Burgoyne repaid the hospitable shelter of Schuyler's mansion by burning it, with its valuable barns and mills, to the ground, under pretence that he might be better able to cover his retreat, but others say, out of mean revenge on the American general."[1]

But the golden moment had fled. On the following morning, the 10th, it was discovered that the Americans under Fellows were in possession of the Batten kil, on the

---

and *Correspondence of General Burgoyne*, recently published, admits this by implication, but seeks to leave the impression that the champagne and the "flirtation," as he calls it, were indulged in by the British general to relieve the mental agony consequent upon his defeat. Mr. Fonblanque's book is characterized by great fairness and liberality—a circumstance which should commend it to American readers.

[1] Lamb who was present at the time of the fire claims, on the contrary, that the burning of the barns was purely accidental, and of the house, the rasult of military necessity. For Lamb's version of the affair which, in justice to Burgoyne, should be read, see Appendix, No. VIII.

The present Schuyler mansion which was rebuilt soon after by Schuyler, stands a few yards northeast of the site of the one burned by Burgoyne. The timber for it was cut down and drawn from the forest, and the house rebuilt and put in complete readiness for the reception of the family in the space of fifteen days! Schuyler, however, had the assistance of the entire army of Gates for this purpose. This fact was related to the author by Mr. Strover, who now owns and occupies the house, and who also was in Gates's army.

opposite side of the Hudson; and Burgoyne, considering it too hazardous to attempt the passage of the river, ordered the army to occupy the same quarters on the heights of Saratoga, which they had used on first crossing the river on the 13th of September. At the same time, he sent ahead a working party to open a road to Fort Edward, his intention being to continue his retreat along the west bank of the Hudson river to the front of that fort, force a passage across and take possession of the post. Col. Cochran, however, had already garrisoned it with two hundred men, and the detachment hastly fell back upon the camp.

XI.

Meanwhile, General Gates, who had begun the pursuit at noon of the 10th with his main army, reached the high ground south of Fish creek, at four the same afternoon. The departure of Burgoyne's working party for Fort Edward led him to believe that the entire British army were in full retreat having left only a small guard to protect their baggage. Acting upon this impression, he ordered Nixon and Glover, with their brigades, to cross the creek early next morning, under cover of the fog which at this time of year usually prevails till after sunrise, and attack the British camp. The English general had notice of this plan, and placing a battery in position, he posted his troops in ambush behind the thickets along the banks of the creek; and concealed also by the fog, waited the attack confident of victory. At early daylight, Morgan, who had again been selected to begin the action, crossed the creek with his men, on a raft of floating logs, and falling in with a British picket, was fired upon, losing a lieutenant, and two privates. This led him to believe that the main body of the enemy had not moved, in which case, with the creek in his rear, enveloped by a dense fog and unacquainted with the ground, he felt his position to be most critical. Meanwhile, the whole army advanced as far as the south bank of the creek and halted. Nixon, however, who was in advance, had already crossed the stream near its confluence with the Hudson, and captured a picket of sixty men, and a number of bateaux, and Glover was preparing to follow him, when a deserter from the enemy confirmed the suspicions of Morgan. This was corroborated a few moments afterward, by the capture of a reconnoitering party of thirty-five men by the advanced guard under Captain Goodale of Putnam's regiment, who, discerning them through the fog just as he neared the opposite bank, charged and took them without firing a gun. Gates was at this time at his headquarters a mile and a half in the rear; and before intelligence could be sent to him, the fog cleared up, and exposed the entire British army under arms. A heavy fire of artillery and musketry was immediately opened upon Nixon's brigade, and they retreated in considerable disorder across the creek.

General Learned had, in the meantime, reached Morgan's corps, with his own and Patterson's brigade, and was advancing rapidly to the attack, in obedience to a standing order issued the day before " that in case of an attack against any point, whether in front, flank or rear, the troops are to fall upon the enemy at all quarters." He had arrived within two hundred yards of Burgoyne's battery, and in a few moments more, would have been engaged at great disadvantage, when Wilkinson reached him with the news that the right wing under Nixon had given way, and that it would be prudent to retreat — The brave old general hesitated to comply. " Our brethren," said he, " are engaged on the right, and the standing order is to attack."

In this dilemma Wilkinson exclaimed to one of Gates's aides standing near, " Tell the general that his own fame and the interests of the cause are at hazard ; that his presence is necessary with the troops." Then turning to Learned, he continued, " our troops on the right have retired, and the fire you hear is from the enemy ; although I have no orders for your retreat, I pledge my life for the general's approbation." By this time several field officers had joined the group, and a consultation being held, the proposition to retreat was approved. Scarcely had they turned about when the enemy, who, expecting their advance had been watching their movements with shouldered arms, fired and killed an officer and several men before they made good their retreat.

Had the plan of the English general succeeded, it is difficult to say what might have been the result. With the brigades of Nixon, Glover, Learned, and Patterson cut off, and with the consequent demoralization of the American army, his retreat would have been rendered less difficult, or, retracing his steps, he might possibly have entered Albany in triumph. He himself called it "one of the most adverse strokes of fortune during the campaign."

The ground occupied by the two armies after this engagement, resembled a vast amphitheatre — the British occupying the arena, and the Americans the elevated surroundings. Burgoyne's camp, upon the meadows and the heights of Saratoga north of Fish creek, was fortified and extended half a mile parallel with the river, most of its heavy artillery being on an elevated plateau, northeast of the village of Schuylerville. On the American side, Morgan and his sharpshooters were posted on still higher ground west of the British, extending along their entire rear. On the east or opposite bank of the Hudson, Fellows, with three thousand men, was strongly entrenched behind heavy batteries; while Gates, with the main body of the Continentals, lay on the high ground south of Fish creek and parallel with it. On the north, Fort Edward was held by Stark with two thousand men, and between that post and Fort George in the vicinity of Glen's Falls, the Americans had a fortified camp; while from the surrounding country, large bodies of yeomanry flocked in, and voluntarily posted themselves up and down the river. The "trap" which Riedesel had foreseen, was already sprung.

. The Americans, impatient of delay, urged Gates to attack the British camp, but that general, now assured that the surrender of Burgoyne was only a question of time, and unwilling needlessly to sacrifice his men, refused to accede to their wishes, and quietly awaited the course of events.

XII.

The beleaguered army was now constantly under fire both in its flanks and rear and in the front. The outposts were continually engaged with those of the Americans; and many of the patrols, detached to keep up communication between the centre and right wing, were taken prisoners. The captured bateaux were of great use to the Americans who were now enabled to transport troops across the river at pleasure and reinforce the posts on the road to Fort Edward. Every hour the position of the British grew more desperate, and the prospect of escape less. There was no place of safety for the baggage, and the ground was covered with dead horses that had been killed by the enemy's round shot and bullets, or by exhaustion, as there had been no forage for four days. Even for the wounded there was no spot that could afford a safe shelter, while the surgeon was binding up their wounds. The whole camp became a scene of constant fighting. The soldier dare not lay aside his arms night or day, except to exchange his gun for the spade, when new entrenchments were to be thrown up. He was also debarred of water although close to Fish creek and the river, it being at the hazard of his life in the day time to get any, from the number of sharpshooters Morgan had posted in trees; and at night he was sure to be taken prisoner if he attempted it. All the water accessible was from a muddy spring, and what could be obtained out of the holes the cattle made with their feet; while by way of luxury, when it rained hard, the men used to catch it in their caps to mix with their flour. Without tents to shelter them from the heavy and incessant rains, the sick and wounded would drag themselves along into a quiet corner of the woods and lie down and die upon the damp ground. Nor were they safe even here, since, every little while, a ball would come crashing down among the trees. The few houses that were at the foot of the heights were nearest to the fire from Fellows's batteries, notwithstanding which the wounded officers and men crawled hither, seeking protection in the cellars. In one of these cellars the Baroness Riedesel ministered to the sufferers like an angel of light and comfort. She made them broth, dressed their wounds, purified the atmosphere by sprinkling vinegar on hot coals, and was ever ready to perform any friendly service, even such from which the sensitive nature of a woman will recoil. Once, while thus engaged, a furious cannonade was opened upon the house under the impression that it was the headquarters of the English commander. "Alas," says Mrs. Riedesel, " it harbored none but wounded men and women." Eleven cannon balls went through the house, and those in the cellar could plainly hear them crashing through the walls over head. One poor fellow, by the name of Jones, a British surgeon whose leg they were about to amputate in the room above, had his other leg taken off by one of these cannon balls in the very midst of the operation. Often General Riedesel wished to withdraw his wife from danger by sending her to the American camp, but the latter remonstrated with him on the ground that to be with people whom she would be obliged to treat with

Present (1877) appearance of the house, in the cellar of which Mrs. Riedesel stayed during the cannonade.

The Cellar.

courtesy, while, perhaps, he was being killed, would be even yet more painful than all she was then forced to suffer. The greatest suffering was experienced by the wounded from thirst, which was not relieved until a soldier's wife volunteered to bring water from the river. This she continued to do with safety, the Americans gallantly withholding their fire whenever she appeared.

Meanwhile, order grew more and more lax, and the greatest misery prevailed throughout the entire army. The commissaries neglected to distribute provisions among the troops, and although there were cattle still left, not one had been killed. More than thirty officers came to the baroness for food, forced to this step from sheer starvation, one of them a Canadian, being so weak as to be unable to stand. She divided among them all the provisions at hand; and having exhausted her store without satisfying them, in an agony of despair, she called to Adjutant General Petersham, one of Burgoyne's aides, who chanced to be passing at the time, and said to him passionately, "Come and see for yourself these officers who have been wounded in the common cause, and are now in want of everything that is due them. It is your duty to make a representation of this to the general." A quarter of an hour afterward, Burgoyne, himself, came to Mrs. Riedesel, and thanked her for reminding him of his duty. In reply, she apologized for meddling with things, she well knew, were out of a woman's province; still, it was impossible, she said, for her to keep silent, when she saw so many brave men in want of food, and had nothing more to give them. "Thereupon," says the baroness, "he thanked me once more (though I believe in his heart, he has never forgiven me the lashing I gave him), and went from me to the officers, and said to them that he was very sorry for what had happened and that he had now, through an order, remedied everything, but why had they not come to him, as his cook was always at their service?" They replied, that English officers were not accustomed to visit the kitchen of their general, and that they had "gratefully received every morsel from Mrs. Riedesel as they felt that she gave it to them directly from her heart."

On the afternoon of the 12th, Burgoyne held a consultation with Riedesel, Phillips, and the two brigadiers, Hamilton and Gall, to whom he submitted the choice of one of the following courses:

"1. To wait in the present position an attack from the enemy, or the chance of favorable events.

"2. To attack the enemy.

"3. To retreat, repairing the bridges as the army moves, for the artillery, in order to force the passage of the ford.

"4. To retreat by night, leaving the artillery and the baggage; and should it be found impracticable to force the passage with musketry, to attempt the upper ford or the passage round Lake George.

"5. In case the enemy, by extending to their left, leave their rear open, to march rapidly upon Albany."

The want of provisions rendered the first proposition inadmissible; while to break through the superior numbers of an enemy strongly posted and entrenched in every point was desperate and hopeless. In view of this, Riedesel strongly urged the adoption of the fourth proposition, and suggested, that the baggage should be left and a retreat begun on the west side of the Hudson; and, as Fort Edward had been reinforced by a strong detachment of the Americans, he further proposed to cross the river four miles above that fort and continue the march to Ticonderoga through the woods, leaving Lake George on the right — a plan which was then feasible, as the road on the west bank of the river had not yet been occupied by the enemy. This proposition was approved, and an order was issued that the retreat should be begun by ten o'clock that night. But when everything was in readiness for the march, Burgoyne, with his usual indecision, suddenly changed his mind and postponed the movement until the next day, when an unexpected maneuver of the Americans made it impossible. During the night, the latter, crossing the river on rafts near the Batten kil,[1] erected a heavy battery on an eminence opposite the mouth of that stream and on the left flank of the army, thus making the investment complete.[2]

Burgoyne was now entirely surrounded; the desertion

---

[1] The Dutch word *kil*, meaning a *channel*, is often used for *creek*, and always erroneously printed *kill*. It is not unusual to meet in American works with such an anomaly for instance as Batten *kill creek*.

[2] The fact of the erection of this battery seems to have escaped the notice of almost every writer upon the subject. The planting of it, however, was as is shown in the text, of vital importance to the complete success of the Americans.

of his German, Indian and Canadian allies,[1] and the losses in killed and wounded had reduced his army one-half; there was not food sufficient for five days; and not a word had been received from Clinton. Accordingly, on the 13th, he again called a general council of all his officers including the captains of companies. The council were not long in deciding, unanimously, that a treaty should be at once opened with General Gates for an honorable surrender — their deliberations being doubtless

---

[1] In justice to Burgoyne it should be stated, that the chief cause of the desertion of his Indian allies was the fact, that they were checked by him in their scalping and plundering of the unarmed. Indeed, the conduct of the English general was in this respect most humane. He said with truth in parliament, that in threatening to let loose his Indians " he spoke daggers but used none;" and yet with strange inconsistency, he was among the first strenuously to urge the employment of the Indians against the colonists. See Fonblanque's work, p. 178.

The desertion of the Canadians, however, had a different cause. In this connection, and to show the everlasting jealousy of professional soldiers towards volunteers, however deserving, consult Edward De Lancey in his address before the N. Y. His. Soc., Jan. 2d, 1877, and note how Burgoyne had to allow his provincial officers and men to escape to avoid penalties they incurred if captured, because not commissioned, although they should have been commissioned, according to agreement, before they entered upon the campaign.

Many of the Germans, also, availed themselves of this opportunity to desert, and settle good farms in the northern portion of New York. There is yet standing (1877) near Hon. John B. Haskin's place on Friend's lake, at Chestertown, Warren Co., N. Y., the cabin of a German deserter from Burgoyne's army, who settled there in the fall of 1777. The cabin was built in 1783, as the figures cut into the stone lintel above the fire-place attest. Mr. Charles H. Faxon, of Chestertown, a gentleman whose patriotic tastes are well known, did his best to have this cabin bought by the state and preserved as an heirloom for the country.

hastened by rifle balls, perforating the tent in which they were assembled, and an eighteen pound cannon ball sweeping across the table at which Burgoyne and his generals were seated.

Accordingly, the following day, the 14th, General Burgoyne sent Lieut. Col. Kingston to the headquarters of General Gates with a proposition for "a cessation of arms, during the time necessary to communicate the preliminary terms; by which in any extremity he and the army mean to abide." Lieut. Col. Kingston was met by Adj. Gen. Wilkinson on the banks of Fish creek, and conducted blindfolded to the American headquarters.[1]

---

[1] "At the hour appointed I repaired to the advanced post, accompanied by Mr. Henry Livingston, of the Upper Manor on the Hudson's river. The bridge across the Fish kil had been destroyed, but the sleepers remained. We did not wait many minutes before the chamade was beat at the advanced guard of the enemy, and an officer descending the hill, stepped across the creek on one of the sleepers of the late bridge; it was 'Major Kingston, with a message from Lieutenant General Burgoyne to Major General Gates.' I named to him 'Colonel Wilkinson, on the part of General Gates, to receive the message.' He paused a moment, pulled out a paper, looked at it, and observed, 'my orders direct me to Major-General Gates.' 'It is to save time and trouble that I am authorized to receive the message you bear.' He then took General Gates's note to General Burgoyne from his pocket, read it, and said 'General Gates has agreed to receive the message, and I am not authorized to deliver it to any other person.' 'Well then, sir, you must submit to be hood-winked.' He affected to start at the proposition, and objected, on the ground of its being an indignity: I could but smile at the expression, and observed, that 'I had understood there was nothing more common, than to blindfold military messengers, when they were admitted within the walls of a place, or the guards of a camp.' He replied, 'Well, sir, I will submit to it, but under the express

General Gates, upon the reception of this communication, authorized a cessation of arms until sunset, and having already prepared a schedule of the terms upon which he was prepared to treat, forwarded them by Kingston to Burgoyne. This schedule evinced that the American general was well acquainted with the distresses of the British, and was drawn up in terms of extreme liberality. It did not, however, satisfy Burgoyne, who returned it with the following answers annexed — Lieut. Col. Kingston, who delivered it, adding the following verbal message.

"If General Gates does not mean to recede from the 6th article, the treaty ends at once. The army will, to a man, proceed to any act of desperation rather than submit to that article."

---

stipulation, that no indignity is intended to the British arms.' I then carefully bound up his eyes with his own handkerchief; he took my arm, and in this way we walked upwards of a mile to head-quarters. Major Kingston appeared to be about forty; he was a well formed, ruddy, handsome man, and expatiated with taste and eloquence on the beautiful scenery of the Hudson's river, and the charms of the season: when I introduced him into General Gates's tent, and named him, the gentlemen saluted each other familiarly, with 'General Gates, your servant,'—'Ah! Kingston, how do you do?' and a shake of the hand. Being seated a few minutes, he arose and observed he had certain communications to make Major General Gates from Lieutenant General Burgoyne, and to guard against inaccuracy of memory, he had committed them to paper, and with permission would read them. The general consented, and the major took from his pocket and read."

MAJOR GENERAL GATES'S PROPOSALS, TOGETHER WITH
LIEUTENANT GENERAL BURGOYNE'S ANSWERS.

PROPOSITION.

I.— General Burgoyne's army being reduced by repeated defeats, by desertion, sickness, etc., their provisions exhausted, their military horses, tents and baggage taken or destroyed, their retreat cut off, and their camp invested, they can only be allowed to surrender as prisoners of war.

II.— The officers and soldiers may keep the baggage belonging to them. The generals of the United States never permit individuals to be pillaged.

III.— The troops, under his Excellency General Burgoyne will be conducted by the most convenient route to New England, marching by easy marches, and sufficiently provided for by the way.

IV.— The officers will be

ANSWER.

Lieut.-General Burgoyne's army, however reduced, will never admit that their retreat is cut off while they have arms in their hands.

Noted.

Agreed.

There being no officer

admitted on parole, and will be treated with the liberality customary in such cases, so long as they, by proper behavior, continue to deserve it, but those who are apprehended having broke their parole, as some British officers have done, must expect to be close confined.

V.—All public stores, artillery, arms, ammunition, carriages, horses, etc., etc., must be delivered to commissaries appointed to receive them.

VI.—These terms being agreed to and signed, the troops under his Excellency's, General Burgoyne's command, may be drawn up in their encampments, where they will be ordered to ground their arms, and may thereupon be marched to the river side on their way to Bennington.

in this army under, or capable of being under, the description of breaking parole, this article needs no answer.

All public stores may be delivered, arms excepted.

This article is inadmissible in any extremity. Sooner than this army will consent to ground their arms in their encampments, they will rush on the enemy determined to take no quarter.

Accompanying this document were counter-proposals from Burgoyne, which Gates returned with the following answers affixed:

General Burgoyne's Preliminary Articles, with General Gates's Answers.

The annexed answers being given to Major General Gates's proposals, it remains for Lieutenant General Burgoyne, and the army under his command, to state the following preliminary articles on their part.

I.—The troops to march out of their camp with the honors of war, and the artillery of the intrenchments, which will be left as hereafter, may be regulated.

I.—The troops to march out of their camp, with the honors of war, and the artillery of the intrenchments to the verge of the river, where the old fort stood, where their arms and the artillery must be left.

II.—A free passage to be granted to this army to Great Britain upon condition of not serving again in North America during the present contest, and a proper post to be assigned for the entry of transports to receive the troops, whenever General Howe shall so order.

II.—Agreed to, for the port of Boston.

Campaign of General John Burgoyne.

III.— Should any cartel take place by which this army or any part of it may be exchanged, the foregoing article to be void as far as such exchange shall be made.

III.— Agreed.

IV.— All officers to retain their carriages, battle-horses and other cattle, and no baggage to be molested or searched, the lieutenant general giving his honor that there are no public stores secreted therein. Major General Gates will of course take the necessary measures for the security of this article.

IV.— Agreed.

V. — Upon the march the officers are not to be separated from their men, and in quarters the officers are to be lodged according to rank, and are not to be hindered from assembling their men for roll callings, and other necessary purposes of regularity.

V. — Agreed to as far as circumstances will admit.

VI.—There are various corps in the army composed of sailors, bateauxmen, ar-

VI. — Agreed to - in the fullest extent.

tificers, drivers, independent companies, and followers of the army, and it is expected that those persons of whatever country, shall be included in the fullest sense and utmost extent of the above articles, and comprehended in every respect as British subjects.

VII. — All Canadians and persons belonging to the establishment in Canada, to be permitted to return there.

VII.— Agreed.

VIII.— Passports to be immediately granted for three officers, not exceeding the rank of captain, who shall be appointed by General Burgoyne to carry despatches to Sir William Howe, Sir Guy Carleton, and to Great Britain by the way of New York, and the public faith to be engaged that these despatches are not to be opened.

VIII.— Agreed.

IX.— The foregoing articles are to be considered only as preliminaries for framing a treaty, in the course

IX. — The capitulation to be finished by 2 o'clock this day, and the troops march from their

of which others may arise to be considered by both parties, for which purpose it is proposed, that two officers of each army shall meet and report their deliberations to their respective generals.

X. — Lieutenant General Burgoyne will send his deputy adjutant-general to receive Major General Gates's answer, to-morrow morning at 10 o'clock.

encampment at five, and be in readiness to move towards Boston to-morrow morning.

X. — Complied with.

These preliminary articles and their answers, being carried back to General Burgoyne, produced an immediate return of his messenger with the following note: " The first preliminary articles of Lieutenant General Burgoyne's proposals, and the 2d and the 3d, and 4th of those of Major General Gates, of yesterday, being agreed to, the formation of the proposed treaty is out of dispute: but the several subordinate articles and regulations necessarily springing from these preliminaries, and requiring explanation, and precision, between the parties, before a definite treaty can be safely executed, a longer time than that mentioned by General Gates in his answer to the ninth article, becomes indispensably necessary. Lieutenant General Burgoyne is willing to appoint two officers immediately, to meet two others from Major General Gates, to propound, discuss, and settle those subordinate articles, in order that the treaty in due form may be executed as soon as possible."

This meeting took place on the afternoon of the 15th, and the parties mutually signed articles of capitulation, or *Convention*, as Burgoyne wished to have it designated. A copy of the Convention was to be formally signed by the English general and delivered the next morning. Meanwhile, during the night, a provincial arrived from below, who stated that he had heard through a third party that Clinton had captured the forts on the Hudson highlands, and arrived at Æsopus eight days previously; and further, that by this time he was very likely at Albany. Burgoyne was so encouraged by this news, that he once more called together a council of war and laid before it the following questions:

1st. Whether a treaty, which was about being completed by his deputies, and which he himself had promised to sign, could be broken? Fourteen votes against eight decided this question in the negative.

2d. Whether the report of a man whom nobody knew was sufficient in our present situation to justify our refusal of so advantageous a treaty? The same number of votes decided this also in the negative.

3d. Whether the common soldiers possessed sufficient spirit to defend the present position of the army to the last man? All the officers of the left wing answered this in the affirmative. Those of the centre and right wings gave a similar answer, provided the enemy were attacked; but the men were too well acquainted with their defective positions to display the same bravery in case they were themselves attacked."

But notwithstanding these votes, Burgoyne was resolved, as the articles of capitulation were not yet signed, to repudiate the informal arrangement with Gates; and in order to gain time he informed him by letter that he had been told by deserters and other reliable persons that he had sent a considerable corps of his army toward Albany, and that this being contrary to all faith, he (Burgoyne) could not give his signature without being convinced that the American army outnumbered his own by at least three or four to one; Gates should therefore name an officer of his army who might see for himself the number of the enemy; and should Burgoyne, after hearing this officer's report, be convinced of the superior numbers of the Americans, he would at once sign the treaty. General Gates received this letter with considerable *nonchalance*, but replied that he would give his word of honor that his army was just as strong now as it was previous to the treaty, and that having since then been reinforced by a few brigades, it certainly did outnumber the English four to one, and this, too, without counting those troops that were on the other side of the Hudson and at Half Moon. He also gave Burgoyne to understand what it meant to break his word of honor, and offered to show his whole army to him after the latter had signed the treaty, when he would find that everything he had stated was true. Being, moreover, in no mood for temporizing, he drew up his troops in order of battle at early dawn of the next day, the 17th, and informed Burgoyne in plain terms, that he must either sign the treaty, or prepare for immediate battle. Riedesel and Phillips added their persuasions, representing to him that the news just received was mere hearsay, but even if it were true, to recede now would be in the highest degree dishonorable. Burgoyne thereupon yielded a reluctant assent, and the articles of capitulation were signed at nine o'clock the same morning.[1] These articles were as follows :

ARTICLES OF CONVENTION BETWEEN LIEUTENANT GENERAL BURGOYNE AND MAJOR GENERAL GATES.

1st. " The troops under Lieutenant General Burgoyne, to march out of their camp with the honors of war, and the artillery of entrenchments, to the verge of the river where the old fort stood, where the arms and artillery are to be left ; the arms to be piled by word of command from their own officers.

2d. A free passage to be granted to the army under Lieutenant-General Burgoyne to Great Britain, on condition of not serving again in North America during the present contest ; and the port of Boston is assigned for the entry of transports to receive the troops, whenever General Howe shall so order.

3d. Should any cartel take place, by which the army under General Burgoyne, or any part of it, may be exchanged, the foregoing articles to be void as far as such exchange should be made.

---

[1] The army of General Gates, which was on the west side of the Hudson, was formed in three lines. Three officers of the royal army (among them Captain Twiss of the engineers), having received orders from Burgoyne to count the troops of the enemy, found them to number between 13,000 and 14,000 men. Subsequently, Gates handed Burgoyne the official list of the men in his army. The American troops on the other side of the Hudson were not counted. These consisted chiefly of militia from the surrounding townships of New Hampshire and Connecticut.

This estimate includes only the number contained in the *immediate* camp and lines of Gates as seen by the three officers in passing through them. The exact number of Gates's army — not counting the troops on the other side of the Hudson — was 22,350 men. This appears by the official list sent by Gates himself to Burgoyne. Counting those on the other or east side of the river, the American army must have been at least 25,000.

4th. The army under Lieutenant General Burgoyne, to march to Massachusetts bay, by the easiest, most expeditious, and convenient route, and be quartered in, near, or as convenient as possible to Boston, that the march of the troops may not be delayed, when the transports shall arrive to receive them.

5th. The troops to be supplied on their march, and during their being in quarters, with provisions by Gen. Gates's orders, at the same rate of rations as the troops of his own army; and if possible, the officers' horses and cattle are to be supplied with forage at the usual rates.

6th. All officers to retain their carriages, battle-horses, and other cattle, and no baggage to be molested or searched; Lieutenant General Burgoyne giving his honor that there are no public stores secreted therein. Major General Gates will of course take the necessary measures for the due performance of this article. Should any carriages be wanted during the march for the transportation of officers' baggage, they are, if possible, to be supplied.

7th. Upon the march, and during the time the army shall remain in quarters in Massachusetts bay, the officers are not, as far as circumstances will admit, to be separated from their men. The officers are to be quartered according to rank, and are not to be hindered from assembling their men for roll-call, and the necessary purposes of regularity.

8th. All corps whatever of General Burgoyne's army whether composed of sailors, bateaux men, artificers, drivers, independent companies, and followers of the army of whatever country, shall be included in every respect as British subjects.

9th. All Canadians, and persons belonging to the Canadian establishment consisting of sailors, bateaux men, artificers, drivers, independent companies, and many other followers of the army, who come under no particular description, are to be permitted to return there; they are to be conducted, immediately by the shortest route to the first British post on Lake George, are to be supplied with provisions in the same manner as the other troops, are to be bound by the same condition of not serving during the present contest in North America.

10th. Passports to be immediately granted for three officers not exceeding the rank of captains, who shall be appointed by Lieutenant General Burgoyne, to carry despatches to Sir William Howe, Sir Guy Carleton, and to Great Britain by the way of New York; and Maj. General Gates engages the public faith, that these despatches shall not be opened. These officers are to set out immediately after receiving their despatches, and are to travel the shortest route, and in the most expeditious manner.

11th. During the stay of the troops in Massachusetts bay, the officers are to be admitted on parole, and are to be allowed to wear their side arms.

12th. Should the army under Lieutenant General Burgoyne find it necessary to send for their clothing and other baggage to Canada, they are to be permitted to do it in the most convenient manner, and the necessary passports granted for that purpose.

13th. These articles are to be mutually signed and exchanged to-morrow morning, at nine o'clock, and the troops under Lieutenant General Burgoyne, are to march out of their entrenchments at three o'clock in the afternoon.

(Signed)   HORATIO GATES, *Maj. Gen.*
(Signed)   J. BURGOYNE, *Lieut. Gen.*

Saratoga, *Oct.* 16, 1777.

To prevent any doubts that might arise from Lieutenant General Burgoyne's name not being mentioned in the above treaty, Major General Gates hereby declares that he is understood to be comprehended in it, as fully as if his name had been specifically mentioned.

HORATIO GATES.

The second clause of this agreement was not carried out by congress; and most of the captured army, with the exception of Burgoyne, Riedesel, Philips and Hamilton were retained as prisoners while the war lasted.

The excuses given by congress for this lack of faith were most paltry and unworthy of a body representing a great cause. The remonstrances to General Gates and congress remained unnoticed; and although Washington himself, earnestly urged a fulfillment of the pledge in which the honor of congress and of the country was involved "the most unworthy counsels prevailed. When, for instance, it was proposed that the embarcation of the troops should take place at Newport, R. I., an intention (perfectly absurd) was imputed to General Howe of breaking faith by causing Burgoyne's army to join him in New York. Again, when the transports were despatched to Boston, the port agreed upon, orders were given that the embarcation should be delayed until all accounts for the subsistence of the captured army had been settled; and on a settlement being offered, it was refused unless payment were made in gold, which, at the time, it was notoriously impossible to procure; and once more congress, driven from both of these positions, gravely stated that all the small arms had not been delivered up at the time of the surrender. Finally, in the beginning of January, 1778, congress passed a resolution indefinitely suspending the embarcation. The true reason for this course was, undoubtedly, the unworthy one that many of the troops might be brought over to the American cause by *desertion;* which, however, was unsuccessful, as — although it has been thought otherwise — not more than eighty Germans deserted from their colors after the surrender. Washington felt this keenly, and seems to have been greatly mortified at the decision of congress. In a letter to Burgoyne, dated at Headquarters, Penn., March 11th, 1778," he writes: "I take pleasure in the opportunity you have afforded me of assuring you that, far from suffering the views of national opposition to be embittered and debased by personal animosity, I am ever ready to do justice to the gentleman and the soldiers, and to esteem where esteem is due, however the idea of a public enemy may interpose."[1] By this action of congress, the Riedesels, Phillips and many other worthy officers as well as

---

[1] See *Life of Madame Riedesel*, also Fonblanque's *Life of Burgoyne*, for the correspondence in full between Washington and Burgoyne.

privates suffered great privation and misery for several years.

The Americans obtained by this victory, at a very critical period, an excellent train of brass artillery, consisting of forty-two guns of various calibre, four thousand six hundred and forty-seven muskets, four hundred set of harness, and a large supply of ammunition. The prisoners numbered five thousand, eight hundred and four, and the entire American force at the time of the surrender, including regulars (Continentals) and militia, was twenty thousand eight hundred and seventeen effective men.[1]

XIII.

At eleven o'clock on the morning of the 17th, the royal army left their fortified camp, and marched to the

---

[1] This does not conflict with the statement on page 110. During the time of the cessation of arms, while the articles of capitulation were preparing, the soldiers of the two armies often saluted, and discoursed with each other from the opposite banks of the river. Among the British was a soldier of the 9th regiment, named Maguire, who came down to the river side, with a number of his companions, and engaged in conversation with a party of Americans on the further shore. In a short time something was observed very forcibly to strike the mind of the honest Hibernian. He suddenly darted like lightning from his companions, and plunged into the stream. At the very same moment, one of the American soldiers, seized with a similar impulse, resolutely dashed into the water. The wondering soldiers on both sides beheld them eagerly swim toward the middle of the river, where they met. They hung on each other's necks and wept: and the loud cries of " my brother! my dear brother!!" which accompanied the transaction, soon cleared up the mystery to the astonished spectators. They were, it seems, both brothers; one had emigrated to America, and the other had entered the army; and both were totally ignorant until that hour that they were engaged in hostile combat against each other's life.

green in front of old Fort Hardy, on the meadow just
north of Fish creek, at its junction with the Hudson.¹
Here in the presence only of Morgan Lewis and Wilkinson, representing the American army, they left their
cannon and small arms. With a longing eye the artilleryman looked for the last time upon his faithful gun,
parting with it as from his bride, and that forever.
With tears trickling down his bronzed cheeks, the
bearded grenadier stacked his musket to resume it no
more. Others in their rage, knocked off the butts of
their arms, and the drummers stamped their drums to
pieces.²

---

¹ Fort Hardy was a military work built by the English, during the governorship of Sir Charles Hardy, and was intended to supersede the old fort which had been erected as early as the war of William and Mary, during the latter part of the 17th century. The lines of the entrenchments embrace about fifteen acres of ground. The outer works yet retain the appearance of a strong fortification, bounded south by the north side of Fish creek, and east by the right bank of the Hudson. Human bones, fragments of fire-arms, swords, balls, tools, implements, and broken crockery, are frequently picked up on this ground. In excavating the earth for the Champlain canal, which passes a few rods west of this fort, such numbers of human skeletons were found, as make it highly probable that this was the cemetery of the garrison.

² "General Riedesel was deeply affected by the sad events. At eight o'clock in the morning of the 17th, he collected all the German troops, and informed them of their fate. In solemnity and in silence, and with drooping heads, the brave and tried warriors heard the words from the mouth of their beloved leader, whose voice, manly at all times, trembled on this occasion, and who was obliged to summon all of his self-control to hide his emotions. 'It was no lack of courage on your part,' said he, among other things, to his men, 'by which this awful fate has come upon you. You will always be justified in the eyes of the world.' He con-

Immediately after the surrender, the British took up their march for Boston, whence they expected to embark, and bivouacked the first night at their old encampment at the base of the hill where Fraser was buried.

---

cluded his address, with the exhortation, that as good soldiers they should bear their misfortune with courage, and do their duty at all times, displaying order and discipline; for in so doing, they would retain the love of their sovereign, and the respect of their enemies.

"General Riedesel's next care was to save the colors. He, therefore, had them taken down from the flag staff, and gave them to his wife, who had them sewed up by a faithful soldier who was a tailor. Henceforth he slept upon them and fortunately saved them. What a dreary future was now in store for the weary soldier in this distant land! Certain of victory a few days ago after so many glorious battles, all prospect for honor and glory was lost in this campaign. In a few hours they were to lay down their arms, those arms with which they had so bravely fought against their enemies, those arms, too, that were now to be surrendered to the enemy, on whose will they were now dependent. Verily, a sadder fate than this cannot be imagined for a soldier!

"Inwardly, however, Riedesel chafed exceedingly at the result and at the bad management which had brought it about. In the first moments of vexation he wrote to the reigning prince at Brunswick as follows:

"'Your serene highness will understand by the accompanying report, now submitted to you, into what a desolate position our fine maneuvers have placed me and the troops of your highness. The reputation I have gained in Germany has been sacrificed to certain individuals, and I consider myself the most unfortunate man on earth.'

"But neither the court nor the public of Brunswick laid anything to the charge of Riedesel, or the troops. On the contrary, they felt the greatest sympathy with them in their unfortunate fate. This is shown, not only by the letters of Duke Charles, and Duke Ferdinand, the hereditary prince of Brunswick, but by the newspapers of that day, in which neither the troops nor their generals are in the slightest degree reproached. On the contrary, they acknowledge their good behavior."—*Memoirs of General Riedesel.*

As they debouched from the meadow, where they had deposited their arms, they passed between the Continentals who were drawn up in parallel lines. But on no face did they see exultation. "As we passed the American army," writes Lieut. Anbury, one of the captured officers, and bitterly prejudiced against his conquerors, "I did not observe the least disrespect, or even a taunting look, but all was mute astonishment and pity; and it gave us no little comfort to notice this civil deportment to a captured enemy, unmarred by the exulting air of victors." [1]

Early the same morning General Wilkinson, before the capitulation, visited Burgoyne in his camp, and accompanied him to the ground where his army were to lay down their arms. Having inspected the place, the two generals rode to the bank of the Hudson, where Burgoyne, surveying it with attention, asked his companion whether it was not fordable at that place? "Certainly, sir," said Wilkinson, "but do you observe the people on the opposite shore?". "Yes," replied Burgoyne, "I have seen them too long!"

The English general having expressed a wish to be formally introduced to his old comrade, Gates, Wilkinson arranged an interview a few moments after the capitulation. In anticipation of this meeting, Burgoyne had

---

[1] "General Gates showed himself on this occasion, exceedingly noble and generous toward the captives. That he might show in some manner the feeling of the Americans, he commanded his troops to wheel round the instant the English laid down their arms. He, himself, drew down the curtains of his carriage in which he had driven to the ground, and in which he was then seated." — *Brunswick Journal.*

bestowed the greatest care upon his toilet. He had attired himself in full court dress, and wore costly regimentals and a richly decorated hat with streaming plumes. Gates, a smaller man and with much less of manner, on the contrary, was dressed merely in a plain blue overcoat, which had upon it scarcely anything indicative of his rank. Upon the two generals first catching a glimpse of each other, they stepped forward simultaneously and advanced, until they were only a few steps apart, when they halted. The English general took off his hat, and making a polite bow, said. "The fortune of war, General Gates, has made me your prisoner." The American general, in reply, simply returned his greeting and said : "I shall always be ready to testify, that it has not been through any fault of your excellency."[1]

As soon as this introduction was over the other captive generals and their suites repaired to the cabin which constituted the head-quarters of Gates, where they

---

[1] A marginal note — supposed to be in the hand-writing of George Clinton — in Burgoyne's orderly book, gives the conversation between the two generals as follows : "'I am glad to see you,' said Gates. 'I am not glad to see you,' replied Burgoyne, 'It is my fortune, sir, and not my fault that I am here.'" Wilkinson, however, an eye-witness of the scene, and generally very accurate, gives the version in the text, which is more in keeping with the urbane manner that invariably characterized the English general.

The place where this meeting took place is about a hundred rods south of Fish creek, and fifty rods north of Gates's head-quarters. The bridge over the Champlain canal at this point probably indicates pretty accurately the precise spot. For the *location* of the headquarters of the American general, see note on pages 122-23.

The head-quarters of Gates was, in the language of Wilkinson, "A

were received with the greatest courtesy, and with the consideration due to brave but unfortunate men. After Riedesel had been presented to Gates, Morgan[1] and other American officers, he sent for his wife and children. It is to this circumstance, that we owe the portraiture of a lovely trait in General Schuyler's character. "In our passage through the American camp," the baroness writes, "I observed with great satisfaction, that no one cast at us scornful glances. On the contrary, they all greeted me, even showing compassion on their countenances at seeing a mother with her little children in such a condition. I confess I feared to come into the enemy's camp, as the thing was so entirely new

---

small hovel, about ten feet square, at the foot of a hill, out of which it had been partially dug; the floor had been prepared by nature; while in one corner four forks with cross-pieces, supported the boards which received the general's pallet."

[1] "Morgan was a large, strong bodied personage, whose appearance gave the idea history has left us of Belisarius. His manners were of the severer cast; but where he became attached he was kind and truly affectionate. This is said, from experience of the most sensitive and pleasing nature; activity, spirit and courage in a soldier, procured his good will and esteem. He was a strict disciplinarian. Permit an anecdote. He had obtained the command of the rifle corps from Arnold without any advertence to the better claim of Hendricks, who, though the younger man was of the three captains, in point of rank, by the dates of commissions, the superior officer. Hendricks, for the sake of peace in the army, and of good order, prudently and good naturedly acquiesced in his assumption of the command, for Morgan had seen more service in our former wars.

At this place Morgan had given it out in orders, that no one should fire. One Chamberlaine, a worthless fellow, who did not think it worth while to draw his bullet, had gone some hundreds of yards into the woods, and discharged his gun. Lieut. Steele happened to be in that quarter at the

to me. When I approached the tents a noble looking man came toward me and took the children out of the wagon; embraced and kissed them; and then with tears in his eyes helped me also to alight. He then led me to the tent of General Gates, with whom I found Generals Burgoyne and Phillips who were upon an extremely friendly footing with him. Presently, the man who had received me so kindly, came up and said to me: 'It may be embarrassing to you to dine with all these gentlemen; come now with your children into my tent, where I will give you, it is true, a frugal meal, but one that will be accompanied by the best of wishes.' 'You are certainly,' answered I, 'a husband and a father since

---

time; Steele had but arrived at the fire, where we sat, when Morgan, who had seen him coming, approached our camp, and seated himself within our circle. Presently Chamberlaine came, gun in hand, and was passing our fire, towards that of his mess. Morgan called to the soldier, accused him as the defaulter; this the man (an arrant liar) denied. Morgan appealed to Steele. Steele admitted he heard the report, but knew not the party who discharged the gun. Morgan suddenly springing to a pile of billets, took one, and swore he would knock the accused down unless he confessed the fact. Instantly, Smith seized another billet, and swore he would strike Morgan if he struck the man. Morgan knowing the tenure of his rank receded. This was the only spirited act I knew of Smith. Such were the rough-hewn characters which, in a few subsequent years, by energy of mind and activity of body, bore us safely through the dreadful storms of the revolution. Morgan was of an impetuous temper, yet withal, prudent in war, as he was fearless of personal danger. His passions were quick and easily excited, but they were soon cooled. This observation is applicable to many men of great talents, and to none more than Morgan. His severity, at times, has made me shudder, though it was necessary, yet it would have been a pleasing trait in his character if it had been less rigid."— *Henry's Journal of Arnold's Expedition against Quebec in* 1775.

you show me so much kindness.' I then learned that he was the American General Schuyler."

The English and German generals dined with the American commander in his tent, on boards laid across barrels. The dinner which was served up in four dishes consisted only of ordinary viands, the Americans at this period being accustomed to plain and frugal meals. The drink, on this occasion, was cider, and rum mixed with water. Burgoyne appeared in excellent humor. He talked a great deal and spoke very flatteringly of the Americans, remarking among other things that he admired the number, dress and discipline of their army and above all the decorum and regularity that were observed. "Your funds of men," he said to Gates, "are inexhaustible. Like the Hydra's head, when cut off, seven more spring up in its stead."

He also proposed a toast to General Washington, an attention that Gates returned by drinking the health of the king of England. The conversation on both sides was unrestrained, affable and free. Indeed the conduct of Gates throughout, after the terms of the surrender had been adjusted, was marked with equal delicacy and magnanimity, as Burgoyne himself admitted in a letter to the Earl of Derby. In that letter, the captive general particularly mentioned one circumstance which he said exceeded all he had ever seen or read of on a like occasion. It was, that when the British soldiers had marched out of their camp to the place where they were to pile their arms, *not a man of the American troops was to be seen*, General Gates having ordered his whole army out of sight, that not one of them should be a spectator of the humiliation of the British troops. This was a refinement of delicacy and of military generosity and politeness reflecting the highest credit upon the conqueror; and was spoken of by the officers of Burgoyne in the strongest terms of approbation.[1]

As the company rose from table, the royal army filed past in their march to the seaboard. Thereupon, by preconcerted arrangement, the generals stepped out, and Burgoyne drawing his sword presented it in the presence of the two armies to General Gates. The latter received it with a courteous bow, and immediately returned it to the vanquished general. Colonel Trumbull has graphically depicted this scene in one of his paintings in the rotunda at Washington.[2]

---

[1] *Remembrancer of* 1777, pages 482 and 3. A letter published in that repository of the American Revolution, at the same time, stated that "some few of the New England men desired to have Burgoyne in their hands for half an hour. Being asked for what purpose, they said they ' would do him no harm; they would tar and feather him, and make him stand on the head of one of his own empty beef-barrels, and read his own proclamation.' " p. 481-82. If made at all, the suggestion must have been merely the sportive sally of a wag.

[2] The headquarters of General Gates — when the surrender took place — were situated *about one hundred and fifty rods south of Fish creek*, very nearly on the west side of the present river road from Schuylerville to Stillwater, in a rude cabin partially dug out of the bank on that side of the road (see note on pages 118-19). By some — and it has given rise to much discussion — it has been supposed, that these head-quarters were on a bluff overlooking the scene of the laying down of arms, just south of Fish creek, and nearly fronting Schuyler's house. This mistake, however, probably arose from the fact, that, during the negotiations between

General Schuyler, as we have seen, was in the camp with Gates at the time of the surrender; and when Burgoyne, with his general officers, arrived in Albany, they were the guests of Schuyler, by whom they were treated with great hospitality. Madame Riedesel, also, speaks with much feeling of the kindness she received on this occasion at the hands of Mrs. Schuyler and her daughters. The urbanity of General Schuyler's manners, and the chivalric magnanimity of his character, smarting as he was under the extent and severity of his pecuniary losses, are attested by General Burgoyne, himself, in his speech in 1778, in the British House of Commons. He then declared that, by his orders, " a very good dwelling house, exceeding large store-houses, great saw-mills, and other out-buildings, to the value altogether perhaps of £10,000 sterling," belonging to General Schuyler, at Saratoga, were destroyed by fire a few days before the

---

the two generals for the surrender, a tent, for the accommodation of General Wilkinson on the part of Gates, and of Major Kingston of Burgoyne, was pitched, says Wilkinson, " *between the advanced* guards of the two armies, on the first bank just above General Schuyler's saw-mill." Thus, very naturally, the mistake arose — that it was a mistake, there can be not the shadow of a doubt, as any one, who will read Wikinson attentively, must at once perceive.— *See General Mattoon's Letter*, Appendix XIII.

" My father, then a small boy, living a mile and a half west of this village (Ballston, N. Y.), which was then a wilderness, remembers to have heard the noise of the artillery in both engagements. Several of the neighbors went over to Saratoga (Schuylerville) to witness the capitulation. He remembered that Judge Beriah Palmer stopped at the house on his return, and said he saw Gen. Burgoyne surrender his sword to Gen. Gates, and gave many particulars of the occurrence."—*Hon. Geo. G. Scott of Ballston, N. Y.*, *to the Author, June* 23, 1877.

surrender to give greater play to his artillery. He said further, that one of the first persons he saw, after the Convention was signed, was General Schuyler; and when expressing to him his regret at the event which had happened to his property, General Schuyler desired him " to think no more of it, and that the occasion justified it according to the rules of war." "He did more," continued Burgoyne; " he sent an aid-de-camp[1] to conduct me to Albany, in order, as he expressed it, to procure better quarters than a stranger might be able to find. That gentleman conducted me to a very elegant house, and to my great surprise, presented me to Mrs. Schuyler and her family. In that house I remained during my whole stay in Albany, with a table of more than twenty covers for me and my friends, and every other demonstration of hospitality."[2]

XIV.

General Burgoyne, until his unfortunate campaign, stood very high in his profession. He had made a brilliant record on the banks of the Tagus for dash, as well

---

[1] The late Col. Richard Varick, then the military secretary of General Schuyler.

[2] *Parliamentary History*, Vol. XIX, p. 1182, as quoted by Chancellor Kent in his address before the N. Y. His. Soc.

During Mrs. Riedesel's stay at Albany, as the guest of Gen. and Mrs. Schuyler, one of her little girls, on first coming into the house, exclaimed, " Oh mama! Is this the palace papa was to have when he came to America?" As the Schuyler family understood German, Madame Riedesel colored at the remark, which, however, was pleasantly got over.— *Life of Peter Van Schaick.*

The Schuyler mansion, which stands on Clinton street facing Schuyler

as judgment, under the eye of a master in the art of war, the famous Count Schaumberg Lippe, who had been selected by Frederic the Great, or the second Frederic, Prince Ferdinand of Brunswick, to save the kingdom of Portugal, on the very verge of ruin. He also added to a prepossessing exterior the polished manners and keen sagacity of a courtier. He was likewise witty and brave. But personal courage alone does not constitute a commander; for of a commander other qualities are expected, especially experience and presence of mind. Burgoyne, in all his undertakings, was hasty and self-willed. Desiring to do everything himself, he rarely consulted with others; and yet he never knew how to keep a plan secret. While in a subordinate position, although continually carping at his military superiors and complaining of his inferior position, yet when given a separate command he was guilty of the same faults which he had

---

street, was not built by Schuyler, himself, but by the wife of General Bradstreet while the latter was on his expedition to Oswego in 1759. The barracks stood some fifteen rods back of the house, between which it is supposed an underground passage existed, though no traces of it have ever been found. The mansion even for this day is a fine one; and for that period must have been superb. It is now (1877) owned and occupied by Mrs. John Tracey. Mrs. Tracey, who cherishes all the traditions of the place, received the author with great courtesy, and kindly acted as his *cicerone* in visiting the interior of the house and the grounds. For the attempt to capture Schuyler by the Indians and Tories see *Lossing's Field Book of the Revolution*. The mark of the tomahawk, which, hurled at Mrs. Schuyler's daughter as she snatched her infant sister from its cradle to bear it to a place of safety, is still clearly seen on the banister.

reprehended in others.[1] Being a great sybarite he often neglected the duties of a general, as well toward his king as his subordinates. He could easily make light of everything, provided he was eating a good meal, or was with his mistress; and while he was enjoying his champagne and choice food his army suffered the keenest want. Thus, immediately after the capitulation, he could eat and drink with the enemy's generals, and talk with the greatest ease of the most important events.

Soon after the surrender, he returned to England and justly threw the failure of the expedition upon the administration. There can be no doubt, that had he been properly supported by Howe, as he had a right to expect, he would, despite his mistakes, have reached Albany; since, in that case, Gates would not have been at Stillwater with an army to oppose him. Mr. Fonblanque, in his life of Burgoyne, draws particular attention for the first time, to a fact that throws entirely new light on the apparent failure of Howe, and clears up all that has hitherto seemed mysterious and contradictory. Orders, fully as imperative as those to Burgoyne, were to have been sent to Howe, but, owing to the carelessness of Germaine — who preferred going to a good dinner in Kent to waiting a few moments to append his signature — they were

---

[1] Had Burgoyne had the experience of his campaign, when he wrote to his friend Sir Gilbert Elliot from Boston, in 1775, he would doubtless have exercised more charity. In that letter he writes, "For God's sake urge the ministry to encourage the general [Gage] in the use of it [money] for the secret service. I am bold to say he has not proper intelligence of what passes within half a mile of us."— *Fonblanque's Burgoyne*, p. 204. See also pp. 142–155 in same connection.

pigeon-holed in London, where they were found, after the convention of Saratoga, carefully docketed, and only wanting the signature of the minister.[1] Hence, Howe acted on the discretionary orders sent to him previously, and concluded to go to Philadelphia instead of to Albany — merely telling Clinton, that if other reinforcements came meanwhile from England, he might make a diversion in favor of Burgoyne. Primarily, then, the failure of the expedition was due to the gross negligence of the war minister, though the failure of Howe does not excuse the blunders through which Burgoyne lost his army in the retreat. It should, moreover, also be stated in justice to

---

[1] Lord E. Fitzmaurice, in his *Life of Lord Shelburne* (Germaine), quotes a memorandum from the hand of that statesman on the subject of that disastrous blunder. He says, "The inconsistent orders given to Generals Howe and Burgoyne could not be accounted for except in a way which it must be difficult for any person who is not conversant with the negligence of office to comprehend. It might appear incredible, if his own secretary and the most respectable persons in office had not assured me of the fact, and what corroborates it, is that it can be accounted for in no other way. It requires as much experience in business to comprehend the very trifling causes which have produced the greatest events, as it does strength of reason to develope the very deepest designs. Among many singularities, Lord Shelburne had a particular aversion to being put out of his way on any occasion. He had fixed to go into Kent at a particular hour and to call on his way at his office to sign the despatches (all of which had been settled) to both these generals. By some mistake those to Gen. Howe were not fair copied, and upon his growing impatient at it, the office, which was a very idle one, promised to send it to the country after him, while they despatched the others to Gen. Burgoyne, expecting that Howe's could be expedited before the packet sailed with the first. By some mistake, however, the ship sailed without them, and they were not signed and were forgotten on his return to town."

Burgoyne that in arranging the campaign with the king, he insisted most strenuously that his success depended upon Howe's coöperation.

On his first arrival in England he was received very coldly by the court and people, the king refusing to see him; but upon a change of the ministry he regained somewhat of his popularity. In 1780, he appeared before the public in a vindication of himself in a work entitled the *State of the Expedition*. Subsequently, he wrote several popular comedies; and was one of the managers of the impeachment of Lord Hastings. He did not live, however, to see the result of that trial. He died on the 4th of August, 1792, and was buried in Westminster Abbey.

In regard to General Gates, the same incapacity, which afterward became so apparent in his unfortunate southern campaign, was manifested from the time of his assuming the command of the northern army until the surrender. It was perhaps no fault of his that he had been placed in command at the north, just at the auspicious moment when the discomfiture of Burgoyne was no longer problematical. He was ordered by congress to the station, and performed his duty passably well. But it is no less true, that the laurels won by him ought to have been worn by Schuyler. Col. Wilkinson, who was a member of Gates's military family, has placed this question in its true aspect. He maintains that not only had the army of Burgoyne been essentially disabled by the defeat of the Germans at Bennington before the arrival of Gates, but that the repulse of St. Leger at Fort Stanwix had deranged

Fac Simile of a stanza from Burgoyne's version of "*As you like it*" in his own hand writing from the original in the author's possession.

The chear, of Old Britons was ever the same
Their sinews it braced — was the inspyring flame
Like theirs shall no vigour of extension slow
Till we turn our pursuit to our Country's Foe
Repeat it should I with I the Women by —

his plans; while safety had been restored to the western frontier, and the panic, thereby caused, had subsided. He likewise maintains that after the reverses at the north, nowise attributable to him, and before the arrival of Gates, the zeal, patriotism and sanitary arrangements of General Schuyler had vanquished the prejudices excited against him; that by the defeat of Baum and St. Leger, Schuyler had been enabled to concentrate and oppose his whole Continental force against the main body of the enemy; and that by him, also before the arrival of Gen. Gates, the friends of the Revolution had been re-animated and excited to manly resistance, while the adherents of the royal cause were intimidated, and had shrunk into silence and inactivity. From these premises, which are indisputable, it is no more than a fair deduction to say "that the same force which enabled Gates to subdue the British army, would have produced a similar effect under the orders of General Schuyler; since the operations of the campaign did not involve a single instance of professional skill, and the triumph of the American arms was accomplished by the physical force, and valor of the troops UNDER THE PROTECTION AND DIRECTION OF THE GOD OF BATTLES.[1]

Gates was a man of great plausibility and address, and,

---

[1] "A Thanksgiving sermon," says Lamb, " was preached on the occasion of the surrender before the American army by the chaplain, from Joel II, 20th. 'But I will remove far from you the Northern army, and will drive him into a land barren and desolate, with his face toward the East sea, and his hinder part toward the utmost sea; and his ill savor shall come up because he hath done great things.'"

withal, a handsome fellow and a great lion in society. It is therefore not surprising, that, flushed with his fortuitous success, or rather with the success attending his fortuitous position, he did not wear his honors with any remarkable meekness. On the contrary, his bearing toward the commander-in-chief was far from respectful. He did not even write to Washington on the occasion, until after a considerable time had elapsed. In the first instance, Wilkinson was sent as the bearer of despatches to congress, but did not reach that body until fifteen days after the articles of capitulation had been signed; and three days more were occupied in arranging his papers before they were presented.[1] The first mention which Washington makes of the defeat of Burgoyne, is contained in a letter written to his brother on the 18th of October, the news having been communicated to him by Governor Clinton. He spoke of the event again on the 19th, in a letter addressed to General Putnam. On the 25th, in a letter addressed to that officer, he acknowledges the reception of a copy of the articles of capitulation *from him* — adding, that it was the first authentic intelligence he had received of the affair, and that he had begun to grow uneasy, and almost to suspect that the previous accounts were premature." And it was not until the 2d of November that Gates deigned to communicate to the commander-in-chief a word upon

---

[1] "It was on this occasion that one of the members made a motion in congress, that they should compliment Colonel Wilkinson with the gift of a pair of spurs."—*Sparks.*

the subject, and then only incidentally, as though it were a matter of secondary importance.[1]

Transferred three years afterward to the chief command of the Southern department, his disastrous defeat and irresolute, not to say cowardly, conduct soon pricked the bubble of his reputation; and after living in comparative obscurity for several years on his farm in Virginia, he died in the city of New York, April 10th, 1806.[2]

---

[1] In the unfortunate battle of Camden, De Kalb, at the sacrifice of his life, played the same role to Gates — though without the same result — that Arnold did in the battle of Saratoga. Colonel, Marquis of Armand, who led the right advance at Camden, accused Gates, openly, of treason and cowardice.

[2] Congress, in the first flush of its gratitude, decreed that Gates should be presented with a medal of gold, to be struck expressly in commemoration of so glorious a victory. On one side of it was the bust of the general, with these words around it: *Horatio Gates, Duci strenuo*; and in the middle, *Comitia Americana*. On the reverse, Burgoyne was represented in the attitude of delivering his sword; and in the back ground, on the one side and on the other, were seen the two armies of England and America. At the top were these words, *Salus regionum Septentrional*; and at the foot, *Hoste ad Saratogam in deditione accepta. Die XVII Oct. M.D.CCLXXVII.* Mr. Benson J. Lossing, who designed the seal of the Saratoga Monument Association, has incorporated in it the reverse of the medal.

In his domestic relation Gen. Gates was an affectionate husband and father. In a letter to his wife, written from Albany three days after the surrender, he says:

"The voice of fame, ere this reaches you, will tell how greatly fortunate we have been in this department. Burgoyne and his whole army have laid down their arms, and surrendered themselves to me and my Yankees. Thanks to the giver of all victory for this triumphant success. I got here night before last, and all now are camped upon the heights to the south of this city. Major General Phillips, who wrote me that saucy note last year from St. Johns, with Lord Petersham, Major Ackland, son of Sir Thomas,

XV.

The Battle of Saratoga has justly been designated by Sir Edward Creasy " one of the fifteen decisive battles of

---

and his lady, daughter of Lord Ilchester, sister to the famous Lady Susan, and about a dozen members of parliament, Scotch lords, etc., are among the captured. I wrote to J. Boone, by Mr. Fluck, an engineer, whom I permitted to pass to Canada, and who goes immediately from thence to England. I could not help, in a modest manner, putting him in mind of the *fete champetre* that I three years ago told him Burgoyne would meet with if he came to America. If Old England is not by this lesson taught humility, then she is an obstinate old slut, bent upon her ruin. I long much to see you, and have, therefore, sent the bearers to Albany by the way of Reading, where you will be received and entertained by Mrs. Potts. Before you leave Reading, you must take advice whether to come by Nazareth or Bethlehem; after that your road up the country by Van Camp's, through the Minisinks, to Hurley and Esopus, is plain and well known to the bearer.

"Don't let Bob's zeal to get to papa, hurry you faster than, considering the length of the journey, you ought to come. If you come by Bethlehem, there is a Mr. Oakley, who holds an office under Mifflin, who will provide you with everything you may have occasion for, and will introduce you to Madame Langton, and the Bishop and Mrs. Ilsley, etc. Perhaps you may get ruffles to your apron; if they are finished I desire you will bespeak them.

"Tell my dear Bob not to be too elated at this great good fortune of his father. He and I have seen many days adverse as well as prosperous. Let us through life endeavor to bear both with an equal mind. General Burgoyne has promised me to deliver any letters I please to commit to his care in England. I think to send a few to some principal men there. Perhaps they may have a good effect for both countries. I would fain have the mother reconciled to her child, and consent, since she is big enough to be married, to let her rule and govern her own house. I hope Lady Harriet Ackland will be here when you arrive. She is the most amiable, delicate little piece of quality you ever beheld. Her husband is one of the prettiest fellows I have seen, learned, sensible, and an Englishman to all

history." It secured for the American colonies the French alliance, and lifted the cloud of moral and financial gloom that had settled upon the hearts of the people, dampening the hopes of the leaders of the Revolution, and wringing despairing words even from the hopeful Washington. From that auspicious day, belief in the ultimate triumph of American liberty never abandoned the nation till it was realized and sealed four years later, almost to a day, in the final surrender at Yorktown.

A century has elapsed since that illustrious event. All the actors in the great drama have passed away, and their descendants are now reaping the rewards of their devotion and suffering. And yet, no monument has arisen to commemorate that turning point of our national destiny. Lexington and Bunker hill have their imposing memorials to tell of the earliest bloodshed in the cause of Cisatlantic freedom ; and, in our own day, the self consecration of Antietam and Gettysburg are made enduring in granite records for the admiration of generations yet to be. The purpose is noble, the tribute deserved, for every such memorial stands as an educator to gratitude and patriotism.

---

intents and purposes; has been a most confounded tory, but I hope to make him as good a whig as myself before we separate. You must expect bad and cold days upon the journey; therefore, prepare against it. I thank God I am pretty well; have had a bad cold, with loss of appetite from being continually harassed with so much business; but I hope to find some rest in winter and much comfort in your's and Bob's company. I will try and get some good tea for you from some of the English officers. Accept my tenderest wishes for your health and safety, and assure my dear Bob how much I am interested in his welfare. Heaven grant us a happy meeting." — *Gates's papers in the New York Historical Society.*

Actuated by these sentiments, in 1859, Hamilton Fish, Horatio Seymour, Benson J. Lossing, John A. Corey, and other patriotic gentlemen organized the Saratoga Monument Association, under a perpetual charter from the state of New York, whose object was the erection of a fitting memorial on the site of Burgoyne's surrender.

It is proposed, whenever sufficient funds are raised, to make the structure of granite, and of the obelisk form and eighty feet square at the base, ten feet at the summit, two hundred and thirty feet in height. Within the monument the first story is one room designed for historical tablets, relics and memorials. On the four corners of the platform are to be mounted four of the large and ornamental brass guns taken from the English at the time of the surrender. Of the large niches in the four gables, three are to be filled with appropriate groups of sculpture in bronze representing the three Generals, Schuyler, Gates, and Morgan, with their accessories, the fourth being vacant, with the word ARNOLD inscribed underneath. The association expect to obtain by purchase five acres of land from the Prospect Cemetery Association of Schuylerville as a site for the monument — the corner stone of which is to be laid, on the centennial of the surrender, Oct. 17th, 1877, with appropriate ceremonies. Hon. Horatio Seymour of Utica, N. Y., will deliver the oration, and Alfred B. Street of Albany, N. Y., the poem. It is a high bluff, sixty feet above the alluvial meadow bordering the river, and overlooks the spot where the British laid down their arms. It is as near, as can conveniently be placed, to where the head-quarters of Gates were situated, which witnessed the formal surrender of Burgoyne's sword, and the unfurling, for the first time, of the stars and stripes.[1]

---

[1] It is true, that a flag, intended for the stars and stripes, and made out of a white shirt and some bits of red cloth from the petticoat of a soldier's wife, first floated on captured standards on the ramparts of Fort Stanwix (Aug. 5th, 1777), but the stars and stripes as we now see them — except as to the number of the stars — was first unfurled to grace the surrender at Saratoga, Oct. 17th, 1777.— Gen. J. Watts De Peyster's *Justice to Schuyler*. The Fort Stanwix flag, is now in the possession of Mrs. Abram Lansing, of Albany, a descendant of Gen. Gansevoort, by whom it is cherished as a most precious relic.

A reliable guide book to the Saratoga battle ground — a work long needed — has been recently written and published by Mrs. Ellen Hardin Walworth, of Saratoga Springs — a grand-daughter of Col. Hardin of Kentucky who was in the battles, and present at the surrender.

SEAL OF THE SARATOGA MONUMENT ASSOCIATION.

PART II.

THE
EXPEDITION OF LIEUT. COLONEL BARRY ST. LEGER.

European Magazine

Engraved by P. Roberts, from a Miniature Painted by
R. Cosway Esq.r R.A.

Col.l S.t Leger

Publish'd March 20.th 1795 by J. Sewell Cornhill

THE EXPEDITION

OF

LIEUT. COLONEL BARRY ST. LEGER.[1]

CONTEMPORANEOUSLY with the descent of Burgoyne upon Northern New York, Colonel Barry St. Leger, as stated in Part First, had been despatched from Montreal, by the way of the St. Lawrence and Lake Ontario, to Oswego, there to form a junction with the Indians and loyalists under Sir John Johnson and Captain Brant. From Oswego, St. Leger was to penetrate by the way of Oneida lake and Wood creek to the Mohawk river, with a view of forming a junction from that direction with Burgoyne, on his arrival in Albany.[2] The alarm everywhere felt on the approach of Burgoyne from the North, was greatly increased in Tryon county, on receiving intelligence of the contemplated invasion by the Indians and loyalists from the West. The news of this movement was first brought

---

[1] This account is taken, in the main, from my father's *Life of Brant* — as being the most accurate and thorough narration of St. Leger's expedition yet written. I have, however, added a number of notes and made a few additions to the text.

[2] *Burgoyne's State of the Expedition*, Appendix, p. xii.

to the inhabitants by an Oneida half-breed sachem named Thomas Spencer, who came therewith direct from Canada, whither he had gone as a secret emissary to obtain information. Spencer stated that he had been present at a council held at the Indian castle of Cassassenny, at which Colonel Claus presided.[1] According to Thomas's relation, Colonel Claus strongly urged the Indians to join in the expedition into the Mohawk valley by the western approach; boasting of the strength of the army under Burgoyne, which had gone against Ticonderoga, and the number of Indians with them, and before whom he assured them Ticonderoga would fall. "Yes," said Colonel Claus, "Ticonderoga is mine. This is true: you may depend on it, and not one gun shall be fired." Singularly enough, though improbable at the time, the prediction, as we have seen, was literally fulfilled. "The same," added the superintendent, "is true of Fort Schuyler. I am sure that when I come before that fort, and the commanding officer shall see me, he also will not fire a shot, but will surrender the fort to me." The Oneida sachem farther informed the people that Sir John Johnson and Colonel Claus were then at Oswego with their families, with seven hundred Indians and four hundred regular troops. There were also six hundred tories on one of the islands above Oswegatchie preparing to join them; and Colonel Butler was to arrive at Oswego on the 14th of July from Niagara, to hold a

---

[1] Colonel Daniel Claus, a brother-in-law of Sir John Johnson, had either superseded Guy Johnson as Indian superintendent in Canada, or been appointed a deputy.

council with the Six Nations, to all of whom he would offer the hatchet to join them and strike the Americans. Thomas thereupon concluded his communication in the following speech :

"BROTHERS: Now is your time to awake, and not to sleep longer; or, on the contrary, it shall go with Fort Schuyler as it went already with Ticonderoga.

"BROTHERS: I therefore desire you to be spirited, and to encourage one another to march on to the assistance of Fort Schuyler. Come up, and show yourselves as men, to defend and save your country before it is too late. Despatch yourselves to clear the brush about the fort, and send a party to cut trees in the Wood creek to stop up the same.

"BROTHERS: If you don't come soon, without delay, to assist this place, we cannot stay much longer on your side; for if you leave this fort without succor, and the enemy shall get possession thereof, we shall suffer like you in your settlements, and shall be destroyed with you. We are suspicious that your enemies have engaged the Indians, and endeavor daily yet to strike and fight against you; and General Schuyler refuses always that we shall take up arms in the country's behalf.

"BROTHERS: I can assure you, that as soon as Butler's speech at Oswego shall be over, they intend to march down the country immediately to Albany. You may judge yourselves that if you don't try to resist, we shall be obliged to join them or fly from our castles, as we cannot hinder them alone. We, the good friends of the country, are of opinion, that if more force appears at

Fort Schuyler, the enemy will not move from Oswego to invade these frontiers. You may depend on it we are willing to help you if you will do some efforts too."

The counsel of the faithful Oneida was neither early enough, nor was it seconded with sufficient promptitude on the part of the inhabitants. Indeed, it must be confessed, that, as the storm of war rolled onward, gathering at once from different directions, and threatening daily to break upon them with increasing fury, many of the yeoman who had hitherto borne themselves nobly, began to falter. A spirit of disaffection had also been more widely diffused among the settlements than could have been supposed from the previous patriotic conduct of the people, while treason lurked in many places where least suspected. Upon this subject, and with special reference to the popular feeling and conduct in Tryon county, John Jay, then sitting in the state convention at Kingston, addressed the following letter to Gouverneur Morris, a member of the council of safety, who was at that time with General Schuyler in the North:

JOHN JAY TO GOVERNEUR MORRIS.

Kingston, July 21*st*, 1777.

"DEAR MORRIS,

"The situation of Tryon county is both shameful and alarming. Such abject dejection and despondency, as mark the letters we have received from thence, disgrace human nature. God knows what to do with, or for them. Were they alone interested in their fate, I should be for leaving their cart in the slough till they would put their shoulders to the wheel.

"Schuyler has his enemies here, and they use these things to his disadvantage. Suspicions of his having been privy to the evacuation of Ticonderoga spread wide; and twenty little circumstances, which perhaps are false, are trumped up to give color to the conjecture.[1] We could wish that your letters might contain paragraphs for the public. We are silent because we have nothing to say; and the people suspect the worst because we say nothing. Their curiosity must be constantly gratified, or they will be uneasy. Indeed, I do not wonder at their impatience, the late northern events having been

---

[1] Reference has already been made, in the text of Part First, to the injustice done towards General Schuyler during this memorable year. There was probably no officer in the service, the commander-in-chief alone excepted, who was considered by the enemy so great an obstacle to the success of their arms. A narrow sectional prejudice existed against him in New England. The failure of the Canadian campaign had been most wrongfully attributed to him in 1776, and with equal injustice the fall of Ticonderoga was now charged to his remissness by his own countrymen. The enemy were not slow to avail themselves of these prejudices and groundless imputations, and through the agency of the tories, the most artful and insidious means were employed to destroy the public confidence in his integrity and capacity. The flame of suspicion was fanned by them until it became general, and was openly avowed. Committees, towns, and districts, assembled, and passed resolves expressing their distrust in him, and both congress and the provincial legislature of New York were addressed upon the subject. General Schuyler, than whom there was not a truer patriot, nor a more earnest or active in the public service, was well aware of these movements. To a committee of the provincial congress, who had formally communicated the charges to him, he returned an answer worthy of a brave and magnanimous soldier. The character of this answer will be understood from this single sentence: "We must bear with the caprice, jealousy, and envy of our misguided friends, and pity them."

such as to have occasioned alarm and suspicion. I have not leisure to add anything more, than that I am, very sincerely, yours, etc.

"JOHN JAY."

As early as the 10th of April, Colonel Robert Van Rensselaer wrote to a friend, that the chairman of the county committee had applied to him for the assistance of his militia, to quell an insurrection of the loyalists in Ballston; but such was the condition of his own regiment, that he was obliged to decline the request. The spirit of disaffection had become so prevalent among his men, that numbers of them had taken the oath of secrecy and allegiance to Great Britain. However, he added that seventeen of the villains had been arrested by the vigilance of the officers, and were then in confinement; and a hope was indulged of being able to detect the whole.[1] Early in the following month the residue of the Roman Catholic Scotch settlers in the neighborhood of Johnstown ran off to Canada, together with some of the loyalist Germans — all headed by two men named M'Donald, who had been permitted by General Schuyler to visit their families. The fact that the wives and families of the absconding loyalists were holding communications with them, and administering to their subsistence on the outskirts of the settlements, had suggested their arrest, and removal to a place of safety, to the number of four hundred — a measure that was approved

---

[1] MS. documents in the Department of State, Albany.

by General Herkimer[1] and his officers.[2] Alarming reports of various descriptions were continually in circulation, and the inhabitants were harassed beyond measure by the necessity of performing frequent tours of military duty — acting as scouts and reconnoitering parties; and standing, some of them, as sentinels around their fields, while others did the labor. No neighborhood felt secure, and all were apprehensive that the whole country would be ravaged by the Indians; while parties of the disaffected were continually stealing away to augment the ranks of the enemy. Thus circumstanced, and at the very moment when they were called upon to reinforce Fort Schuyler, the committee both of Palatine and Schoharie, feeling that they were not strong enough even for self-defence, were calling upon the council of safety at Albany to send additional forces for their protection. Mr. Paris wrote repeatedly upon the subject. The Schoharie committee, on the 17th of July, wrote very frankly, that "the late advantages gained by the enemy had such an effect, that many who had been counted as friends of the state were drawing back. "Our situation," he added, " is deplorable — excepting those who have sought protection from the enemy. We are entirely open to the Indians and tories, whom we expect every hour to come upon us. Part of our militia are at Fort Edward;

---

[1] Herkheimer (*Ergheimer*), by which name he was known — was a man in the prime of years, between forty-six and fifty, and a son of the soil — a tiller of it who had amassed an honest independence by labor and frugality.

[2] MS. documents in the Department of State, Albany — Letter of Isaac Paris.

and of the few that are here, many are unwilling to take up arms to defend themselves, as they are unable to stand against so many enemies. Therefore if your honors do not grant us immediate relief to the amount of about five hundred men, we must either fall a prey to the enemy, or take protection also."[1] On the 18th of July, General Schuyler wrote to the Hon. Pierre Van Courtlandt, from Saratoga, and again on the 21st from Fort Edward, to the same effect. "I am exceedingly chagrined," he says, " at the pusillanimous spirit which prevails in the county of Tryon. I apprehend much of it is to be attributed to the infidelity of the leading persons of that quarter." " If I had one thousand regular troops, in addition to those now above and on the march, I should venture to keep only every third man of the militia, and would send them down." " The substance of Colonel Harper's information had been transmitted about a month ago. In consequence whereof, I sent Colonel Van Schaick into Tryon county with as many troops as I could collect. After the improper agreement made by General Herkimer,[2] these troops were marched back; but as soon as I was informed of the march, I ordered them to remain in Tryon county, where they are still, and I have sent up Colonel Wesson's regiment to reinforce them. But if I may be allowed to judge of the temper of General Herkimer and the committee of Tryon

---

[1] MS. correspondence with the Provincial Congress — Secretary's office, Albany.

[2] Probably referring to the interview between Herkimer and Brant at Unadilla.

county, from their letters to me, nothing will satisfy them unless I march the whole army into that quarter. With deference to the better judgment of the council of safety, I cannot by any means think it prudent to bring on an open rupture with the savages at the present time. The inhabitants of Tryon county are already too much inclined to lay down their arms, and take whatever terms the enemy may please to afford them. Half the militia from this (Tryon) county, and the neighboring state of Massachusetts, we have been under the necessity of dismissing; but the whole should go." " I enclose you the proceedings of a council of general officers, held at this place on the 20th instant. You will perceive that we have been driven to the necessity of allowing some of the militia to return to their plantation. The remainder have promised to remain three weeks longer — that is to say, unless they choose to return sooner, which will doubtless be the case, and for which they have many reasons."[1]

The complaints of General Schuyler were not without just foundation, as the reader has already seen. Indeed, both regulars and militia in Tryon county, seemed for the moment to have lost all the high qualities of soldiers or citizens. Of two hundred militiamen ordered to muster and join the garrison of Fort Schuyler, only a part obeyed; while two companies of regular troops, receiving the like orders, entered upon the service with great reluctance, and not without urging various ex-

---

[1] MS. Cor. Council of Safety — Secretary's office, Albany.

cuses — complaining that service in scouting parties had unfitted them for garrison duty.[1] Under circumstances of such discouragement, it was a time of peculiar trial to the officers and committee of safety. Tryon county had early espoused the cause of freedom, and apparently with greater unanimity than any other county in the state; and the extensive defection, or criminal apathy, which we have just been contemplating, was altogether unexpected. But a crisis was approaching, which necessity soon obliged them to meet. Accordingly, on the 17th of July, General Herkimer issued a patriotic proclamation to the inhabitants of the county, announcing the gathering of the enemy at Oswego, " Christians and savages," to the number of two thousand strong, with the intention of invading the frontier, and calling upon the people *en masse*, to be ready at a moment's warning to repair to the field, with arms and accoutrements, on the approach of the enemy. Those in health, from sixteen to sixty years of age, were designated for actual service; while those above sixty years of age, or invalids, were directed to arm for the defence of the women and children at whatever place they might be gathered in for safety. Concerning the disaffected, and those who might refuse to obey the orders, it was directed in the proclamation that they should be arrested, their arms secured, and themselves placed under guard to join the main body. All the members of the committee, and all those who, by reason of having formerly held commissions, had become

---

[1] *Annals of Tryon County.*

exempts from service, were invited to repair to the rendezvous, and aid in repulsing the foe: "not doubting that the Almighty Power, upon our humble prayers, and sincere trust in Him, will then graciously succor our arms in battle for our just cause, and victory cannot fail on our side."

The Oneida Indians, who were sincerely disposed to favor the cause of the United States, but who, pursuant to the humane policy of congress and the advice of General Schuyler, had determined to preserve their neutrality, beheld the approaching invasion from Oswego with no small degree of apprehension. The course they had marked out for themselves, as they were well aware, was viewed with displeasure by their Mohawk brethren, while the other members of their confederacy were obviously inclined to side with their "Uncle."[1] Living, moreover, in the immediate neighborhood of Fort Schuyler, where St. Leger's first blow must be struck, they were not a little troubled in the prospect of what might happen to themselves. The watchful Thomas Spencer, therefore, despatched the following letter to the committee on the 29th of July which was received on the 30th:

"At a meeting of the chiefs, they tell me that there is but four days remaining of the time set for the king's troops to come to Fort Schuyler, and they think it likely they will be here sooner.

---

[1] In the Six Nations, the Mohawks — the head tribe — were called "uncle." The Oneidas were "the elder brother," etc.

"The chiefs desire the commanding officers at Fort Schuyler not to make a Ticonderoga of it ; but they hope you will be courageous.

"They desire General Schuyler may have this with speed, and send a good army here ; there is nothing to do at New York ; we think there is men to be spared — we expect the road is stopped to the inhabitants by a party through the woods ; we shall be surrounded as soon as they come. This may be our last advice, as these soldiers are part of those that are to hold a treaty. Send this to the committee — as soon as they receive it, let the militia rise up and come to Fort Schuyler.

"To-morrow we are a-going to the Three rivers[1] to the treaty. We expect to meet the warriors, and when we come there and declare we are for peace, we expect to be used with indifference and sent away.

"Let all the troops that come to Fort Schuyler take care on their march, as there is a party of Indians to stop the road below the fort, about 80 or 100. We hear they are to bring their cannon up Fish creek. We hear there is 1000 going to meet the enemy. We advise not — the army is too large for so few men to defend the fort — we send a belt of eight rows to confirm the truth of what we say.

"It looks likely to me the troops are near — hope all friends to liberty, and that love their families, will not be backward, but exert themselves ; as one resolute blow

---

[1] The junction of the Oneida, Seneca, and Oswego rivers — not Three Rivers in Canada.

would secure the friendship of the Six Nations, and almost free this part of the country from the incursions of the enemy." [1]

The certainty that the invaders were thus approaching, the earnestness of the appeals of the committee to the patriotism of the people, the influence of the proclamation of the German general, who was a much better man than officer, save only in the single attribute of courage; and, above all, the positive existence of a common danger from which there was no escape; were circumstances, together, not without their effect. And although the eleventh hour had arrived, yet the militia, and all upon whom the call to arms had been made, now began to move with a degree of alacrity and an exhibition of spirit that went far to atone for the unpatriotic, if not craven, symptoms already noticed.

Meantime, having completed his organization at Oswego, Lieut. Colonel St. Leger commenced his march upon Fort Schuyler, moving by the route already indicated, though with great circumspection. The name of this place of rendezvous has already recurred more than once, or twice, in the preceding pages. Its position was important, and it had been a place of renown in the earlier wars of the colony. The river bearing the same name, which here pours northwardly into Lake Ontario, is the outlet both of the Oneida and

---

[1] MS. letter among the papers of General Gansevoort. Thomas Spencer was a blacksmith, who had resided among the Cayugas, and was greatly beloved by the Indians.— *Letter from General Schuyler to Colonel Dayton — Gansevoort papers.*

Seneca rivers, through which, and their tributary streams, it is connected with the chain of small lakes bearing the names of Oneida, Cazenovia, Skaneateles, Owasco, Cayuga, Seneca, and Canandaigua. Its estuary, of course, forms the natural opening into the rich district of country surrounding these lakes, which, down to the period of the present history, contained the principal towns of four of the five nations of Indians. During the wars between the French and Five Nations, Oswego was repeatedly occupied by the armies of the former. It was here that Count Frontenac landed, on his invasion of the Onondaga country in 1692, at which time, or subsequently, a considerable military work was erected on the western side of the river. During the war with France, which was closed in America by the conquest in Canada, it was in the occupancy of the Provincials and English. The expedition destined to descend the St. Lawrence upon Montreal, was assembled at this point in 1759, after the fall of Niagara, under General Shirley and Sir William Johnson. The army was encamped here several weeks, and finally broke up without attempting its main object — owing, as Sir William Johnson intimates in his private diary, to a want of energy on the part of Shirley. After the fall of Quebec and Montreal into the hands of the English, a battalion of the 55th regiment was stationed at Oswego, under Major Duncan, a brother of the naval hero of Camperdown. A new and far more formidable work was constructed upon the eastern or northeastern promontory, formed by the embouchure of the river

Expedition of Lt. Col. Barry St. Leger. 153

into the lake. The new position was far better chosen for a fortress than the old; and, ultimately, before the Britons were dispossessed of it by the Americans, it became a work of somewhat formidable strength and dimensions. The situation is one of the most beautiful that can be imagined; and during the two or three years in which Major Duncan was in command, by the cultivation of a large garden, the laying out and improving of a bowling-green and other pleasure-grounds, it was rendered a little paradise in the wilderness.[1]

All told, the army of St. Leger consisted of seventeen hundred men — Indians included. These latter were led by Thayendanegea. The order of their march as beautifully drawn and colored, was subsequently taken, with the escritoire of the commanding general. The advance of the main body, was formed of Indians, marching in five Indian columns; that is, in single files, at large distances from each other, and four hundred and sixty paces in front of the line. From these columns of Indians, files were stretched at a distance of ten paces from each other, forming a line of communication with the advanced guard of the line, which was one hundred paces in front of the column. The right and left flanks were covered by Indians at one hundred paces, forming likewise lines of communication with the main body. The king's regiment moved from the left by Indian file, while the 34th moved in

---

[1] See Mrs. Grant's delightful book—*Memoirs of an American Lady*, chapters xliv to xlvii inclusive, Munsell's edition, 1876.

the same order from the right. The rear guard was formed of regular troops, while the advance guard, composed of sixty marksmen, detached from Sir John Johnson's regiment of Royal Greens, was led by Sir John's brother-in-law, Captain Watts. Each corps was likewise directed to have ten chosen marksmen in different parts of its line, in case of attack, to be pushed forward to any given point as circumstances might require.[1]

From these extraordinary precautions, it may well be inferred that Lt. Col. St. Leger, who probably acted much under the advice of Sir John Johnson and the refugee Provincials, who must have been best acquainted with the country and the character of the enemy they were going to encounter, was not a little apprehensive of an attack by surprise while on his march.

In addition to the arrangements already indicated, a detachment from the 8th regiment, with a few Indians, was sent a day or more in advance, under the command of Lieutenant Bird. This officer pushed forward with spirit, but was somewhat annoyed by the insubordination and independent action of his allies. The following extracts from his private diary[2] will not only disclose his own embarrassments, but illustrate the character of Indian warriors acting in concert with regular troops:

---

[1] MS. directions found among the captured papers of St. Leger.

[2] MS. Diary of Lt. Henry Bird, captured from Lt. Col. St. Leger by Col. Gansevoort.

"*Tuesday*, 28th *July*, 1777.— After going two miles, and no savages coming up, waited two hours for them. Sixteen Senecas arriving, proceeded to the Three rivers [1]— waited there two hours — seventy or eighty Messesaugues coming up, I proposed moving forward. They had stolen two oxen from the drove of the army, and would not advance, but stayed to feast. I advanced without Indians seven miles farther — in all nineteen miles. Posted four sentinels all night from a sergeant's guard of twelve men — relieved every hour — visited every half hour. All fires put out at nine o'clock.

"*Wednesday.*— Set off next morning at six, having waited for the savages till that time, though none arrived. Ordered the boats to keep seventy rods behind each other — half the men keeping their arms in their hands, while the other half rowed. Ordered, on any of the boats being fired upon, that the men should jump ashore. The rest to support them with all expedition. Rowed all night. Encamped at Nine-mile point.

"*Thursday, July* 30.—With twenty-seven Senecas and nine Messesaugues joined Mr. Hair's party.[2] Many savages being with us, proceeded to Wood creek, a march of fifteen miles.   *   *   *   *   *

"*Friday.*—The savages hinted an intention to send parties to Fort Stanwix, but to proceed in a body no farther. I called a council of the chiefs — told them I had orders to approach near the fort — that if they

---

[1] The junction of the Oneida, Seneca and Oswego rivers.

[2] Lieut. Hair — afterward killed.

would accompany me, I should be content; but if they would not go, I should take the white people under my command, and proceed myself. The Messesaugues said they would go with me. The Senecas said I had promised to be advised by their chiefs — that it was their way to proceed with caution. I answered, that I meant only as to fighting in the bush, but that I had communicated my intentions to them in the former camp, of preventing them (the Americans meaning) from stopping the creek,[1] and investing their fort. But since I had promised to be advised by them, I would take it so far as to wait till next morning — and would then certainly march by daybreak. After some counselling, they seemed pleased with what I had said, and said they would send out large scouts to prepare the way. Accordingly eighteen or twenty set off this evening."

On the 2d of August, however, Bird wrote back to his general that no savages would advance with him except Henriques, a Mohawk, and one other of the Six Nations, an old acquaintance of his. The letter continues: "Those two, sir, I hope to have the honor to present to you. A savage, who goes by the name of Commodore Bradley, was the chief cause of their not advancing to-day. Twelve Messesaugues came up two or three hours after my departure. Those, with the scout of fifteen I had the honor to mention to you in

---

[1] General Schuyler had directed the commanding officer of Fort Stanwix to obstruct the navigation of Wood creek by felling trees therein.

my last, are sufficient to invest Fort Stanwix, if you favor me so far as not to order to the contrary."[1]

St. Leger received this letter on the same day, at Nine-mile point, whence he immediately despatched the following reply :

GENERAL ST. LEGER TO LIEUT. BIRD.
" *Nine Mile Point*, Aug. 2, 1777.

"SIR: "I this instant received your letter containing the account of your operations since you were detached, which I with great pleasure tell you have been sensible and spirited ; your resolution of investing Fort Stanwix is perfectly right ; and to enable you to do it with greater effect, I have detached Joseph (Thayendanegea) and his corps of Indians to reinforce you. You will observe that I will have nothing but an investiture made ; and in case the enemy, observing the discretion and judgment with which it is made, should offer to capitulate, you are to tell them that you are sure I am well disposed to listen to them ; this is not to take any honor out of a young soldier's hands, but by the presence of the troops to prevent the barbarity and carnage which will ever obtain where Indians make so superior a part of a detachment ; I shall move from hence at eleven o'clock, and be early in the afternoon at the entrance of the creek.

"I am, sir, your most obt. and humble ser't,
" *Lieut. Bird*, 8*th reg't*."[2]   " BARRY ST. LEGER.

---

[1] MS. of the original letter, among the Gansevoort papers.

[2] MS. of the original letter, among the Gansevoort papers —Vide, also, Campbell's Annals.

The investment of the fort was made by Lieut. Bird forthwith — Brant arriving to his assistance at the same time. But the result of the siege that followed proved that the British commander had grievously miscalculated the spirit of the garrison of Fort Stanwix, in his anticipations of a speedy capitulation. Still, his prudential order, the object of which was to prevent an unnecessary sacrifice of life at the hands of his Indian allies, calculating, of course, upon an easy victory, was not the less commendable on that account.

The situation of Fort Stanwix itself — or rather Fort Schuyler, as it must now be called — next demands attention. At the beginning of the year, as we have already seen, the post was commanded by Colonel Elmore of the state service. The term of that officer expiring in April, Colonel Peter Ganesvoort, also of the state troops, was designated as Colonel Elmore's successor, by an order from General Gates, dated the 26th of that month. Notwithstanding the labors of Colonel Drayton, in repairing the works, the preceding year, Colonel Gansevoort found them in such a state of dilapidation, that they were not only indefensible, but untenable. A brisk correspondence ensued between that officer and General Schuyler upon the subject, from which it is manifest that, to say nothing of the miserable condition of his defences, with the prospect of an invasion from the West before him, his situation was in other respects sufficiently deplorable. He had but a small number of men, and many of those were sick by reason of destitution.[1] Added to all which was the responsibility of the Indian relations confided to him by special order of General Schuyler on the 9th of June.[2]

Colonel Marinus Willett was soon afterward directed to join the garrison at Fort Schuyler with his regiment, and most fortunate was the selection of such an officer as Willett to coöperate with such another as Gansevoort; since all the skill, and energy, and courage of both were necessary for the situation. The work itself was originally a square fort, with four bastions, surrounded by a ditch of considerable width and depth, with a covert way and glacis around three of its angles; the other being sufficiently secured by low, marshy ground. In front of the gate there had been a drawbridge, covered by a salient angle raised in front on the glacis. In the centre of the ditch a row of perpendicular pickets had been erected, with rows of horizontal pickets fixed around the ramparts under the embrasures. But since the conclusion of the French war, the fort had fallen into decay; the ditch was filled up, and the

---

[1] Letters among the Gansevoort papers.

[2] "You will keep up a friendly intercourse with the Indians, and suffer no speeches to be made to them by any person not employed in the Indian department; and when you have occasion to speak to them, let your speech be written, and a copy transmitted to me, that the commissioners may be informed of every transaction with those people."—*Schuyler's letter to Colonel Gansevoort.* Colonel G. lost no time in holding a council with such of the chiefs and warriors as yet remained friendly, and he seems to have fully acquired their confidence. He delivered a sensible speech on the occasion, but it contains nothing requiring farther note.

pickets had rotted and fallen down;[1] nor had any suitable progress been made in its reparation. Immediate exertions, energetic and unremitting, were necessary to repair, or rather to renew and reconstruct, the works, and place them in a posture of defence, should the long anticipated invasion ensue from that quarter. A more correct idea of the wretched condition of the post, even down to the beginning of July, may be found from the annexed letter:[2]

COL. GANSEVOORT TO GEN. SCHUYLER.

"*Fort Schuyler*, *July* 4*th*, 1777.

SIR :

Having taken an accurate review of the state of the garrison, I think it is incumbent on me to inform your Excellency by express of our present circumstances. Every possible assistance is given to Captain Marquizee, to enable him to carry on such works as are deemed absolutely necessary for the defence of the garrison. The soldiers are constantly at work—even such of them as come off guard are immediately turned out to fatigue. But I cannot conceal from your Excellency the impossibility of attending fully to all the great objects pointed out in the orders issued to the commanding officer on the station, without farther assistance. Sending out sufficient parties of observation, felling the timber into Wood creek, clearing the road from Fort

---

[1] *Willett's Narrative.*

[2] MS. copy preserved among General Gansevoort's papers.

Dayton, which is so embarrassed, in many parts, as to be impassable, and prosecuting, at the same time, the internal business of the garrison, are objects of the greatest importance, which should, if possible, be immediately considered. But while no exertions compatible with the circumstances we are in, and necessary to give your Excellency satisfaction with respect to all these interesting matters, shall be omitted, I am very sensible it is not in our power to get over some capital obstructions without a reinforcement. The enclosed return, and the difficulties arising from the increasing number of hostile Indians, will show to your Excellency the grounds of my opinion. One hundred and fifty men would be needed speedily and effectually to obstruct Wood creek; an equal number will be necessary to guard the men at work in felling and hauling of timber. Such a deduction from our number, together with smaller deductions for scouting parties, would scarcely leave a man in the garrison, which might, therefore, be easily surprised by a contemptible party of the enemy. The number of inimical Indians increases. On the affair of last week only two made their appearance. Yesterday a party of at least forty, supposed to be Butler's emissaries, attacked Ensign Sporr with sixteen privates, who were out on fatigue, cutting turf about three quarters of a mile from the fort. One soldier was brought in dead and inhumanly mangled; two were brought in wounded — one of them slightly and the other mortally. Six privates and Mr. Sporr are missing. Two parties were immediately sent to pursue the enemy, but they returned without being able to come up with them. This success will, no doubt, encourage them to send out a greater number; and the intelligence they may possibly acquire, will probably hasten the main body destined to act against us in these parts. Our provision is greatly diminished by reason of the spoiling of the beef, and the quantities that must be given from time to time to the Indians. It will not hold out above six weeks. Your Excellency will perceive, in looking over Captain Savage's return of the state of the artillery, that some essential articles are very scarce. As a great number of the gun-bullets do not suit the fire-locks, some bullet-moulds of different sizes for casting others, would be of great advantage to us. Our stock of powder is absolutely too little; a ton, in addition to what we have, is wanted as the lowest proportion for the shot we have on hand. We will, notwithstanding every difficulty, exert ourselves to the utmost of our power; and if your Excellency will be pleased to order a speedy reinforcement, with a sufficient supply of provision and ammunition to enable us to hold out a siege, we will, I hope, by the blessing of God, be able to give a good account of any force that will probably come against us."

The picture is gloomy enough; and was rendered the more so from the mistakes of the engineer, a Frenchman, who had been employed by General Schuyler, and whom it was ultimately found necessary to arrest and send back to head-quarters.[1] Colonel Willett had from the first

---

[1] *Willett's Narrative.*

doubted the capacity of Marquizee, and after his dismissal the work proceeded for the most part under his own immediate direction.

The garrison had likewise other difficulties to encounter. With the gathering of St. Leger's motley forces at Oswego, preparatory to his descent upon the Mohawk, the Indians, as has already been seen by Gansevoort's letter, began to appear in scouting parties in the circumjacent forests. The utmost caution was therefore necessary on leaving the fort, even for a short distance. It was during this critical period that the familiar incident of Captain Gregg and his faithful dog occurred, of which the following brief account was given by Colonel Gansevoort:

COL. GANSEVOORT TO GEN. SCHUYLER (EXTRACT).

"*Fort Schuyler*, *June* 26, 1777.

"I am sorry to inform your Honor that Captain Gregg and Corporal Madison, of my regiment, went out a gunning yesterday morning, contrary to orders. It seems they went out just after breakfast, and at about ten o'clock Corporal Madison was killed and scalped. Captain Gregg was shot through his back, tomahawked and scalped, and is still alive. He informs me that the misfortune happened about ten o'clock in the morning. He looked at his watch after he was scalped. He saw but two Indians. He was about one mile and a half from the fort, and was not discovered until two o'clock in the afternoon. I immediately sent out a party and had him brought into the fort, just after three o'clock; also the corpse of Madison. Gregg is perfectly in his senses, and speaks strong and hearty, notwithstanding that his recovery is doubtful." [1]

There was little of romance in Colonel Gansevoort, and he related the incident with military brevity. The story, however, has often been told, with a variety of amplifications, particularly in regard to the wounded soldier's faithful dog, to whose affectionate sagacity he is said to have been indebted for his discovery, if not his life. According to the narrative of President Dwight, it appears that Gregg and his companion had been seduced into a fatal disobedience of orders, by the clouds of pigeons appearing in the adjoining woods. Immediately upon their fall, the Indians rushed upon them for their scalps, which they took — giving each a simultaneous cut upon the head with their tomahawks. The corporal had been killed by the shot, but Captain Gregg was only wounded.[2] Feigning death, however, he had the presence of mind, and the fortitude, to submit to the subsequent torture without betraying himself by a groan or the quivering of a muscle. The Indians departing immediately, Captain Gregg crawled to his lifeless companion, and pillowed his head upon his body; while his

---

[1] MS. of the original draught, among Col. Gansevoort's papers.

[2] It has been asserted in history, that St. Leger encouraged these isolated murders by large bounties for scalps. Twenty dollars is said to have been the price he paid; but his despatch to Lieut. Bird, before cited, does not corroborate the charge of such inhumanity. That despatch was a private document, moreover, not written for the light, or for effect, and must therefore be received as true. It was found among Col. Gansevoort's papers.

faithful dog ran to a place at no great distance thence, where two men were engaged in fishing, and by his imploring looks and significant actions, induced them to follow him to the spot where lay his wounded master. Hastening to the fort, the fishermen reported what they had seen, and a party of soldiers being forthwith despatched to the place, the bodies of the wounded and the dead were speedily brought into the garrison, as we have seen from the colonel's official account. Captain Gregg was severely wounded, independently of the scalping; and his case was for a long time critical.

The friendly Indians, then chiefly, if not exclusively, Oneidas, though still acting and speaking in the name of the Six Nations, presented an address of condolence to Colonel Gansevoort on this occasion, to which the latter made a suitable reply, which alone has been preserved, and reads as follows:

"Brother Warriors of the Six Nations: I thank you for your good talk.

"Brothers: You tell us you are sorry for the cruel usage of Captain Gregg, and the murder of one of our warriors; that you would have immediately pursued the murderers, had not General Schuyler, General Gates, and the French general, desired you not to take any part in this war; and that you have obeyed their orders, and are resolved to do so. I commend your good inclination and intention.

"Brothers: You say you have sent a runner to the Six Nations, to inform them of what has happened, and that you expect some of your chiefs will look into the affair, and try to find out the murderers. You have done well. I shall be glad to smoke a pipe with your chiefs, and hope they will do as they speak.

"BROTHERS: I hope the mischief has been done, not by any of our good friends of the Oneida nation, but by the tories, who are enemies to you as well as to us, and who are ready to murder yourselves, your wives, and children, if you will not be as wicked as themselves.

BROTHERS: When your chiefs shall convince me that Indians of the Six Nations have had no hand in this wicked thing, and shall use means to find out the murderers and bring them to justice, you may be assured that we will strengthen the chain of friendship, and embrace you as our good brothers. I will not suffer any of our warriors to hurt you."

The address contained two or three additional paragraphs in reference to other subjects. Captain Gregg recovered, and resumed his duties; and having served to the end of the war, lived many years afterward.

Another tragic incident occurred at nearly the same time. About noon, on the 3d of July, the day being perfectly clear, Colonel Willett was startled from his *siesta* by the report of musketry. Hastening to the parapet of the glacis, he saw a little girl running with a basket in her hand, while the blood was trickling down her bosom. On investigating the facts, it appeared that the girl, with two others,[1] was picking berries, not two

---

[1] One of the girls was Caty Steese, a servant of Capt. Johannis Roff (Roof) which was the cause of his attempt to do violence to Cornplanter when, in 1797, he confessed to having killed her (*Brant*, vol. II, p. 411, note).—*Letter from Col. Gansevoort to Col. Van Schaick, July 25th,* 1777.

hundred yards from the fort, when they were fired upon by a party of Indians, and two of the number killed. Happily, she who only was left to tell the tale, was but slightly wounded. One of the girls killed, was the daughter of an invalid, who had served many years in the British artillery. He was entitled to a situation in Chelsea hospital, but had preferred rather to remain in the cultivation of a small piece of ground at Fort Stanwix, than again to cross the ocean.[1]

By the middle of July, the Indians hovering about the fort became so numerous, and so bold, as to occasion great annoyance. Large parties of soldiers could only venture abroad on the most pressing emergencies; and even one of these was attacked, several of its numbers killed and wounded, and the officer in command taken prisoner. The force of the garrison, at this time, consisted of about five hundred and fifty men — ill-supplied, as we have already seen, both with provisions and munitions of war. Fortunately, however, on the 2d of August, the very day of the investiture of the fort by the advance of St. Leger's army, under Thayendanegea and Bird, Lieutenant Colonel Mellon, of Colonel Weston's regiment, arrived with two hundred men, and two bateaux of provisions and military stores. Not a moment was lost in conveying these opportune supplies into the fort. Delay would, indeed, have been dangerous; for at the instant the last loads arrived at the fort, the enemy appeared on the skirt of the forest, so near to the boats,

---

[1] *Willett's Narrative.*

that the captain who commanded them became their prisoner.¹

The command of Colonel Gansevoort now consisted of seven hundred and fifty men, all told; and upon examination it was ascertained that they had provisions for six weeks — with fixed ammunition enough for the small arms. But for the cannon they were lamentably deficient — having barely enough for nine rounds per diem during the period specified. A besieging army was before the fort, and its garrison was without a flag! But as necessity is the mother of invention, they were not long thus destitute. Stripes of white were cut from ammunition shirts; blue from a camblet cloak captured from the enemy; while the red was supplied from such odds and ends of clothes of that hue as were at hand.² And, thus furnished, commenced the celebrated defence of Fort Schuyler.

Such was the condition of Fort Schuyler at the commencement of the memorable siege of 1777 — an event, with its attending circumstances, forming an important feature in the northern border warfare of the Revolution. Colonel St. Leger³ himself arrived before the fort on the

---

¹ *Willett's Narrative.*

² Idem.

³ It is difficult, from the books, to determine what was at that time the precise rank of St. Leger. He has usually been called a *brigadier general*. By some contemporary writers he was called *Colonel* St. Leger. But in General Burgoyne's despatches to Lord George Germaine, of August 20, 1777, he is repeatedly denominated *Lieutenant Colonel* St. Leger. He is also called Colonel St. Leger by Bissett. But he, nevertheless, signed his name as a brigadier general in a letter to Col. Gansevoort, on the 9th of August.

3d of August, with his whole force — a motley collection of British regulars, Hessian auxiliaries, New York loyalists, usually denominated Johnson's Greens, together with numbers of the Canadians, and the Indians under Thayendanegea. Sir John Johnson, and Colonels

SIR JOHN JOHNSON.

Claus and Butler,[1] were also engaged with him in the expedition. A flag was sent into the fort on the morning of that day, with a copy of a rather pompous proclamation from St. Leger, which, it was probably supposed, from its vaunting threats and lavish promises, might pro-

---

[1] At the breaking out of the war, John Butler was lieutenant colonel of a regiment of the Tryon county militia, of which Guy Johnson was the colonel and Jelles Fonda the major. Sir John had been commissioned a general after the decease of his father.

duce a strong impression upon the garrison. "The forces intrusted to my command are designed to act in concert, and upon a common principle, with the numerous armies and fleets which already display, in every quarter of America, the power, the justice, and, when properly sought, the mercy of the king." So commenced the proclamation. After denouncing "the unnatural rebellion" as having already been made the "foundation for the completest system of tyranny that ever God in his displeasure suffered for a time to be exercised over a froward and stubborn generation," and charging that "arbitrary imprisonment, confiscation of property, persecution and torture, unprecedented in the inquisitions of the Roman church, were among the palpable enormities tha verified the affirmation"—and after denouncing "the profanation of religion," and other "shocking proceedings" of the civil authorities and committees in rebellion, the proclamation proceeded—"animated by these considerations; at the head of troops in the full powers of health, discipline, and valor; determined to strike where necessary, and anxious to spare when possible, I, by these presents, invite and exhort all persons in all places where the progress of this army may point, and by the blessing of God I will extend it far, to maintain such a conduct as may justify me in protecting their lands, habitations, and families." The object of his address was to hold forth security, and not depredation; he offered employment to those who would join his standard; security to the infirm and industrious; and payment in coin for all the supplies the people would bring to his camp. In conclusion, he said — "If, notwithstanding these endeavors and sincere inclinations to effect them, the frenzy of hostility should remain, I trust I shall stand acquitted in the eyes of God and men, in denouncing and executing the vengeance of the state against the wilful outcasts. The messengers of justice and of wrath await them in the field ; and devastation, famine, and every concomitant horror that a reluctant, but indispensable prosecution of military duty must occasion, will bar the way to their return."

This manifesto, however, produced no effect, then or afterward. The siege had been anticipated, and the brave garrison, officers and men, had counted the cost and determined to defend the fortress to the last. Accordingly, hostilities commenced actively on the morning of the following day. The Indians, concealing themselves behind clumps of shrubbery and stumps of trees, annoyed the men who were employed in raising the parapets not a little with their rifles. Several were wounded; and it was found necessary immediately to station sharp-shooters at suitable points, to watch opportunities, and fire in return. The 5th was spent in much the same manner, with the addition of the throwing of a few shells by the enemy — several of which fell within the fort, and some in the barracks. "On the evening of this day, soon after it was dark, the Indians, who were at least one thousand in number, spread themselves through the woods, completely encircling the fort, and commenced a terrible yelling, which was continued at intervals the greater part of the night."

Having thus commenced his operations,[1] Colonel St. Leger found means of conveying the intelligence to General Burgoyne — not for a moment anticipating the distressing circumstances in which the northern commander-in-chief already found himself involved, though but mid-way in the career of victory. Harassed incessantly by the foes he had vanquished; unable to obtain supplies, except by sending back for them to Fort George, in which service his troops were already greatly fatigued; not one-third of his horses arrived from Canada; the roads excessively bad, and rendered all but impassable by a deluge of rain; with only four days of provisions on hand; the vaunting general, who had boasted in the British capital that, with ten thousand men, he could march through the whole rebel country at pleasure, already found himself in an unenviable situation. But on learning the advance of Lt. Col. St. Leger, he instantly and justly considered that a rapid movement forward, at this critical juncture, would be of the utmost importance. If the retreating Americans should proceed up the Mohawk with a view of relieving Fort Schuyler, in the event of St. Leger's success against that place they would place themselves between two fires; or perhaps Burgoyne supposed that were such a movement to be made on the part of the Americans, he might yet throw his army between them and Albany, and thus compel them either to stand a general engagement or to strike off to the right, and by recrossing the Hudson higher up, secure

---

[1] *Willett's Narrative.*

a retreat into New England. If, on the other hand, the Americans should abandon Fort Schuyler to its fate, and themselves fall back upon Albany, he argued that the Mohawk country would of course be entirely laid open to him ; his junction with St. Leger established, and the combined army be at liberty to select its future line of operation. But his supplies were inadequate to such an extensive operation, and his army was too weak to allow him to keep up such a chain of posts as would enable him to bring them up daily from the *depôt* at Lake George. With a view, therefore, of obtaining immediate relief, and of opening a new source of supply, especially of cattle, from the upper settlements of New England, the expedition to Bennington, the place of deposit of provisions for the provincial forces, was planned, and committed to a detachment of the Brunswicker troops, under Colonel Baum, for execution. The signal failure of this expedition was calculated still farther both to embarrass and depress the invaders ; while the brilliant success of the militia under General Stark on that occasion, proving, as it had done, that neither English nor German troops were invincible, revived the drooping spirits of the disheartened ; reinspired the people with confidence of ultimate success ; and was the source of universal exultation.

The progress of events brings us back to the lower valley of the Mohawk. No sooner was the advance of St. Leger upon Fort Schuyler known to the committee and officers of Tryon county, than General Herkimer, in conformity with the proclamation heretofore cited, summoned the militia of his command to the field, for the purpose of marching to the succor of the garrison. Notwithstanding the despondency that had prevailed in the early part of the summer, the call was nobly responded to, not only by the militia, but by the gentlemen of the county, and most of the members of the committee, who entered the field either as officers or private volunteers. The fears so generally and so recently indulged seemed all to have vanished with the arrival of the invader, and the general soon found himself at the head of between eight hundred and a thousand men, all eager for action and impatient of delay. Their place of rendezvous was at Fort Dayton (German Flats), in the upper section of the Mohawk valley — and the most beautiful. The regiments were those of Colonels Klock, Visscher, Cox, and one or two others, augmented by volunteers and volunteer officers, who were pushing forward as though determined at all hazards to redeem the character of the county. Indeed, their proceedings were by far too impetuous, since they hurried forward in their march without order or precaution, without adequate flanking parties, and without reconnoitering the ground over which they were to pass. They moved from Fort Dayton on the 4th, and on the 5th reached the neighborhood of Oriskany,[1] where they encamped. From this point, an express[2] was sent forward by General Herkimer

---

[1] Probably the site of Whitestown. One of the MS. narratives in the author's possession says they crossed the river at old Fort Schuyler (now Utica).

[2] Adam Helmer accompanied by two other men.

to apprise Colonel Gansevoort of his approach, and to concert measures of coöperation. The arrival of the express at the fort was to be announced by three successive discharges of cannon, the report of which, it was supposed, would be distinctly heard at Oriskany — only eight miles distant. Delays, however, intervened, so that the messengers did not reach the fort until ten or eleven o'clock on the following morning; previous to which the camp of the enemy being uncommonly silent, a portion of their troops had been observed by the garrison to be moving along the edge of the woods down the river, in the direction of the Oriskany creek.[1] The concerted signals were immediately fired;[2] and as the proposition of Herkimer was to force a passage to the fort, arrangements were immediately made by Colonel Gansevoort to effect a diversion of the enemy's attention, by making a sally from the fort upon the hostile camp, for which purpose two hundred men were detailed, consisting one-half of Gansevoort's, and one-half of the Massachusetts troops, and one field-piece — an iron three pounder. The execution of the enterprise was entrusted to Colonel Willett.[3]

It appears that on the morning of that day, which was

---

[1] Letter of Colonel Willett to Governor Trumbull of Cannecticut.

[2] MS. of Captain Henry Seeber, in the author's possession. See, also, *Willett's Narrative.*

[3] Willett's letter to Governor Trumbull. The officers serving in this detachment were Captain Van Benschoten and Lieutenant Stockwell, who led the advance guard; Captain Allen (of Massachusetts), Bleecker, Johnson, and Swartwout; Lieutenant Diefendorf, Conyne, Bogardus, M'Clenner, and Ball; Ensign Chase, Bailey, Lewis, Dennison, Magee, and Arnent. The rear guard was commanded by Major Badlam.

the 6th of August, General Herkimer had misgivings as to the propriety of advancing any farther without first receiving reinforcements. His officers, however, were eager to press forward. A consultation was held, in which some of the officers manifested much impatience at any delay, while the general still urged them to remain where they were until reinforcements could come up, or at least until the signal of a sortie should be received from the fort. High words ensued, during which Colonels Cox and Paris, and many others, denounced their commander as a tory and coward. The brave old man calmly replied that he considered himself placed over them as a father, and that it was not his wish to lead them into any difficulty from which he could not extricate them. Burning, as they now seemed, to meet the enemy, he told them roundly that they would run at his first appearance.[1] But his remonstrances were unavailing. Their clamor increased, and their reproaches were repeated, until, stung by imputations of cowardice and a want of fidelity to the cause,[2] and somewhat irritated withal, the general immediately gave the order — " March on ! "[3] The words were no sooner heard than the troops gave a shout, and moved, or rather rushed forward. They marched in files of two deep, preceded by an advanced guard and keeping flanks upon each side.[4]

---

[1] *Travels* of President Dwight, vol. III, p. 192.

[2] MS. statement of George Walter, in possession of the author; also of Henry Seeber.

[3] Statement of Adam Miller, in possession of the author.

[4] It has been charged by most writers that even these ordinary precautions were not observed. Miller and Walter, however, both assert the fact.

Having, by ten o'clock, proceeded rapidly forward to the distance of only two or three miles,[1] the guards, both front and flanks, were suddenly shot down, the forest rang with the war whoops of a savage foe, and in an instant the greater part of the division found itself in the midst of a formidable ambuscade. Colonel St. Leger, it appeared, having heard of the advance of General Herkimer, in order to prevent an attack in his entrenchments, had detached a division of Sir John Johnson's regiment of Greens, under Sir John's brother-in-law, Major Watts, Colonel Butler with his rangers, and Joseph Brant with a strong body of Indians, to intercept his approach.[2] With true Indian sagacity, Thayendanegea had selected a position admirably fitted for his purpose, which was, to draw the Americans, whom he well knew to be approaching in no very good military array, into an ambuscade. The locality favored his design.[3]

---

[1] The battle ground is about two miles west of Oriskany, and six from Whitesborough.

[2] In every account of this battle which has fallen under the author's observation, excepting that of Colonel Willett, Sir John Johnson is made the British commander at this battle. He was not in it at all, as will appear a few pages forward. Even the cautious and inquisitive President Dwight falls into error, and carries it through his whole account.

[3] "The country presented ample opportunities for such a stratagem; and its advantages were not neglected. The ambush was set about two miles from Fort Stanwix, where a primitive corduroy road was the sole method of traversing a swampy hollow or ravine, drained by a little affluent of that stream. This road was completely commanded by heights on either hand, covered with dense woods, in which Sir John Johnson stationed his marksmen, both whites and savages. It was as handsome a trap as that which Hermann or Arminius set for the Legions of Verus in the Teutoberger

There was a deep ravine crossing the path which Herkimer with his undisciplined array was traversing, "sweeping toward the east in a semi-circular form, and bearing a northern and southern direction. The bottom of this ravine was marshy, and the road crossed it by means of a causeway. The ground, thus partly enclosed by the ravine, was elevated and level. The ambuscade was laid upon the high ground west of the ravine."[1]

The enemy had disposed himself adroitly, in a circle, leaving only a narrow segment open for the admission of the ill starred Provincials on their approach. The stratagem was successful. Unconscious of the presence of the foe, Herkimer, with his whole army excepting the rear-guard, composed of Colonel Visscher's regiment, found himself encompassed at the first fire — the enemy closing up the gap at the instant of making himself known. By thus early completing the circle, the baggage and ammunition wagons, which had just descended into the ravine, were cut off and separated from the main body, as also was the regiment of Colonel Visscher, yet on the eastern side of the ravine; which, as their general had predicted, instantly and ingloriously fled, leaving their companions to their fate. They were pursued, however, by a portion of the Indians, and suffered more severely,

---

forest, eighteen centuries previous — an ambush which determined the fate of Roman progress into the free German land, just as the issue of Oriskany, reversing the case, checked the progress of the British into the free German flatlands of the Mohawk."—*Gen. J. Watts De Peyster, in His. Mag, New Series,* vol. v, No. 1.

[1] *Campbell's Annals.*

probably, than they would have done, had they stood by their fellows in the hour of need, either to conquer or to fall.[1]

Being thrown into irretrievable disorder by the suddenness of the surprise and the destructiveness of the fire, which was close and brisk from every side, the division was for a time threatened with annihilation. At every opportunity the savages, concealed behind the trunks of trees, darted forward with knife and tomahawk to ensure the destruction of those who fell; and many and fierce were the conflicts that ensued hand to hand. The veteran Herkimer fell, wounded, in the early part of the action — a musket ball having passed through and killed his horse, and shattered his own leg just below the knee.[2] The general was placed upon his saddle, how-

---

[1] Believing, as stated in a preceding note, that my father's account of this battle is the most reliable of any extant, I have preferred to keep the text as much as possible intact. I cannot, however, refrain from saying, in this connection, that I think the imputation of cowardice in regard to Col. Visscher's regiment is hardly justified in view of all the circumstances. Perhaps no body of men were as ready and anxious to perform their duty as were the patriotic members of Col. Visscher's regiment. It must be remembered that it was composed of farmers who had never seen service; and it is scarcely to be wondered at that when they saw themselves cut off, flanked, fired upon by an unseen foe accompanied by most hideous yells, they were panic-stricken, and did not wheel into line in the dense woods and fire upon enemies immediately in range of friends. Neither could the voice of their brave commander have been heard under the circumstances any more than as if they had been in the cave of the winds. It is strange, too, that Col. Visscher's regiment should have suffered as they did, had it given danger such a wide berth; for the fact is undisputed that a very large proportion of the regiment was either killed or wounded.

[2] Walton's MS. account.

ever, against the trunk of a tree for his support, and thus continued to order the battle. Colonel Cox, and Captains Davis and Van Sluyck, were severally killed near the commencement of the engagement; and the slaughter of their broken ranks, from the rifles of the tories and the spears and tomahawks of the Indians, was dreadful. But even in this deplorable situation the wounded general, his men dropping like leaves around him, and the forest resounding with the horrid yells of the savages, ringing high and wild over the din of battle, behaved with the most perfect firmness and composure. The action had lasted about forty-five minutes in great disorder, before the Provincials formed themselves into circles in order to repel the attacks of the enemy, who were concentrating, and closing in upon them from all sides.[1] From this moment the resistance of the Provincials was more effective, and the enemy attempted to charge with the bayonet. The firing ceased for a time, excepting the scattering discharges of musketry from the Indians; and as the bayonets crossed, the contest became a death struggle, hand to hand and foot to foot. Never, however, did brave men stand a charge with more dauntless courage, and the enemy for the moment seemed to recoil — just at the instant when the work of death was arrested by a heavy shower of rain, which suddenly broke upon the combatants with great fury. The storm raged for upward of an hour, during which time the enemy sought such

---

[1] The first movement of this kind was made by Jacob Seeber, without orders, according to the narrative of Henry Seeber.

shelter as might be found among the trees at a respectful distance; for they had already suffered severely, notwithstanding the advantages in their favor.[1]

During this suspension of the battle, both parties had time to look about, and make such new dispositions as they pleased for attack and defence, on renewing the murderous conflict. The Provincials, under the direction of their general, were so fortunate as to take possession of an advantageous piece of ground, upon which his men formed themselves into a circle, and as the shower broke away, awaited the movements of the enemy. In the early part of the battle, the Indians, whenever they saw a gun fired by a militia-man from behind a tree, rushed upon and tomahawked him before he could reload. In order to counteract this mode of warfare, two men were stationed behind a single tree, one only to fire at a time — the other reserving his fire until the Indians ran up as before.[2] The fight was presently renewed, and by the new arrangement, and the cool execution done by the fire of the militia forming the main circle, the Indians were made to suffer severely; so much

---

[1] "At this crisis of the day, when a dropping or drizzling rain of death was covering the narrow field with dead and wounded, the crash and horror of the battle were suspended by the fierce tumult of a thunder-storm of tropical violence — as fierce as that which broke upon the battle-field of Chantilly, on the first of September, 1862, converting the afternoon into night, amidst whose charm another republican hero, Kearny, passed like Herkimer from earthly fame to eternal glory. offering up his great life for the rights of man and for freedom."— *Gen. J. Watts De Peyster.*

[2] *Campbell's Annals.*

so that they began to give way, when Major Watts [1] came up with a reinforcement, consisting of another detachment of Johnson's Greens.[2] These men were mostly loyalists who had fled from Tryon county, now returned in arms against their former neighbors. As no quarrels are so bitter as those of families, so no wars are so cruel and passionate as those called civil. Many of the Provincials and Greens were known to each other; and as they advanced so near as to afford opportunities of mutual recognition, the contest became, if possible, more of a death struggle than before. Mutual resentments, and feelings of hate and revenge, raged in their bosoms. The Provincials fired upon them as they advanced, and then, springing like chafed tigers from their covers, attacked them with their bayonets and the butts of their muskets, or both parties in closer contact throttled each other and drew their knives; stabbing, and sometimes literally dying in one another's embrace.

At length a firing was heard in the distance from the fort, a sound as welcome to the Provincials as it was astounding to the enemy. Availing themselves of the hint, however, a *ruse de-guerre* was attempted by Colonel Butler, which had well-nigh proved fatal. It was the sending, suddenly, from the direction of the fort, a detachment of the Greens disguised as American troops,

---

[1] Brother of the late venerable John Watts, of New York.

[2] Campbell. The enemy, as on the march from Oswego, had posted a line of sentinels at short distances from each other, extending from St. Leger's intrenchments to the scene of action; so that communications could be interchanged rapidly and at pleasure.

in the expectation that they might be received as a timely reinforcement from the garrison. Lieutenant Jacob Sammons was the first to descry their approach, in the direction of a body of men commanded by Captain Jacob Gardenier — an officer who, during that memorable day, performed prodigies of valor. Perceiving that their hats were American, Sammons informed Captain Gardenier that succors from the fort were coming up. The quick eye of the captain detected the *ruse*, and he replied — " Not so : they are enemies ; don't you see their green coats ! " [1] They continued to advance until hailed by Gardenier, at which moment one of his own soldiers, observing an acquaintance, and supposing him a friend, ran to meet him, and presented his hand. It was grasped, but with no friendly gripe, as the credulous fellow was dragged into the opposing line informed that he was a prisoner. He did not yield without a struggle ; during which Gardenier, watching the action and the result, sprang forward, and with a blow from his spear levelled the captor to the dust and liberated his man.[2] Others of the foe instantly set upon him, of whom he slew the second and wounded a third. Three of the disguised Greens now sprang upon him, and one of his spurs becoming entangled in their clothes, he was thrown to the ground. Still contending, however, with almost super-

---

[1] Manuscript narrative of William Gardenier, in the possession of the author.

[2] Idem.

human strength, both of his thighs were transfixed to the earth by the bayonets of two of his assailants, while the third presented a bayonet to his breast, as if to thrust him through. Seizing this bayonet with his left hand, by a sudden wrench he brought its owner down upon himself, where he held him as a shield against the arms of the others, until one of his own men, Adam Miller, observing the struggle, flew to his rescue. As the assailants turned upon their new adversary, Gardenier rose upon his seat; and although his hand was severely lacerated by grasping the bayonet which had been drawn through it, he seized his spear lying by his side, and quick as lightning planted it to the barb in the side of the assailant with whom he had been clenched. The man fell and expired — proving to be Lieutenant McDonald, one of the loyalist officers from Tryon county. All this transpired in far less time than is necessarily occupied by the relation. While engaged in the struggle, some of his own men called out to Gardenier — "for God's sake, captain, you are killing your own men!" He replied — "they are not our men — they are the enemy — fire away!" A deadly fire from the Provincials ensued, during which about thirty of the Greens fell slain, and many Indian warriors. The parties once more rushed upon each other with bayonet and spear, grappling and fighting with terrible fury; while the shattering of shafts and the clashing of steel mingled with every dread sound of war and death, and the savage yells, more hideous than all, presented a scene which

Expedition of Lt. Col. Barry St. Leger.

can be more easily imagined than described.[1] The unparalleled fortitude and bravery of Captain Gardenier infused fresh spirits into his men, some of whom enacted wonders of valor likewise. It happened during the *melee*, in which the contending parties were mingled in great confusion that three of Johnson's Greens rushed within the circle of the Provincials, and attempted to make prisoner of a Captain Dillenback. This officer had declared he would never be taken alive, and he was not. One of his three assailants seized his gun, but he suddenly wrenched it from him, and felled him with the butt. He shot the second dead, and thrust the third through with his bayonet.[2] But in the moment of his triumph at an exploit of which even the mighty Hector, or either of the sons of Zeruiah might have been proud, a ball laid this brave man low in the dust.

Such a conflict as this could not be continued long; and the Indians, perceiving with what ardor the Provincials maintained the fight, and finding their own numbers sadly diminished, now raised the retreating cry of " *Oonah!* " and fled in every direction, under the shouts

---

[1] MS. of William Gardenier. It was in reference to these individual deeds of prowess, that the eloquent Gouverneur Morris thus spoke in his address before the New York Historical Society:—" Let me recall, gentlemen, to your recollection, that bloody field in which Herkimer fell. There was found the Indian and the white man born on the banks of the Mohawk, their left hand clenched in each other's hair, the right grasping in a grasp of death, the knife plunged in each other's bosom; thus they lay frowning."

[2] George Walter relates this incident, in his narrative, in the possession of the author. Walter was himself a witness of the fact, while lying wounded with two balls, by the side of General Herkimer.

and hurrahs of the surviving Provincials and a shower of bullets. Finding, moreover, from the firing at the fort, that, their presence was necessary elsewhere, the Greens and Rangers now retreated precipitately, leaving the victorious militia of Tryon county masters of the field.[1]

Thus ended one of the severest, and, for the numbers engaged, one of the most bloody battles of the Revolutionary war. Though victorious, the loss of the Provincials was very heavy ; and Tryon county long had reason to mourn that day. Colonel Paris was taken prisoner by the enemy, and afterward murdered by the Indians. Several other prisoners were also killed by the savages, after they had been brought into Colonel Butler's quarters ; and, as it was said, by the colonel's own tacit consent, if not permission in terms. But the general character of that officer forbids the imputation.[2]

---

[1] It is an extraordinary fact, that every historian who has written of the battle of Oriskany, has recorded it as a defeat of the Provincials, from Marshall and Ramsay down, to say nothing of the British chroniclers. Such was also the author's impression until he undertook the present investigation. Captain Brant himself, in conversation with Samuel Woodruff, Esq., admitted that they were the victors; and all the written statements which the author has been able to procure from the survivors of the battle, bear the same testimony.

[2] The late Doctor Moses Younglove of Hudson, Columbia county, was the surgeon of General Herkimer's brigade. He was taken prisoner in this battle by a sergeant of Sir John Johnson's regiment. After his release he made a deposition setting forth many grievous barbarities committed, both by the Indians and tories, upon the prisoners who fell into their hands that day. They were cruelly tortured, several of them murdered; and, as the doctor had reason to believe, some of them were subsequently taken to an island in Lake Ontario, and eaten. This is scarcely to be believed.

Major John Frey, of Colonel Klock's regiment, was likewise wounded and taken; and to show the more than savage fury burning in the bosoms of the men brought into conflict on this occasion, the disgraceful fact may be added, that his own brother, who was in the British service, attempted to take his life after he had arrived in Butler's camp. The major saw his brother approaching in a menacing manner, and called out — " Brother, do not kill me! Do you not know me?" But the infuriated brother rushed forward, and the major was only saved by the interposition of others.[1] The whole number of the Provincial militia killed was two hundred, exclusive of wounded and lost as prisoners. Such, at least, was the American report. The British statements claimed that four hundred of the Americans were killed, and two hundred taken prisoners.[2]

Retaining possession of the field, the survivors immediately set themselves at work in constructing rude litters, upon which to bear off the wounded. Between forty and fifty of these, among whom was the commanding general, were removed in this manner. The brave old

---

[1] MS. statement of Jacob Timmerman, in the author's possession.

[2] " On the 5th I learned, from discovering parties on the Mohawk river, that a body of one thousand militia were on their march to raise the siege. On the confirmation of this news, I moved a large body of Indians, with some troops, the same night, to lay in ambuscade for them on their march. They fell into it. The completest victory was obtained. Above four hundred lay dead on the field, amongst the number of whom were almost all the principal movers of rebellion in that country." — *Letter of Colonel St. Leger to General Burgoyne, Aug.* 11, 1777.

man, notwithstanding the imprudence of the morning — imprudence in allowing a premature movement at the dictation of his subordinates — had nobly vindicated his character for courage during the day. Though wounded, as we have seen, in the onset, he had borne himself during the six hours of conflict, under the most trying circumstances, with a degree of fortitude and composure worthy of all admiration. Nor was his example without effect in sustaining his troops amid the perils by which they were environed. At one time during the battle, while sitting upon his saddle raised upon a little hillock, being advised to select a less exposed situation, he replied — "I will face the enemy." Thus, "surrounded by a few men, he continued to issue his orders with firmness. In this situation, and in the heat of the onslaught, he deliberately took his tinder-box from his pocket, lit his pipe, and smoked with great composure."[1] At the moment the soldiers were placing him on the litter, while adjusting blankets to the poles, three Indians approached, and were instantly shot down by the unerring rifles of three of the militia. These were the last shots fired in that battle.[2]

---

[1] Campbell. An officer, who was in the general staff at the battle of Leipzig, has related to the author a very similar incident in the conduct of old Blucher. He was not wounded; but he sat upon a hillock, issuing his orders and smoking his pipe, while the cannon balls were ploughing up the earth about him.

[2] Narrative of Jacob Sammons, MS. The officers of the Tryon county militia killed or wounded in this battle were as follows : — In Colonel Frederick Visscher's regiment, Captains John Davis and Samuel Pettingill,

The loss of the enemy in this engagement was equally, if not more severe, than that of the Americans. Th Greens and Rangers of Sir John Johnson and Colonel Butler must have suffered badly, although no returns were given in the contemporaneous accounts. Major Watts was severely wounded and left on the field, as was supposed, among the slain. His death was reported by Colonel Willett, in his letter to Governor Trumbull, and by other authorities. But such was not the fact. Reviving from faintness produced by loss of blood, some hours after the action, he succeeded in crawling to a brook, where, by slaking his thirst, he was preserved from speedy death, and in the course of two or three days was found by some Indian scouts, and brought into

---

killed; Major Blauvelt and Lieut. Groat taken prisoners and never heard of afterwards; Captain Jacob Gardenier and Lieut. Samuel Gardenier wounded. In Colonel Jacob Klock's regiment, Major John Eisenlord, and Major Van Sluyck, and Captain Andrew Dillenback, killed; Captains Christopher Fox and John Breadbeg, wounded; Brigade Major John Frey, wounded and taken prisoner. In Colonel Peter Bellinger's regiment, Major Enos Klepsattle, Captain Frederic Helmer, and Lieut. Petrie, were killed. Lieutenant Colonel Frederick Bellinger and Henry Walradt were taken prisoners. In Colonel Ebenezer Cox's regiment, Colonel Cox and Lieut. Col. Hunt were killed; Captains Henry Diefendorf, and Robert Crouse, and Jacob Bowman, killed. Captain Jacob Seeber and Lieut. William Seeber mortally wounded. The surgeon, Moses Younglove, was taken prisoner. Among the volunteers not belonging to the militia, who were killed, were Isaac Paris (then a member of the legislature), Samuel Billington, John Dygert, and Jacob Snell, members of the committee of safety. There was likewise a Captain Graves who fell, but to which regiment he belonged the author has not ascertained.

St. Leger's camp.[1] But the Indians were the most roughly handled, they having lost nearly one hundred warriors, several of whom were sachems in great favor. Frederick Sammons, who had been detached upon a distant scout previous to the battle, returning some days

---

[1] This statement respecting Major Watts was derived from the late Mr. John Watts, of New York, his brother. As mentioned in the text, St. Leger, in his official report, did not state the number of his own killed and wounded. Colonel Butler, however, wrote to Sir Guy Carleton — " Of the New Yorkers, Captain M'Donald was killed, Captain Watts dangerously wounded, and one subaltern. Of the Rangers, Captains Wilson and Hare killed, and one private wounded. The Indians suffered much, having thirty-three killed and twenty-nine wounded; the Senecas lost seventeen, among whom were several of their chief warriors, and had sixteen wounded. During the whole action the Indians showed the greatest zeal for his majesty's cause; and had they not been a little too precipitate, scarcely a rebel of the party would have escaped. Most of the leading rebels are cut off in the action, so that any farther attempts from that quarter are not to be expected. Captain Watts, of the Royal New Yorkers, whose many amiable qualities deserved a better fate, lay wounded in three places upon the field two days before he was found." — *Parliamentary Register.*

" Major Watts was wounded through the leg by a ball, and in the neck by a thrust from a bayonet which passed through the back of the windpipe, and occasioned such an effusion of blood as to induce not only him but his captors to suppose (after leading him two or three miles) that he must die in consequence. He begged his captors to kill him; they refused and left him by the side of a stream (Oriskany creek) under the shade of a bridge, where he was found two days subsequently, covered with fly-blows, but still alive. He was borne by some Indians to Schenectady where he remained (after losing his leg) until sufficiently recovered to bear a voyage to England." — *Mrs. Bonney's Legacy of Historical Gleanings,* vol. 1, p. 69. "Major Watts," says his grand nephew, Gen. J. Watts De Peyster, in a letter to the author, " died in elegant retirement surrounded by a noble family of equally brave sons." The sash taken from him is still in possession of the Sander's family.

afterward, crossed the battlefield, where, he says — "I beheld the most shocking sight I had ever witnessed. The Indians and white men were mingled with one another, just as they had been left when death had first completed his work. Many bodies had also been torn to pieces by wild beasts."[1]

It has been affirmed that the Indians were persuaded to join in this battle only with great difficulty, and not until they had been induced to sacrifice their reason to their appetites. It was very manifest that during the action many of them were intoxicated. The consequence was, that they suffered more severely than ever before.[2] According to the narrative of Mary Jemison, the Indians (at least the Senecas), were deceived into the campaign. "They were sent for to see the British whip the rebels. They were told that they were not wanted to fight, but merely to sit down, smoke their pipes, and look on. The Senecas went to a man; but, contrary to their expectation, instead of smoking and looking on, they were obliged to fight for their lives; and in the end of the battle were completely beaten, with a great loss of killed and wounded."[3]

The whole Indian force was led by Thayendanegea in person — "the great captain of the Six Nations," as he was then called — and as the Cayugas had now likewise joined the Mohawks in alliance with the arms of Eng-

---

[1] MS. narrative of Frederick Sammons, in the author's possession.

[2] *Journal of General Lincoln.*

[3] *Life of Mary Jemison.*

land — the Onondagas adopting a doubtful policy, but always, in fact, acting against the Provincials — he must have had a large force in the field. Of the Senecas alone thirty-six were killed and a great number wounded. Captain Brant was accustomed, long years afterward, to speak of the sufferings of his "poor Mohawks" in that battle. Indeed, the severity with which they were handled on that occasion, rendered them morose and intractable during the remainder of the campaign; and the unhappy prisoners were the first to minister with their blood to their resentment.[1] "Our town," says Mary Jemison, "exhibited a scene of real sorrow and distress when our warriors returned and recounted their misfortunes, and stated the real loss they had sustained in the engagement. The mourning was excessive, and was expressed by the most doleful yells, shrieks, and howlings, and by inimitable gesticulations."

It was unfortunate that General Herkimer formed his

---

[1] In Mr. Samuel Woodruff's memoranda of his conversations with Brant, it is noted as the admission of the latter, that "he and his Mohawks were compelled to flee in a dispersed condition through the woods, all suffering from fatigue and hunger before they arrived at a place of safety. Their retreat began at nightfall. They were pursued by a body of Oneidas, who fought with General Herkimer. The night was dark and lowery. Exhausted by the labors of the day, and fearful he might be overtaken by the pursuing Oneidas, Brant ascended a branching tree, and planting himself in the crotch of it, waited somewhat impatiently for daylight." There is evidently somewhat of error in this statement. The field of battle was not more than five miles from St. Leger's entrenchments, and the battle was ended at two o'clock P.M. Judge W. probably confounded this battle with another — perhaps that of the Chemung.

line of march with so little judgment that, when attacked, his men were in no situation to support each other ; and more unfortunate still, that he marched at all, so long before he could expect to hear the concerted signal for the diversion to be made in his favor by the sortie of Colonel Willett. The heavy rain storm, moreover, which caused a suspension of the battle, had likewise the effect of delaying the sally for nearly an hour. It was made, however, as soon as it was practicable, and was not only completely successful, but was conducted with such ability and spirit by the gallant officer to whom it was confided, as to win for him the applause of the foe himself.[1] In addition to the two hundred men detailed for this service, under Colonel Willett's command, as before stated, fifty more were added to guard the light iron three pounder already mentioned. With these troops, and this his only piece of mounted ordnance, Colonel Willett lost not a moment, after the cessation of the rain, in making the sally. The enemy's sentinels being directly in sight of the fort, the most rapid movements were necessary. The sentinels were driven in, and his advanced guard attacked, before he had time to form his troops. Sir John Johnson, whose regiment was not more than two hundred yards distant from the advanced guard, it being very warm, was in his tent, divested of his coat at the moment, and had not time to put it on before his camp was assailed. Such, moreover, were the celerity of Willett's movement and the im-

---

[1] *London Universal Magazine*, 1782.

petuosity of the attack, that Sir John could not bring his troops into order, and their only resource was in flight. The Indian encampment was next to that of Sir John, and in turn was carried with equal rapidity. The larger portion of the Indians, and a detachment from the regiment of Sir John, were, at the very moment of this unexpected assault upon their quarters, engaged in the battle of Oriskany. Those who were left behind now betook themselves — Sir John and his men to the river — and the Indians to their natural shelter, the woods — the troops of Colonel Willett firing briskly upon them in their flight. The amount of spoil found in the enemy's camp was so great, that Willett was obliged to send hastily to the fort for wagons to convey it away. Seven of these vehicles were three times loaded and discharged in the fort, while the brave little Provincial band held possession of the encampments. Among the spoils thus captured, consisting of camp equipage, clothing, blankets, stores, etc., were five British standards, the baggage of Sir John Johnson, with all his papers, the baggage of a number of other officers, with memoranda, journals, and orderly books, containing all the information desirable on the part of the besieged.[1] While Colonel Willett

---

[1] " Among other things taken from the enemy, were several bundles of papers, and a parcel of letters belonging to our garrison, which they had taken from our militia, but not yet opened. Here I found one letter for myself: there were likewise papers belonging to Sir John Johnson, and several others of the enemy's officers, with letters to and from General St. Leger, the commander. These letters have been of some service to us." — *Colonel Willett's letter to Governor Trumbull.*

was returning to the fort, Colonel St. Leger, who was on the opposite side of the river, attempted a movement to intercept him. Willett's position, however, enabled him to form his troops so as to give the enemy a full fire in front, while at the same time he was enfiladed by the fire of a small field-piece. The distance was not more than sixty yards between them; and although St. Leger was not backward in returning the fire, his aim was nevertheless so wild as to be entirely without effect. The assailants returned into the fortress in triumph without having lost a man — the British flags were hoisted on the flag-staff under the American — and the men, ascending the parapets, gave three as hearty cheers as were ever shouted by the same number of voices. Among the prisoners brought off by the victors, was Lieutenant Singleton, of Sir John Johnson's regiment. Several Indians were found dead in their camp, and others were killed in crossing the river. The loss of the enemy, particularly in stores and baggage, was great; while the affair itself was of still more importance, from the new spirit of patriotic enthusiasm with which it inspired the little garrison.[1] For this chivalrous exploit congress passed a resolution of thanks, and directed the commissary general of military stores to procure an elegant sword, and present the same to Colonel Willett in the name of the United States.

---

[1] In the account of the sortie, the author has adopted almost the very language of the brave colonel himself, in his Narrative. As he led the affair, and was of course the best qualified to describe it, the author could do no better than take his own words. In tracing the progress of the siege, it will be often necessary to draw from the same indisputable source.

General Herkimer did not long survive the battle. He was conveyed to his own house[1] near the Mohawk river, a few miles below the Little falls; where his leg, which had been shattered five or six inches below the knee, was amputated about ten days after the battle, by a young French surgeon in the army of General Arnold, and contrary to the advice of the general's own medical adviser, the late Dr. Petrie. But the operation was unskilfully performed,[2] and it was found impossible by his attendants to stanch the blood. Colonel Willett called to see the general soon after the operation. He was sitting up in his bed, with a pipe in his mouth, smoking, and talking in excellent spirits. He died the night following that visit. His friend, Colonel John Roff, was present at the amputation, and affirmed that he bore the operation with uncommon fortitude. He was likewise with him at the time of his death. The blood continuing to flow — there being no physician in immediate attendance — and being himself satisfied that the time of his departure was nigh, the veteran directed the Holy Bible to be brought to him. He then opened it and read, in the presence of those who surrounded his bed, with all the composure which it was possible for any man to exhibit, the thirty-eighth psalm — applying it to his own situation.[3] He soon afterward expired; and it

---

[1] Yet standing, 1837. See *Benton's Herk. Co.*, 151.

[2] Col. Roff's statement — MS. in possession of the author.

[3] Statement of Colonel John Roff (Roof), a god-son of General Herkimer, and who was in the action, to the author's father.

may well be questioned whether the annals of man furnish a more striking example of Christian heroism — calm, deliberate, and firm in the hour of death — than is presented in this remarkable instance. Of the early history of General Herkimer but little is known. It has already been stated that his family was one of the first of the Germans who planted themselves in the Mohawk valley. And the massive stone mansion, yet standing at German Flats, bespeaks its early opulence. He was an uneducated man — with, if possible, less

---

The father of Colonel John Roof (Johannis Roof) held a captain's commission in the militia, and, with his son, was in the battle of Oriskany. He was a prominent man in his day; and it is not a little singular that, up to this time, he has never received the recognition to which he is entitled. Johannis Roof came over from Germany in 1758, and being a man of enterprise and of means, he was, soon after his arrival in this country, given the charge of the carrying-place at Fort Stanwix; and afterwards — such was his industry and integrity — was made storekeeper and inn-keeper at that fort. He traded quite extensively with the Indians, furnishing supplies to the garrison, etc. When finally driven thence, he sold his buildings to the United States, but before he was paid for them, they were burned (by order of the government) to prevent the tories from taking possession. Nor, by the way, did he ever obtain (owing to his papers being destroyed by the burning of the Patent-office) compensation. After the destruction of his buildings, he settled at Canajoharie — expecting to return to Fort Stanwix (Rome), after peace was established — but the garrison being withdrawn, he remained at Canajoharie, and soon after bought up a large tract of land at that place, laid it out in streets and village lots, and erected a store-house, combining therewith a hotel (*vide* Stone's *Brant*, vol. II, p. 411, note), for the accommodation of the travelling public and those desiring to settle in the vicinity. For many years Canajoharie was known as Roof's village.—*Letter from grandson of Johannis Roof* (Dr. F. H. Roof, *of Rhinebeck, N. Y.*), *to the author, June* 12*th*, 1877.

skill in letters, even than General Putnam, which is saying much. But he was, nevertheless, a man of strong and vigorous understanding — destitute of some of the essential requisites of generalship, but of the most cool and dauntless courage. These traits were all strikingly disclosed in the brief and bloody expedition to Oriskany. But he must have been well acquainted with that most important of all books — the Bible. Nor could the most learned biblical scholar, lay or clerical, have selected a portion of the sacred Scriptures more exactly appropriate to the situation of the dying soldier, than that to which he himself spontaneously turned. If Socrates died like a philosopher, and Rousseau like an unbelieving sentimentalist, General Herkimer died like a Christian hero. Congress passed a resolution requesting the governor and council of New York to erect a monument at the expense of the United States, to the memory of this brave man, of the value of five hundred dollars. This resolution was transmitted to the governor of New York, George Clinton, in a letter from which the following passage is quoted: " Every mark of distinction shown to the memory of such illustrious men as offer up their lives for the liberty and happiness of their country, reflects real honor on those who pay the tribute ; and by holding up to others the prospect of fame and immortality, will animate them to tread in the same path." Governor Clinton thus wrote to the committee of Tryon county on the occasion: " Enclosed you have a letter and resolves of congress, for erecting a monument to the memory of your late gallant general. While with you I lament the cause, I am impressed with a due sense of the great and justly merited honor the continent has, in this instance, paid to the memory of that brave man." Such were the feelings of respect for the services and memory of the deceased entertained by the great men of that day. Sixty years have since rolled away, and the journal of congress is the only monument, and the resolution itself the only inscription, which as yet testify the gratitude of the republic to General Nicholas Herkimer.

Though in fact defeated at Oriskany, the enemy claimed, as we have seen, a victory. In one sense, it is true, the achievement was theirs. They had prevented the advance of the Americans to the succor of the fort; and on their retreat the Americans were unable to pursue. Still the field was won, and retained by them.[1] Availing himself of his questionable success, however, and well knowing that days must probably elapse before the garrison could become apprised of the whole circumstances of the engagement and its issue, St. Leger lost no time in endeavoring, by false representations, to press the besieged to a capitulation. On the same night of the battle, therefore, at nine o'clock, Colonel Bellinger and Major Frey, being in St. Leger's camp as prison-

---

[1] It was alleged, in some of the contemporaneous accounts, that the forces engaged with Herkimer were ordered back in consequence of the sortie of Willett. That circumstance, however, does not alter the essential facts of the case. The victory was the same.

ers, were compelled to address a note to Colonel Gansevoort, greatly exaggerating the disasters of the day, and strongly urging a surrender. In this letter they spoke of the defeat at Oriskany, of the impossibility of receiving any farther succor from below — of the formidable force of St. Leger, together with his train of artillery — announced the probable fact that Burgoyne and his army were then before Albany, and stated that longer resistance would only result in "inevitable ruin and destruction." The letter was transmitted to Colonel Gansevoort by St. Leger's adjutant-general, Colonel Butler, who, in delivering it, made a verbal demand of surrender. Colonel Gansevoort replied that he would give no answer to a verbal summons, unless delivered by Colonel St. Leger himself, but at the mouth of his cannon.

On the following day a white flag approached the garrison, with a request that Colonel Butler, and two other officers, might be admitted into the fort as bearers of a message to the commanding officer. Permission being granted, those officers were conducted blindfolded into the fort, and received by Colonel Gansevoort in his dining-room. The windows of the room were shut, and candles lighted; a table was also spread, upon which were placed some slight refreshments. Colonels Willett and Mellen were present at the interview, together with as many of the American officers as could be accommodated in the quarters of their commander. After the officers were seated and the wine had been passed around, Major Ancrom, one of the messengers, addressed Colonel Gansevoort in substance as follows:

"I am directed by Colonel St. Leger, the officer commanding the army now investing this garrison, to inform the commandant that the colonel has, with much difficulty, prevailed upon the Indians to agree, that if the garrison, without farther resistance, shall be delivered up, with the public stores belonging to it, to the investing army, the officers and soldiers shall have all their baggage and private property secured to them. And in order that the garrison may have a sufficient pledge to this effect, Colonel Butler accompanies me to assure them, that not a hair of the head of any one of them shall be hurt." (Here turning to Colonel Butler, he said, "That, I think, was the expression they made use of, was it not?"—to which the colonel answered, "Yes.") "I am likewise directed to remind the commandant, that the defeat of General Herkimer must deprive the garrison of all hopes of relief, especially as General Burgoyne is now in Albany; so that, sooner or later, the fort must fall into our hands. Colonel St. Leger, from an earnest desire to prevent farther bloodshed, hopes these terms will not be refused; as in this case it will be out of his power to make them again. It was with great difficulty that the Indians consented to the present arrangement, as it will deprive them of that plunder which they always calculate upon on similar occasions. Should, then, the present terms be rejected, it will be out of the power of the colonel to restrain the Indians, who are very numerous and exasperated, not only from plundering the property, but of destroying the lives, probably, of the greater part of the garrison. Indeed, the Indians are so exceedingly provoked and mortified by the losses they have sustained in the late actions, having had several of their favorite chiefs killed, that they threaten — and the colonel, if the present arrangements should not be entered into, will not be able to prevent them from executing their threats — to march down the country, and destroy the settlement, with its inhabitants. In this case, not only men, but women and children, will experience the sad effects of their vengeance. These considerations, it is ardently hoped, will produce a proper effect, and induce the commandant, by complying with the terms now offered, to save himself from future regret, when it will be too late."

This singular oration was of course delivered extemporaneously, as also was the following reply by Colonel Willett, with the approbation of Colonel Gansevoort:

"Do I understand you, sir? I think you say, that you come from a British colonel, who is commander of the army that invests this fort; and by your uniform, you appear to be an officer in the British service. You have made a long speech on the occasion of your visit, which, stripped of all its superfluities, amounts to this — that you come from a British colonel, to the commander of this garrison, to tell him, that if he does not deliver up the garrison into the hands of your colonel, he will send his Indians to murder our women and children. You will please to reflect, sir, that their blood will be on your head, not on ours. We are doing our duty ; this garrison is committed to our charge, and we will take care of it. After you get out of it, you may turn round and look at its outside, but never expect to come in again, unless you come a prisoner. I consider the message you have brought, a degrading one for a British officer to send, and by no means reputable for a British officer to carry. For my own part, I declare, before I would consent to deliver this garrison to such a murdering set as your army, by your own account, consists of, I would suffer my body to be filled with splinters, and set on fire, as you know has at times been practiced, by such hordes of women and children killers as belong to your army."

Colonel Willett observes in his narrative, whence these facts are drawn, that in the delivery he looked the British major full in the face ; and that he spoke with emphasis is not doubted. The sentiments contained in this reply were received with universal applause by the Provincial officers, who, far from being intimidated by the threats of the messengers, were at once impressed with the idea that such pressing efforts to induce a capitulation could only be the effect of doubt, on the part of the enemy himself, of his ability either to sustain the siege or carry the works by assault. Before the interview was closed, Major Ancrom requested that an English surgeon, who was with him, might be permitted to visit the British wounded in the garrison, which request was granted. Major Ancrom also proposed an armistice for three days, which was likewise agreed to by Colonel Gansevoort — the more readily, probably, because of his scanty supply of ammunition.

On the 9th of August, Colonel Gansevoort having refused to recognize any verbal messages from the British commander, Colonel St. Leger transmitted the substance of Major Ancrom's speech in the form of a letter — protesting that no indignity was intended by the delivery of such a message — a message that had been insisted upon categorically by the Indians — and formally renewing the summons of a surrender — adding, that the Indians were becoming exceedingly impatient, and if the proposition should be rejected, the refusal would be attended with very fatal consequences, not only to the garrison, but to the whole country of the Mohawk river.

The reply of Colonel Gansevoort was written with soldierly brevity, in the following words:

COL. GANSEVOORT TO COL. ST. LEGER.

"*Fort Schuyler, Aug 9th,* 1777.

"SIR: "Your letter of this day's date I have received, in answer to which I say, that it is my determined resolution, with the forces under my command, to defend this fort to the last extremity, in behalf of the United American States, who have placed me here to defend it against all their enemies.

"I have the honor to be, sir,
"Your most ob't humble serv't,
"PETER GANSEVOORT,
"*Col. commanding Fort Schuyler.*
"Gen. Barry St. Leger."[1]

---

[1] Copied, by the author, from the original draft, found among the Gansevoort papers.

Expedition of Lt. Col. Barry St. Leger. 205

Failing in these attempts to induce a surrender, the besiegers, four days afterward, had recourse to another expedient. It was the issuing of an appeal to the inhabitants of Tryon county, signed by Sir John Johnson, Colonel Claus, and Colonel John Butler, similar in its tenor to the verbal and written messages of St. Leger to Colonel Gansevoort. The appeal commenced with strong protestations of a desire for the restoration of peace, with a promise of pardon, and oblivion for the past, notwithstanding the many and great injuries the signers had received, upon a proper submission by the people. They, too, were threatened with the ravages of a victorious army, and the resentment of the Indians for the losses they had sustained at Oriskany, in the event of rejecting this appeal. In regard to the garrison of Fort Schuyler, its longer resistance was pronounced "mulish obstinacy," and the people of the Mohawk valley were urged to send up a deputation of their principal men, to oblige the garrison to do at once what they must be forced to do soon — surrender. If they did not surrender, the threat was again repeated that every soul would be put to death by the Indians.[1] Messengers were despatched with this document into Tryon county, but to no good purpose; while, as will soon appear, some of those messengers were involved in serious difficulty by their errand.

But if Colonel Willet's success in the brilliant exe-

---

[1] I have found this document only in *The Remembrancer* for 1777, page 451.

cution of the sortie on the 6th, entitled him, as it unquestionably did, to the commendations he received, a still more perilous enterprise, undertaken by him a few days afterward, was thought, alike by friends and foes, to entitle him to still greater applause. The artillery of the besiegers was not sufficiently heavy to make any impression upon the works, and there was every probability that the garrison might hold out until succors should be obtained, could their situation be made known. Col. Willett was not only well acquainted, but exceedingly popular, in Tryon county; and it was supposed that, should he show himself personally among the militia of that district, notwithstanding the extent of their suffering in the late expedition, he might yet rally a force sufficient to raise the siege. The bold project was therefore conceived by him of passing by night, in company with another officer, through the enemy's works, and, regardless of the danger from the prowling savages, making his way through some forty or fifty miles of sunken morasses and pathless woods, in order to raise the county and bring relief.[1] Selecting Major Stockwell for his companion, Colonel Willett undertook the expedition on the 10th, and left the fort at ten o'clock that night, each armed with nothing but a spear, and provided only with a small supply of crackers and cheese, a small canteen of spirits, and in all other respects unincumbered, even by a blanket. Having escaped from the sally-port, they crept upon their hands and knees along the edge of a morass to the river,

---

[1] *British Universal Magazine.*

which they crossed by crawling over upon a log, and succeeded in getting off unperceived by the sentinels of the enemy, although passing very near to them. Their first advance was into a deep-tangled forest in which, enveloped in thick darkness, they lost their direction, and found it impossible to proceed. While in this state of uncertainty, the barking of a dog added little to their comfort, inasmuch as it apprised them that they were not far from a new Indian encampment, formed subsequent to the sortie a few days before. They were, therefore, compelled to stand perfectly still for several hours, and until the morning star appeared to guide their way. Striking first in a northern direction for several miles, and then eastwardly, they traced a zigzag course, occasionally adopting the Indian method of concealing their trail by walking in the channels of streams, and by stepping on stones along the river's edge. In this way they travelled the whole of the ensuing day without making a single halt. On the approach of night they dared not to strike a light, but lay down to sleep, interlocked in each other's arms. Pursuing their journey on the 12th, their little stock of provisions being exhausted, they fed upon raspberries and blackberries, of which they found an abundance in an opening occasioned by a windfall. Thus refreshed, they pushed forward with renewed vigor and at an accelerated pace, and arrived at Fort Dayton at three o'clock in the afternoon.[1]

---

[1] "So successful was Col. Willett in all his movements, that the Indians, believing him to be possessed of supernatural power, gave to him the name of the Devil." — *Campbell.*

The colonel and his friend received a hearty welcome from Colonel Weston, whose regiment was then in charge at Fort Dayton, and from whom he obtained the agreeable intelligence that, on learning the news of General Herkimer's disaster, General Schuyler had ordered Generals Arnold and Larned, with the Massachusetts brigade, to march to the relief of Colonel Gansevoort. Colonel Willett thereupon took horse immediately for Albany to meet General Arnold, who was to command the expedition; and in four days afterward accompanied Arnold back to Fort Dayton, where the troops were assembling. The first New York regiment had been added to the brigade of General Larned, who was yet in the rear, bringing up the heavy baggage and stores.

During Willett's brief absence to Albany an incident occurred in the neighborhood of Fort Dayton, showing that if he had been active in his attempts to bring succors to the fort, the enemy, on the other hand, had not been idle. About two miles above Fort Dayton resided a Mr. Shoemaker, a disaffected gentleman, who had been in his majesty's commission of the peace. Having heard of a clandestine meeting of tories at the house of that gentleman, Colonel Weston despatched a detachment of troops thither, which came upon the assemblage by surprise, and took them all prisoners. Among them was Lieutenant Walter N. Butler, from St. Leger's army, who, with fourteen white soldiers and the same number of Indians,[1] had

---

[1] *The Remembrancer* for 1777, page 395.

visited the German Flats secretly, with the appeal of Sir John Johnson, Claus, and the elder Butler, referred to in a preceding page, for the purpose of persuading the timid and disaffected inhabitants to abandon the Provincial cause, and enrol themselves with the king's army before Fort Schuyler. Butler was in the midst of his harangue to the meeting at the moment of the unwelcome surprise. General Arnold ordered a court-martial, and caused him to be tried as a spy.[1] Of this tribunal Colonel Willett officiated as judge advocate. The lieutenant was convicted, and received sentence of death; but at the intercession of a number of officers, who had known him while a student at law in Albany, his life was spared by a reprieve. He was, however, removed to Albany and closely imprisoned until the spring of the following year. When General the Marquis de Lafayette assumed the command of the Northern department, the friends of the Butler family, in consequence, as it was alleged, of his ill-health, interceded for a mitigated form of imprisonment. He was then removed to a private house and kept under guard, but shortly afterward effected his escape — owing, it was reported, to treachery — and was subsequently distinguished as one of the severest scourges of the beautiful valley which had given him birth.

The address of Johnson, Claus, and Butler, having been thus introduced among the people of the county,

---

[1] *The Remembrancer* states that Butler came "on a truce to the inhabitants of the county." But if he did bear a flag, it could be no protection for *such* a mission — as it was not.

Arnold issued a proclamation from Fort Dayton for the purpose of counteracting its influence. It was couched in severe language in regard to St. Leger and his heterogeneous army — denounced those of the people who might be seduced by his arts to enrol themselves under the banner of the king — but promised pardon to all, whether Americans, savages, Germans, or Britons, who might return to duty to the states.

Meantime Colonel St. Leger was pushing his operations before the fort with considerable vigor. Every effort to intimidate the garrison having failed, and the commander exhibiting an unsubmitting spirit, St. Leger "commenced approaching by sap, and had formed two parallels, the second of which brought him near the edge of the glacis; but the fire of musketry from the covert way rendered his farther progress very difficult."[1] The fire of his ordnance producing no effect, his only means of annoying the garrison was by throwing shells; but these proved of so little consequence as to afford a discouraging prospect of success. Having advanced, however, within one hundred and fifty yards, it is not to be denied that some uneasiness began to be manifested within the garrison. Ignorant of the fate of Colonel Willett and Major Stockwell, and entirely cut off from all communication from without, their provisions daily exhausting, and having no certain prospect of relief, some of the officers commenced speaking in whispers of the expediency of saving the garrison from a reënact-

---

[1] *Willett's Narrative.*

ment of the Fort William Henry tragedy, by acceding to St. Leger's proffered terms of capitulation. Not so the commander. After weighing well the circumstances of the case, he came to the deliberate resolve, in the event of obtaining no succor from without, when his provisions were about exhausted, to make a sally at night, and cut his way through the encampment of the besiegers, or perish in the attempt.

Fortunately, the necessity of executing the bold determination did not arrive. The siege had continued until the 22d of August, when suddenly, without any cause within the knowledge of the garrison, the besiegers broke up their encampment, and retired in such haste and confusion as to leave their tents, together with a great part of their artillery, camp equipage, and baggage behind. What was the motive for this unexpected flight of a vaunting and all but victorious foe, was a problem they were unable to solve within the garrison, although their joy was not, on that account, the less at their deliverance. It subsequently appeared that the panic which produced this welcome and unexpected change in the situation of the garrison, was caused by a *ruse-de-guerre*, practiced upon the forces of St. Leger by General Arnold, who had been waiting at Fort Dayton several days for the arrival of reinforcements and supplies.[1] But having heard that St. Leger

---

[1] "I wrote you, the 21st instant, from German Flats, that from the best intelligence I could procure of the enemy's strength, it was much superior to our's; at the same time I inclosed you a copy of the resolutions of a council of war, and requested you to send me a reinforcement of one thou-

had made his approaches to within a short distance of the fort, Arnold, on the 22d of August, determined at all events to push forward and hazard a battle, rather than see the garrison fall a sacrifice.[1] With this view, on the morning of the 23d, he resumed his march for Fort Schuyler, and had proceeded ten miles of the distance from Fort Dayton when he was met by an express from Colonel Gansevoort, with the gratifying intelligence that the siege had been raised. The cause of this sudden movement was yet as great a mystery to the colonel and his garrison, as was the flight of the host of Ben-hadad from before Samaria to the king of Israel, when the Syrian monarch heard the supernatural sound of chariots, and the noise of horses, in the days of Elisha the prophet. Arnold was, of course, less in the dark. The circumstances were these :

Among the party of tories and Indians captured at Shoemaker's under Lieutenant Butler, was a singular being named Hon-Yost Schuyler. His place of residence was near the Little falls, where his mother and a brother named Nicholas, were then residing. Hon-Yost Schuyler was one of the coarsest and most ignorant

---

sand light troops."— *Letter of Arnold to Gen. Gates, Aug.* 23, 1777.— " I have been retarded by the badness of the roads, waiting for some baggage, and ammunition, and for the militia, who did not turn out with that spirit which I expected. They are now joining me in great numbers A few days will relieve you."— *MS. letter from Arnold to Col. Gansevoort, Aug.* 22, 1777.

[1] Letters above cited from Arnold to Gen. Gates.— *Vide Remembrancer,* 1777, page 444.

men in the valley, appearing scarce half removed from idiocy; and yet there was no small share of shrewdness in his character. Living upon the extreme border of civilization, his associations had been more with the Indians than the whites; and tradition avers that they regarded him with that mysterious reverence and awe with which they are inspired by fools and lunatics. Thus situated and thus constituted, Hon-Yost had partially attached himself to the royalist cause, though probably, like the cow-boys of West Chester, he really cared little which party he served or plundered; and had he been the captor of the unfortunate Andre, would have balanced probabilities as to the best way of turning the prize to account. Be these things, however, as they may, Hon-Yost was captured, with Walter Butler, and, like him, was tried for his life, adjudged guilty, and condemned to death. His mother and brother, hearing of his situation, hastened to Fort Dayton, and implored General Arnold to spare his life. The old woman strongly resembled the gipsey in her character, and the eloquence and pathos with which she pleaded for the life of her son, were long remembered in the unwritten history of the Mohawk valley. Arnold was for a time inexorable, and the woman became almost frantic with grief and passion on account of her wayward son. Nicholas, likewise, exerted himself to the utmost in behalf of his brother. At length General Arnold proposed terms upon which his life should be spared. The conditions were, that Hon-Yost should hasten to Fort Schuyler, and so alarm the camp of St. Leger as to induce him to raise the seige and fly. The convict-traitor gladly accepted the proposition, and his mother offered herself as a hostage for the faithful performance of his commission. Arnold, however, declined receiving the woman as a hostage, preferring and insisting that Nicholas should be retained for that purpose. To this the latter readily assented, declaring that he was perfectly willing to pledge his life that Hon-Yost would fulfil his engagements to the utmost. Nicholas was, therefore, placed in confinement, while Hon-Yost departed for the camp of Colonel St. Leger — having made an arrangement with one of the Oneida Indians, friendly to the Americans, to aid him in the enterprise. Before his departure several shots were fired through Schuyler's clothes, that he might appear to have had a narrow escape; and the Oneida Indian, by taking a circuitous route to Fort Schuyler, was to fall into the enemy's camp from another direction, and aid Hon-Yost in creating the panic desired. The emissary first presented himself among the Indians, who were in a very suitable state of mind to be wrought upon by exactly such a personage. They had been moody and dissatisfied ever since the battle of Oriskany — neither the success nor the plunder promised them had been won, and they had previously received some vague and indefinite intelligence respecting the approach of Arnold. They had likewise just been holding a pow-wow, or were actually convened in one, for the purpose of consulting the Manito touching the dubious enterprise in which they were engaged, when Hon-Yost arrived. Knowing their character well, he communicated his intelligence to them in the most mysterious and imposing manner. Pointing to his riddled garments, he proved to them how narrow had been his escape from the approaching army of the rebels. When asked the number of the troops that Arnold was leading against them, he shook his head mysteriously, and pointed upward to the leaves of the trees. The reports spread rapidly through the camps, and reaching the ears of the commander, Hon-Yost[1] was sent for to the tent of St. Leger himself. Here he was interrogated, and gave information that General Arnold, with two thousand men, was so near that he would be upon them within twenty-four hours. He gave St. Leger a pitiable narrative of his captivity, trial, and condemnation to the gallows. It was while on his way to execution, as he alleged, that, finding himself not very closely guarded, he took an opportunity to effect his escape — thinking, at the worst, that he could only die, and it would be as well to be shot as hanged. A shower of bullets had indeed been let fly at him, but fortunately had only wounded his clothes, as the general might see.[2] Meantime the Oneida messenger arrived with a belt, and confirmed to the Indians all that Schuyler had said; adding, that the Americans had no desire to injure the Indians, and were intent only upon attacking the British troops and rangers. While making his way to the camp of the besiegers, the ingenious Oneida had fallen in with some

---

[1] *Jobannes Justus*, Dutch for John Joost, pronounced *Hon-Yost*.
[2] *Remembrancer*, for 1777 — p. 447-448.

two or three straggling Indians of his acquaintance, to whom he communicated his business, and whose assistance in furthering the design he engaged. These sagacious fellows dropped into the Indian camp at different points, and threw out alarming suggestions — shaking their heads mysteriously, and insinuating that a bird had brought them intelligence of great moment.[1] They spoke of warriors in great numbers advancing rapidly upon them, and used every indirect method of infusing a panic into the minds of the listeners who gathered around them. The Indians presently began to give signs of decamping, and St. Leger assayed in vain to reassure them. He convened a council of their chiefs, hoping that by the influence of Sir John Johnson, and Colonels Claus and Butler, he should be able to retain them. Other reports, of a yet more terrifying tendency, getting afloat, not only among the Indians but in the other camp, the former declared that "the pow-wow said they must go;" and a portion of them took their departure before the council broke up. The result was a general and precipitate flight. It has been stated, that in the commencement of the retreat the Indians made themselves merry at the expense of their white allies, by raising a shout that the Americans were upon them, and then laughing at the groundless terror thus created.[1] According to the account derived by Gordon from the Rev. Mr. Kirkland, an altercation took place between Colonel St. Leger and Sir John Johnson, the former re-

---

[1] *Travels* of President Dwight, vol. III, p. 195-197.

proaching the latter with the defection of the Indians, while the baronet charged his commander with but an indifferent prosecution of the siege. It was in the gray of twilight, when a couple of sachems, standing upon a little eminence not far in the rear, and overhearing the interchange of sharp words between them, put an end to the unpleasant colloquy by raising the shout — "*they are coming! — they are coming!*" Both St. Leger and Sir John recommenced their retreat with all possible expedition upon hearing such an alarm. Their troops were equally nimble of foot on the occasion, throwing away their knapsacks and arms, and disencumbering themselves of every hindrance to the quick-step; while the Indians, enjoying the panic and confusion, repeated the joke by the way until they arrived at the Oneida lake. It is believed, however, that it was not the Americans alone of whom St. Leger began to stand in fear, being quite as apprehensive of danger from his own dusky allies as he was of the approaching army of Arnold. There is British authority for stating that the Indians actually plundered several of the boats belonging to their own army; robbing the officers of whatsoever they liked. Within a few miles of the camp, they first stripped off the arms, and afterward murdered, with their own bayonets, all those British, German, and American soldiers who were separated from the main body.[1]

---

[1] *British Universal Magazine.* Indeed, St. Leger's report of this disastrous retreat, addressed to General Burgoyne from Oswego, on the 27th of August, corresponds very closely with the American accounts whence the present narrative has been drawn. He states that the Indians fell

218 *Campaign of General John Burgoyne.*

Thus were the threats of savage vengeance sent by Colonel St. Leger to the garrison, in some degree wreaked upon his own army. Hon-Yost Schuyler accompanied the flying host to the estuary of Wood creek, where he deserted, threading his way back to Fort Schuyler the same evening — imparting to Colonel Gansevoort his first information of the advance of Arnold.[1] From Fort Schuyler, Hon-Yost proceeded back to the German Flats. On presenting himself at Fort Dayton, his brother was discharged, to the inexpressible joy of his mother and their relatives. But he proved a tory in grain, and embraced the first opportunity subsequently presented, which was in October, of running away to the enemy, with several of his neighbors, and attaching himself to the forces of Sir John Johnson.[2]

Immediately on the receipt of Colonel Gansevoort's despatch announcing St. Leger's retreat, General Arnold pushed forward a detachment of nine hundred men, with directions, if possible, to overtake the fugitives, and render their flight still more disastrous. On the day following, Arnold himself arrived at the fort, where he was

---

treacherously. upon their friends, and became more formidable than the enemy they had to expect. He leaves no room, however, to suppose that there was any difficulty between Sir John Johnson and himself — calling him " his gallant coadjutor," etc., and commending his exertions to induce the Indians again to meet the enemy, as also those of Colonels Claus and Butler.

[1] Letter of Colonel Gansevoort to General Arnold.

[2] After the close of the contest, Hon-Yost returned to the Mohawk valley, and resided there until his death — which event occurred about twenty years since.

Expedition of Lt. Col. Barry St. Leger. 219

received with a salute of artillery and the cheers of the brave garrison. He, of course, found that Gansevoort had anticipated his design of harassing the rear of the flying enemy, and had brought in several prisoners, together with large quantities of spoil.[1] So great was their panic, and such the precipitancy of their flight, that they left their tents standing, their provisions, artillery, ammunition, their entire camp equipage, and large quantities of other articles enhancing the value of the booty.[2]

Thus ended the siege of Fort Schuyler, or Fort Stanwix, as the public have always preferred calling it. St. Leger hastened with his scattered forces back to Oswego, and thence to Montreal. From that post he proceeded to Lake Champlain, passing up the same to Ticonderoga, for the purpose of joining the army of Burgoyne. Finding that the enemy had evacuated the country between the fort and Lake Ontario, and that the post could be in no immediate danger from that direction, Colonel Gansevoort took the opportunity of visiting his friends at Albany, and at the seat of the state government, then just organized at Kingston. His reception was most cordial, as appears not only from contemporaneous accounts, but from the following modest address to his fellow-soldiers of the garrison, on his return to resume his command:

"I should be wanting in justice to you, if I did not

---

[1] Letter of Arnold to General Gates, Aug. 24, 1777.

[2] Among other articles was the escritoire of St. Leger himself, containing his private papers, several of which have been used by the author in writing this and the preceding chapters.

give some testimony of your good conduct during the time you have been in this garrison, and especially while we were besieged by the enemy. Believe me, that I am impressed with a proper sense of the behavior by which you have done essential service to your country, and acquired immortal honor to yourselves. Nothing can equal the pleasure I have experienced since my absence, in hearing and receiving the public approbation of our country for our services, which is, and must be, to every soldier, a full and ample compensation for the same. Permit me to congratulate you upon the success of the American arms, both to the southward and northward. Every day terminates with victory to America; and I make not the least doubt, but in this campaign we shall effectually establish the Independence of the United States, and thereby secure to ourselves the rights and liberties for which we have so nobly stood forth." [1]

As an evidence of the value placed upon the services of the colonel in the defence of Fort Schuyler, he was shortly afterward promoted in the state line to the rank of brigadier general, while his gallantry was farther rewarded by a colonel's commission from congress in the army of the United States.[2] On leaving his regiment, its officers

---

[1] Copied by the author from the original manuscript. It was filed away among the colonel's papers, with the following inscription :— " A laconic address to my fellow officers and soldiers after our success at Fort Stanwix."

[2] There seems to have been something peculiar and special in this commission. In a letter which Colonel Gansevoort wrote jointly to William Duer and Gouverneur Morris, a copy of which is preserved among his papers, he observes: "Congress have done me the honor of appointing me

presented him with an affectionate letter of congratulation on his promotion, mingled with an expression of their regret at the loss to the regiment of " so worthy a patron." To which the colonel returned an appropriate letter of thanks.[1] The people of Tryon county were of

---

colonel commander of Fort Schuyler. I should esteem it as a favor if you would inform me whether I am to receive any pay for that commission, other than as colonel of the third regiment of New Yorkers; and if not, I should be glad if you would endeavor to get something allowed me, as my present pay will not reimburse my table liquors, which you may well conceive to be something considerable as commanding officer. I am not solicitous to make money by my commission; but I could wish not to sink by it, as I am obliged to do now. The commission which congress has sent me *as commandant of Fort Schuyler*, subjects me as much to the command of my superior officers, as any former one. If that was the intention of congress, the appointment is nugatory. If not, I wish congress to alter the commission."

[1] The following is a copy of the address referred to in the text: "Honored Sir: From a just sense of that conduct which has hitherto been so conspicuously shown to advance the third New York regiment to honor and public notice, we congratulate you that those characteristics which so eminently point out the gentleman and soldier, have by your personal bravery been deservedly noticed by our bleeding country. Although we rejoice at your promotion, yet we cannot but regret the loss of so worthy a patron. That the prosperity which has crowned your conduct with victory may still be continued, is the sincere wish and prayer of, honored sir, your most obedient and very humble servants." It was signed by twenty-six officers. Colonel Gansevoort replied as follows:— "Gentlemen: Your polite address on my promotion merits my sincere thanks. Gratitude, I hope, shall never be wanting in me to the third N. Y. regiment, who have, by their firmness and discipline, been the chief authors of my promotion. Therefore, gentlemen, please accept my warmest wishes for the prosperity of the corps, that all their virtuous endeavors in the defence of their bleeding country may be crowned with honor and success, which will always be the earnest prayer of, gentlemen, your most obliged, humble servant."

course rejoiced, that the blow, directed, as the enemy supposed, with unerring certainty against them, had been averted. They had suffered severely in the campaign; but there were enough of her sons yet left to swell the ranks of General Gates not a little; and they pressed ardently to join his standard, although circumstances did not then require them long to remain in the field.

In October following, when Sir Henry Clinton was ascending the Hudson for the purpose either of succoring, or of coöperating with, Burgoyne, Colonel Gansevoort was ordered to Albany by General Gates, to take command of the large force then concentrating at that place. Happily, there was no occasion to test his prowess in his new and temporary command.

APPENDIX.

APPENDIX.

No. I.

ANECDOTES OF BURGOYNE'S CAMPAIGN — PERSONAL REMINISCENCES, ETC., BY THE LATE CHAS. NEILSON.

ON the near approach of Burgoyne with so powerful, and as yet successful an army, with his horde of unrestrained savages, who were continually in advance and on his flanks, prowling about the country, plundering, murdering, and scalping all who refused loyalty to the British king; the inhabitants on both sides of the river, in the wildest consternation and alarm, fled in every direction. The horrors of war, however mitigated by the laws and usages of civilization, are at all times sufficiently terrific; but when to these the fierce cruelties of a cloud of savages are superadded, those only who are familiar with an American border warfare, can form an adequate opinion of its atrocities. In one place a long cavalcade of ox carts occasionally intermixed with wagons, filled with all kinds of furniture hurriedly thrown in, and not often selected by the owners with reference to their use or value, on occasions of such alarm, were stretched for some distance along the road; while in another might be seen a number on horseback, and here and there two mounted at once on a steed panting under the weight of a double load, closely followed by a crowd of pedestrians, and some perhaps weeping mothers, with a child or two screaming in their arms or on their backs, trudging along with fearful and hurried step. These found great difficulty in keeping up with the rapid flight of their mounted friends. Here and there would be seen some humane person assisting the more unfortunate, by relieving them of their burdens with which they were encumbered; but generally a principle of selfishness prevented much interchange of friendly offices — every one for himself was the common cry.

To those who now sit quietly under their own shady bowers, or by the fireside long endeared by tranquility and happiness, it is left to imagine, with what feelings they hastened to abandon their homes and their all, as it were, and fly for safety, they knew not whither. The men of this generation can never know what were the sorrows of those fathers that saw their children exposed to dangers and death, and what the agonies of those kind mothers, of whom my own respected mother was one, who pressed their offspring to their bosom in the constant apprehension of seeing them torn from their embraces, to become the victims of savage cruelty, and it is impossible with sufficient force to describe the appalling distress that many families experienced at that moment of peril and alarm.

*   *   *   *

Often, when a boy, have I sat long and silent, in the family group, by the side of my much respected, now sainted mother, listening to her tales of alarm, suffering and distress, that pervaded this part of the country, in those troublous times; and the dangers to which she herself had frequently been exposed. And often while reciting the tragic fate of her friend and acquaintance, Miss Jane M'Crea, and other equally savage cruelties, have I seen the big tear roll from her glistening eye and trickle down her cheek, glowing with the emotions of her heart. And even to this day, when I reflect on those scenes of savage cruelty, and with what emotion they were then recited, a sympathetic tear will insensibly steal from my eye, and I am involuntarily led to exclaim O! my mother! my much loved mother! could I have been present to have witnessed those scenes of danger and alarm to which thou hast been exposed, and from which thou barely escaped with thy life, with one arm would I have encircled that brow, around which the Indian's tomahawk thrice was brandished, preparatory to the fatal stroke; and with the other would I have *dashed* to the earth, that ferocious savage, whose scalping-knife, reeking with the blood of thy friends, was already drawn to execute on thee its threatened deed! But a mightier arm was interposed for thy protection. He in whom thou trusted was there — for at the critical moment, when there seemed no possible escape, a file of men approached, as if specially and providentially directed — the sharp crack of rifles was heard in the distance — the fatal balls were sped — two cruel savages fell dead at thy feet, and thou alone, the joy of thy friends, wast saved, to relate the sad story of thy three murdered companions!

It may be supposed, from my relation of so many of the numerous scenes, and some of them heart-rending, through which my own friends have passed, that *they* were the only persons who suffered in those trying times. My intention is not to be so understood, nor do I suppose that the many trials through which they passed, were greater than those of many others; yet the relation of them, by being often repeated, have become more familiar, and consequently better enables me to give a correct account of them.

The subsequent tragic scene, though I do not now recollect all the particulars, I will recount in substance, as follows:

My step-grandfather, had been very active among the Indians and tories, and understood their manner of warfare so well that he was often selected to head volunteer parties, who went in pursuit of them, in their marauding expeditions, and was generally very successful; for which they owed him a grudge, and tried many ways to decoy and take him; but he had always eluded them.

It happened on a time when it was supposed there were no Indians in the vicinity, and the inhabitants all felt secure, that my father was gone from home on business with the committee of safety, leaving my grandfather, grandmother, and mother, at home alone — they all occupying the same house at the time. Soon after dark, a little dog, which they had, and which was then in the house, for some moments seemed to express considerable uneasiness, and at last ran to the door, and with a kind of howl, or unusual expression, immediately turned and looked up, with much seeming concern, to my grandfather, whose keen perception in a moment led him to exclaim, " Indians !" He immediately caught his rifle, which lay horizontally on hooks attached to a beam overhead, and opening the door stepped out. But he had no sooner passed the threshold, than the sharp crack of three rifles were heard in rapid succession, and he staggered back, exclaiming, " run for your lives !" and fell into the room. My mother and grandmother, already horror-stricken, gave a sudden scream and immediately sprang out of an opposite window, and ran to a neighboring house, about eighty rods distant, to give the alarm. It so happened that two distant neighbors, who had been out that day on a hunting excursion, called at the same house some ten or fifteen minutes before, and hearing the firing, were, in company with the occupant, listening to ascertain its direction, if repeated. At the same time a horse was heard at a distance rapidly approaching, which soon proved to be my father's on which, having heard the firing, and suspecting mischief, he was riding at the top of his speed, and arrived at the moment the alarm was given. Springing from his horse, and being furnished with a rifle, the four men immediately hurried on, regardless of any danger they might be rushing into. On approaching the house, it being then quite dark, they caught the glimpse of persons running in the direction of a piece of woods near by ; upon whom they, in their hurry, fired at random.

Having pursued on to the skirt of the wood, and seeing no more of the enemy, they returned to the house, where a mournful spectacle presented itself. There lay the mangled and lifeless corpse of my grandfather, drenched in his own blood; and tomahawked and scalped; and on examination it was found that three balls had passed through his body. In searching, the next morning, at the place where the Indians, for such were they supposed to be, were fired upon, they found blood in several places leading into the woods, evincing that some *one* of them, at least, had been wounded. It was supposed that the hostile party consisted of four tories, and five Indians, as that number was seen next day, near Fort Edward, traveling north with a hurried step; one of which limped considerably and lagged behind.

A short time previous to the foregoing tragedy, my grandfather, at the head of fifty men, had a desperate encounter with about eighty Indians and tories at Sabbathday point,[1] in which the enemy were defeated, with the loss of forty killed and wounded. It was supposed that, in consequence of so signal a defeat, which was effected by means of an ambuscade, the Indians and tories were determined, at all hazards, to destroy the man, who in this, as in many other instances, had been so great a

---

[1] Sabbathday point is a low neck of land stretching into Lake George from the western shore, three miles from the little village of Hague. On Sabbathday point, Lord Amherst with his army stopped for refreshment upon the morning of the Sabbath, and gave this beautiful spot the name by which it is now known. It is a charming spot, and susceptible of great embellishment. In the summer of 1756, a small body of Provincials who had retreated to this point, defeated a superior force of French and Indians, who had attacked them in gun-boats.

scourge to them, and which they finally accomplished, in the manner already related.

At the time the American army under General Schuyler was retreating down the Hudson from Fort Edward, small parties of tories and Indians kept pace with them along the opposite bank, and when an opportunity presented, where the road was on or near the margin of that stream, along which the army passed, they would secrete themselves near the bank and fire across at the officers and men ; and in this manner they pursued them as far down as Stillwater, wounding many on the way. When the army was thus passing near E. Vandenburgh's, and opposite a shoal place in the river, an Indian waded out some distance and fired, hitting a soldier and badly wounding him in the hand. Another soldier, by the name of Dirk Van Vechten, who was marching in the same platoon, was so vexed at it that he was determined to avenge the injury. Accordingly he kept a sharp look out, and watching his opportunity, as soon as he saw an Indian approach the river, he crept along on the ground, and laid himself down on the margin of the bank, behind some open bushes ; and as an Indian arrived at a spot in the river, from which he raised his piece to fire, Van Vechten let drive at him, when the Indian bounded, with a horrid screech, three feet out of water, and fell, and he saw no more of him. After that, the Indians were very careful how and where they showed themselves.

*　　　*　　　*　　　*

Several anecdotes in connection with the battle of Bennington have been recorded, of which the following is one.

Among the reinforcements from Berkshire county came a clergyman, the Rev. Mr. Allen, of Pittsfield, with a portion of his flock, resolved to make bare the arm of flesh against the enemies of the country. Before daylight on the morning of the 16th, he addressed the commander as follows: "We the people of Berkshire have been frequently called upon to fight, but have never been led against the enemy. We have now resolved, if you will not let us fight, never to turn out again." General Stark asked him if he wished to march then, when it was dark and rainy. "No," was the answer. "Then," continued Stark, "if the Lord should once more give us sunshine, and I do not give you fighting enough, I will never ask you to come again." The weather cleared up in the course of the day, and the men of Berkshire followed their spiritual guide into action.

Another — On General Stark's approach to the Hessian camp, and pointing out the enemy to his soldiers, he declared to them that "he would gain the victory over them in the approaching battle, or Molly Stark should be a widow that night."

Some two or three days previous to the time that Colonel Baum was detached to Bennington, a party of Indians and tories were sent on for the purpose of scouring the country between that place and Fort Edward. On their way they captured and took with them Mrs. Hannah Coon (now Mrs. Grandy), wife of Mr. Elisha Coon, a captain in the American militia, and who was then absent on duty. Mrs. Coon was then in a very delicate situation, and such as required momentary attention; but notwithstanding, she was compelled, as incapacitated as she was, to travel on foot with these ferocious savages and more brutal tories. The second day after her capture her *accouchement* took place, where they halted for the night. In the morning after her confinement, she, with two other women who had also been captured, was again compelled to walk and carry her child, to the place where the troops under Colonel Baum encamped, previous to the action with the Americans under General Stark. Before the battle, she says, the troops were in high spirits, and boasted much of their ability to subdue the "rebel Yankees," as they called the Americans, and vainly endeavored to persuade a number, whom they had taken prisoners on the way, to join in the cause of the British king. But during the action, and while the soldiers were repeatedly bringing the wounded into camp, she would laugh at, and ridicule them. Soon after the action commenced, she saw the Indians, she says, flying in all directions, and skulking behind trees, rocks, and other places of concealment. On the retreat of the Indians, after the defeat of Colonel Baum, she was taken with them, and soon met the reinforcements under Colonel Breymann; when she returned to camp and remained during the second battle, and was again compelled to travel on foot with them on their retreat to the place where they encamped during the night. Here, owing to her recent confinement and constant fatigue, she was taken sick, and whether it was on that account, or on account of the hurry and bustle the troops were in at the time, being in momentary expectation of pursuit by the Americans, she does not know, but she was left without a guard, and managed to conceal herself and child until they had departed, when she made her escape.

During those days of extreme suffering, distress, and alarm that she experienced, while in her delicate state of health, she was often threatened with instant death, if she refused to proceed or complained of inability; and once, in particular, an Indian chief approached her with much ferocity, at a time when she was tantalizing them on their defeat, and actually clenched up her child, which was lying on her lap, and drew his scalping knife around its head, and brandished his tomahawk over her, in token of what he would do if she did not desist; and she thinks would have carried his threats into execution, had it not been for the interference of a humane officer. After her escape, and having undergone all the horrors of a cruel death, she with much difficulty returned home, where she remained alone (excepting her infant child), and in the midst of the wilderness, about three weeks, with nothing to subsist upon but a little salt pork, which had been concealed, and some old or seed cucumbers, that were left undisturbed in the garden, all of their other provisions and even her cooking and other furniture having been taken away by the Indians and tories. The cucumbers she scraped the seeds from and peeled, then roasted them in the embers, and though she was fearful they might kill her, yet, she says, she thought she might as well die by eating them as to starve to death — as the salt pork she could not eat alone.

At the expiration of three weeks she was again taken by the Indians and tories, who, she thinks, vented their malice particularly upon her, on account of her husband having taken sides with the Americans, as they would often speak of it. At this time she was compelled to cross the river with them, in advance of the British army, and was taken as far as Stillwater, but managed to make her escape during the action of the 19th of September, having suffered much during the time.

But little do the junior matrons of these times of luxury and ease, know or feel of the suffering and deprivations of those who inhabited this part of the country in those days of peril and alarm ; and there are but few, who sufficiently realize the price at which the dear bought liberties of our now happy country were purchased.

Mrs. Coon (Grandy), now (1844) lives on the same farm that her husband owned and occupied when she was taken prisoner — about two miles from Union Village, in Washington county, New York. She is, at the time of writing this narrative, ninety-three years of age, quite active, and her step uncommonly firm for a person of her advanced age ; and she bids fair to live yet a number of years. On the recital of her sufferings, a glow of resentment suffused her matronly cheek; and the fire of indignation would sparkle in her keen black eye ; but in a moment she sprang upon her feet, with the seeming activity of youth, and broke out in raptures of joy, as though no sacrifice for her country had been too great, and exclaimed with much energy of feeling: " But they got well paid for it! the first army," as she called it, " were most all taken prisoners, and the second got defeated and had to run for their lives;" and " Oh," she said, " how I rejoiced to see it, though I knew my own sufferings would be increased." And who is there so lost to his country's weal as not to exclaim with the patriot poet?

"Amor (patriæ) vincit omnia, et nos cedamus amori."

The following incident took place while Colonel Warner had the command of the garrison at Fort Edward:

While the Americans held undisputed possession of the posts at the north, it was a very common thing for the different commanders to exchange visits. Colonel Warner occasionally visited the commander at Fort George. On one of these occasions, he was returning with two officers, all of them on horseback. As they were passing the Bloody pond, where some hostile Indians had hid themselves behind an old tree, they received a volley of musketry from their concealed enemies. The two officers fell lifeless to the ground, and Colonel Warner was wounded, as was also the horse he rode. He put spurs to the bleeding animal and endeavored to escape. One of the officer's horses accompanied him, and the Indians pursued. As he rode on, his own occasionally seemed ready to fall under him, and at other times would revive and appear to renew his strength. The other horse kept up with them, alternately increasing and relaxing his speed, to keep pace with his wounded companion. The colonel in vain tried to seize the bridle which hung over his neck, an expedient which promised to save him if his own steed should fail. In this manner, and with all the horrid anticipation of a cruel death before him, he managed to outstrip his pursuers until he reached Glen's Falls. There, as the uninjured horse came along side, he made another attempt to seize his bridle, and succeeded. He instantly dismounted, unslung his own saddle, threw it over the fence, mounted the other horse and rode off at full speed. He saw no more of his pursuers from this moment, but reached Fort Edward in safety. Not however, without being really overcome by his exertion, fatigue, and loss of blood. What was also singular, was the arrival of his wounded horse, which lived to do good service in the field.

* * * *

During the time (nearly a month [1]) that Burgoyne, with his army, lay at and near the Batten kil, an incident took place, which I think worthy of notice, as showing the spirit and ardor of the whigs in those troublous times, and their determination to cut off all supplies from the invading army.

The tories, or *cow boys* as they were then called, were in the constant habit of plundering the inhabitants

---

[1] An error, unless Fort Miller, ten miles above, is considered as a portion of the encampment at the Batten kil.— *W. L. Stone.*

on both sides of the river, of their grain, poultry, and other kinds of eatables, and driving off their cattle, hogs, and sheep, whenever they could find them, for the purpose of supplying the British army with provisions, for which no doubt they were well paid. Though often pursued, and sometimes roughly handled by the whigs, they still persisted. At one time in particular, they had collected and secreted in a deep dark ravine, branching off from Mill creek, a large quantity of provisions, such as beef, pork, flour, and other articles of consumption, with the intention of transporting them, at some favorable opportunity, to the British camp. By accident it was found out, and the place of concealment discovered; upon which my father, at the head of about twenty resolute fellows, which he had collected together and well armed, went on in the night, for the purpose of taking or destroying their plunder. On their arrival within a short distance of the depot, one of them crept slily along, when he discovered the tories, about thirty in number; five of whom appeared to be armed and keeping guard, while the others were in the act of loading four wagons which stood a short distance from the depot, and which they had brought for the purpose of conveying away their stores. The assailing party then held a secret council of war, to consult whether, the enemy being so much superior in number, it was advisable to proceed; whereupon it was unanimously agreed that they should go ahead, and made their arrangements accordingly.

The place where the stores were concealed, was behind a point projecting from the opposite side, around which the ravine curved, forming the bank on the side of the assailants into a semicircle, around which, it was preconcerted, they should extend themselves in couples, and silently approach the bank or brow of the hill, and at the word of command, " *Come on, boys !*" they were all to give a whoop, and rush on, though not to fire unless the tories made resistance ; but in that case, to fight their way through in the best way they could. All preliminaries being arranged, they formed themselves in order of battle, and silently moved on to the brow of the hill forming the ravine; and when my father, who was at the head, and as previously agreed, gave the word, " Come on boys!" they gave such horrid, continued, and frightful yells, and at the same time rushing down the hill like a mighty torrent, that by the time they had got to the bottom of the ravine, the enemy had all decamped, leaving their arms and baggage a prey to the victors. The assailants not yet satisfied, pursued on a considerable distance, shouting, whooping, and making the woods ring with their horrid yells, as though a thousand Indians had been let loose upon the frightened fugitives. Having found no enemy in their pursuit, the assailants returned to the deserted camp, to examine their booty ; but as the tories had not yet brought, or had concealed their horses, and having no means of bringing off the wagons, they went to work and broke them in pieces, as much as they could. Having stove in the barrels, and scattered and otherwise destroyed the flour and other provisions, they all returned home safe and sound, and much to the joy and gratification of their families and friends; bringing with them twenty-five stand of arms, with which Burgoyne had furnished the tories, and which the victors considered lawful prize.

Thus ended this hazardous and praiseworthy exploit, and for which my father was honored with the title of *captain*, a title, as is now well known to many, by which for a number of years, he was addressed, until he was appointed a civil magistrate, when the title was exchanged for *esquire*.

About the same time, small parties of Indians were seen prowling about the vicinity, of whom my father and a few resolute fellows had been in pursuit. On their return, he had occasion, while the others passed on, to call at a Mr. Ezekiel Ensign's, who afterwards, and for a number of years, kept a public house a little north of Wilbur's basin. While sitting there about nine o'clock in the evening, in conversation with Mr. Ensign, a ferocious looking giant-like Indian, armed and accoutred in the usual costume of an aboriginal warrior, ushered himself into the room, and after eyeing them sharply for a moment, he with one hand drew from his belt a huge tomahawk, which he flourished about his head in true Indian style, and with the other a long scalping-knife, whose glittering steel became more brilliant in the dazzling glare of a bright torch-light, and with which he exhibited, in pantomime, his dextrous manner of taking scalps. At the same time, with eyes flashing fire, and turning alternately from one to the other, as they sat in opposite directions, he accompanied his daring acts in broken English, with threats of instant death, if they attempted to move or speak. Ensign being a cripple in one arm, having at some former time accidentally received a charge of shot through his shoulder, and feeling his own weakness, should resistance become necessary, and being in momentary expectation of receiving the fatal blow, became fixed and immovable in his chair, with a countenance of ashy paleness,

Obstupuit, steteruntque comæ, et vox faucibus hæsit.

On the other hand, my father, being a man of great muscular strength, and of uncommon agility, and having had many encounters with the Indians, for which they owed him a grudge, prepared himself, with much presence of mind, for a desperate event. To this effect, while the Indian, in his threatening manner, would momentarily direct his attention to Ensign, he would imperceptibly and by degrees, turn himself in his chair, and in this manner would from time to time, keep silently moving by little and little, until he succeeded in placing himself in a position in which he could grasp with both hands, the back posts of his chair. Thus situated, and knowing the lives of both of them depended altogether on his own exertions, he watched his opportunity, and the moment the Indian turned his eye from him, he grasped the chair, and with almost the rapidity of lightning, sprang upon his feet, whirled the chair over his head, and aimed at him a desperate blow: but the chair taking the ceiling above, and the Indian at the same time, and almost as quick as thought, dodging the blow, he missed his aim. The Indian, having recovered his position, immediately sprang with a hideous yell, and with his tomahawk uplifted, ready to strike the fatal blow; but before he could effect his direful purpose, the chair was brought around the second time, and with redoubled force, athwart his head and shoulders, which brought him to the floor.

No sooner had he fallen, than his assailant, dropping his chair, sprang upon him, and wrenched from his firm grasp, the dreadful weapons of death; and would have disabled him on the spot, but Ensign, who by this time had recovered the power of speech, and supposing he intended to take the Indian's life, begged of him not to kill him in the house. He then, holding him in his firm grasp, called for a rope, which was soon procured, and with the assistance of Ensign, he succeeded, though not without a dreadful struggle, in binding the savage monster. By this time, two of the neighbors who had been alarmed by some female of the family, came in, when he was shut up in an out-house, with the doors barred, and left in their keeping during the remainder of the night; to be disposed of in the morning as circumstances might require. In the night, the guard believing him secure, and allowing themselves to fall asleep, he made his escape, by removing some portion of the floor and under wall, on the opposite side of the prison to which his guard was posted, much to the regret, not only of his victor, but to many of the neighbors, who had flocked together to obtain a sight of the *conquered savage.*

At another time seven of those maurauding tories, who had distinguished themselves by a series of desperate acts not to be patiently endured by the community, were

Appendix. 243

taken prisoners, conveyed to Albany, and confined in the city prison, which also served for the court house and the meetings of the common council, and from which they once made their escape, but only to enjoy their liberty a few hours, for they were soon retaken and condemned to the gallows. The public indignation was much excited by their conduct in prison, and the circumstances attending their being brought to suffer the sentence of the law. They were confined in the right hand room of the lower story of the prison. The door of their apartment swung in a place cut out lower than the level of the floor. When the sheriff came to take them out he found the door barricaded. He procured a heavy piece of timber with which he in vain endeavored to batter down the door, although he was assisted in the operation by some very athletic and willing individuals. During the attempt, the voices of the prisoners were heard threatening death to those who persevered in the attempt, with the assertion that they had a train of powder to blow up themselves and their assailants. Indeed it was well ascertained, that a quantity of powder had passed into their possession, but how, could not be known. It was afterwards found placed under the floor, and arranged to produce the threatened result. The sheriff could not effect his entrance, while a crowd of gazers looked on to see the end of this singular contest. Some one suggested the idea of getting to them through the ceiling, and immediately went to work to effect a passage by cutting a hole through. While this was going on, the prisoners renewed their threats, with vows of vengeance speedy, awful and certain. The assailants, however, persevered, and having procured a fire-engine, placed it so as to introduce the hose suddenly to the hole in the ceiling, and at a given signal inundated the room beneath. This was dextrously performed. The powder and its train were in an instant rendered useless. Still, however, to descend was the difficulty, as but one person could do so at a time. The disproportion of physical strength that apparently awaited the first intruder, prevented, for some time, any further attempt. At last an Irishman, by the name of McDole, who was a merchant, exclaimed, "give me an Irishman's gun, and I will go first!" He was instantly provided with a formidable cudgel, and with this in his hand he descended, and at the same moment in which he struck the floor, he levelled the prisoner near him, and continued to lay about him violently until the room was filled with a strong party of citizens, who came to his assistance through the hole in the ceiling. After a hard struggle they were secured, and the door, which had been barricaded by brick taken from the fireplace, was opened.

They were almost immediately taken out for execution, and the mob was sufficiently exasperated to have instantly taken their punishment into their own hands. The prisoners while moving up the hill to the place of execution, wore an air of great gloom and illnature. No one appeared to pity them, and their own hopes of being released by some fortunate circumstance, as by the intervention of the enemy, had now vanished forever.

Having arrived at the summit of the hill, near, or at

the very place now covered with elegant and substantial edifices, near the present academy, they there, upon one gallows of rude construction, ended their miserable lives together, and were buried in front of it.

The transaction created considerable excitement, and was considered by the tories as a cruel and unnecessary waste of life, and a sacrifice to the unnatural feelings which had dictated the unhappy rebellion. By the whigs, it was considered as a necessary example, demanded by the nature of the times and the enormity of the offences they had committed, and they considered it not only a justifiable, but an imperious act of necessity, to inflict upon the offenders the full penalties of the law.[1]

*   *   *   *

At one time while the two armies were encamped near each other (after the battle of Freeman's farm) about twenty of the most resolute inhabitants in the vicinity, collected together for the purpose of having a frolic, as they termed it, of some kind or other. After their arrival at the place of rendezvous, and a number of propositions had been logically discussed, they finally concluded, with more courage than prudence, that, by a *coup-de-main*, they would go and bring in one of the British advance pickets, which was posted on the north bank of the middle ravine. Having with much formality, selected their several officers, and furnished themselves with suitable arms and other equipments, they marched off in *ir*-regular military style. The martial costume of the captain, for by such title he was addressed, exhibited

---

[1] *The Sexagenary*, by S. D. W. *Bloodgood*, p. 100, Munsell's edition.

the extremes of continental etiquette, personified in one instance, by a sharp and huge three cocked hat, profusely trimmed with the threadbare fragments of thrown-off gold lace, surmounting a well pomatumed and powdered head. A long waisted blue coat, turned up with rather sun-bleached buff, that met and parted at the same time on his breast; a black silk neck-kerchief drawn tightly around his throat, discovering the balance of power, or rather the center of gravity, to be lying some where in the region of the olfactory organ, completed the upper half of this mischief-bent volunteer officer. A pair of buckskin small clothes drawn tightly over a muscular thigh, were met at the knee by a pair of straight-sided boots, that, doubtless, by their stiffness and want of pliability prevented any thing like an attack upon the limb inside. An old white belt thrown over the whole man, and a heavy sabre with a leather scabbard, completed the brilliant costume of this son of chivalry, and *ir*-regular friend of the continental congress.

The other *com*-missioned officers, for such by way of distinguishment, were they called, were fully armed and accoutred in a similar manner, but somewhat inferior in brilliancy.

Brown tow shirts were the panoply of the *farmer*-soldiers; over their broad shoulders hung powder horns and shot bags, manufactured during the long winter evenings, and now and then stopped up with a corn cob, which had escaped the researches of the swinish multitude. Muskets were rather uncommon among the inhabitants in those days of martial exploit, and in their stead, long fowling-pieces were substituted.

In such a group of combatants just escaped, as it were, from the tomahawk, hastily equipped for the present emergency, and bearing a grotesque appearance, the name of Steuben was of no more weight than the feather that danced in the breeze. Thus armed and accoutred, these sons of daring intrepidity, marched off about ten o'clock at night, with more courage than order, fully determined to conquer or die in the glorious cause of their beloved country, then bleeding at every pore.

As they approached within musket-shot distance of their unsuspecting enemy, they were formed, or rather formed themselves in order of battle, and advanced in three *grand* divisions — one by a circuitous route, to gain their rear, while the other two posted themselves on their flanks. After giving time for each party to gain their several positions, the resolute captain, who was prepared for the purpose, gave the preconcerted signal, by a deafening blast on an old horse trumpet, whose martial sound had often cheered the mounted troops to fierce and bloody combat, when all, with fearless step "rushed bravely on" with clattering arms, through rustling leaves and crackling brush, with the usual parade of a hundred men. As they closed in, the leaders of each division, in a bold and commanding voice, and before the guard could say "Who comes there?" called, or rather bawled out, "Ground your arms, or you are all dead men!" Supposing they were surrounded by a much superior force, and deeming resistance, under such circumstances, of no avail, the officer of the guard gave the orders, when their arms were immediately grounded, and thirty British soldiers surrendered themselves "prisoners of war" to only two-thirds of their number, and those undisciplined American farmers.

*   *   *   *

Accompanying the American army were a great number of women, principally foreigners, many of whom had husbands or brothers in the action, and many who followed merely for the sake of plunder, as was manifested during the night after the action of the 7th October. The next morning after the battle, every man that was left dead on the field, and even those who were supposed to be mortally wounded, and not yet dead, but helpless, were found stripped of their clothing, which rendered it almost impossible to distinguish between American and British. But *during* the action, a heart-rending, and yet to some a laughable, scene took place in the American camp, and probably the same in the British. In the heat of the battle, and while the cannon were constantly roaring like oft peals of distant thunder, and making the earth to quake from its very foundation, some of those women, wringing their hands, apparently in the utmost distress, and frantically tearing their hair in the agony of their feelings, were heard to cry out, in the most lamentable exclamations, " Och, my husband! my poor husband! Lord Jesus, spare my poor husband!" which would be often repeated, and sometimes by fifteen or twenty voices at once ; while the more hardened ones, and those rejoicing in the prospects of plunder, would break out in blasphemous imprecations, exclaiming, " D—n your poor husband, you can get another !" And in this manner the scene continued during the action; and I have heard it observed by those who were present, that they could not help smiling, even through their tears, at the pitiful exhibition.

*   *   *   *

The soldier who shot General Fraser, was Timothy Murphy, a Virginian, who belonged to Morgan's rifle corps, in which he distinguished himself as a marksman, and excited much interest while in camp. After the capture of Burgoyne, the company to which he belonged was ordered to Schoharie, where it remained until their term of service expired. When the company was disbanded, Murphy and some others remained, and served in the militia; his skill in the desultory war which the Indians carry on, gave him so high a reputation, that though not nominally the commander, he usually directed all the movements of the scouts that were sent out, and on many important occasions the commanding officers found it dangerous to neglect his advice; his *double rifle*, his skill as a marksman, and his fleetness either in retreat or pursuit, made him an object both of dread and of vengeance to the Indians: they formed many plans to destroy him, but he always eluded them, and sometimes made them suffer for their temerity.

He fought the Indians with their own weapons. When circumstances permitted, he tomahawked and scalped his fallen enemy; he boasted after the war that he had slain forty of the enemy with his own hand; more than half of whom he had scalped; he took delight in perilous adventures, and seemed to love danger for danger's sake. Tradition has preserved the account of many of his exploits; but there are so many versions of the same story, and so much evident fiction mixed with the truth, that the author will give but a single instance as proof of the dread with which he was regarded by the Indians.

They were unable to conjecture how he could discharge his rifle twice without having time to reload; and his singular good fortune in escaping unhurt, led them to suppose that he was attended by some invisible being, who warded off *their* bullets, and sped *his* with unerring certainty to the mark. When they had learned the mystery of his doubled-barrelled rifle, they were careful not to expose themselves too much until he had fired twice, knowing that he must have time to reload his piece before he could do them further injury.

One day having separated from his party, he was pursued by a number of Indians, all of whom he outran excepting one; Murphy turned round, fired upon this Indian, and killed him. Supposing that the others had given up the pursuit he stopped to strip the dead, when the rest of his pursuers came in sight. He snatched the rifle of his fallen foe, and with it killed one of his pursuers; the rest, now sure of their prey, with a yell of joy heedlessly rushed on, hoping to make him their prisoner; he was ready to drop down with fatigue, and was likely to be overtaken, when turning round, he discharged the remaining barrel of his rifle, and killed the foremost of the Indians; the rest, astonished at his firing three times in succession, fled, crying out that he could shoot all day without loading.

In stature, Murphy was about five feet six inches, and very well proportioned, with dark complexion, and an eye that would kindle and flash like the very lightning when excited. He was exceedingly quick in all his motions, and possessed an iron frame that nothing apparently could affect: And what is very remarkable, his body was never wounded or scarred during the whole war.[1]

*   *   *   *

The following facts respecting Col. Cochran, I obtained through the politeness of Miss Caroline Ogden, an interesting maiden lady, and grand-daughter of the colonel, who now (1844) resides with J. T. M'Cown, Esq., in the city of Troy.

Colonel Cochran having been sent to Canada as a spy, his mission was suspected, and a large bounty offered for his head. While there he was taken sick, and knowing that he was suspected, concealed himself, for the space of a few days, in a brush heap, within about two miles of the American lines, unable to make his escape, or even to walk. Having suffered much from his sickness and want of nourishment, and having discovered a log cabin at considerable distance from where he was concealed, and the only one in sight, he crept to it on his

---

[1] At the close of the war, Murphy became a farmer and settled in Schoharie Co., N. Y. He was a capital stump speaker, and was a political power in the county. He brought William C. Bouck into political life, which in time, carried him into the gubernatorial chair of the Empire state. He died in 1818, full of years and honors, of cancer occasioned by the recoil of his rifle on his cheek.— *Ed.*

hands and knees, for the purpose of soliciting assistance. On his approach to the rear of the cabin, he heard three men in earnest conversation, and as it happened he was the subject of their discourse. Having heard of the heavy bounty that was offered for the colonel, and having seen a man in the vicinity a few days before, answering the description of him, they were then forming their plans, and expressing their determination to find his whereabouts, and take him for the sake of the bounty. One of the men was the owner of the cabin, whose wife was also present, and the others were his brother and brother-in-law. Soon after this conversation took place, and the three men having departed in pursuit, he crept into the cabin, and frankly told the woman, who seemed favorably impressed towards him, on account of his almost helpless condition, that he had overheard the conversation, and that *he* was the man of whom they were in search, and that he should throw himself entirely upon her mercy, and trust to her fidelity for protection, which she very kindly promised him, to the utmost of her ability. Having administered some restoratives, which seemed to give relief, and given him some suitable nourishment, he lay down on a bed in the room, for the purpose of taking some repose, which he very much needed. After the men had been absent some three hours, they again returned, when she concealed him in a closet, or sort of cupboard, standing by the side of the fire place, and shut the door, taking good care while the men were in the house, to keep near it herself, that if anything should be wanted from within, she might be ready to get it herself.

During the time the men were in the cabin, they expressed much confidence in the belief that the colonel was concealed somewhere in the vicinity, and named many places in which they intended to search for him; all of which he, in his place of concealment, overheard. Having taken some food, and otherwise prepared themselves, the men again departed, in order to renew their search.

Soon after they retired, and the woman considering the colonel's present situation not long safe, she proposed that he should conceal himself at some distance from the cabin, where she might clandestinely bring him food, and render him such other assistance as he needed, and accordingly directed him to take post on a certain hill about half a mile off, where he might be able to discover any person on their approach, and to flee, if he was able, and it became necessary. On his manifesting an inclination to resume his former position in the brush heap, which was in the midst of quite a patch of ground that had been cut over for a fallow, she told him that her husband intended to burn it over the next day, and in that case he would certainly be discovered, or perish in the conflagration; upon which he submitted entirely to her proposition and directions, and crept along to the hill in the best way he could. He remained sometime in this place of concealment, undiscovered by any one except this faithful Rahab of the forest, who rendered him suitable and timely assistance, and like a good Samaritan poured in the "oil and the wine," until his strength was in a measure restored, and he was again enabled to return to his country and his home.

Some years, after the close of the war, and while the colonel lived at Ticonderoga, he accidentally came across this kind hearted woman, whose name, I much regret, I have not been able to ascertain, and rewarded her handsomely for her fidelity.

Colonel Cochran died 1822, near Sandy Hill, Washington county, New York, much lamented by a large circle of friends and acquaintances, and was buried in the family burying-ground at Fort Edward.

*   *   *   *

The Germans were found almost totally unfit for the business they were engaged in. They were unable to march through the woods and encounter the difficulties incident to our then almost unsettled country. Many of them deserted to our army before and after the convention at Saratoga.

Among those of the German troops who surrendered, were the Hesse-Hanau regiment, Riedesel's dragoons and Specht's regiment, the most remarkable of the whole. The Hessians were extremely dirty in their persons, and had a collection of wild animals in their train — the only thing American they had captured. Here could be seen an artillery-man leading a black grizzly bear, who every now and then would rear upon his hind legs as if he were tired of going upon all fours, or occasionally growl his disapprobation at being pulled along by his chain. In the same manner a tamed deer would be seen tripping lightly after a grenadier. Young foxes were also observed looking sagaciously at the spectators from the top of a baggage wagon, or a young racoon securely clutched under the arm of a sharp shooter. There were a great many women accompanying the Germans, and a miserable looking set of oddly dressed, gypsey featured females they were.

It is said that no insults were offered to the prisoners as they marched off, and they felt grateful for it. However, after they got out of the camp, many of the British soldiers were extremely abusive, cursing the rebels and their own hard fate. The troops were escorted by some of the New England militia, and crossed the river at Stillwater, on a bridge of rafts, which had been constructed by the Americans while the army was encamped on Bemis's heights.

On the night of the surrender, a number of Indians and squaws, the relics of Burgoyne's aboriginal force, were quartered under a strong guard for safe keeping. Without this precaution their lives would not have been safe from the exasperated militia.

* * * *

Among these savages were three, that were between six and seven feet in height, perfect giants in form, and possessing the most ferocious countenances. And among them, was recognized the same Indian with whom my father had the encounter at Ensign's.

Blood and carnage were now succeeded by success and plunder. The clouds of battle rolled away, and discovered hundreds of searchers after the relics of the tented field.

* * * *

While the British army lay on the north bank of

Fish creek, the east side of the river, in addition to the regular troops, was lined with American militia. One of them, an expert swimmer, discovered a number of the enemy's horses feeding in a meadow of General Schuyler's, opposite, and asked permission of his captain to go over and get one of them. It was given, and the man instantly stripped, and swam across the river. He ascended the bank and selecting a fine bay horse for his prize, approached the animal, seized, and mounted him instantly. This last was the work of a moment. He forced the horse into a gallop, plunged down the bank and brought him safely over to the American camp, although a volley of musketry was fired at him from a party of British soldiers posted at a distance beyond. His success was hailed with enthusiasm, and it had a corresponding effect on his own adventurous spirit. After he had rested himself, he went to his officer and remarked, that it was not proper that a private should ride, whilst his commander went on foot. "So, sir," added he, "if you have no objections, I will go and catch another for you, and next winter when we are home, we will have our own fun in driving a pair of Burgoyne's horses." The captain seemed to think it would be rather a pleasant thing, and gave a ready consent. The fellow actually went across the second time, and with equal success, and brought over a horse that matched exceedingly well with the other. The men enjoyed this prank very much, and it was a circumstance familiar to almost every one in the army at that time.

Another circumstance happened about the same time, and shows that families were not only divided in feeling on the subject of the war, but that the natural ties which bind the same kith and kin together, were not always proof against the political animosities of the times. When Burgoyne found his boats were not safe, and in fact much nearer the main body of the American army than his own, it became necessary to land his provisions, of which he had already been short for many weeks, in order to prevent his army being actually starved into submission. This was done under a heavy fire from the American troops, who were posted on the opposite side of the river. On one of these occasions, a person by the name of Mr. ——, at Salem, and a foreigner by birth, and who had at the very time a son in the British army, crossed the river at De Ridder's with a person by the name of M'Neil; they went in a canoe, and arriving opposite to the place intended, crossed over to the western bank, on which a redoubt called Fort Lawrence had been erected. They crawled up the bank with their arms in their hands, and peeping over the upper edge, they saw a man in a blanket coat, loading a cart. They instantly raised their guns to fire, an action more savage than commendable. At the moment the man turned so as to be more plainly seen, old Mr. —— said to his companion, now that's my own son Hughy, but I'll d—'d for a' that if I sill not gi' him a shot. He then actually fired at his own son, as the person really proved to be, but happily without effect. Having heard the noise made by their conversation, and the cocking of their pieces, which the nearness of his position rendered perfectly practicable, he ran round the cart, and the balls lodged in the felloe of the wheel. The report drew the attention of the neighboring guards, and the two marauders were driven from their lurking place. While retreating with all possible speed M'Niel was wounded in the shoulder and while alive carried the wound about him unhealed to his last day. Had the ball struck the old Scotchman, it is questionable whether any one would have considered it more than even-handed justice, commending the chalice to his own lips.

At the time Governor George Clinton, to whose indefatigable exertions the state of New York owes more than she could repay, ordered out the militia of the different counties, and at their head proceeding northward in hopes of cutting off the retreat of Sir John Johnson, he advanced as far as Crown point without meeting the enemy. On his arrival at that post, and hearing nothing of Sir John, my father and John Benson, known and distinguished as *bare foot* Benson, who were volunteers at the time, were selected by Governor Clinton, as scouts, to proceed from that post through a dense howling wilderness, as far as Schroon lake, for the purpose of ascertaining by the trail of the Indians whether Sir John had passed between the two lakes. With only one ration for each, and nothing for their guide but a small pocket compass, they set out with their usual firmness and intrepidity. After traveling over steep and rugged mountains, and through deep, dark, and dismal ravines, they at length reached Schroon lake,

Appendix. 259

without making any discovery, in time to return as far back as the Beaver meadows, about two miles west of the head of Brant lake, the first night. During the night, by way of precaution, they deemed it advisable to separate, that, in case they should be discovered by Indians, who were constantly lurking about the country, there might be a better chance, for *one* of them at least, to make his escape and give the alarm. Accordingly they lay down in the tall grass about fifteen or twenty rods apart, for their repose, during the night. About three o'clock in the morning, as near as they could judge, they heard a rustling in the grass, about equi-distant from them both, and soon after heard a stepping, like some person cautiously approaching, which they supposed at the time to be the step of some Indian who might have discovered them at the time they concealed themselves in the grass. On the approach of the object within the circle of their faint vision, they both, as if by concert, though ignorant of each others intentions, being determined to sell their lives as dear as possible, raised themselves on one knee, levelled their pieces, and fired at the same instant. As soon as they fired, they heard a groan and momentary struggle in the grass, when all again was still as the abodes of death. They then reloaded, and resumed their former positions, but there was no more sleep for them during the remainder of that night. Soon after day break, and when there was light sufficient to discern objects at a distance, they took an observation, and seeing no enemy near, they advanced to ascertain the result of their encounter in the night, when behold, to their surprise, they found they had killed a famous great — deer!

After having their own sport for a while, they started on their return for the camp, by a different route from the one they came, and which they supposed would be nearer, but they had not gone far among the mountains, before the needle to their compass refused to perform its duty, owing no doubt to some neighboring *mineral*, which operated more powerfully than the pole. After wandering about for some time, in a dark and dismal forest, it being a dark and cloudy day, they became bewildered and finally got lost. Thus they continued to travel through the day, and found themselves at night near the place where they started from in the morning. By this time, having fasted twenty-four hours, their appetites became so sharp they thought they would make a meal out of the deer they had fortuitously killed the night before; but on their arrival at the spot they found that the wolves or some other animals had devoured it, and left not even a bone. They then laid themselves down for repose, on the same bed of grass they had occupied the night of the encounter. The next morning they again started for the camp, by the same route they came the first day, though somewhat faint for the want of food. About ten o'clock they came across a knapsack, which had been lost or left in the woods, by some person to them unknown, containing a lot of boiled pork, bread and cheese promiscuously thrown in together, and out of which Benson made a hearty meal; but my father, having so strong an aversion even to the *smell* of cheese that he refused to taste a mouthful of any of the contents of the knapsack ; and accordingly stood it out until he arrived at camp, about three o'clock in the afternoon of the third day, where they were received, with much joy, by the governor and his staff, who had given them up for lost. It was thus ascertained that Sir John, with his horde of Indians, had not retreated in that direction, and the governor gave up all hopes of intercepting them on this occasion, and returned home.

As I have pledged myself, in my introduction, to give all the principal facts connected with Burgoyne's campaign, as far as they have come to my knowledge, and as I am not writing to please any particular individual or class of readers, I will relate the following incident, which is often spoken of even to this day.

The inhabitants throughout this part of the country, having been much harassed by the Indians and tories, and in constant danger of their lives, were consequently under the necessity, for their own safety, of building, at different stations, what they termed block-houses.

These buildings were constructed of logs flattened on two sides and locked or halved together at the angles or corners, which rendered them strong and proof against rifle or musket balls. On each side, about six feet from the bottom, was an interstice or narrow space between the logs, for the purpose, in case of a siege or an attack, of thrusting their guns through to fire on the besiegers, below this open space a platform was erected about two feet from the floor, to stand upon while firing. The buildings were constructed without windows, and with but one door, which was made strong, and when occupied, this was strongly barricaded. To these buildings, when it was known or suspected there were Indians or tories in the vicinity, a number of families would resort during the night, leaving their own dwellings much exposed, and many of which were plundered and consumed.

The block-houses were often attacked, and sometimes with considerable force, but as near as I have been able to learn, without much success, though with some loss to the assailants.

It happened during a considerable interval of time, in which no Indians had been seen in the neighborhood, that the inhabitants ceased resorting to their block-houses. At this time a man by the name of Joseph Seely, whose vicious habits generally led him more to the gratification of his own evil propensities, than the public weal, and who had been out one day on a hunting excursion, for which he was very famous, and not fastidious about the kind of game he bagged, even if it was a turkey or a fowl that might *accidentally* come in his way, returned from the woods, saying he had come across a party of Indians and tories, at whom he had fired, and as he thought, killed one. The alarm was immediately spread throughout the neighborhood, and the men all armed themselves, and flocked together, for the purpose of going in pursuit. On being led by Seely to the place where he said he had shot at the Indians, they found a trail of blood extending some distance through the woods, which led them on the course they concluded it best to pursue, not doubting, from the circumstances of the blood, that he had severely wounded, if not killed, one of the Indians or tories.

After traveling some miles and finding no enemy, they concluded they might have secreted themselves in the neighborhood, with the intention of committing their savage deeds during the following night. Accordingly they all returned home, it being near night, and for safety, after secreting as much of their effects as they conveniently could, they and their families resorted to their block-houses, and by turns kept watch for the enemy during the night; but none appeared to molest them.

The next morning they very cautiously returned to their several homes, and many of them with the expectation of finding their property destroyed, and their dwellings in ashes. About ten o'clock, this mischief-bent hero of the forest, after having his own sport at the expense of his neighbors, and feeling conscious he had carried the joke too far, finally disclosed the whole secret. Having spent the whole forenoon of the previous day, and finding no game, on his return came across a flock of sheep, and from his natural propensity to mischief, he fired among them, and badly wounded one, when they all ran into the woods. On pursuing them some distance to see if the wounded sheep died, he observed the blood trickled along on the leaves; upon which he thought he would raise a "hue and cry," and alarm the neighborhood, by the horrible story he told of having seen and shot an Indian.

The following daring feat was performed by the author's great-uncle, Captain Hezekiah Dunham, who commanded a militia company in the vicinity of Bemis's heights, a staunch whig, and a firm friend to the American cause.

One evening as he was at a public entertainment, a boy was seen emerging from the woods in the neighborhood on horseback, and presently approaching the place where the people were collected, asked if he could purchase a little rum. When he was answered no, he immediately mounted, returned a considerable distance, and then was seen galloping down the main road by the river. On seeing this Dunham exclaimed, "This means something, I am sure of it." He then watched for the boy's return, and in a few minutes he repassed at full speed. He then reëntered the wood, and was gone from their sight in an instant. Dunham's penetration induced him to say, "The enemy is near us; the tories are in our neighborhood, and not far off." He separated from his company, with a determination to act immediately.

Dunham, when he reached home, immediately went to a person by the name of Green, who was a son of Vulcan and of Mars, and an able-bodied, bold, and persevering fellow. He was the pride of his settlement, and the safe-guard of the people around him — always ready for action, never desponding, and fearless to an extent that was remarkable. He was always relied upon in trying emergencies by the leading men in the vicinity, and what completed his merits, he was never backward. Dunham related the circumstance to him, and declared his belief that there was a party of tories in the neighborhood.

Three other persons were called upon the same night for assistance, and when the rest of their neighbors were asleep, these hardy men commenced their reconnaissance. Every suspected spot was carefully approached in hopes of finding the objects of their search. Every hollow that could contain a hiding place was looked into; but in a more particular manner the outhouses and barns of those persons who were suspected for their attachment to the enemy, were examined by them. It seemed all in vain. No traces of a concealed foe were discovered, when toward day-break it was proposed to separate and make one final search for that time. Dunham took two men with him, and Green but one. The former as a last effort returned to the house of one ———, who it was probable would be in communication with an enemy if near him. As he approached the house he had to pass a meadow adjoining, and observed a path leading from the house to a small thicket of about three acres in extent. Dunham immediately suspected it led to his enemy. He pursued it, and found it passed around the thicket, and when it almost met the place where it turned off, the path entered the wood. Dunham paused, and turning to his companions said, " Here they are, will you follow me?" They instantly agreed to accompany him, and the party moved on in single file, with light and cautious steps. As they got nearly to the centre,

Dunham in advance, a log stopped up the path, and seemed to prevent any farther approach. With a motion that indicated the necessity of their remaining still, he mounted the log, and looking over, discovered, sure enough, at once a desired and yet imposing sight. Around the remains of a watch-fire, which day-break rendered less necessary, sat a group of five fierce looking men, with countenances relaxed from their usual fixedness; but yet betokening boldness, if not savageness of purpose. They were dressing themselves, and putting on their shoes and stockings, which stood beside their rude couches. Their clothes were much worn, but had a military cut, which making their stout and muscular forms more apparent, gave them a peculiar snug fit, and distinguished them from the loose, slovenly, scarecow figures which the homely character of our country seamstresses imposed upon everything rural or rusticated among our people. Their hats or caps were set carelessly on their heads, with the air of regulars; and what made them still more observed was, that every man of them had his musket at his side on the ground, ready to be used at an instant's notice. Dunham surveyed this scene a few moments, and then drew back cautiously to his companions. In a tone not above a whisper, he said, " Shall we take 'em ?" A nod from his companions decided him — each now examined his musket, and reprimed it. The captain took the right of the little band, and they moved forward to the log. They mounted it at the same instant, and as they did so, Dunham cried out, "surrender or you are all dead men!" The group that thus found themselves almost under the "muzzles of their enemies' guns," were indeed astonished. All but their leader, Thomas Lovelass, seemed petrified and motionless. This resolute man seemed disposed to make an effort for their lives. Twice amid the silence and stillness of the perilous moment, he stretched out his hand to seize his gun. Each time he was prevented by the near approach of the muzzle that pointed at his head, and beyond which he saw an unflinching eye steadfastly fixed upon him; at the same instant he was told, that if he touched it he was a dead man.

At this critical period of the rencontre, Dunham peremptorily ordered the party to come out, one by one, which they reluctantly did, fearing perhaps that they were surrounded by and in contact with a superior force. As fast as one came over the log he was secured by the most powerful man of the three, while the other two kept their pieces steadily pointed at the prisoners. Some young women who proved to be sisters of some of the party, gave way to the most violent grief. Well aware of the danger they were in, and the speedy vengeance inflicted upon tories and spies, they anticipated the most dreadful consequences to their unhappy brothers, and no words can express the frantic sorrow to which they abandoned themselves. The young men themselves assumed an air of firmness, but it was easily penetrated. They confessed that their intention was to capture and take off some of the most active whigs in the neighborhood. One of the prisoners, upon promise of quarter, informed that he belonged to a party of fifteen, who had come down from Canada on the same business — who were then, in various disguises, scattered through the country to ascertain the state of affairs for the benefit of the British general in Canada, who was planning an inroad, and that they had left their boats concealed on the shores of Lake George. The country was at that time overrun with spies and traitors. Robberies were frequent, and the inhabitants (non-combatants), carried prisoners to Canada. General Schuyler's house was robbed and two of his servants or life-guards carried there. The general saved himself by retiring to his chamber, barricading the door, and firing upon the marauders.

Lovelass and his companions, were taken to the barracks at Saratoga, where they were tried and condemned at a court-martial, of which the celebrated General Stark was president. Lovelass alone suffered death. He was considered too dangerous a man to be permitted to escape. He complained that being found with arms in his hands he was only a prisoner, and many thought that such being the fact he was scarcely punishable as a spy. Indeed he even bewailed his hard fate, and the injustice done him, but found he had nothing to expect from the judges. In two or three days he was brought out of his place of confinement, and suffered death upon the gallows, during a tremendous storm of rain and wind, accompanied with heavy and often repeated claps of thunder, and the most vivid flashes of lightning.[1]

*   *   *   *

---

[1] The skull of Lovelass is now (1877) in the possession of George Strover Esq., who lives in the old Schuyler mansion at Schuylerville. The spy was hung a few rods south of his, Mr. Strover's, house.

The following incident, which took place near Oriskany, may be interesting to the reader, as showing the unlimited confidence which might, in those days, be placed in the Indians, when pledged to perform any certain act within their power.

An old Indian named Han-Yerry, who during the war had acted with the royal party, and now resided at Oriskany in a log wigwam which stood on the bank of the creek, just back of the house until recently occupied by Mr. Charles Green, one day called at Judge White's with his wife and a mulatto woman who belonged to him, and who acted as his interpreter. After conversing with him a little while, the Indian asked him,

" Are you my friend ? "

" Yes," said he.

" Well, then," said the Indian, " do you believe I am your friend ? "

" Yes, Han-Yerry," replied he, " I believe you are."

The Indian then rejoined, " well, if you are my friend, and you believe I am your friend, I will tell you what I want, and then I shall know whether you speak true words."

" And what is it that you want ? " said Mr. White.

The Indian pointed to a little grandchild, the daughter of one of his sons, then between two and three years old, and said,

" My squaw wants to take this pappoose home with us to stay to-night, and bring her home to-morrow: if you are my friend, you will now show me."

The feelings of the grandfather at once uprose in his

bosom, and the child's mother started with horror and alarm at the thought of entrusting her darling prattler with the rude tenants of the forest. The question was full of interest. On the one hand, the necessity of placing unlimited confidence in the savage, and entrusting the welfare and the life of his grandchild with him; on the other the certain enmity of a man of influence and consequence in his nation, and one who had been the open enemy of his countrymen in their recent struggle. But he made the decision with a sagacity which showed that he properly estimated the character of the person he was dealing with. He believed that by placing implicit confidence in him, he should command the sense of honor which seems peculiar to the uncontaminated Indian. He told him to take the child; and then as the mother, scarcely suffering it to be parted from her, relinquished it into the hands of the old man's wife, he soothed her fears with his assurances of confidence in their promises. That night, however, was a long one; and during the whole of the next morning, many and often were the anxious glances cast upon the pathway leading from Oriskany, if possible to discover the Indians and their little charge, upon their return to its home. But no Indians came in sight. It at length became high noon; all a mother's fears were aroused; she could scarcely be restrained from rushing in pursuit of her loved one. But her father represented to her the gross indignity which a suspicion of their intentions would arouse in the breast of the chief; and half frantic though she was, she was restrained. The afternoon slowly wore away, and still nothing was seen of her child. The sun had nearly reached the western horizon, and the mother's heart had swollen beyond further endurance, when the forms of the Indian chief and his wife, bearing upon her shoulders their little visitor, greeted its mother's vision. The dress which the child had worn from home had been removed, and in its place its Indian friends had substituted a complete suit of Indian garments, so as completely to metamorphose it into a little squaw. The sequel of this adventure was the establishment of a most ardent attachment and regard on the part of the Indian and his friends for the white settlers. The child, now Mrs. Eells of Missouri, the widow of the late Nathaniel Eells of Whitesboro, still remembers some incidents occurring on the night of her stay at the wigwam, and the kindness of her Indian hostess.

Another — which occurred in relation to the siege of Fort Stanwix, and which evinced the fortitude and prowess of General Schuyler, in moments of difficulty.

When Colonel Willett and his companion Lieutenant Stockwell left the fort and got beyond the investing party, which was not done without passing through sleeping groups of savages, who lay with their arms at their side, they crossed the river, and found some horses running wild in the woods. They were soon mounted, and with the aid of their bark bridles, stripped from the young trees, they made considerable progress on their journey. It is well known that they reached Stillwater village, and begged a reinforcement. General Schuyler, who then quartered in the house of Dirck Swart, Esq., now standing at the foot of the hill, and occupied by Mrs. Williams, called a council of his officers, and asked their advice. It is perhaps not generally known that he was opposed by them. As he walked about in the greatest anxiety, urging them to come to his opinion, he overheard some of them saying, " he means to weaken the army." The emotions of the veteran were always violent at the recollection of this charge. At the instant when he heard the remark, he found that he had bitten a pipe, which he had been smoking, into several pieces, without being conscious of what he had done. Indignantly he exclaimed, " Gentlemen, I shall take the responsibility upon myself; where is the brigadier that will take command of the relief? I shall beat up for volunteers to-morrow." The brave, the gallant, the ill fated Arnold started up with his characteristic quickness, and offered to take command of the expedition. In the morning the drum beat for volunteers, and two hundred hardy fellows capable of standing great fatigue, offered their services and were accepted. The result of his efforts is well known. To General Schuyler's promptness and fearlessness, therefore, due credit should be given.

*   *   *   *

Another—in relation to the same siege may be interesting to the reader.

A man by the name of Baxter, who resided in the vicinity of the fort, being a disaffected man, had been sent to Albany, to be watched by the committee of safety. Two sons of his remained behind, and were extremely industrious, taking every opportunity to keep their farm in order, notwithstanding its being in the vicinity of the hostile parties. They were so successful, and so little disturbed by the British, that the Americans began to suspect that they were on too good terms with the enemy. Their father's character kept up the suspicion. One day, as it subsequently appeared, one of the sons, who was working with a wheel plough, in cutting his furrows, would every few minutes approach a fence which was between him and the enemy. After several turns, as he was making his last cut across the field, he felt his hands suddenly grasped with violence. Impelled by a natural desire to escape, he jumped forward, and seizing his plough cleaver, he turned on his antagonist, who was an Indian, and felled him to the ground. But a second approached, and with equal dexterity and nerve he dealt a second blow, which levelled the savage. Both were stunned, their heads being too obvious to escape the terrible blow of the plough cleaver.

As they lay on the ground, he alternately struck them over their heads with all his might, and then setting his horses clear from the plough, he came to the fort and told them what had happened. His tale was not believed, and when he offered to lead them to the spot, they suspected further treachery. They detained him to abide the event, and sent out a detachment to ascertain how the fact was; and these found two savages lying dead at the place he mentioned. This brave feat procured the release of the father, and indeed rescued the whole family from the imputation of toryism forever.

Another — respecting Abraham D. Quackenboss, as

being connected with the battle of Oriskany, may also be interesting.

Abraham D. Quackenboss, resided in the Mohawk country on the south side of the river, at the breaking out of the war. Living as it were among the Indians, he spoke their language as well as he did his own. Among them he had a friend, named Bronkahorse — who, though an Indian, had been his playmate, and they had served in the French war together under Sir William Johnson. When the revolutionary troubles came on, Bronkahorse called upon Quackenboss, and endeavored to persuade him to espouse the cause of the king — assuring him that their *Great Father* could never be conquered. Quackenboss refused, and they parted. The Indian, however, assuring him that they parted as friends, although, since they had fought in one war together he had hoped they might do so in the other. Mr. Quackenboss saw no more of his friend until the battle of Oriskany. During the thickest of the fight he heard his name called in the well known voice of Bronkahorse, from behind a large tree near by. He was himself sheltered by a tree; but in looking out for the warriors he saw his Indian friend. The latter now importuned Quackenboss to surrender, assuring him of kind treatment and protection, but also assuring him unless he did so, he would inevitably be killed. Quackenboss refused, and the Indian thereupon attempted to kill him. For a moment they watched each other endeavoring to obtain the first and best chance of a shot. The Indian at length fired, and his ball struck the tree, but had nearly been fatal. Springing from his covert upon the Indian, Quackenboss fired, and his friend Bronkahorse fell dead on the spot. It was the belief of Mr. Quackenboss that the loss of the enemy during that battle equalled that of Herkimer's command. The latter suffered the most severely in the early part of the engagement — the enemy in the latter part.

No. II.
Force employed under Lieutenant General Burgoyne in the Campaign of 1777.

The army which took the field in July, 1777, consisted of seven battalions of British infantry; viz.: 9th, 20th, 21st, 24th, 47th, 53d, and 62d regiments, of each of which (as also of three regiments left in Canada) the flank companies were detached to form a corps of grenadiers and light infantry, under Majors Ackland and the Earl of Balcarras. The German troops consisted of a few Hessian rifles (the regiment of Hesse-Hanau), a corps of dismounted dragoons, and a mixed force of Brunswickers. The artillery was composed of 511 rank and file, including 100 Germans, with a large number of guns, the greater part of which, however, were employed only on the lakes. The ordnance which accompanied the force on their line of march, consisted of thirty-eight pieces of light artillery attached to columns, and a pair of six twenty-four pounders, six twelve pounders, and four howitzers.

The royal army was divided into three brigades under

Major General Phillips,[1] of the royal artillery, and Brigadier Generals Fraser and Hamilton. The German troops were distributed among the three brigades, with one corps of reserve under Colonel (Brigadier General) Breymann, and were immediately commanded by Major General Riedesel, Colonel Kingston, and Captain Money acted as adjutant and quarter-master general, and Sir James Clerke (killed at Saratoga in the action of Oct. 7th), and Lord Petersham (afterward Earl of Harrington), were aides-de-camp to General Burgoyne.

The total force was — rank and file:

British,.. 4,135
German, ... 3,116
Canadian militia,........................... 148
Indians, ... 503

Total,............ 7,902

Of these numbers General Burgoyne was obliged to detach nearly 1,000 men to garrison Ticonderoga before he crossed the Hudson. —*Fonblanque's Burgoyne.*

---

[1] The employment of artillery officers in command of infantry brigades was at that time contrary to regulation, and General Burgoyne, in a letter to General Hervey of 11 July, '77, excuses himself for having made this arrangement by the statement that "the service must suffer in the most material degree if the talents of General Phillips were not suffered to extend beyond the artillery; and I hold myself fully justified in continuing this great use."

Remarks on the Employment of German Troops by the English Government.

A great deal has been written in condemnation of the English government employing Germans in the war for the subjugation of her revolted American colonies. But does any soldier work for pure patriotism and not for hire? Besides, at that time, the German soldier belonged body and soul to him to whom he had sold himself: he had no country; he was severed from every tie — in fact, he was, in every sense of the word, the *property* of his military lord, who could do with him as he saw fit. Again, it may well be asked, wherein did this action of the British government differ from that of the United States, employing in our late civil war recruiting agents in the different German ports for the express purpose of filling up her depleted armies, and also purchasing substitutes in Canada.

No. III.

Instructions for Lieutenant Colonel Baum, on a Secret Expedition to the Connecticut River.

[*The erasures were made by General Burgoyne.*[1]]   *Amendments made by General Burgoyne.*

The object of your expedition is to try the affections of the country, to

---

[1] The erasures are printed in italics, and the amendments in the opposite column.

disconcert the councils of the enemy, to mount the Riedesel's dragoons, to complete Peters's corps, and to obtain large supplies of cattle, horses and carriages.

The several corps, of which the inclosed is a list, are to be under your command.

The troops must take no tents, and what little baggage is carried by officers must be on their own bat horses.

You are to proceed *by the route* from Batten kil to Arlington, and take post there, *so as to secure the pass from Manchester. You are to remain at Arlington* till the detachment of the Provincials, under the command of Captain Sherwood, shall join you from the southward.

You are then to proceed to Manchester, where you take post so as to secure the pass of the mountains on the road from Manchester to Rockingham; hence you will detach the Indians and light troops to the northward, toward Otter creek. On their return, and also receiving intelligence that no enemy is in force *in the neighborhood of Rockingham*, (1) you will proceed by the road over the mountains to Rockingham, where you will take post. This will be the most distant part on the expedition. (2)

You are to remain there *as long as necessary to fulfill the intention of the expedition from thence*, (3) and you are afterwards to descend *by* the *Connecticut* river to Brattlebury, and from that place, by the quickest march, you are to return by the great road to Albany.

During your whole progress, your detachments are to have orders to bring in to you all horses fit to

(1) upon the Connecticut river.

(2) And must be proceeded upon with caution, as you will have the defile of the mountains behind you, which might make a retreat difficult; you must therefore endeavor to be well informed of the force of the enemy's militia in the neighboring country. Should you find it may with prudence be effected.

(3) while the Indians and light troops are detached up the river.

mount the dragoons under your command, or to serve as bat horses to the troops, *they are likewise to bring in (4) saddles and bridles as can be found.* (5)

Your parties are likewise to bring in wagons and other convenient carriages, with as many draft oxen as will be necessary to draw them, and all cattle fit for slaughter (milch cows excepted), which are to be left for the use of the inhabitants. Regular receipts, in the form hereto subjoined, are to be given, in all places where any of the above mentioned articles are taken, to such persons as have remained in their habitations, and otherwise complied with the terms of General Buryoyne's manifesto; but no receipts to be given to such as are known to be acting in the service of the rebels. (6)

(4) together with as many.

(5) The number of horses requisite, besides those necessary for mounting the regiments of dragoons, ought to be 1300. If you can bring more for the use of the army, it will be so much the better.

(6) As you will have with you persons perfectly ac-

quainted with the abilities of the country, it may perhaps be advisable to tax the several districts, with the portions of the several articles, and limit the hours for their delivery; and, should you find it necessary to move before such delivery can be made, hostages of the most respectable people should be taken, to secure their following you the ensuing day. All possible means are to be used to prevent plundering.

As it is probable that Captain Sherwood, who is already detached to the southward and will join you at Arlington, will drive in a considerable quantity of cattle and horses to you, you will therefore send in this cattle to the army, with a proper detachment from Peters's corps to cover them, in order to disincumber yourself; but you must always keep the regiments of dragoons compact.

The dragoons themselves must ride, and take care of the horses of the regiment. Those horses which are destined for the use of the army must be tied together by strings of ten each, in order that one man may lead ten horses. You will give the unarmed men of Peters's corps to conduct them, and inhabitants whom you can trust. You must always take your camps in good position; but at the same time where there is pasture; and you must have a chain of sentinels round your cattle and horses when grazing.

Colonel Skeene will be with you as much as possible, in order to assist you with his advice, to help you to distinguish the good subjects from the bad, to procure you the best intelligence of the enemy, and to choose those people who are to bring me the accounts of your progress and success.

When you find it necessary to halt for a day or two, you must always entrench the camp of the regiment of dragoons, in order never to risk an attack or affront from the enemy.

As you will return with the regiment of dragoons mounted, you must always have a detachment of Captain Fraser's or Peters's corps in front of the column, and the same in the rear, in order to prevent your falling into an ambuscade when you march through the woods.

You will use all possible means to make the country believe that the troops under your command are the advanced corps of the army, and that it is intended to pass the Connecticut on the road to Boston. You will likewise *have it insinuated*,

(7) that the main army from Albany is to be joined at Springfield by a corps of troops from Rhode island.

You will send off occasionally cattle or carriages, to prevent being too much incumbered ; and will give me as frequent intelligence of your situation as possible.

It is highly probable that the corps under Mr. Warner, now supposed to be at Manchester, will retreat before you ; but, should they, contrary to expectation, be able to collect in great force, and post themselves advantageously, it is left to your discretion to attack them or not ; always bearing in mind, that your corps is too valuable to let any considerable loss be hazarded on this occasion.

Should any corps be moved from Mr. Arnold's main army, in order to intercept your retreat, you are to take as strong a post

(7) insinuate,

as the country will afford, and send the quickest intelligence to me; and you may depend on my making such a movement as shall put the enemy between two fires, or otherwise effectually sustain you.

It is imagined the progress of the whole of this expedition may be effected in about a fortnight; but every movement of it must depend upon your success in obtaining such supply of provisions as will enable you to subsist till your return to the army, in case you can get no more. (8)

All persons acting in committees, or any officers acting under the directions of congress, either civil or military, are to be made prisoners.

(8) And, should not the army be able to reach Albany before your expedition should be completed, I will find means to send you notice of it, and give your route another direction.

NARRATIVE OF A PARTICIPITATOR IN THE BATTLE OF BENNINGTON.

BROOKLYN, *September* 27, 1866.

WM. L. STONE, ESQ.,

My Dear Sir: The following narrative was communicated to me in 1828, by Mr. Stafford of Albany, the son of an American captain, who was in the battle of Bennington. I send you herewith my original notes of the conversation, taken down at the time from the lips of the narrator, which you may cheerfully make use of (if you so desire), in your forthcoming translation.

Respectfully yours,
THEODORE DWIGHT.

" My father lived in the western part of Massachusetts, and when Colonel Warner called upon the militia to come out and defend the public stores at Bennington, he set off at once with many of his neighbors, and hurried his march. He was well known to his townsmen; and so much esteemed, that the best men were ready to go with him; many of them pious people, long members of the church, and among them young and old, and of different conditions.

" When they reached the ground, they found the Hessians posted in a line; and on a spot of high ground, a small redoubt was seen formed of earth just thrown up, where they understood a body of loyalists or Provincial troops, that is, tories, was stationed. Colonel Warner had command under General Stark; and it is generally thought that he had more to do than his superior in the business of the day. He was held in high regard by the Massachusetts people ; and my father soon reported himself to him, and told him he awaited his orders. He was soon assigned a place in the line, and the tory fort was pointed out as his particular object of attack.

"When making arrangements to march out his men, my father turned to a tall, athletic man, one of the most vigorous of the band, and remarkable for size and strength among his neighbors. 'I am glad,' said he, 'to see you among us. You did not march with the company ; but, I suppose, you are anxious for the business of the day to begin.' This was said in the hearing of the rest, and attracted their attention My father was surprised and mortified, on observing the man's face turn pale, and his limbs tremble. With a faltering voice, he replied : ' Oh no, sir, I didn't come to fight, I only came to drive back the horses !' 'I am glad,' said my father, ' to find out we have a coward among us, before we go into battle. Stand back, and do not show yourself here any longer.'

" This occurrence gave my father great regret, and he repented having spoken to the man in the presence of his company. The country you know, was at that time in a very critical state. General Burgoyne had come down from Canada with an army, which had driven all the American troops before it ; Crown point and Ticonderoga, the fortresses of Lake Champlain, in which the northern people placed such confidence, had been deserted at his approach ; and the army had disgraced itself by a panic retreat, without fighting a battle, while Burgoyne was publishing boastful and threatening proclamations, which frightened many, and induced some to declare for the king. Just at such a time, when so many bad examples were set, and there were so many dangers to drive others to follow, it was a sad thing to see a hale, hearty, tall man shake and tremble in the presence of the enemy, as we were just going to fight them. However, an occurrence happened, fortunately, to take place immediately after, which made amends. There was an aged and excellent old man present, of a slender frame, stooping a little with advanced age and hard work, with a wrinkled face, and well known as one of the oldest persons in our town, and the oldest on the ground. My father was struck with regard for his aged frame, and much as he felt numbers to be desirable in the impending struggle, he felt a great reluctance at the thought of leading him into it. He therefore turned to him, and said: 'The labors of the day threaten to be severe, it is therefore my particular request, that you will take your post as sentinel yonder, and keep charge of the baggage.' The old man stepped forward with an unexpected spring, his face was lighted with a smile, and pulling off his hat, in the excitement of his spirit, half affecting the gayety of a youth, whilst his loose hair shone as white as silver, he briskly replied: 'Not till I've had a shot at them first, captain, if you please.' All thoughts were now directed towards the enemy's line; and the company, partaking in the enthusiasm of the old man, gave three cheers. My father was set at ease again in a moment;

and orders being soon brought to advance, he placed himself at their head, and gave the word: 'Forward, march!'

"He had observed some irregularity in the ground before them, which he had thought might favor his approach; and he soon discovered that a small ravine, which they soon entered, would cover his determined little band from the shot of the enemy, and even from their observation, at least for some distance. He pursued its course; but was so far disappointed in his expectations, that, instead of terminating at a distance from the enemy's line, on emerging from it, and looking about to see where he was, he found the fresh embankment of the tory fort just above him, and the heads of the tories peeping over, with their guns leveled at him. Turning to call on his men, he was surprised to find himself flat on the ground without knowing why; for the enemy had fired, and a ball had gone through his foot into the ground, cutting some of the sinews just as he was stepping on it, so as to bring him down. At the same time, the shock had deafened him to the report of the muskets.

The foremost of his soldiers ran up and stooped to take him in their arms, believing him to be dead or mortally wounded; but he was too quick for them, and sprang on his feet, glad to find he was not seriously hurt, and was able to stand. He feared that his fall might check his followers; and, as he caught a glimpse of a man in a red coat running across a distant field, he cried out, 'Come on, my boys! They run! They run!' So saying, he sprang up, and clambering to the top of the fort, while the enemy were hurrying their powder into the pans and the muzzles of their pieces, his men rushed on shouting and firing, and jumping over the breastworks, and pushing upon the defenders so closely, that they threw themselves over the opposite wall, and ran down the hill as fast as their legs would carry them.

"Those raw soldiers, as most of them were, were ready to laugh at themselves, when they turned round and saw themselves, their new position, masters of a little fort which their enemies had been hard at work to construct, they knew not how long; but out of which they had so easily been set a scampering, merely because they had shown some resolution and haste in assaulting it.

"The result of the day's battle is well known. The Hessians and other troops with them, suffered a total defeat; and not only were the stores at Bennington protected and saved, and the army of Burgoyne weakened by the loss of a considerable body of troops, but the spirits of the people greatly encouraged, and the hope of final success revived. From that time there was less difficulty found in collecting troops; and the recruiting of our army at Bemis's heights, or Saratoga, as it is often called, was more easily effected.

"It so happened that many years after the close of the war, and when I heard my father tell this story many times over, I became acquainted with an old townsman of his, who was a loyalist, and took an active part as a soldier in the service of King George; and he told me a story of the battle of Bennington which I think you would like to hear.

Appendix.

Story told by one who was in the Tory Fort.

"I lived not far from the western borders of Massachusetts when the war began, and knew your father very well. Believing that I owed duty to my king, I became known as a loyalist, or, as they called me, a tory; and soon found my situation rather unpleasant. I therefore left home, and soon got among the British troops who were come down with Burgoyne, to restore the country to peace, as I thought. When the Hessians were sent to take the military stores at Bennington, I went with them; and took my station with some of the other loyalists in a redoubt or small fort in the line. We were all ready when we saw the rebels coming to attack us; and were on such a hill and behind such a high bank, that we felt perfectly safe, and thought we could kill any body of troops they would send against us, before they could reach the place we stood upon. We had not expected, however, that they would approach us under cover; but supposed we should see them on the way. We did not know that a little gully which lay below us, was long and deep enough to conceal them, but they knew the ground, and the first we saw of the party coming to attack us, they made their appearance right under our guns. Your father was at the head of them. I was standing at the wall at the time, with my gun loaded in my hand; and several of us leveled our pieces at once. I took as fair aim at them as I ever did at a bird in my life, and thought I was sure of them; though we had to point so much downwards, that it made a man but a small mark. We fired together, and he fell. I thought he was dead to a certainty; but to our surprise he was on his feet again in an instant, and they all came jumping into the midst of us, with such a noise, that we thought of nothing but getting out of the way of their muskets as fast as possible. I saw all my companions were going over the wall on the other side, and I went too. We had open fields before us, and scattered in all directions, some followed by our enemies. I ran some distance with another man, and looking around saw several of your father's soldiers who were coming after us, level their muskets to fire. We had just reached a rail fence, and both of us gave a jump at the same instant to go over it. While I was in the air I heard the guns go off. We reached the ground together, but my companion fell and lay dead by the fence, while I ran on with all my might, finding I was not hurt.

"I looked back, hoping to see no one following, but I was frightened on discovering a tall rawboned fellow, running like a deer, only a short distance behind, and gaining on me every step he took. I immediately reflected that my gun was only a useless burden, for it was discharged, and had no bayonet; and although a valuable one, I thought my only chance of saving my life, lay in lightening myself as much as possible. I therefore gave my gun a throw off to one side, so that if my pursuer should choose to pick it up he should lose some distance by it; and then without slackening my speed, I turned my head to see how he took the maneuver; and found he had not only taken advantage of my hint, and thrown away his own gun, but was also just

Appendix. 293

kicking off his shoes. I tried to throw off my own in the same way, but they were fastened on with a pair of old fashioned buckles. I strained myself to the utmost to reach a wood which lay a little way before me, with the desperate hope of finding some way of losing myself in it. I ventured one look more; and was frightened almost out of my senses at finding the bare-legged fellow, almost upon me, and ready to gripe, and perhaps strangle me by main force. I did not like to stop and give myself up as a prisoner; for I supposed he must be in a terrible passion, or he would not have taken such extraordinary pains to overtake me; and even if he should spare my life and do me no injury, in that solitary spot, I did not know what to expect from the rebels, as we called them. So I ran on, though but an instant more; for I had hardly turned my head again before I found the appearance of a wood which I had seen was only the tops of some trees growing on the borders of Walloomsac creek, which ran at the foot of a frightful precipice, the edge of which I had reached. I felt as if it were almost certain death to go farther; but I had such a dread of my pursuer, that I set but lightly by my danger, and instead of stopping on the brink, I ran right off, without waiting even to see where I was going.

"I fell like a stone, and the next instant struck on my feet in soft mud, with a loud, spatting noise, which I heard repeated close by me. Spat! spat! for down came the fierce fellow after me, and struck close by me in the wet clay, by the edge of the water. I looked at him with perfect dismay; for what could I do then? I had sunk into the mud up to my knees, and was entirely unarmed. It was some relief to see, that he had no pistol to shoot me, and was not quite near enough to reach me. He, however, was beginning to struggle to get his legs out, and I expected to see him free and springing upon me in a moment more. I struggled too, but found it was no easy work to extricate myself, and began to think, that it would probably be as bad for him. This encouraged me to try with all my might; and I thought I found my neighbor was much slower in getting out than I had feared. Indeed I could not perceive, for some time, that either of us made any advances, although we had wasted almost all our remaining strength. I now remarked, that my enemy was standing much deeper in the mud than myself. Oh, thought I, the fellow was barefooted; that is the reason: the soles of my shoes had prevented me from sinking quite so deep; there is a good chance of my getting out before him. Still neither of us spoke a word. So I struggled again most violently; but the straps of my shoes were bound tight across my ancles, and held them to my feet, while I felt that I had not strength enough to draw them out. This made me desperate; and I made another effort, when the straps gave way, and I easily drew out one bare foot, and placed it on the top of the ground. With the greatest satisfaction I found the other slipping smoothly up through the clay; and, without waiting to regret my shoe buckles (which were of solid silver), or to exchange a blow or a word with my enemy, whom I was still dreadfully afraid of, I ran down the shore of the brook, as fast as my legs could carry me.

"A man who has never been frightened as I was, with the expectation of instant death, cannot easily imagine how far he will run, or how much he can do, to get out of danger. I thought for some time, that my long-legged enemy was coming, and ran on, afraid almost to look behind me. But he did not come; and I never saw or heard of him again. How he could have got out, I cannot imagine; and there seemed to be no chance of his finding help very soon, so that I think he must have spent the night in that uncomfortable condition, and may have stayed, for aught I know, till he starved to death.

"However, my fears were not dispelled; for I knew our whole detachment had been entirely routed; Germans, Englishmen, tories, and all; and, as I thought there would be a pursuit by our conquerors, I expected every moment to meet some of them, with arms in their hands. Indeed, at any moment I might be discovered by some of them, and fired upon before I could see them; so I chose the most secret paths and courses I could find, keeping among the thickest trees and bushes, and avoiding every house and sign of inhabitants, under a constant fear of being dead or a prisoner the next moment. Who can tell what I suffered in that one day? I had been delivered from the imminent danger of musket balls, bayonets, the close pursuit of a rancorous enemy, a leap from a precipice and a long and most fatiguing run through a wild and unknown region, traversed, as I presumed, by many men thirsting for my blood. Night was now approaching, and I felt almost faint with the want of food as well as weariness. But I soon reached a region which I began to recognize as one I had before seen ; and, knowing that the house of my brother-in-law was not far distant, I determined to visit it, and get such food and clothes as I now greatly needed. On second thoughts I concluded that I might be in danger even there. There might be a party of my enemies in the neighborhood, if not in possession of the house ; for in such times, in a region overrun by war, one party often occupies a position one day or one hour which they give up to their enemies the next. I therefore determined to proceed with great caution ; and, although I soon came in sight of the house, and was suffering greatly from the want of rest and refreshment, I concealed myself, and watched the neighborhood as long as I could see, and then, after remaining quiet till late in the night, stole out softly, and walked round the house, listening carefully, and scrutinizing everything, to discover traces of any change unfavorable to my wishes.

"Finding no signs of danger, I at length mustered up courage and entered the house, where I found the family had not all retired to rest ; and was very glad to see my sister coming towards me with an air of unconcern, which showed the household had not been disturbed. When she approached me, however, she addressed me as a stranger ; and then, for the first time, I began to think of my appearance. There had been powder enough burnt in the fort to blacken my face as dark as an Indian's and the perspiration which had started out during my races had washed it partly off in streaks, so that the expression of my countenance was strangely altered. At the same time I was without a coat, and my few remaining garments we e torn by thorns and spattered with mud.

"I was treated with the utmost kindness by my sister as soon as she recognized me, and, after eating a good meal, and taking a long night's rest, I felt quite well and strong. She kept me as long as I was willing to stay; but I did not feel safe out of the army, which then seemed sure of soon reaching Albany and finishing the war. I soon set off on foot, reaching Burgoyne's lines, and was placed in the tory fort on the eastern brow of Bemis's heights. There I thought myself safe once more. The abatis, formed of rough trees, with their branches on, which had been laid on the sides of the fort, appeared absolutely impassable by any body of the enemy. But in this I was disappointed; for, when the battle came on, the Yankees rushed upon our fortification with impetuosity, and in such numbers that they soon covered the ground and trees, that they were as thick as the hair on a dog. Again I was glad to save myself by a rapid retreat."

DESCRIPTION OF ST. LUKE'S BRIDGE, AND OF THE ATTEMPT TO BURN IT ON THE APPROACH OF BAUM.

"12 CLINTON PLACE, NEW YORK,
25th *July*, 1877.
"WM. L. STONE,

"My Dear Sir : Since my last visit to your house, when an interesting conversation was had upon the subject of *Bennington battle*, I have looked more fully into the account of the same, as contained in your "Memoirs etc., of Maj. Gen. Reidesel." My long residence in the vicinity of that now famous battle-field, and my personal acquaintance with many of the men engaged in the fight, gives me especial interest in the story as told in your book.

"On page 121, I find an allusion to the '*bridge of St. Luke*.' This bridge is a very familiar object to me. I used to go to mill there when I was a boy. In '77 it's *name* may have been St. Luke's; but in 1815 it's name was Van Schaick, from the little Dutch village on the margin of Hoosick river, a short distance below the bridge. It spanned the stream then called Little White creek, a few rods above its debouch into Walloomsac (or Bennington) river. The three streams — White creek, Walloomsac and Hoosick — unite near this bridge. The road passing over the bridge, was the *great market road*, leading to the North river, Albany, Halfmoon, etc A branch road led off in a northwesterly direction to Cambridge, Batten kil, Fort Edward, etc.

"At the point where the bridge spans the creek, there

Appendix. 299

is a *deep, narrow* ravine, extending for a considerable distance both *above* and *below* the bridge. Hence the bridge was important, indeed it was *indispensable* to Baum's marching army. It was a *wooden* bridge, covered with loose plank, not very long but *very high*.

"A little skirmishing adventure occurred at this bridge, the circumstances of which were as follows:

"On the 15th of August, '77, the day previous to Bennington battle, a small scouting party from the American camp, or to speak more truly, a party of volunteer scouts from the country near Bennington, were exploring the country along the road towards Cambridge. They were met and driven back by Col. Baum's advancing troops. Some of the party were taken prisoners. But most of them escaped. Being on foot and well acquainted with the country, they took to the fields and made a safe retreat to Bennington, ready for the battle next day. On their way home they were obliged to pass over St. Luke's (Van Schaick's) bridge, crossing the stream — Little White creek, near its termination in the Walloomsac river.

"As our Yankee boys were crossing the bridge, they wished they could destroy it to embarrass the invading foe; but they did not dare stop to do it because *British guns* were close to their heels, and they hurried forward. At this critical juncture, one man more heroic than the rest, Eleazur Edgerton, declared that the bridge ought to be destroyed, and he would go back and *burn* it, if any one would join him. Two of his associates volunteered. Those three returned, threw the plank off into the chasm below and set fire to the timbers. Whilst they were doing this heroic work, British balls were whizzing about their ears; but all three safely escaped, and soon rejoined their more *discreet* companions. I have ever esteemed this daring feat as one of the *heroic* acts of those trying times.

"The inspiring leader of this patriotic trio, Eleazur Edgerton, resided in the town of Bennington, where he spent his after life. He was a man quite above the medium size, very strong and athletic, devoting his energies to peaceful and useful pursuits. He was a farmer and a carpenter. He had peculiar characteristics that gave him a distinguished local reputation among his neighbors. As a carpenter he was noted for the mechanical strength of his work. His neighbors used to call him the *strong builder*, and that the Green mountain winds had a hard job to blow down one of Uncle Lezur's barns.

"He always went bare-headed and bare-handed summer and winter. This gave him a very rough appearance. They used to say his face was all made out doors.

"Notwithstanding this rough exterior, he was a man of very gentle nature, much beloved by children. He was the king of children in his neighborhood. He often visited them at their homes, carrying his pockets full of apples and other little presents. But the special favor that the children liked the best, and which they waited for with the most anxiety, was his pocket full of sticks and straws for them to play *jack straws.*

"Yours very truly,
"J. W. RICHARDS."

Appendix.

Mr. E. W. B. Canning of Stockbridge, Mass., writes to the author concerning the alarm through the county as follows:

"When I became a citizen of the town in 1850, there were a few persons still living who remembered the memorable occasion of the alarm that pervaded Berkshire at the time of the descent of the British on Bennington; and I desire more particularly to refer to it here in order to correct a version of the story by some who have wrongly connected it with the battle of Lexington.

"Early one Sunday morning in August, '77, our village was startled by the sound of three musket shots fired in succession. On looking out, there were seen Esq. Woodbridge — then living in the present residence of Mr. Samuel Lawrence — Dea. Nash, his next neighbor, and Dea. Edwards, on the street corner near the latter's house — now Mrs. Owens's — each with a musket in his hand. So strictly was the day kept at that time, that the sight of these men so situated provoked as much astonishment as would now the discovery of a quartette of our reverend clergy prefacing divine service by a game of euchre over the pulpit cushion. Something unusual and very important must be in the wind, or these fathers of the town and church had gone daft. Matters were soon explained to the fast gathering citizens, for a courier had just brought news that the British were marching on Bennington, and that every able-bodied man was needed to repel the invasion. Anon, forth came the yeoman soldiery, equipped as well as haste and alarm permitted, and took their way northward to the scene of danger.

With this body went Dr. Oliver Partridge, whom many of us remember, and who told me he dressed the mortal wound of Col. Baum, who commanded the enemy in that battle. The courier, having notified the above named gentlemen, pushed on down the county to rouse the lower towns. He arrived in New Marlboro just as the minister had announced the text of his morning sermon. The commander of the minute-men being summoned from his pew and told the news, forthwith strode up the broad aisle and, addressing the clergyman, exclaimed: 'Mr. Turner, the British are at Bennington, and I forbid Sabby-day! Minute men, turn out and follow me!' The militia of the northern portion of the county alone arrived in time to share in the glory of the victory, the courier having been despatched by Gen. Stark on the day before the battle, which had already been fought and won when our volunteers came to aid in gathering the spoils."

No. IV.

THE JANE MCCREA TRAGEDY.

Probably no event, either in ancient or modern warfare, has received so many versions as the killing of Miss Jane McCrea, during the revolutionary war. It has been commemorated in story and in song, and narrated in grave histories, in as many different ways as there have been writers upon the subject. As an incident merely, of the Revolution, accuracy in its relation is not, perhaps, of much moment. When measured, however, by its results, it at once assumes an importance which justifies such an investigation as shall bring out the truth.

The slaying of Miss McCrea was, to the people of New York, what the battle of Lexington was to the New England colonies. In each case, the effect was to consolidate the inhabitants more firmly against the invader. The blood of the unfortunate girl was not shed in vain. From every drop, hundreds of armed yeomen arose; and, as has been justly said, her name was passed as a note of alarm along the banks of the Hudson, and as a rallying cry among the Green mountains of Vermont brought down her hardy sons. It thus contributed to Burgoyne's defeat, which became a precursor and principal cause of American independence.

The story, as told by Bancroft, Irving and others is, that as Jane McCrea was on her way from Fort Edward to meet her lover, Lieutenant Jones, at the British camp, under the protection of the Indians, a quarrel arose between the latter as to which should have the promised reward; when one of them, to terminate the dispute, "sunk," as Mr. Bancroft says, "his tomahawk into the skull" of their unfortunate charge. The correct account, however, of the Jane McCrea Tragedy, gathered from the statement made by Mrs. McN_al to General Burgoyne on the 28th of July, 1777, in the *marquee* of her cousin, General Fraser, and corroborated by several people well acquainted with Jane McCrea, and by whom it was related to the late Judge Hay, of Saratoga Springs — a veracious and industrious historian — and taken down from their lips, is different from the version given by Mr. Bancroft.

On the morning of the 27th of July, 1777, Miss McCrea and Mrs. McNeal were in the latter's house at Fort Edward, preparing to set out for Fort Miller for greater security, as rumors had been rife of Indians in the vicinity. Their action was the result of a message sent to them early in the morning by General Arnold, who had, at the same time, despatched to their assistance Lieutenant Palmer, with some twenty men, with orders to place their furniture and effects on board a *bateau* and row the family down to Fort Miller

Lieutenant Palmer, having been informed by Mrs. McNeal that nearly all her household goods had been put on board the *bateau*, remarked that he, with the soldiers, was going up the hill as far as an old blockhouse, for the purpose of reconnoitering, but would not be long absent. The lieutenant and his party, however, not returning, Mrs. McNeal, and Jane McCrea concluded not to wait longer, but to ride on horseback to Col. McCrea's ferry, leaving the further lading of the boat in charge of a black servant. When the horses, however, were brought up to the door, it was found that one side-saddle was missing, and a boy[1] was accordingly despatched to the house of a Mr. Gillis for the purpose of borrowing a side-saddle or a pillion.

---

[1] His name was Norman Morrison. It is not known what became of him, though tradition states, that being small and active, he escaped from the savages and reached his house in Hartford, Washington Co., N. Y.

Appendix. 305

While watching for the boy's return, Mrs. McNeal heard a discharge of fire arms,[1] and looking out of a window, saw one of Lieutenant Palmer's soldiers running along the military road toward the fort, pursued by several Indians. The fugitive, seeing Mrs. McNeal, waved his hat as a signal of danger, and passed on; which the Indians perceiving, left off the pursuit, and came toward the house.

Seeing their intention, Mrs. McNeal, screamed; "get down cellar for your lives!" On this, Jane McCrea and the black woman, Eve, with her infant, retreated safely to the cellar, but Mrs. McNeal was caught on the stairs by the Indians, and dragged back by the hair of her head by a powerful savage, who was addressed by his companions, as the " Wyandot Panther." A search in the cellar was then begun, and the result was the discovery of Jane McCrea, who was brought up from her concealment,[2] the Wyandot exclaiming upon seeing her. " My squaw, me find um agin — me keep um fast now, forebet, ugh!"

By this time the soldiers had arrived at the fort, the alarm drum was beaten, and a party of soldiers started in pursuit. Alarmed by the noise of the drum — which

---

[1] So fatal was this discharge, that out of Lieutenant Palmer's party of twenty men, only eight remained, Palmer himself being killed on the spot.

[2] Judge Hay was informed by Adam, after he became a man, that his mother, Eve, had often described to him how she continued to conceal him and herself in an ash-bin beneath a fire-place; he luckily not awaking to cry while the search was going on around them in the cellar. This was also confirmed by the late Mrs. Judge Cowen.

they, in common with Mrs. McNeal and Jenny, heard — the Indians, after a hurried consultation, hastily lifted the two women upon the horses which had been waiting at the door to carry them to Colonel McCrea's ferry, and started off upon a run. Mrs McNeal, however, having been placed upon the horse on which there was no saddle, slipped off and was thereupon carried in the arms of a stalwart savage.

At this point, Mrs. McNeal lost sight of her companion, who, to use the language of Mrs. McNeal, " was there ahead of me, and appeared to be firmly seated on the saddle, and held the rein, while several Indians seemed to guard her — the Wyandot still ascending the hill and pulling along by bridle-bit the affrighted horse upon which poor Jenny rode." The Indians, however, when half way up the hill, were nearly overtaken by the soldiers, who, at this point, began firing by platoons. At every discharge the Indians would fall flat with Mrs. McNeal. By the time the top of the Fort Edward hill had been gained, not an Indian was harmed, and one of them remarked to Mrs. McNeal; " wagh! um no kill — um shoot too much high for hit." During the firing, two or three of the bullets of the pursuing party hit Miss McCrea with a fatal effect, who, falling from her horse, had her scalp *torn* off by her guide, the Wyandot Panther, in revenge for the loss of the reward given by Burgoyne for any white prisoner — a reward considered equal to a barrel of rum.

Mrs. McNeal, however, was carried to Griffith's house, and there kept by the Indians until the next day, when she was ransomed and taken to the British camp.

"I never saw Jenny afterwards," says Mrs. McNeal, "nor anything that appertained to her person until my arrival in the British camp, when an aide-de-camp showed me a fresh scalp-lock which I could not mistake, because the hair was unusually fine, luxuriant, lustrous, and dark as the wing of a raven. Till that evidence of her death was exhibited, I hoped, almost against hope, that poor Jenny had been either rescued by our pursuers (in whose army her brother, Stephen McCrea, was a surgeon), or brought by our captors to some part of the British encampment."

While at Griffith's house, Mrs. McNeal endeavored to hire an Indian, named Captain Tommo, to go back and search for her companion, but neither he nor any of the Indians could be prevailed upon to venture even as far back as the brow of the Fort Edward hill to look down it for the " white squaw," as they called Jenny.

The remains of Miss McCrea were gathered up by those who would have rescued her, and buried — together with those of Lieutenant Palmer — under the supervision of Colonel Morgan Lewis (then deputy quartermaster general), on the bank of the creek, three miles south of Fort Edward, and two miles south of her brother John McCrea's farm, which was across the Hudson, and directly opposite the principal encampment of General Schuyler.

The only statements which, while disproving Mr. Bancroft's relation, seems to conflict with the above account of the *manner* of her death, is the one made by Dr. John Bartlett, a surgeon in the American army. This occurs in his report to the director-general of the hospitals of the Northern department, dated at Moses creek at headquarters, at ten o'clock of the night of July 27, 1777, and is as follows:

"I have this moment returned from Fort Edward, where a party of hell-hounds, in conjunction with their brethren, the British troops, fell upon an advanced guard, inhumanly butchered, scalped and stripped four of them, wounded two more, each in the thigh, and four more are missing.

"Poor Miss Jenny McCrea, and the woman with whom she lived, were taken by the savages, led up the hill to where there was a body of British troops, and there the poor girl was shot to death in cold blood, scalped and left on the ground; and the other woman not yet found.

"The alarm came to camp at two P.M. I was at dinner. I immediately sent off to collect all the regular surgeons, in order to take some one or two of them along with me, but the devil a bit of one was to be found. * * * * There is neither amputating instrument, crooked needle, nor tourniquet in all the camp. I have a handful of lint and two or three bandages, and that is all. What in the name of wonder I am to do in case of an attack, God only knows. Without assistance, without instruments, without anything!"

This statement, however, was made, as is apparent on its face, hurriedly, and under great excitement. A thousand rumors were flying in the air, and there had been no time in which to sift the kernels of truth from the chaff. But, in addition to this, the story of the surgeon is flatly contradicted by testimony, both at the time of the occurrence and afterward. General Burgoyne's famous "Bouquet order" of the 21st of May, and his efforts, by appealing to their fears and love of gain, to prevent any species of cruelty on the part of his savage allies — facts well known to his officers and men — render it simply impossible to believe the statement of Surgeon Bartlett, that a "body of British troops" stood calmly by and witnessed the murder of a defenceless maiden — and a maiden, too, between whom and one of their comrades-in-arms there was known to be a betrothment. Leaving, however, probabilities, we have the entirely different and detailed account of Jenny's companion, Mrs. McNeal, "the woman with whom she lived," and who, as "the woman not yet found," was endeavoring — while the surgeon was penning his account — to prevail upon the Indians to go back and search for Jenny's body, left behind in their hurried flight.

The entire matter, however, seems to be placed beyond all doubt, not only by the corroborative statement of the Wyandot Panther, when brought into the presence of Burgoyne — to the effect that it was not he, but the enemy, that had killed her — but by the statement of General Morgan Lewis, afterward governor of New York state. His account is thus given by the late Judge Hay in a letter to the writer:

"Several years after Mrs. Teasse had departed this — to her — eventful life, I conversed (in the hearing of

Mr. David Banks, at his law-book store in New York) with Governor Lewis. Morgan Lewis then stated his distinct recollection that there were three gun-shot wounds upon Miss McCrea's corpse, which, on the day of her death, was, by direction of himself — and, in fact, under his own personal supervision — removed, together with a subaltern's remains, from a hill near Fort Edward to the Three Mile creek, where they were interred. The fact of the bullet wounds — of which I had not before heard, but which was consistent with Mrs. Teasse's statement — was to me 'confirmation strong as proof from Holy writ,' that Jane McCrea had not been killed exclusively by Indians, who would have done that deed either with a tomahawk or scalping-knife, and would not, therefore, be likely (pardon the phrase in this connection) to have wasted their ammunition. In that opinion Governor Lewis, an experienced jurist — if not general — familiar with rules of evidence, concurred."

This opinion of two eminent lawyers, as well as the statement of the Wyandot, receives, moreover, additional confirmation in the fact that when the remains of Jane McCrea, a few years since were disinterred and removed to the old Fort Edward burial ground, and consigned to Mrs. McNeal's grave, Dr. William S. Norton, a respectable and highly intelligent practitioner of physic and surgery, examined her skull, and found no marks whatever of a cut or a gash.[1]

---

[1] Miss McCrea's remains have recently again been removed, for the third time, to the new Union cemetery, situated half way between Fort Edward and Sandy Hill. A large slab of white marble has been placed over the spot by Miss McCrea's niece, Mrs. Sarah H. Payne.

Appendix. 311

This fact, also, strongly confirms the opinion expressed at the time by General Fraser,[1] at the *post-mortem* camp investigation, that Jane McCrea was accidentally, or rather unintentionally, killed by American troops pursuing the Indians, and, as General Fraser said he had often witnessed, aiming too high, when the mark was on elevated ground, as had occurred at Bunker's (Breed's) hill.

It thus appears, first, that Jane McCrea was accidentally killed by the Americans, and, secondly, that the American loyalist, David Jōnes, did not send the Indians, much less the ferocious Wyandot Panther, whom he abhorred and dreaded, on their errand.

Indeed, the falsity of this latter statement (which, by the way, General Burgoyne never believed) is also susceptible of proof. The well established fact that Jones had sent Robert Ayers (father-in-law of Mr. Ransom Cook, now residing at Saratoga Springs, N. Y.), with a letter to Miss Jane McCrea asking her to visit the British encampment and accompany its commander-in-chief, with his lady guests, on an excursion to Lake George, clearly shows how the charge against Jones had crept into a whig accusation concerning misconduct and meanness; and the dialogue (also well authenticated) between two of her captors, in relation to the comparative value of a white squaw — estimated at a barrel of rum — and her scalp-lock, accounts perhaps, for the story of the pretended proffered reward (a barrel of rum), alleged to have caused the quarrel among the Indians which resulted in

---

[1] Afterwards killed at the battle of Saratoga, Oct. 7th, 1777.

the supposed catastrophe. All who had been acquainted with David Jones knew that he was incapable of such conduct, and so expressed themselves at the time.

The rumor, also, which is slightly confirmed in Burgoyne's letter to General Gates, that Miss McCrea was on her way to an appointed marriage ceremony, originated in Jones's admission that he had intended, on the arrival of his betrothed at Skenesborough (now Whitehall, N. Y.), to solicit her consent to their immediate nuptials — Chaplain Brudenell officiating. But Jones explicitly denied having intimated such a desire, in a letter to Miss McCrea or otherwise. "Such," he added, " was, without reference to my own sense of propriety, my dear Jenny's sensibility, that the indelicacy of this supposed proposal would, even under our peculiar circumstances, have thwarted it."

Indeed, this question was often a topic of conversation between General Fraser and his cousin, Mrs. McNeal, who, with Miss Hunter (afterwards Mrs. Teasse), accompanied him from Fort Edward to Saratoga, and on his death, in that battle, returned to Fort Edward, after witnessing the surrender of the British general. Jones frankly admitted to his friends that in consequence of the proximity of the savages to Fort Edward, he had engaged several chiefs who had been at the Bouquet encampment, to keep an eye upon the fierce Ottawas, and especially upon the bloodthirsty Wyandots, and persuade them not to cross the Hudson; but if they could not be deterred from so doing by intimations of danger from rebel scouts, his employés were to watch over the safety of his mother's residence, and also that of Colonel

McCrea. For all which, and in order the better to secure their fidelity, Jones promised a suitable but not specified reward; meaning thereby such trinkets and weapons as were fitted for Indian traffic, and usually bestowed upon savages, whether in peace or war.

But partisanship was then extremely bitter, and eagerly seized the opportunity thus presented of magnifying a slight and false rumor into a veritable fact, which was used most successfully in stirring up the fires of hatred against loyalists in general, and the family of Jones in particular. The experiences of the last few years afford fresh illustrations of how little of partisan asseveration is reliable; and there is so much of the terrible in civil war which is indisputably true, that it is not difficult, nor does it require habitual credulity, to give currency to falsehood.

One, who a hundred years hence, should write a history of the late Rebellion, based upon the thousand rumors, newspaper correspondence, statements of radical and fierce politicians on one or another side, would run great risk of making serious misstatements. The more private documents are brought to light, the more clearly they reveal a similar, though even more intensified state of feeling between the tories and the whigs during the era of the Revolution. Great caution should therefore be observed, when incorporating in history any accounts as facts, which seem to have been the result of personal hatred or malice.

No. V.
A Visit to the Battle-Ground in 1827.

The following account of a visit to the field of Saratoga, on the fiftieth anniversary of that battle, viz: October 17th, 1827, was written immediately afterward for the use of the late Col. William L. Stone, for his *Life of Brant*. The writer, the late venerable Samuel Woodruff, Esq., of Windsor (Conn.), was a participator in the battle:

Windsor, Conn., *Oct.* 31, 1827.

My dear Sir:

You may remember when I had the pleasure to dine with you at New York, on the 14th inst., I had set out on a tour to Saratoga to gratify a desire I felt, and which had long been increasing, to view the battle-grounds at that place, and the spot on which the royal army under the command of General Burgoyne surrendered to General Gates on the 17th of October, 1777.

I thought it would add something to the interest of that view to me, to be there on the 17th, exactly half a century after that memorable event took place, You will excuse me for entering a little into the feelings of Uncle Toby respecting Dendermond in the compressed and hastily written journal I kept of my tour, especially as you will take into consideration that I had the honor to serve as a volunteer under General Gates part of that campaign, and was in the battle of the 7th of October.

I take the liberty to enclose you an extract of that

part of my journal which embraces the principal object of my tour.

Oct. 17th. After a short stop in Troy, took another stage for Saratoga ; at Lansingburgh, a neat and handsome village, about three miles from Troy, crossed the Hudson on a covered bridge of excellent workmanship, over to Waterford (Old Half Moon point), another rich and flourishing village. Arrived at Fish creek in Saratoga at half past two P.M. through a beautiful, well cultivated interval of alluvial land on the west side of the Hudson — everything from Albany to this place wears the appearance of wealth and comfort. Put up at Mr. Barker's tavern. After dinner viewed the ruins of the British fortifications and head-quarters of Gen. Burgoyne. He kept his quarters for several days at a house, now standing and in good repair, about a mile north of Fish creek, on the west side of the road, owned by Mr. Busher, an intelligent farmer about seventy-five years of age. While Burgoyne held his head-quarters at this house, Baron Riedesel, of the royal army, obtained leave of the commander-in-chief to place his lady the baroness and their three small children under the same protection ; these were also accompanied by lady Ackland and some other ladies, wives of British officers. At that time some of the American troops were stationed on the east bank of the Hudson, opposite the house, in fair view of it, and within cannon-shot distance. Observing considerable moving of persons about the house, the Americans supposed it the *rendezvous* of the British officers, and commenced a brisk cannonade upon it. Several shot struck and shattered the house. The baroness with her children fled into the cellar for safety, and placed herself and them at the northeast corner, where they were well protected by the cellar wall. A British surgeon by the name of Jones, having his leg broken by a cannon ball, was at this time brought in, and laid on the floor of the room which the baroness and the other ladies had just left. A cannon ball entered the house near the northeast corner of the room, a few inches above the floor, and passing through, broke and mangled the other leg of the poor surgeon. Soon after this he expired. Mr. Busher very civilly conducted me into the room, cellar, and other parts of the house, pointing out the places where the balls entered, etc. From hence I proceeded to, and viewed with very great interest, the spot where Gen. Burgoyne, attended by his staff, presented his sword to Gen. Gates; also, the ground on which the arms, etc., of the royal army were stacked and piled. This memorable place is situated on the flat, north side of Fish creek, about forty rods west of its entrance into the Hudson, and through which the Champlain canal now passes.

Contiguous to this spot is the N. W. angle of old Fort Hardy, a military work thrown up and occupied by the French, under Gen. Dieskau, in the year 1755. The lines of intrenchment embrace, as I should judge, about fifteen acres of ground. The outer works on the north side of Fish creek, and east on the west bank of the Hudson. Human bones, fragments of fire-arms, swords, balls, tools, implements, broken crockery, etc., etc., are frequently picked up on this ground.

In excavating the earth for the Champlain canal, which passes a few rods west of this fort, such numbers of human skeletons were found as render it highly probable this was the cemetery of the French garrison.

About twenty or thirty rods west of the aqueduct for the canal over Fish creek, stood Gen. Schuyler's mills, which were burned by order of Gen. Burgoyne.

Gen. Schuyler's dwelling-house also, and his other buildings, standing on a beautiful area a little southeast of the mills on the south side of the creek, suffered the same fate. The mills have been rebuilt and are now in operation, at the same place where the former stood. The grandson of Gen. Schuyler now lives in a house erected on the site of the former dwelling of his father — a covered bridge across the creek adjoining the mills.

I cannot, in this place, omit some short notices of Gen. P. Schuyler. It seems he was commander-in-chief of the northern army until the latter part of August, 1777, at which time he was superseded by Gen. Gates.

I remember at that time there was some excitement in the public mind, and much dissatisfaction expressed on account of that measure; and with my limited means of knowledge, I have never been able to learn what *good* reason induced his removal. Few men in our country at that time ranked higher than Gen. Schuyler in all the essential qualities of the patriot, the gentleman, the soldier, and scholar. True to the cause of liberty, he made sacrifices which few were either able or willing to bear. The nobility of soul he possessed, distinguished him from ordinary men, and pointed him out as one deserving of public confidence.

At the surrender of the royal army, he generously invited Gen. Burgoyne, his suite, and several of the principal officers, with their ladies, to his house at Albany; where, at his own expense, he fed and lodged them for two or three weeks with the kindest hospitality.

This is the man, who, a few days before, had suffered immense loss in his mills and other buildings at Fish creek, burned by order of the same Burgoyne who had now become his guest.

Respecting Gen. Gates, I will only say *finis coronat opus.*

Oct. 18th. At seven A.M., started on foot to view some other and equally interesting places connected with the campaign of 1777. Three miles and a half south of Fish creek, called at the house of a Mr. Smith, in which Gen. Fraser died of wounds received in the battle of the 7th October, and near which house, in one of the British redoubts, that officer was buried. This house then stood by the road on the west margin of the intervale, at the foot of the rising ground. A turnpike road having since been constructed, running twenty or thirty rods east of the old road, the latter has been discontinued, and Mr. Smith has drawn the house and placed it on the west side of the turnpike.

Waiving, for the present, any farther notices of this spot, I shall attempt a concise narrative of the two hostile armies for a short period anterior to the great battle of the 7th of October.

The object of the British general was to penetrate as far as Albany, at which place, by concert, he was to meet Sir Henry Clinton, then with a fleet and army lying at New York. In the early part of September, Gen. Burgoyne had advanced with his army from Fort Edward, and crossed the Hudson with his artillery, baggage wagons, etc., on a bridge of boats, and intrenched the troops on the highlands in Saratoga. On the 19th of September they left their intrenchments, and moved south by a slow and cautious march toward the American camp, which was secured by a line of intrenchments and redoubts on Bemis's heights, running from west to east about half a mile in length, terminating at the east end on the west side of the intervale.

Upon the approach of the royal army, the American forces sallied forth from their camp, and met the British about a mile north of the American lines. A severe conflict ensued, and many brave officers and men fell on both sides. The ground on which this battle was fought was principally covered with standing wood. This circumstance somewhat embarrassed the British troops in the use of their field artillery, and and afforded some advantage to the Americans, particularly the riflemen under the command of the brave Col. Morgan, who did great execution. Night, which has so often and so kindly interposed to stop the carnage of conflicting hosts, put an end to the battle. Neither party claimed a victory. The royal army withdrew in the night, leaving the field and their slain, with some of their wounded, in possession of the Americans. The loss of killed and wounded, as near as could be ascertained, was, on the part of the British, 600; and on that of the Americans, about 350. The bravery and firmness of the American forces displayed this day, convinced the British officers of the difficulty, if not utter impossibility, of continuing their march to Albany. The season for closing the campaign in that northern region was advancing — the American army was daily augmenting by militia, volunteers, and the "two months men," as they were then called. The fear that the royal armies might effect their junction at Albany, aroused the neighboring states of New England, and drew from New Hampshire, Massachusetts, Connecticut, and Vermont, a large body of determined soldiers. Baum's defeat at Bennington had inspired them with new hopes and invigorated their spirits.

Under these circumstances, inauspicious to the hostile army, the British commander-in-chief summoned a council of war; the result of which was to attempt a retreat across the Hudson to Fort Edward. Gen. Gates, apprehending the probability of this measure, seasonably detached a portion of his force to intercept and cut off the retreat, should that be attempted.

Many new and unexpected difficulties now presented themselves. The boats which had served the British army for a bridge, being considered by them as of no further use, had been cut loose, and most of them floated down the river. The construction of rafts sufficient for conveying over their artillery and heavy baggage, would be attended with great danger as well as loss of time. The bridges over the creeks had been destroyed; great quantities of trees had been felled across the roads by order of the American general; another thing, not of

Appendix. 321

the most trifling nature, Fort Edward was already in possession of the Americans. In this perplexing dilemma the royal army found themselves completely *checkmated*. A retreat, however, was attempted, but soon abandoned. Situated as they now were, between two fires, every motion they made was fraught with danger and loss. They retired to their old intrenched camp.

Several days elapsed without any very active operations on either side. This interval of time was, however, improved by the royal army in preparations to make one desperate effort to force the line of the American camp, and cut their way through on their march to Albany. The American army improved the meantime in strengthening their outer works, arranging their forces, and placing the *Continentals* on the north side of the intrenchments, where valiant men were expected; thus preparing to defend every point of attack; Morgan, with his riflemen, to form the left flank in the woods.

During these few days of " dreadful preparation," information daily arrived in our camp, by deserters and otherwise, that an attack would soon be made upon the line of our intrenchments at Bemis's heights, near the head-quarters of Gen. Gates.

The expected conflict awakened great anxiety among the American troops, but abated nothing of that sterling intrepidity and firmness which they had uniformly displayed in the hour of danger; all considered that the expected conflict would be decisive of the campaign at least, if not of the war in which we had been so long engaged. Immense interests were at stake. Should

Gen. Burgoyne succeed in marching his army to Albany, Gen. Clinton, without any considerable difficulty, would there join him with another powerful English army, and a fleet sufficient to command the Hudson from thence to New York. Should this junction of force take place, all the states east of the Hudson would be cut off from all efficient communication with the western and southern states.

In addition to this there were other considerations of the deepest concern. The war had already been protracted to a greater length of time than was expected on either side at the commencement. The resources of the country, which were at first but comparatively small in respect to those things necessary for war, began to fail; the term of enlistment of many of the soldiers had expired.

We had no public money, and no government to guaranty the payment of wages to the officers and soldiers, nor to those who furnished supplies for the troops.

Under these discouraging circumstances it became extremely difficult to raise recruits for the army. During the year 1776 and the fore part of '77, the Americans suffered greatly by sickness, and were unsuccessful in almost every rencontre with the enemy. Men's hearts, even the stoutest, began to fail. This was indeed the most gloomy period of the war of the Revolution.

On the 7th of October, about ten o'clock A.M., the royal army commenced their march, and formed their line of battle on our left, near Bemis's heights, with Gen. Fraser at their head. Our pickets were driven in about one o'clock P.M., and were followed by the British troops on a quick march to within fair musket shot distance of the line of our intrenchments. At this moment commenced a tremendous discharge of cannon and musketry, which was returned with equal spirit by the Americans.

For thirty or forty minutes the struggle at the breastworks was maintained with great obstinacy. Several charges with fixed bayonets were made by the English grenadiers with but little effect. Great numbers fell on both sides. The ardor of this bloody conflict continued for some time without any apparent advantage gained by either party. At length, however, the assailants began to give way, preserving good order in a regular but slow retreat — loading, wheeling, and firing, with considerable effect. The Americans followed up the advantage they had gained, by a brisk and well-directed fire of field-pieces and musketry. Col. Morgan with his riflemen hung upon the left wing of the retreating enemy, and galled them by a most destructive fire. The line of battle now became extensive, and most of the troops of both armies were brought into action. The principal part of the ground on which this hard day's work was done, is known by the name of Freeman's farm. It was then covered by a thin growth of pitch-pine wood without under brush, excepting one lot of about six or eight acres, which had been cleared and fenced. On this spot the Britsh grenadiers, under the command of the brave Major Ackland, made a stand, and brought together some of their field artillery; this little field soon became literally "the field of blood." These grenadiers, the flower of the royal army, unaccustomed to yield to any opposing force in fair field, fought with that obstinate spirit which borders on madness. Ackland received a ball through both legs, which rendered him unable to walk or stand. This occurrence hastened the retreat of the grenadiers, leaving the ground thickly strewed with their dead and wounded.

The battle was continued by a brisk running fire until dark. The victory was complete; leaving the Americans masters of the field. Thus ended a battle of the highest importance in its consequences; and which added great lustre to the American arms. I have seen no official account of the numbers killed and wounded; but the loss on the part of the British must have been great, and on the part of the Americans not inconsiderable. The loss of general officers suffered by the royal army was peculiarly severe. But to return to the Smith house. I made known to the Smith family the object of my calling upon them; found them polite and intelligent, and learned from them many interesting particulars respecting the battle of the 7th of October. For several days previous to that time Gen. Burgoyne had made that house his head-quarters, accompanied by several general officers and their ladies, among whom were Gen. Fraser, the Baron and Baroness Riedesel, and their children.

The circumstances attending the fall of this gallant officer have presented a question about which military men are divided in opinion. The facts seem to be agreed, that soon after the commencement of the action, Gen.

Arnold, knowing the military character and efficiency of Gen. Fraser, and observing his motions in leading and conducting the attack, said to Col. Morgan, "that officer upon a grey horse is of himself a host, and must be disposed of. Direct the attention of some of the sharpshooters among your riflemen to him." Morgan, nodding his assent to Arnold, repaired to his riflemen, and made known to them the hint given by Arnold. Immediately upon this, the crupper of the grey horse was cut off by a rifle bullet, and within the next minute another passed through the horse's mane, a little back of his ears. An aid of Fraser noticing this, observed to him, " Sir, it is evident that you are marked out for particular aim ; would it not be prudent for you to retire from this place ?" Fraser replied, " my duty forbids me to fly from danger ; " and immediately received a bullet through his body. A few grenadiers were detached to carry him to the Smith house.

Having introduced the name of Arnold, it may be proper to note here, that although he had no regular command that day, he volunteered his service, was early on the ground, and in the hottest part of the struggle at the redoubts. He behaved (as I then thought), more like a madman than a cool and discreet officer. Mounted on a brown horse, he moved incessantly at a full gallop back and forth, until he received a wound in his leg, and his horse was shot under him. I happened to be near him when he fell, and assisted in getting him into a litter to be carried to head-quarters.

Late in the evening Gen. Burgoyne came in, and a

tender scene took place between him and Fraser. Gen. Fraser was the idol of the British army, and the officer on whom, of all others, Burgoyne placed the greatest reliance. He languished through the night, and expired at eight o'clock the next morning. While on his deathbed he advised Burgoyne, without delay, to propose to Gen. Gates terms of capitulation, and prevent the further effusion of blood; that the situation of his army was now hopeless; they could neither advance nor retreat. He also requested that he might be buried in the *Great redoubt* — his body to be borne thither between sunset and dark, by a body of the grenadiers, without parade or ceremony. This request was strictly complied with.

After viewing the house to my satisfaction, I walked up to the place of interment. It is situated on an elevated piece of ground, commanding an extensive view of the Hudson, and a great length of the beautiful interval on each side of it. I was alone; the weather was calm and serene. Reflections were awakened in my mind which I am wholly unable to describe. Instead of the bustle and hum of the camp, and *confused* noise of the battle of the warrior, and the shouts of victory which I here witnessed fifty years ago, all was now silent as the abodes of the dead. And indeed far, far the greatest part of both those armies who were then in active life at and near this spot, are now mouldering in their graves, like that valiant officer whose remains are under my feet — "their memories and their names lost," while God, in his merciful Providence, has preserved my life, and after the lapse of half a century has afforded me an opportunity of once more viewing those places which force upon my mind many interesting recollections of my youthful days.

Oct. 19th. On my return down the river from Albany to New York, in the steam boat North America, I had leisure and opportunity for reflecting upon the immense wealth and resources of the state of New York — greater, I believe, at this time than that of any other two states in the Union. It would be hazarding nothing to say, that this single state possessses more physical power, and more of the " sinews of war," than were employed by the whole thirteen states through the war of the Revolution. This among other considertions, led me to the reflection how honorable it would be to the state, and how deserving of the occasion, that a monument be erected at or near the place where the royal army surrendered by capitulation on the 17th of October, 1777, in commemoration of an event so important in our national history. The battle of the 7th of October may be considered, in its effects and consequences, as the termination of the war, with as much propriety as that of Bunker's hill was the commencement of it.

   I am, Sir,
     Very respectfully yours,
        SAMUEL WOODRUFF.
William L. Stone, Esq.

No. VI.
FRASER'S REMAINS, PROBABLE ORIGIN OF THE TRADITION OF THEIR HAVING BEEN REMOVED.

The following incident, printed in *The Old Settler* in 1851 is certainly most curious; nor have I any doubt but that the tradition held to this day at Wilbur's basin of the remains of General Fraser having been removed to England, had its rise in the circumstances here related. This opinion, moreover, receives, in my mind, additional confirmation in the fact that P. Stansbury, who published an account of his visit to the battle ground in 1821, states that the farmers there told him that Fraser's body had " lately been taken to England." This date, it will be observed (1821) corresponds exactly with the one mentioned by Peter Barker.

AN INCIDENT OF BURGOYNE'S CAMPAIGN.

MR. ALLEN — About thirty years ago, the late Peter Barker, then of Schuylerville, Saratoga county, related to me an extraordinary circumstance which occurred in that village, during the time he was proprietor of the hotel, and also land agent of Philip Schuyler, Esq. 'Tis an *old* affair, and may perhaps be interesting to the readers of *The Old Settler*. From a memorandum made at the time, I am enabled to give you the precise language of Mr. Barker. He said: " One morning a carriage drove up to my door, from which there alighted three gentlemen — one very aged, the other two much younger. On learning that Mr. Schuyler was absent (for whom they inquired), they informed me that their business with him was to obtain permission to remove the remains of a relative, who was many years ago buried on his land. I replied, that as agent of Mr. Schuyler, I would not only grant the permission, but would render them any assistance in my power to effect the object of their visit. They thanked me, and requested me to order a box to be made, sufficiently large to contain the bones of a person, and also to engage six men to be in attendance when wanted, with implements for digging; and after ordering an early dinner, they left the house, on foot. They were absent about two hours. On their return, they intimated to me that they had discovered the grave. After eating a hasty dinner, we summoned the men; and having obtained the box, started under the guidance of the old gentleman. He led us to the plain east of the house, and about half way to the river, to a large primitive elm tree, where he ordered us to stop. He then, with a pocket compass, ascertained the due north course from the tree, and measured off a certain distance from the tree by pacing: there he stuck a stake. After spending half an hour or more in measuring and remeasuring, he marked on the surface of the ground an oblong square of about five by eight feet, and directed the workmen to there commence digging, giving them particular directions if they should discover anything like rotten or decayed wood to stop. At the depth of four feet such a discovery was made. The old gentleman, much agitated, got into the pit, and under his direction the earth was carefully removed from off the decayed wood, which was in length about seven feet. Beneath the wood was another decayed substance, which the old gentleman said was the remains of woolen blankets; and, on removing that covering, human bones were discovered; with them, the remains of two bayonets, which appeared to have been crossed on the breast — a silver stock buckle, a gold masonic medal, and several musket balls, by which the remains were fully identified by the old gentleman, who, with his own hands, the tears streaming down his cheeks, and with the greatest care and reverence, gathered up all the bones and ashes, and placed them in the box which was carefully closed.

"It was dark when we returned to the house. After supper, the two young gentlemen invited me to their room, to give me an explanation of the singular events of the day. They said the remains they had removed, were those of a British officer in Burgoyne's army, in the war of the Revolution, and the old gentleman who accompanied them was the servant of that officer. The officer was mortally wounded in the battle of Saratoga. His servant (the old gentleman) and three of his soldiers carried him off the field of battle in blankets, and as far north as the elm tree, under which he died. The servant was determined, and did most effectually mark the place, that the grave might be found, should occasion ever afterwards require. They hastily dug a grave, laid the body in it in full dress, covered it first with several blankets, then with three or four boards, and filled it up with earth.

"After peace the servant returned to England, and for many years afterwards importuned the family of that officer to send him over for the remains. They placed but little reliance upon his representations and declined

Appendix.

doing it; and so the matter rested until that time, when the old gentleman became so importunate, giving them no peace, that they, grandsons of the officer, finally decided to gratify him by bringing him over to this country, but without, they said, the least hope or expectation of success; and they attributed the finding of the remains more to accident, than to the recollection of the old gentleman. J.
Troy, May, 1851.

No. VII.

LADY ACKLAND.

The following remarks on Lady Harriet Ackland — says Mr. Fonblanque in his *Life of Burgoyne* — are extracted from a letter written by Miss Warburton (Burgoyne's niece) to her nephew, the late Sir John Burgoyne of Crimean fame, while a boy at school:

"You will be curious, I do not doubt, to know the sequel of this incomparable woman's history, and as far as I am able I will give it you. She had the happiness to see her husband perfectly recovered from his wounds, shortly after which he was unfortunately involved in an affair of honor in consequence of some disagreement with a brother officer in America during the preceding campaign. They fought with swords, and Major Ackland, in making a pass at his adversary, slipped and fell forward with great violence. It happened that a small pebble lay within reach of his fall, and he struck his temple upon it with such force that instant death ensued. Imagine to yourself the wretchedness of Lady Harriet on this unhappy event. Attached to him as she was, having suffered so much for his sake, and having, as she hoped, brought him home to safety and a life of future happiness, to have all this cheering prospect dashed at once in so miserable a manner, was, one would have thought, more than human nature could support or sustain. But she had a mind superior to every trial, and even this, her severest infliction, she bore up under with resignation and fortitude. I saw her again many years afterwards, when her sorrows had been somewhat tempered by time. She was still handsome, but her bloom and vivacity were gone. I placed myself where I could unobserved contemplate the change she had undergone since I had first seen her. Her countenance was mild and placid, but there was a look of tender melancholy mingled with resignation that made her the most interesting object I had ever beheld. * * Whilst we render this tribute to the virtue of Lady Harriet, let us not overlook the heroic conduct of Mr. Brudenell. I cannot conceive courage and fortitude exceeding that which he displayed at the funeral of General Fraser. There was on that occasion every thing to appal the strongest mind; that under such circumstances he should not only go through the solemn service with deliberation, but that his voice should preserve its firmness, is I think, an instance of the most determined resolution that ever was exhibited."[1]

Lady Ackland, or rather Mrs. Brudenell, died on the 21st of July, 1815.

---

[1] "There is a sequel to this romantic story which Miss Warburton forgot to mention; Lady Harriet Ackland ultimately became the wife of Mr. Brudenell."—*Note by Fonblanque.*

No. VIII.

STATEMENT BY SERGEANT LAMB OF THE ROYAL WELSH FUSILEERS IN REGARD TO THE BURNING OF GENERAL SCHUYLER'S HOUSE AND BARNS.

Some letters passed between the opposed generals. The first was from General Burgoyne, by Lady Ackland, whose husband was dangerously wounded and a prisoner, recommending her ladyship to the care and protection of General Gates. Gates's answer was pointed with the sharpest irony, in which he expresses his surprise that his excellency, after considering his preceding conduct, should think that he could consider the greatest attention to Lady Ackland in the light of an obligation. These epistles, although mere communications between individuals, and frequently on private affairs, yet serve to portray the *disposition of the times*, and unveil the cause that gave rise to the unhappy contest.

"The cruelties," added he, "which mark the retreat of your army, in burning the gentlemen's and farmer's houses as they went along, are almost, among civilized nations, without a precedent; they should not endeavor to ruin those they cannot conquer; this conduct betrays more the vindictive malice of a monk, than the generosity of a soldier."

What gave rise to this charge was the following circumstance. On the west bank of Hudson's river, near the height of Saratoga, where the British army halted after their retreat, stood General Schuyler's dwelling house, with a range of barracks, store-houses, etc. The evening the army arrived at these buildings, the weather being very wet and cold, the sick and wounded were directed to take possession of these barracks, while the troops took post on the height above it. In the course of the night, the barracks took fire by accident, and, being built of wood, were soon consumed. It was with the greatest difficulty that the wounded soldiers were rescued from the flames.[1] Two days after this, the enemy had formed a plan of attack ; a large column of troops was approaching to pass the river, preparatory to a general action. This column was entirely covered from the fire of the British artillery by some of these buildings. General Burgoyne ordered them to be set on fire ; but so far was the sufferer from putting an invidious construction upon that action, that one of the first persons General Burgoyne saw after the convention was signed was the owner, General Schuyler ; who, instead of blaming the English general, owned he would have done the same upon the like occasion, or words to that effect.

CORRESPONDENCE BETWEEN GATES AND BURGOYNE.

The following is the correspondence between the two generals referred to by Sergeant Lamb. It will be seen to differ somewhat from the copy extract given by him.

---

[1] The author was in the house when it took fire, and it was with the greatest difficulty he escaped.

General Burgoyne to General Gates.

" Sir : Lady Harriet Ackland, a lady of the first distinction by family rank and by personal virtues, is under such concern on account of Major Ackland her husband, wounded and a prisoner in your hands, that I cannot refuse her request to commit her to your protection.

" Whatever general impropriety there may be in persons acting in your situation and mine to solicit favors, I cannot see the uncommon perseverance in every female grace, and exaltation of character of this lady, and her very hard fortune without testifying that your attentions to her will lay me under obligation.

" I am Sir,
" Your obedient servant,
" J. Burgoyne.
" *Oct. 9th*, 1777.
" Maj. Gen. Gates."

General Gates to General Burgoyne.

"Saratoga, *Oct.* 11*th*, 1777.

" Sir : I have the honor to receive your excellency's letter by Lady Ackland. The respect due to her ladyship's rank, the tenderness due to her person and sex were alone sufficient securities to entitle her to my protection if you consider my preceding conduct with respect to those of your army whom the fortune of war has placed in my hands. I am surprised that your excellency should think that I could consider the greatest attention to Lady Ackland in the light of an obligation.

"The cruelties which mark the retreat of your army, in burning gentlemen's and farmers' houses as they pass along, is almost, among civilized nations, without a precedent. They should not endeavor to ruin those they could not conquer. This conduct betrays more of the vindictive malice of a bigot, than the generosity of a soldier.

"Your friend, Sir Francis Clerke, by the information of Dr. Potts, the director-general of my hospital, languishes under a dangerous wound. Every sort of tenderness and attention is paid him, as well as to all the wounded who have fallen into my hands, and the hospital, which you were obliged to leave to my mercy.

"At the solicitation of Major Williams I am prevailed upon to offer him and Major Wiborn in exchange for Colonel Ethan Allen. Your excellency's objections to my last proposals for the exchange of Colonel Ethan Allen I must consider trifling, as I cannot but suppose that the generals of the royal armies act in equal concert with those of the generals of the armies of the United States.

"The bearer delivers a number of letters from the officers of your army taken prisoners in the action of the 7th.

"I am, Sir,
"Your Excellency's most humble servant,
"HORATIO GATES.
"Lt. General Burgoyne."

Memorandum of a Message delivered by Major Kingston from Lieutenant General Burgoyne to General Gates in answer to the above letter.

"The general from a great deal of business did not yesterday answer your letter about the officers, but intended it.

"In regard to the reproaches made upon this army of burning the country, they are unjust; General Schuyler's house, and adjacent buildings remained protected till General Gates's troops approached the ford. General Burgoyne owns the order for setting fire at *that time* to any thing that covered the movement.

"The barracks, particularly took fire by mere accident, and measures were taken, though ineffectual, to save them. If there has been any vindictive spirit in burning other buildings on the march, it has probably been employed by some secret well-wishers to the American cause, as General Burgoyne has been informed some of the buildings belonged to supposed friends of the king. The general does not think that General Gates has a right, from any thing that has appeared in his conduct or reasoning, to make use of the term TRIFLING; and he still persists, that he cannot interfere with the prisoners in General Howe's army, and more especially in a case that has been under negotiation between General Howe and General Washington."

No. IX.
Jane McCrea and Sketch of Fort Edward.

Fort Edward, a short distance from which the death of Jane McCrea took place, has an important place in American history. In colonial times it was a central point of interest both to the whites and Indians. In the wars of Queen Anne, the Old French, and Seven Years War, both sides were equally anxious to possess it, and, in consequence, many thrilling adventures occurred in its vicinity.

The first white man, says Sir William Johnson, who settled in the town, was Colonel John Henry Lydius son of a Dutch minister of Albany. Lydius was a man of extensive acquaintance with the Indians, having resided much among them, in Canada for several years where he married, and again at Lake George. He erected several mills on an island opposite the present village; and hence the names the place long went by — Lydius's Mills. IIis daughter Catherine Lydius was the first white child born in Washington Co. The street in the village of Fort Edward, now Broadway, was formerly called Lydius after the founder. Col. Lydius carried on an extensive trade with the Indians at this point for several years. He was, however, extremely unpopular with these people, who justly accused him of having, on various occasions, cheated them in land transactions. This feeling on the part of the Indians, at length culminated in 1749, in which year they burned his house on the island and took his son prisoner.

Appendix. 339

Old Fort Edward stood on the east bank of the Hudson, a few rods below the present rail road bridge. Nothing now remains of it except, as in the case of Fort Hardy, a few slight mounds, where were the earth works, and the broken bricks and pottery which are mixed plentifully with the soil. At the best, it consisted only of a square fortified by two bastions on the east side, and by two demi-bastions on the side toward the river. It was built in 1700, by the English, for the protection of the northern frontier, and was called Fort Nicholson, after Col. Nicholson. After the failure, however, of that officer's remarkable though entirely abortive, expedition for the subjugation of Canada — an expedition the organization of which cost the colonies and that of New York in particular a vast amount of money — the fort was abandoned and allowed to go to decay.

In 1755, the English, under General, and afterward Sir William Johnson, made a forward movement toward Canada. As one of the preliminary steps to this expedition General Phineas Lyman, with 600 men was sent forward to the site of Fort Lydius in the beginning of August of that year, to rebuild the fort. The site of the old fortification was abandoned, because it was too much commanded, and a large redoubt, with a simple parapet and a wretched palisade, was built on a more elevated spot not far distant. Within were small barracks for 200 men. The ramparts of earth and timber were sixteen feet high and twenty-two feet thick, and mounted six cannon. On the island opposite, were also barracks and store-houses. It received the name of Fort Lyman, and was a most important depot for the munitions of war in the northern movement of the English forces; besides which it was a general rendezvous of the army and became after a large hospital for the sick and wounded. It also received the name of "The Great carrying-place"—the reason for this designation being that the rapids and falls in the river above the fort made it impossible to ascend any further with the bateaux. Consequently, the goods, arms and ammunition were here unloaded, and carried overland either to Wood creek at Fort Anne, when they were reshipped, and taken to Lake Champlain, or else to the head of Lake George and thence down the lake to the carrying-place at its foot.

In 1755, Israel Putnam was in Gen. Lyman's regiment, as the captain of a company, and was probably with him at the rebuilding of the fort. He was frequently there during that and two succeeding years, and formed a headquarters for himself and his rangers. In 1757 he performed some heroic feats in its behalf. A band of Indians approached it with the secrecy and craftiness so characteristic of the race, and attempted to surprise and capture the garrison, but Putnam, then a major, was not easily taken. He and his men were ready for the savages and put them speedily to flight. In the winter of the same year, the fort was accidentally set on fire. The flames spread rapidly, and for a time it looked as though everything would be destroyed. The powder magazine was in great danger, as the flames were getting very near it. Putnam placed himself between the fire and the magazine, and for an hour and a half fought with the flames until they were finally subdued. The covering of the magazine was scorched and blackened, and the brave Putnam came out of the conflict with his face, arms and hands fearfully burned. Many weeks passed before he recovered from his injuries. Two years afterward, 1758, Putnam and a few of his followers were again chased by the Indians in their canoes to a short distance below the fort. They were in a bateau and rapidly rowed down the river with their pursuers close behind them; approaching the falls at Fort Miller, there seemed to be no way of escape but by going over them. So the bateau was steered to the falls and went over the verge. The Indians fired, and looked for the utter destruction of the crew, when to their amazement they were seen gliding rapidly away unharmed. Neither the leap over the falls, nor the rapids below, nor their bullets had harmed their supposed victims; and henceforth, the Indians considered Putnam under the special protection of the Great Spirit.

The fort retained the name of Fort Lyman but a few years, when it was changed to Fort Edward in honor of Edward, Duke of York, a grandson of George II and brother of George III. During the revolutionary war it was at times held by the British but was the greater portion of the time in the hands of the Americans, affording protection to the farmers of the surrounding country who frequently flocked into it when fearful of the incursions of Indians and tories.

On the approach of Burgoyne's army from Fort Anne it was evacuated by the Americans, by order of Schuyler until after the surrender of the British army at Saratoga.[1] While Burgoyne lay at Fort Miller, it was occupied a portion of the time by General Riedesel with his Brunswickers. While here Riedesel buried two large bateaux inside of the fort for the benefit of Col. St. Leger in case the latter should retreat by way of this place, marking the spot by two crosses to give the appearance of two graves. St. Leger, however, fell back on Oswego; and the bateaux were afterward found by the Americans (*see Life of Reidesel and Gordon*). Reidesel was also quartered for three weeks on the garrison ground at Fort

---

[1] It was while Schuyler lay at Fort Edward, before he fell back, that he resorted to a trick or expedient to delay Burgoyne's march.

"Frederick the Great, after Liegnizt, 16th August, 1760, caused a letter or despatch to fall into the hands of the Russian General Chernicheff, which induced the Muscovite, with every chance of success before him, to retire precipitately. In Schuyler's case he likewise by astuteness, turned the tables on his enemy. A communication had been sent by one Mr. Levins, from Canada, to Gen. Sullivan. It was concealed under the false bottom of a canteen. Schuyler substituted an answer worded in such a manner that if it reached Burgoyne it would cause him the greatest perplexity. Its purport he confided to certain parties around him, and then sent it forward by a messenger who was to conduct himself so as to be captured. The bearer was taken prisoner, and the paper which he bore was soon placed in the hands of Burgoyne. This had greater effect than even Schuyler could have expected. Stedman, the British staff officer and historian, acknowledged that Burgoyne ' was so completely duped and puzzled by it for several days that he was at a loss whether to advance or retreat.' This result, so flattering to Schuyler's sagacity, was communicated to one of Schuyler's staff, after Burgoyne's surrender, by an English officer. In justice to Schuyler let this be noted."—*Gen. J. Watts de Peyster*.

Appendix. 343

Amherst [1] at the half-way brook between the present village of Glen's Falls and Lake George.

Schuyler was greatly blamed for not defending Fort Edward.[2] Ticonderoga had to be evacuated, without resistance because it was commanded by Sugar-loaf mountain. Fort Edward was in like manner commanded on all sides. Major General, the Marquis de Chastellux, who visited it shortly after the surrender, described it as situated in a basin or valley both as to ground and encircling forests. "*Such is Fort Edward*," he writes, "*so much spoken of in Europe*, although it could in no time have been able to resist 500 men, with four pieces of cannon." "The fact is Fort Edward was not a strong position;" and Kalm criticised both of these forts justly in 1758-9. "They were the result of jobs, badly located and badly built, with the design to put money into some favorite's pockets."

The Marquis de Chastellux closes his description of his trip to the fort as follows:

"I stopped here (Fort Edward) an hour to refresh my horses, and about noon set off to proceed as far as the *cataract* (Glen's Falls,) which is eight miles beyond

---

[1] The Fort Amherst here mentioned, was the fortified camp spoken of on page 92 as being held by the Americans.

[2] Mrs. Riedesel joined her husband at Fort Edward. "The following day passed Ticonderoga, and about noon arrived at Fort George, where we dined with Col. Anstruther, an exceedingly good and amiable man, who commanded the 62d regiment. In the afternoon we seated ourselves in a calash, and reached Fort Edward on the same day, which was the 14th of August."— *Journal of Mrs. General Riedesel.*

it. On leaving the valley, and pursuing the road to Lake George, is a tolerable military position, which was occupied in the war before the last. It is a sort of intrenched camp, adapted to abatis, guarding the passage from the woods, and commanding the valley. I had scarcely lost sight of Fort Edward, before the spectacle of devastation presented itself to my eyes, and continued to do so as far as the place I stopped at. Peace and industry had conducted cultivators amidst these ancient forests, men content and happy before the period of this war. Those who were in Burgoyne's way alone experienced the horrors of his expedition; but on the last invasion of the savages, the desolation has spread from Fort Schuyler (or Fort Stanwix) to Fort Edward. I beheld nothing around me but the remains of conflagrations; a few bricks proof against the fire, were the only indications of ruined houses; whilst the fences still entire and cleared out lands, announced that these deplorable habitations had once been the abode of riches and of happiness.

" Arrived at the height of the cataract it was necessary for us to quit our sledges and walk a mile to the bank of the river. The snow was fifteen inches deep, which rendered this walk rather difficult and obliged us to proceed in Indian file in order to make a path. Each of us put ourselves alternately at the head of this little column, as the wild geese relieve each other to occupy the summit of the angle they form in their flight. But had our march been still more difficult, the sight of the cataract was an ample recompense. It is not a sheet of

Appendix. 345

water as at Cohoes. The river confined and interrupted in its course by different rocks, glides through the midst of them, and precipitating itself obliquely forms several cascades. That of Cohoes is more majestic; this, more terrible. The Mohawk river seems to fall from its own dead weight; that of the Hudson frets and becomes enraged. It foams and forms whirlpools, and flies like a serpent making its escape, still continuing its menaces by horrible hisses.

"It was near two when we regained our sledges, having two and twenty miles to return to Saratoga, so that we trod back our steps as fast as possible, but we still had to halt at Fort Edward to refresh our horses. We employed this time as we had done in the morning, in warming ourselves by the fires of the officers who commanded the garrison. They are five in number, and have about one hundred and fifty soldiers. They are stationed in this desert for the whole winter, and I leave the reader to imagine whether this garrison be much more gay than the two most melancholy ones of Gravalines or Briançon, our own in France. We set off again in an hour, and night soon overtook us; but before it was dark I had the satisfaction to see the first game I had met in my journey. It was a bevy of quails. (Partridges?) They were perched to the number of seven upon a fence. I got out of my sledge to have a nearer view of them. They suffered me to approach within four paces, and to make them rise I was obliged to throw my cane at them; they all went off together in a flight similar to that of partridges, and like them they are sedentary."

346 Campaign of General John Burgoyne.

No. X.

THE FIGHT AT DIAMOND ISLAND,[1] AND AN INCIDENT
OF BURGOYNE'S CAMPAIGN.

On page 54 mention is made of the British army hearing shouting in the American camp, which proved to be rejoicing at the capture of some bateaux, and a part of the 53d regiment of the English. It was at this time, Sept. 24, 1777, that the fight at Diamond island near the head of Lake George occurred. Burgoyne on pushing south from Skenesborough had left small garrisons at Ticonderoga, Fort George and Diamond island; there being at the latter post, particularly, a large accumulation. Seizing the opportunity thus afforded, General Lincoln, acting under the direction of the commander-in-chief, resolved, if possible, to break Burgoyne's line of communication and capture his supplies. Col. John Brown was accordingly sent with a force to attack Ticonderoga. Meeting with but partial success in this enterprise, he returned by way of Lake George; and it was while on his way up the lake that the fight at Diamond island occurred.

A recent writer has taken pains to gather up all the

---

[1] So called from the innumerable beautiful crystals which are there found. Silliman, who was here in 1819, says: "The crystals are hardly surpassed by any in the world for transparency and perfection of form. They are, as usual, the six-sided prism, and are frequently terminated at both ends by six-sided pyramids. These last of course, must be found loose, or, at least, not adhering to any rocks; those which are broken off have necessarily only one pyramid." — *Silliman's Travels*, p. 153.

documents and throw light on Col. Baum's attacks on Ticonderoga and Diamond island, and we quote from him as follows:

"Since the printed accounts of the attack upon Ticonderoga are almost as meagre as those of the struggle at the island, we will here give the official report, which is likewise to be found among the *Gates Papers*, now in the possession of the Historical Society of New York, prefacing the report, however, with the English statement of Burgoyne.

"In the course of a vindication of his military policy, Gen. Burgoyne writes as follows:

"During the events stated above, an attempt was made against Ticonderoga by an army assembled under Major-General Lincoln, who found means to march with a considerable corps from Huberton undiscovered, while another column of his force passed the mountains Skenesborough and Lake George, and on the morning of the 18th of September a sudden and general attack was made upon the carrying place at Lake-George, Sugar-Hill, Ticonderoga, and Mount-Independence. The sea officers commanding the armed sloop stationed to defend the carrying place, as also some of the officers commanding at the post of Sugar-Hill and at the Portage, were surprised, and a considerable part of four companies of the 53d regiment were made prisoners; a block-house, commanded by Lieutenant Lord of the 53d, was the only post on that side that had time to make use of their arms, and they made a brave defence till cannon taken from the surprised vessel was brought against them.

"After stating and lamenting so fatal a want of vigilance, I have to inform your Lordship of the satisfactory events which followed.

"The enemy having twice summoned Brigadier General Powell, and received such answer as became a gallant officer entrusted with so important a post, and having tried during the course of four days several attacks, and being repulsed in all, retreated without having done any considerable damage.

"Brigadier General Powell from whose report to me I extract this relation, gives great commendations to the regiment of Prince Frederick, and the other troops ſtationed at Mount-Independence. The Brigadier alſo mentions with great applauſe the behaviour of Captain Taylor of the 21ſt regiment, who was accidentally there on his route to the army from the hoſpital, and Lieutenant Beecroft of the 24th regiment, who with the artificers in arms defended an important battery."[1]

"Such is Burgoyne's account of the attack upon Ticonderoga; next to which comes that of Col. Brown, who, for the second time in the course of his military experience, had an opportunity of exhibiting his valor in connection with the fort. His report to Gen. Lincoln runs as follows:

"North end of lake George landing.
"thurſday Sept. 10th 1777

"Sir: With great fatigue after marching all laſt night I arrived at this place at the break of day, after the beſt diſpoſition of the men, I could make, immediately began the attack, and in a few minutes, carried the place. I then without any loſs of time detached a conſiderable part of my men to the mills, where a greater number of the enemy were poſted, who alſo were ſoon made priſoners, a ſmall number of whom having taken poſſeſſion of a block houſe in that Vicinity were with more difficulty bro't to ſubmiſſion; but at a ſight of a Cannon they ſurrendered. during this ſeaſon of ſucceſs, Mount Defiance alſo fell into our hands. I have taken poſſeſſion of the old french lines at Ticonderoga, and have ſent a flag demanding the ſurrender of Ty: and mount independence in ſtrong and peremptory terms. I have had as yet no information of the event of Colº. Johnſons attack on the mount. My loſs of men in theſe ſeveral actions are not more than 3 or 4 killed and 5 wounded. the enemy's loſs: is leſs. I find myſelf in poſſeſſion of 293 priſoners. Viz. 2 captains, 9 ſubs. 2 Commiſſaries non Commiſſioned officers and privates 143. Britiſh 119, Canadians 18 artificers and retook more than 100 of our men. total 293, excluſive of the priſoners retaken.— The watercraft l have taken, is 150 batteaus, below the falls on lake Champlain 50 above the falls including 17 gun boats and one armed ſloop. arms equal to the number of priſoners. Some ammunition and many other things which I cannot now aſcertain.

---

[1] *State of the Expedition from Canada*, by Burgoyne, p. xciv. Ed. 1780.

I muſt not forget to mention a few Cannon which may be of great ferv'ce to us. Tho. my succeſs has hitherto anſwered my moſt ſanguine expectations, I cannot promiſe myſelf great things, the events of war being ſo dubious in their nature, but ſhall do my beſt to diſtreſs the enemy all in my power, having regard to my retreat — There is but a ſmall quantity of proviſſions at this place which I think will neceſſitate my retreat in caſe we do not carry Ty and independence — I hope you will uſe your utmoſt endeavor to give me aſſiſtance ſhould I need in croſſing the lake &c — The enemy but a very ſmall force at fort George. Their boats are on an iſland about 14 miles from this guarded by ſix companies, having artillery — I have much fear with reſpect to the priſoners, being obliged to ſend them under a ſmall guard — I am well informed that conſiderable reinforcements is hourly expected at the lake under command of Sir John Johnſon — This minute received Gen[l]. Powals anſwer to my demand in theſe words, ' The garriſon intruſted to my charge I ſhall defend to the laſt.' Indeed I have little hopes of putting him to the neceſſity of giving it up unleſs by the force under Colonel Johnſon.

"I am &

" Gen[l]. Lincoln.[1]   " JOHN BROWN."

"We now turn to the fight at Diamond island, giving first the English version, simply remarking as a preliminary, that the postcript of a letter addressed, by Jonas Fay to Gen. Gates, dated Bennington, Sept. 22, 1777, is the following:

" By a person juſt arrived from Fort George — only 30 men are at that place and 2 Gun Boats anchor'd at a diſtance from land and that the enemy have not more than 3 weeks proviſion."[2]

" Writing from Albany after his surrender, Gen. Burgoyne says, under the date of Oct. 27th, that

" On the 24th inſtant, the enemy, enabled by the capture of the gun boats and bateaux which they had made after the ſurpriſe of the ſloop, to embark upon Lake George, attacked Diamond Iſland in two diviſions.

---

[1] *Gates Papers*, p. 154.
[2] *Ibid*, p. 208.

Campaign of General John Burgoyne.

"Captain Aubrey and two companies of the 47th regiment, had been pofted at that ifland from the time the army paffed the Hudfon's River, as a better fituation for the fecurity of the ftores at the fouth end of Lake George than Fort George, which is on the continent, and not tenable againft artillery and numbers. The enemy were repulfed by Captain Aubrey with great lofs, and purfued by the gunboats under his command to the eaft fhore, where two of their principal veffels were retaken, together with all the cannon. They had juft time to fet fire to the other bateaux, and retreated over the mountains."[1]

"This statement was based upon the report made by Lieut. Irwine, the commander at Lake George, whose communication appears to have fallen into the hands of Gates, at the surrender of Burgoyne.

Lieut. Geo. Irwine, of the 47th, reports thus to Lieut. Francis Clark (Clerke), aid-de-camp to Gen. Burgoyne:

"Fort George 24th Septr. 1777.

" Sir

" I think it neceffary to acquaint you for the information of General Burgoyne, that the enemy, to the amount of two or three hundred men came from Skenefborough to the carrying place near Ticonderoga and there took feventeen or eighteen Batteaus with Gunboats — Their defign was firft to attack the fort but confidering they could not well accomplifh it without cannon they defifted from that fcheme, they were then refolved to attack Diamond Ifland (which Ifland Capt. Aubrey commands) and if they fucceeded, to take this place, they began to attack the Ifland with cannon about 9 o'clock yefterday morning, I have the fatiffaction to inform you that after a cannonading for near an hour and a half on both fides the enemy took to their retreat. Then was Gun boats fent in purfuit of them which occafioned the enemy to burn their Gun boats and Batteaus and made their efcape towards Skenefborough in great confufion — we took one Gun boat from them with a twelve pounder in her and a good quantity of ammunition — we have heard there was a few kill'd and many wounded of them. There was not a man killed or hurt during the whole action of his Majefty's

---

[1] *State of the Expedition from Canada*, p. 53.

Troops. I have the honor to be Sir your moſt obedient and moſt humble Serᵗ

"Geoᵉ Irwine Com at Fort George
"Lᵗ 47ᵗʰ"[1]

"We next give the report of Col. Brown, who writes as follows, and not without chagrin:

"Skeenſboro Friday 11 o'clock, a m. Sepᵗ 26ᵗʰ 1777
"Dear Sir

"I this minute arrived at this place by the way of Fort Ann, was induced to take this route on acᵗ of my Ignorance of the ſituation of every part of the continental Army ——

"On the 22 inſt at 4 o'clk P.M. I ſet ſail from the north end Lake George with 20 ſail of Boats three of which were armed, Viz one ſmall ſloop mounting 3 guns. and 2 Britiſh Gun Boats having on Board the whole about 420 Men officers included with a Determined reſolution to attack Diamond Iſland which lies within 5 miles Fort George at the break of Day the next Morning, but a very heavy ſtorm coming on prevented — I arrived Sabbath Day point abt midnight where I tarried all night, during which time I [sic] ſmall Boat in the fleet taken the Day before coming from Fort George, conducted by one Ferry lately a ſutler in our army, I put Ferry on his Parole, but in the night he found Means to eſcape with his Boat, and informed the Enemy of our approach, on the 23d I advanced as far as 12 Mile Iſland, the Wind continuing too high for an attack I ſuſpended it until the Morning of the 24ᵗʰ at 9 oclock at which Time I advanced with the 3 armed Boats in front and the other Boats, I ordered to wing to the Right and left of Iſland to attempt a landing if practicable, and to ſupport the Gun Boats in caſe they ſhould need aſſiſtance, I was induced to make this experiment to find the ſtrength of the Iſland as alſo to carry it if practicable — the enemy gave me the firſt fire which I returned in good earneſt, and advanced as nigh as I thought prudent, I ſoon found that the enemy had been advertiſed of our approach and well prepared for our reception having a great number of cannon well mounted with good Breaſt Works, I however approached within a ſmall Diſtance giving the Enemy as hot a fire as in my Power. untill the ſloop was hulled between wind and Water and obliged to toe her off and one of the boats ſo damaged as I was obliged to quit her in the action. I had two men killed two Mortally wounded

---

[1] *Gates Papers*, p. 212.

and several others wounded in such Manner as I was obliged to leave them under the Care of the Inhabitants, who I had taken Prisoners giving them a sufficient reward for their services.

"I Run my Boats up a Bay a considerable distance and burnt them with all the Baggage that was not portable— The Enemy have on Diamond Island as near as could be collected are about three hundred, and about 40 at Fort George with orders if they are attacked to retreat to the Island — Gen. Borgoine has about 4 Weeks Provision with his army and no more, he is determined to cut his Road through to Albany at all events, for this I have the last authority, still I think him under a small mistake — most of the Horses and Cattle taken at Ty and thereabouts were left in the Woods. Genl Warner has put out a party in quest of them.

"I am Dear S^r wishing you and the
"Main Army
"great Success your most ob^t
"hum^l Ser^t

"Genl Lincoln   "J<small>NO</small> B<small>ROWN</small>

"NB You may Depend on it that after the British Army were supply with six Weeks provision which was two weeks from the Communication between Lake George and Fort Edward was ordered by Genl Burgoine to be stor'd and no passes given ——

"The attack on the Island continued with interruption 2 Hours."[1]

"Thus ended the fight at Diamond island; a fight which, if attended with better success, might have perhaps hastened the surrender of Burgoyne, and resulted in other advantages to the American arms. As it was, however, the British line of communication on Lake George was not broken, while the American leaders took good care to prevent this failure from reaching the public ear through the press. Thus Col. Brown's reports to Gen. Lincoln remained unpublished. They have now been brought out and put on permanent record, as interesting material for American history."

---

[1] *Gates Papers*, p. 220.

Appendix. 353

No. XI.
ALEXANDER BRYAN, THE SCOUT.

" Bryan was a shrewd and somewhat of an ecentric character ; and the events of his life, if generally known, would undoubtedly place his name among the patriots of his time and furnish a deserved monument to his memory." The hint which Dr. Steel thus throws out was acted upon by his grandson, John Alexander Bryan, who, a few years since, erected to his memory a monument in Greenridge cemetery, bearing this inscription :

" In memory of Alexander Bryan. Died April 9th, 1825, aged 92 years. The first permanent settler, and the first to keep a public-house, here, for visitors. An unpaid patriot, who, alone and at great peril, gave the first and only information of Burgoyne's intended advance on Stillwater, which led to timely preparations for the battle of September 19th — followed by the memorable victory of October 7th, 1777."

Alexander Bryan was born in 1733. He was a native of Connecticut, and emigrated to New York early in life, fixing his residence in Dutchess county, where he married Martha Tallmadge, a sister of Senator Tallmadge's father. Some years afterward he removed to the town of Half-Moon, Saratoga county, where he kept an inn about two miles north of Waterford, on what was then the great road between the northern and southern frontiers. Here he continued to reside during the war of the American Revolution ; and his house, naturally, was frequently the resort of the partisans of the contending powers — towards whom he conducted himself so discretely that he was molested by neither, but was confided in by both. His patriotism, however, was well known to the committee of safety of Stillwater, who through him were enabled to thwart many machinations of the tories.

When General Gates took command of the northern army, he applied to the committee to furnish him with a suitable person who might act as a scout, and by penetrating within the enemy's lines report their strength and intended movements. Bryan was at once selected " as the best qualified to undertake the hazardous enterprise." Nor was the choice of the committee ill advised. Bryan was a person endowed with great physical powers of endurance; well acquainted with the country; shrewd, discreet, and reticent; gifted with a fine address and presence; and, considering the meagre educational advantages of the time, possessed of much more than ordinary intelligence. By pursuing a circuitous route, he arrived unmolested at the camp of the enemy, which, at this time, was situated in the vicinity of Fort Edward. He tarried in the neighborhood until he obtained the required information, and was convinced that preparations were making for an immediate advance. Then, on the 15th of September, in the early gray of the autumn morning, he started with the tidings. He had not proceeded many miles before he discovered that he was hotly pursued by two troopers, from whom, after an exciting chase, he adroitly managed to escape, and arrived safely at the head-quarters of General Gates late in the following night. The intelligence he communicated, of the crossing of the Hudson by Burgoyne, with the evident intention on the part of that general to surprise the American army at Stillwater, was of the greatest importance, and led immediately to the preparations which resulted in the sanguinary engagement of the 19th of September. It is handed down as a tradition in the Bryan family, that Gates was in such haste to profit by this information — on which, from his knowledge of Bryan, he implicitly relied — that he forgot either to reward or thank his faithful scout; and, what is worse, he never mentioned the exploit in any of his despatches.[1] This circumstance is thus alluded to by Dr. Steel: "The numerous and essential services which Bryan thus rendered to his country continued for a long time to excite the admiration and gratitude of his few remaining associates, to whom alone they were known, and by whom their importance could only be properly estimated; and it is to be regretted that to the day of his death they remained unacknowledged and unrewarded by any token or profession of gratitude by his country."

Mr. Bryan left five sons, Daniel, Jehial, Robert, John, and Alexander, and two daughters, all of whom are now dead. None of these, except Daniel, ever made any effort to have the services of their father acknowledged

---

[1] Gates seemed to have a habit of forgetting to mention in his despatches those to whom he was indebted for his successes. Arnold, for instance, who did such signal service in the action of October 7th, was never alluded to by him.

and rewarded by the United States government. We have seen a letter from Daniel, accurately written, in 1853, at the age of eighty-two, in a clear, bold hand, in which he speaks of an application made in his behalf, as the only surviving legal representative (by the Hon. John M. Parker, M.C., from that district), for an appropriation to pay the services of his father in the Burgoyne campaign. The application failed because, as it is supposed, no witnesses could be found except those who had heard the facts traditionally, which was not deemed to be within the rules laid down by congress in such cases. For these reasons it is the more fitting that we should here permanently record and give prominence to the patriotic deeds of this early settler of Saratoga.

While, however, Bryan was the chief scout upon whom Gates relied, and who, as has been seen, was the first to furnish intelligence, yet the American general had others in his employ. John Strover (the father of the present George Strover of Schuylerville, N. Y.), had also the command of a party of scouts well acquainted with the country. " He was present," says General Bullard, " at the execution of Thomas Lovelace, a malignant tory, who was hung upon an oak tree, about thirty rods south of where George Strover now resides. At that date the gravel ridge extended east as far as where the canal now is, and the oak tree stood upon the east point of the gravel ridge near where the store house of the Victory company now stands. When the Waterford and Whitehall turnpike was constructed through there, about 1813, the stump of the old oak was removed

Appendix. 357

by the excavation. John Strover had frequently informed his son George that Lovelace was buried in a standing posture, near the tree. When the excavation took place, George stood by and saw the bones, yet in a standing posture, removed from the very spot which had been pointed out by his father. During the campaign Burgoyne employed Lovelace and other tories as spies, and they were generally secreted in the woods between here and Saratoga lake. One day Capt. Dunham, then residing near the lake, in company with Daniel Spike and a colored man, was scouring the woods, and while crossing upon a tree which had fallen over the brook east of the Wagman farm, discovered five guns stacked in the hiding place of the spies. With a sudden rush, Dunham and his associates seized the guns and captured all five of the spies, bound and brought them into the American camp. We have not been able to give the date of the arrest or execution of Lovelace, but think it was after the close of Burgoyne's campaign. Gen. Stark was then at Schuylerville and presided at the court martial before which he was tried. With a vindictive tory element in their midst, and the Indians on the borders, but little progress was made in permanently settling this county, until after peace was declared.

Great and crushing as was the defeat at Saratoga, the war was not yet ended, and the struggle continued for five years longer. Nor did this locality escape the trials and hardships of those times which tried men's souls. The march and counter march of this hostile army with its barbarous allies, had completely desolated the whole region hereabouts. This county had been richly laden with the golden harvest and domestic animals for the use of the husbandman. As a specimen, the farm of James Brisbin had sufficient wheat and cattle to have paid the purchase price, but it was all taken and consumed by Burgoyne's army without compensation, notwithstanding the fair promises made in his proclamation of July 10, before stated. We should except a single cow, which escaped from her captors, returned home and was afterwards secreted and saved. After the surrender, the farmers gradually returned to their rural homes, erected new log houses, and began again to till the soil. But little progress, however, was made, until the close of the war, as this valley lay in the track of the Indians and tories, who had fled to Canada, and made repeated raids into this county."

No. XII.

SKETCH OF CHARLES DE LANGLADE AND HIS RELATIONS WITH BURGOYNE.[1]

When the war of the American Revolution broke out, Charles de Langlade was forty-six years old, but his age sat lightly upon him. At the solicitation of Captain De Peyster of Michilimakinac, he resolved, if his services were required, to take an active part in the war, which, according to the *Miscellanies* of this officer, " secured in our interest all the western Indians." Indeed, he was very soon authorized to raise an Indian

---

[1] From the *Wisconsin Hist. Col.*, vol. VII.

force, and "attack the rebels every time he met them," to use the language of Captain De Peyster's orders.

Embodying a numerous force of Sioux, Sacs, Foxes, Menominees, Winnebagoes, Ottawas and Chippewas, Langlade marched for Montreal. Upon their arrival in that city, a grand council was held with all the ceremonies so dear to the Indians. Larocque, the interpreter of the Sioux, being unable to fulfill his functions, Langlade translated the speeches of the chiefs of that tribe into the Chippewa dialect, which was familiar to almost all the Indians of the northwest, interpreting afterwards into French all that was said in Chippewa. It is well known that a war feast preceded most Indian expeditions ; and care was taken on this occasion, that this ancient and solemn custom should not be omitted. At the banquet which was given, an ox was roasted whole, and served to these voracious guests, who speedily devoured it. Grignon's Memoir does not designate any of the particular services rendered by Langlade at the head of the warriors. It simply says that he took part in engagements under the orders of Major Campbell, in the English army commanded by General Burgoyne, upon the borders of Lake Champlain, and that he went with new recruits to Canada several times during the war.

The army of General Burgoyne, about eighty-five hundred soldiers, and five hundred savages strong, was to invade New York and effect its junction with General Howe at Albany. It assembled at Crown point the thirtieth of June, 1777, and began its movement early in July. It had been proposed, says the Canadian historian Garneau, to join with them a large number of Canadians; but in spite of their coldness and uncertainty as to the future, the mass of the people were but little disposed to fight against the Revolution. Thus Burgoyne was able to induce only one hundred and fifty inhabitants to follow him,[1] the others were overwhelmed with fatigue duties at home.[2]

Langlade rejoined Burgoyne's army with his savages at Skenesborough, now Whitehall, at the end of July, 1777. He was accompanied by his brave old friend, Chevalier Luc du la Corne St. Luc,[3] who though sixty-

---

[1] Anburey, in his travels, affirms that three hundred Canadians were enrolled in the army of Burgoyne. "This nation," says he, "sought not to be involved in a war of invasion which would expose them to reprisals on their own territory." But Burgoyne, in his *State of the Expedition from Canada*, page 10, declares positively that the number of Canadians who served in his army did not exceed one hundred and fifty.

[2] *Histoire du Canada*, vol. III, p. 29.

[3] Luc de la Corn St. Luc, Chevalier de St. Louis, is one of the Canadians who exercised the greatest influence over the savages. One of his first exploits was the capture of Fort Clinton, in 1747. He distinguished himself at the battle of Ticonderoga, where he carried off a convoy of one hundred and fifty of Gen. Abercrombie's wagons. He took part in the battle on the plains of Abraham; then at the victory of St. Foy, near Quebec, where he was wounded. He wished to go to France after the conquest of Canada; but the vessel l'Auguste, on which he embarked, was lost upon the coast of Cape Breton, November 15, 1761; and after this shipwreck of melancholy celebrity, in which, out of one hundred and twenty-one passengers, only seven escaped death, he returned to Canada, making a long and painful march through the woods, and remained permanently in the country. After the American war, St. Luc was appointed legislative councillor, and stoutly defended the political rights of the Canadians at an epoch when they were not always respected. He died at an advanced age.

Appendix. 361

six years old, had not hesitated at the request of the governor of Canada, Sir Guy Carleton, to take the direction of the savage bands which had come to reinforce the English army.

According to Burgoyne, these children of the wilderness did not render all the assistance that was expected of them. They delighted only in pillage and theft, and were guilty of frightful murders. When there was the most need of their service, they began to disband, and very soon not one remained in camp. On this subject we adduce the testimony of Anburey, an officer of the English army, whose account is based entirely upon that of Burgoyne:

"The general showed great resentment to the Indians upon this occasion,[1] and laid restraints upon their dispositions to commit other enormities. He was the more exasperated, as they were Indians of the remoter tribes who had been guilty of this offence, and whom he had been taught to look upon as more warlike. I believe, however, he has found equal depravity of principle reigns throughout the whole of them, and the only preëminence of the remoter tribes consists in their ferocity. From this time, there was an apparent change in their temper; ill-humor and mutinous disposition strongly manifested itself, when they found the plunder of the country was controlled; their interpreters, who had a *douceur* in the capacity, being likewise debarred from those emoluments, were profligate enough to promote dissension, desertion and revolt.

---

[1] The supposed murder of Miss Jane McCrea.

"In this instance, however, Monsieur St. Luc is to be acquitted of those factions, though I believe he was but too sensible of their pining after the accustomed horrors, and that they were become as impatient of his control as of all others, however, through the guide and interest of authority, and at the same time, the affectionate love he bore to his old associates, he was induced to cover the real cause under frivolous pretences of complaint.

"At the pressing instance of St. Luc, a council was called, when to the general's great astonishment, those nations he had the direction of, declared their intention of returning home, at the same time demanding the general to concur with and assist them. This event was extremely embarrassing, as it was giving up part of the force which had been obtained at a great expense to government, and from whose assistance so much was looked for; on the other hand, if a cordial reconciliation was made with them, it must be by indulgence in all their excesses of blood and rapine. Nevertheless the general was to give an immediate answer, he firmly refused their proposal, insisted upon their adherence to the restraints that had been established; and at the same time, in a temperate manner represented to them their ties of faith, of generosity, and honor, adding many other persuasive arguments, to encourage them in continuing their service.

"This answer seemed to have some weight with them, as many of the tribes nearest home only begged, that some part of them might be permitted to return to their harvest, which was granted. Some of the remote tribes seemed to retract from their proposal, professing great zeal for the service. Notwithstanding this, to the astonishment of the general, and every one belonging to the army, the desertion took place the next day, when they went away by forces, loaded with such plunder as they had collected, and have continued to do so daily, till scarce one of those that joined us at Skenesborough is left."[1]

If Burgoyne was unable to obtain more efficient aid from the savages, he had only himself to blame ; for, if we may believe the testimony of their principal commandant, La Corne St. Luc, Burgoyne had fallen into the fatal errors of more than one of his predecessors, and had not acted in such a manner as to gain the confidence of the Indian tribes, who had come many hundreds of leagues to fight under the English flag.

We know that having won some easy triumphs, Burgoyne afterwards suffered many defeats, and was at length ignominiously beaten at Saratoga, October 7th, 1777, when he with his army was obliged to capitulate. On the 17th this disaster caused an immense sensation in England, and public opinion almost unanimously condemned the unfortunate general for the incapacity and improvidence he had shown. Burgoyne tried to justify his conduct by pamphlets, and by speeches in the House of Commons, where he had powerful friends. Desirous to throw the responsibility of his reverses upon others, he attacked with severity the conduct of the Canadians and

---

[1] *Anburey's Travels*, Lond. edition, 1791, I, p. 329–332.

Indians, complaining bitterly of their indifference or desertion, and involving their intrepid commander in the same blame.[1]

We have before us a speech pronounced by Burgoyne in the House of Commons on the 26th of May, 1778, in which he brings the most injurious accusations against the character of La Corne St. Luc. This latter officer passed a part of the preceding winter in London, and had not hesitated to declare that Burgoyne did not seem to him so superior a commander as had been believed; hence the resentment of the unfortunate general against this Canadian officer:

"Sir, a gentleman has been in London great part of the winter, who I wish had been called to your bar. It is for the sake of truth only I wish it; for he is certainly no friend of mine. His name is St. Luc le Corne, a distinguished partisan of the French in the last war, and now in the British service as a leader of the Indians. He owes us, indeed, some service, having been formerly instrumental in scalping many hundred British soldiers upon the very ground where, though with a different sort of latitude, he was this year employed. He is by nature, education, and practice, artful, ambitious and a courtier. To the grudge he owed me for controlling him in the use

---

[1] This general, says Garneau, wished to throw the blame upon the Canadians; but in his army of eight thousand men, there were but one hundred and fifty combatants from our province. Burgoyne complained also in unmeasured terms of the conduct of M. de Luc, commandant of the savages; but this officer easily repelled the attacks of a man who was a better talker than captain.

Appendix. 365

of the hatchet and scalping-knife, it was natural to his character to recommend himself to ministerial favor, by any censure in his power to cast upon an unfashionable general. He was often closeted by a noble lord in my eye (Lord George Germain); and with all these disadvantages, as he has not been examined here, I wish the noble lord to inform the House, what this man has presumed to say of my conduct with the Indians. I know, in private companies, his language has been, that the Indians might have done great services, but they were discharged. Sir, if to restrain them from murder was to discharge them, I take with pride the blame — they were discharged. That circumstance apart, I should say that the Indians and Mr. St. Luc at the head of them deserted."[1]

To this summons Lord Germain responded, that he had indeed had interviews with M. St. Luc, in which the latter had declared that General Burgoyne was a good officer with regular troops; but that he did not seem to like Indians, nor to have taken the measures necessary to retain their good will. In short, St. Luc had said to him,[2] " General Burgoyne is a brave man; but he is as heavy as a German."

When intelligence of the speech of Gen. Burgoyne reached de la Corne St. Luc, he replied to it by a very vigorous letter, dated at Quebec, October 23, 1778, which appeared in French, in the London papers. It

---

[1] *Parliamentary History of England*, vol. XIX, p. 1181.
[2] *Ibid.*, p. 1195.

produced an impression far from favorable to the cause of his accuser. In this letter, St. Luc says to General Burgoyne, that he has no right to treat him so indecorously; that his origin is as good as his own — his adversary was a natural son[1]— that his fifty years of service were ample demonstration that he had never shrank from the dangers of war, and that he had achieved a reputation long before he, Burgoyne, had had an opportunity to destroy one of the finest armies that had ever come into the country. He added, that if the Indians had little by little deserted the English army, it was because Burgoyne had not given them enough attention, nor taken sufficient care of them. In the affair at Bennington, August 16, 1777, when several hundred of the English were killed or taken prisoners, among whom were a good number of savages, the Indians were astonished to see, for instance, that Burgoyne sent no detachment to rally the stragglers of the vanquished body, or to succor the wounded, of whom many died.

"This conduct," says St. Luc, "did not give them a very high idea of the care that you would take of those who fought under your orders. The indifference which you manifested as to the fate of the Indians who took part in this (Bennington) expedition, to the number of a hundred and fifty, disgusted them to the last degree with the service; for a large number of savages had per-

---

[1] An error. General Burgoyne was born in lawful wedlock — and the gossip at the time was as cruel as it was unjust. For proof of this in full, see *Fonblanque's Life of Burgoyne.*— *W. L. S.*

Appendix. 367

ished on the battle-field with their redoubtable chief, and of sixty-one Canadians, forty-five only escaped death."[1]

In the council which was held after this unfortunate affair, St. Luc informed Burgoyne of the discontent of the savages, which very soon broke out in so open a manner, that they left the English camp altogether, because Burgoyne refused them provisions, shoes, and the services of an interpreter.

" Respecting the reason for having deserted the army," says St. Luc to Burgoyne, "you should recollect that it is you who were the cause of my departure; for, two days after the savages had left, you saw your error, and Brigadier General Fraser had already foreseen the consequences of your conduct in regard to the savages. You then sent for me to come to the brigadier's tent, and you asked me to return to Canada, bearing despatches to General Carleton praying his excellency to treat the Indians with kindness, and to send them back to you. This I did, and I should have joined the army, had not the communications been interrupted. * * * *

" Be that as it may, notwithstanding my advanced age, sixty-seven years, I am ready to cross the ocean to justify myself before the king, my master, and before my country, from the ill-founded accusation that you have brought

---

[1] Captain F. Montague, who took part in Burgoyne's campaign, declared, when questioned by a committee of the House of Commons, on the 1st of June, 1779, that many savages quitted the army at different times after the defeat at Bennington, which corroborates the assertion of St. Luc on this point. See *State of the Expedition from Canada*, p. 75.

against me, although I do not at all care what you personally think of me."

This letter, full of noble pride, received no reply that we know of, and Burgoyne contented himself with making a soothing allusion in a speech which he made before the House of Commons, the fourteenth of the following December.

While justifying himself thus completely, St. Luc at the same time revealed in its true light Langlade's conduct in this campaign; for, bound together by a close friendship, holding similar positions, they acted under the same inspiration, and had in view only the true interests of the cause for which they fought. If neither was well understood by General Burgoyne, his want of tact and justice towards them, were only too fully avenged at a later period.

No. XIII.

LETTER OF GENERAL EBENEZER MATTOON, A PARTICIPANT IN THE BATTLE, WITH NOTES BY THE AUTHOR.[1]

The following account of the battle at Satatoga is from the pen of E. Mattoon, Esq., of Amherst, Mass. He was an officer in the army, and took a very active part in that memorable contest "which tried men's souls." The description is given in lively colors, and contains some important facts which have never before

---

[1] For this valuable letter from the *Saratoga Sentinel* of November 10th, 1835, I am indebted to the courtesy of my friend Mr. Lyman C. Draper of Madison, Wis., who first directed my attention to it.

been published. It cannot fail to be read with deep interest.

AMHERST, MASS., *Oct.* 7, 1835.

PHILIP SCHUYLER, ESQ.

Sir: Yours of the 17th ult., requesting me to give you a detailed account of what I recollect of the battle at Saratoga, surrender of Gen. Burgoyne, etc., was duly received.

When I left home on a visit to my friend Frost, at Union Village, it was my intention to have visited the ground on which the army of Gen. Burgoyne was met and compelled to surrender. But the absence of Mr. Frost prevented. Had I known, however, that a descendant of that venerable patriot and distinguished commander, Gen. Schuyler, was living on the ground, I should have procured means to pay him my respects.

Gen. Gates, indeed, obtained the honor of capturing Burgoyne and his army; but let me tell you, sir, that it was more through the wise and prudent counsels of your brave and distinguished ancestor, and the energy and intrepidity of Generals Lincoln and Arnold, than through the ability and foresight of Gates.

In my narrative, I shall confine myself to what transpired from the 7th to the 17th day of October, 1777, both days included. This will necessarily lead me to correct the statement of Gen. Wilkinson and a Mr. Buel[1] in your neighborhood, respecting the fall of Gen. Fraser. By confounding the two accounts of the 19th

---

[1] For an account of Mr. Buel see Prof. Silliman's visit to the battle ground in the Appendix.

of September, and 7th of October, neither of them is correctly described.

The action of the 19th of September, commenced about ten o'clock, A.M., and continued during the day, each army alternately advancing and retiring. On that day, Col. Morgan posted a number of his riflemen to take off the officers as they appeared out of the woods; but no such posting of riflemen occurred on the 7th of October, Gen. Wilkinson to the contrary notwithstanding.

On the 7th of October the American army was posted, their right wing resting on the North river, and their left extending on to Bemis's heights, Generals Nixon and Glover commanding on the right; Lincoln, the centre, and Morgan and Larned the left.[1] The British army, with its left resting on the river, commanded by Phillips; their centre by Gen. Redhiesel,[2] and the extreme right

---

[1] "The position thus selected lay between the Hudson river on the east and Saratoga lake only six miles to the west; the high lands west of the river valley were cut by three deep ravines leading easterly, forming strong natural barriers against an approaching army; the whole country in this vicinity was a wilderness, and the high ground approaches so near the river there, that it was the most advantageous point in the whole valley to dispute the passage of the British army moving from the north. Such was the place selected by the experienced Polish patriot Koscuisko, and approved by Gen. Gates, as the Thermopylæ of the struggle for American freedom."— *General E. F. Bullard's Centennial Address at Schuylerville*, July 4, 1876.

[2] Ried-esel, pronounced Re-day-zel, with accent on second syllable. The Cockneys in the British army pronounced it Red-hazel — whence General Mattoon's spelling of it is doubtless derived.— *Author*.

extending to the heights, was commanded by Lord Balcarras[1] where he was strongly fortified. Their light troops were under the command of Gen. Fraser and Lord Auckland.[2]

About one o'clock of this day, two signal guns were fired on the left of the British army which indicated a movement. Our troops were immediately put under arms, and the lines manned. At this juncture Gens. Lincoln and Arnold rode with great speed towards the enemy's lines. While they were absent, the picket guards on both sides were engaged near the river. In about half an hour, Generals Lincoln and Arnold returned to headquarters, where many of the officers collected to hear the report, General Gates standing at the door.

Gen. Lincoln says, "Gen. Gates, the firing at the river is merely a feint; their object is your left. A strong force of 1500 men are marching circuitously, to plant themselves on yonder height. That point must be defended, or your camp is in danger." Gates replied, "I will send Morgan with his riflemen, and Dearborn's infantry."

Arnold says, "That is nothing; you must send a strong force." Gates replied, "Gen. Arnold, I have nothing for you to do; you have no business here." Arnold's reply was reproachful and severe.

---

[1] Balcarras, it may be remembered, was the officer who got into a serious altercation with Arnold in England — refusing to speak or recognize him.

[2] Ackland.

Gen. Lincoln says, "You must send a strong force to support Morgan and Dearborn, at least three regiments."

Two regiments from Gen. Larned's brigade, and one from Gen. Nixon's, were then ordered to that station, and to defend it, at all hazards. Generals Lincoln and Arnold immediately left the encampment, and proceeded to the enemy's lines.

In a few minutes, Capt. Furnival's company of artillery, in which I was lieutenant, was ordered to march towards the fire, which had now opened upon our picket in front, the picket consisting of about 300 men. While we were marching, the whole line, up to our picket or front, was engaged. We advanced to a height of ground which brought the enemy in view, and opened our fire. But the enemy's guns, eight in number, and much heavier than ours, rendered our position untenable.

We then advanced into the line of infantry. Here Lieutenant M'Lane joined me. In our front there was a field of corn, in which the Hessians were secreted. On our advancing towards the corn field, a number of men rose and fired upon us. M'Lane was severely wounded. While I was removing him from the field, the firing still continued without abatement.

During this time, a tremendous firing was heard on our left. We poured in upon them our canister shot, as fast as possible, and the whole line, from left to right, became engaged. The smoke was very dense, and no movements could be seen; but as it soon arose, our infantry appeared to be slowly retreating, and the Hessians slowly advancing, their officers urging them on with their hangers.

Just at this moment, an elderly man, with a long hunting gun, coming up, I said to him, "Daddy, the infantry mustn't leave, I shall be cut to pieces." He replied, "I'll give them another gun." The smoke then rising again, several officers, led by a general, appeared moving to the northward, in rear of the Hessian line. The old man, at that instant, discharged his gun, and the general officer pitched forward on the neck of his horse, and instantly they all wheeled about, the old man observing, "I have killed that officer, let him be who he will." I replied, "you have, and it is a general officer, and by his dress I believe it is Fraser." While they were turning about, three of their horses dropped down; but their further movements were then concealed by the smoke.

Here I will offer the reasons why I think this officer was Gen. Fraser, and that he was killed by the shot of this old man. In the first place, the distance, by actual measurement, was within reach of a gun. For the next morning, a dispute arising about the distance, some contending that it was eight rods, and others fifteen, two respectable sergeants, both of whom have since been generals in the militia of Massachusetts, Boardman and Lazell, were selected to decide the dispute, by pacing the ground. They did so, and found the distance from the stump where the old man stood to the spot where the horses fell, just twelve rods. In the next place, the officer was shot through the body from left to right as was afterwards ascertained. Now from his relative position to the posted riflemen, he could not have been shot through in this direction, but they must have hit him in front. Moreover the riflemen could not have seen him, on account of the smoke in which he was enveloped.[1]

The troops continuing warmly engaged, Col. Johnson's regiment coming up, threw in a heavy fire, and compelled the Hessians to retreat. Upon this we advanced with a shout of victory. At the same time Auckland's corps gave way.

We proceeded but a short distance before we came upon four pieces of brass cannon, closely surrounded with the dead and dying; at a few yards further we came upon two more. Advancing a little further, we were met by a fire from the British infantry, which proved very fatal to one of Col. Johnson's companies, in which were killed one sergeant, one corporal, fourteen privates — and about twenty were wounded.

They advanced with a quick step, firing as they came on. We returned them a brisk fire of canister shot, not allowing ourselves time even to sponge our pieces. In a short time they ceased firing, and advanced upon us with trailed arms. At this juncture Arnold came up with a part of Brooks's regiment, and gave them a most deadly fire, which soon caused them to face about and retreat with a quicker step than they advanced.

---

[1] Still, there seems no doubt that Murphy, by the orders of Morgan, shot Fraser; see Silliman's visit in the Appendix where he speaks of Morgan having told his friend, Hon. Richard Brent, to this effect.

Appendix. 375

The firing had now principally ceased on our left, but was brisk in front and on the right. At this moment, Arnold says to Col. Brooks (late governor of Massachusetts), "Let us attack Balcarras's works." Brooks replied, " No. Lord Auckland's detachment has retired there, we can't carry them." " Well, then, let us attack the Hessian lines." Brooks replies, " With all my heart." We all wheeled to the right, and advanced. No fire was received, except from the cannon, until we got within about eight rods, when we received a tremendous fire from the whole line. But a few of our men, however, fell. Still advancing, we received a second fire, in which a few men fell, and Gen. Arnold's horse fell under him, and he himself was wounded. He cried out, " Rush on, my brave boys." After receiving the third fire, Brooks mounted their works, swung his sword, and the men rushed into their works. When we entered the works, we found Col. Bremen dead, surrounded with a number of his companions, dead or wounded. We still pursued slowly ; the fire, in the mean time, decreasing. Nightfall now put an end to this day's bloody contest. During the day, we had taken eight cannon, and broken the centre of the enemy's lines.

We were ordered to rest until relieved from the camps. The gloom of the night, the groans and shrieks of the wounded and dying, and the horrors of the whole scene baffle all description

Under cover of this night (the 7th) the British army changed their position, so that it became necessary to reconnoitre on the ground.[1] While Gen. Lincoln was doing this, he was severely wounded, so that his active services were lost to the army during that campaign. A powerful rain commenced about 11 o'clock, which continued without abatement till the morning of the 9th. In this time, information came that Gen. Burgoyne had removed his troops to Saratoga. At 9 o'clock A.M., of October 8th, Captain Furnival received orders to march to the river, to cross the floating bridge, and repair to the fording place, opposite Saratoga, where we arrived at dusk. There we found Gen. Bailey of New Hampshire, with about 900 men, erecting a long range of fires, to indicate the presence of a large army. The British troops had covered the opposite heights with their fires.

In the early part of the evening Col. Moseley arrived with his regiment of Massachusetts militia, when our company was directed by Gen. Bailey to make a show of our field pieces at the river. We soon extinguished their lights. Then we were ordered to pass Battenkill river, and erect works there, during the night. In the morning we perceived a number of officers on the stairs, and on the east side of the house, on the hill, a little north

---

[1] During a retreat, a " Mr. Willard, residing near the foot of the mountain opposite the battle ground, by night would display signals from its top by different lights, in such manner as from time to time to give the Americans the location and movements of the British army. That mountain tain is plainly visible from Albany and Fort Edward. It has ever since been known by the name of " Willard's mountain " That is certainly one of the earliest systems of telegraphing known to have been put in practice.

of the Battenkill river, apparently surveying our situation and works.

My captain being sick at the time, I levelled our guns, and with such effect as to disperse them. We took the house to be their head-quarters.[1] We continued our fire till a nine or twelve pounder was brought to bear upon us, and rendered our works useless. Next we were ordered to repair, in haste, to Fort Edward, to defend the fording place. Col. Moseley's regiment accompanied us. Some slight works were thrown up by us; and while thus employed, a number of British officers appeared on the opposite side of the river. We endeavored to salute them according to their rank. They soon disappeared.

---

[1] This was the house, mentioned in the text, as the one in which Riedesel was stationed. Speaking of this house, Gen. Bullard, in his centennial address says: "At that time this house belonged to the Lansing family, of Albany and was probably occupied by them as a summer residence. It was deserted before the British army arrived from the north in September. It was a two story house, having a gable or French roof, fronting east with a hall in the middle and a room at each end. One of the old rafters and the plank of the partition, each shattered by a cannon ball, are still carefully preserved on the spot by Mrs. Marshall. She has kindly placed in my hands a gold piece, found by Samuel Marshall on those premises about fifty years ago, which is stamped, " Georgius III, *Dei Gratia*," with his profile on the one side, and on the other the British crown, 1776. This was evidently a coin lost by the officers in 1777." The house stands a short distance from the road on a gentle eminence, directly opposite the mouth of the Batten kil, and one mile north of the Fish kil. The room in which the wounded man lay, as narrated in the text, is the north east angle of the house; and the visiter can see on casting an eye across the river, that the cannon that did the mischief must have stood on a small eminence still visible on the eastern bank.

378 Campaign of General John Burgoyne.

During this day (the 10th) we captured fifty Indians, and a large number of Canadians and tories. We remained at Fort Edward till the morning of the 13th. Being then informed of the armistice which had been agreed upon, we were ordered to return to our position upon the Battenkill and repair our works. Here we remained till the morning of the 17th, when we received orders to repair to Gen. Gates's head quarters on the west side of the river.

THE BATTEN KIL.

As we passed along we saw the British army piling (not stacking) their arms; the piles of arms extending from Schuyler's creek northward nearly to the house on the hill before mentioned. The range of piles ran along the ground west of the road then traveled, and east of the canal as, I am informed, it now runs.

Just below the island we passed the river, and came to Gen. Gates's marquee, situated on a level piece of ground, from 130 to 150 rods south of Schuyler's creek. A little south and west of this there is a rising ground, on which our army was posted, in order to appear to the best advantage. A part of it was also advantageously drawn upon the east side of the river. About noon on the 17th, Gen. Burgoyne, with a number of his officers, rode up near to the marquee, in front of which Gen. Gates was sitting, attended with many of his officers. The sides of the marquee were rolled up, so that all that was transacted might be seen. Gen. Burgoyne dismounted and approached Gen. Gates, who rose and stepped forward to meet him. Gen. Burgoyne then delivered up his sword to Gen. Gates, who received it in his left hand, at the same time extending his right hand to take the right hand of Gen. Burgoyne.

After a few minutes conversation, Gen. Gates returned the sword to Gen. Burgoyne, who received it in the most graceful and gentlemanly manner. The rest of Burgoyne's officers then delivered up their swords, and had them restored to them likewise. They then all repaired to the table and were seated; and while dining, the prisoners were passing by.[1]

---

[1] Our favorite Yankee Doodle was also here first adopted as the hymn of freedom. Although some four verses of it were composed by a British surgeon about twenty years earlier at East Albany to ridicule the Connecticut brigade which then appeared under Col. Thomas Fitch, we do not find that it was ever adopted by our side earlier than October, 1777. After the British army had stacked their arms in Fort Hardy, October 17, they crossed

After they had all passed by, a number of us went in search of a gun which was upon a carriage the day previous to the 17th, near what was called the Hessian burying ground. But the tracks of the carriage were so confused, and the stench from the dead bodies was so offensive, that the search was discontinued.

Thus I have replied to your inquiries, as far as my recollection extends. I should be very happy to meet you, and spend a day or two in walking over the battle ground, and entering into other particulars concerning that engagement, which however, are of minor importance.

    With much esteem,
     I am, dear sir, yours,
       E. MATTOON.[1]

Fish creek and passed south through the long lines of the American army. As our victorious host did not feel like insulting a fallen foe it was suggested that a lively tune be played for their consolation, and by common consent, the melodious Yankee Doodle was given by the whole American lines, while the rank and file of the British were passing between them. Unless some other locality shall prove an older title, you can justly claim that our famous Yankee Doodle was first sung in this valley, as the national tune of free America. The 4th Connecticut regiment did gallant service in the Revolutionary war at White Plains, Trenton and Saratoga, and Andrew Fitch, a son of Col. Thomas Fitch, was a lieut. col. in that regiment and probably had the pleasure of hearing that tune under different circumstances, from those under which his father heard it in derision twenty years earlier.

[1] Ebenezer Mattoon was born at Amherst, Mass., Aug. 19, 1755, and died there Sept. 17, 1843. The son of a farmer, he graduated at Dartmouth College in 1776, and then joined the artillery company at the battle of Saratoga, and left the service with the rank of major. He was a delegate from Amherst to the conventions; and was several times a member of the legislature. From 1797 to 1816 major general 4th division; ad-

Letter from the Duc de la Rochefoucauld-Liancourt, who visited the Surrender Ground in 1795.

"In 1795, the then Duc de La Rochefoucauld-Liancourt visited the famous battle fields of Saratoga, and in his published account of his travels in the new world upon his return gives a graphic account of the scenes of Burgoyne's surrender.

"I have seen," says the Duc, "John Schuyler, the eldest son of the general. For a few minutes I had already conversed with him at Schenectady, and was now with him at Saratoga. The journey to this place was extremely painful, on account of the scorching heat; but Saratoga is a township of too great importance to be passed by unobserved. If you love the English, are fond of conversing with them, and live with them on terms of familiarity and friendship, it is no bad thing if occasionally you can say to them, '*I have seen Saratoga.*'

"Yes, I have seen this truly *memorable* place, which may be considered as the spot where the independence of America was sealed; for the events which induced Great Britain to acknowledge that independence were obviously consequences of the capture of General Bur-

---

jutant general of the state 1816; state senator 1795-6; 20 years sheriff of Hampshire; M. C. 1801-3; and in 1820, although blind, was a member of the state constitutional convention. He commanded the A. & H. artillery company in 1817. Gen. Mattoon was a scientific farmer.— *Drake's Biographical Dictionary.*

goyne, and would, in all probability, never have happened without it. The dwelling-house of John Schuyler stands exactly on the spot where this important occurrence took place.[1] Fish creek, which flows close to the house, formed the line of defence of the camp of the English general, which was formed on an eminence a quarter of a mile from the dwelling. The English camp was also entirely surrounded with a mound of earth to strengthen its defence. In the rear of the camp the German troops were posted by divisions on a commanding height communicating with the eminence on which General Burgoyne was encamped. The right wing of the German corps had a communication with the left wing of the English, and the left extended towards the river. General Gates was encamped on the other side of the creek at the distance of an eighth of a mile from General Burgoyne, his right wing stretched towards the plain; but he endeavored to shelter his troops as much as possible from the enemy's fire until he resolved to form the attack. General Nelson, at the head of the American militia, occupied the heights on the other side of the river, and engaged the attention of the left wing of the English while other American troops observed the movements of the right wing. In this position Gen. Burgoyne surrendered his army. His provisions were nearly consumed, but he was amply supplied with artillery and ammunition. The spot remains exactly as it then was, excepting the sole circumstance that the bushes

---

[1] This is of course, an error.—*Author.*

Appendix. 383

which were cut down in front of the two armies are since grown up again. Not the least alteration has taken place since that time. The entrenchments still exist ; nay, the footpath is still seen on which the adjutant of Gen. Gates proceeded to the English general with the ultimatum of the American commander ; the spot on which the council of war was held by the English officers, remains unaltered. You see the way by which the English column, after it had been joined by the Germans, filed off by the left to lay down their arms within an ancient fort which was constructed in the war under the reign of Queen Anne ; you see the place where the unfortunate army was necessitated to ford the creek in order to reach the road to Albany, and to march along the front of the American army. You see the spot where Gen. Burgoyne surrendered up his sword to Gen. Gates ; when the man, who two months before had threatened all the rebels, their parents, their wives and their children with pillage, sacking, firing and scalping, if they did not join the English banner, was compelled to bend British pride under the yoke of these rebels, and when he underwent the two fold humiliation as a ministerial agent of the English government to submit to the dictates of revolted subjects and a commanding general of disciplined regular troops, to surrender up his army to a multitude of half-armed and half-clothed peasants. To sustain so severe a misfortune and not to die with despair exceeds not, it seems therefore, the strength of man. This memorable spot lies in a corner of the court yard of John Schuyler ; he was then a youth twelve years old, and placed on an eminence at the foot of which stood Gen. Gates, and near which the American army was drawn up to see their disarmed enemies pass by. His estate includes all the tract of ground on which both armies were encamped and he knows as it were their every step. How happy must an American feel in the possession of such property if his bosom be anywise susceptible of warm feelings! It is a matter of astonishment that neither congress nor the legislature of New York should have erected a monument on this spot reciting in plain terms this glorious event and thus calling it to the recollection of all men who should pass this way to keep alive the sentiments of intrepidity and courage and the sense of glory which for the benefit of America should be handed down among Americans from generation to generation."

No. XIV.

Professor Silliman's Visit to the Battle Ground in 1820.

The following account of the visit of Professor Silliman to the battle ground — although he was not a participant in the battle — has value, from the fact that his relation is derived mainly from his guide, Major Buel, who was in the conflict. In the course of his narrative — to avoid repetition — wherever he has quoted from Wilkinson or Mrs. Reidesel, passages which are familiar to the readers of the text, I have placed stars. — *W. L. S.*

House in which Gen. Fraser Died.

Ten o'clock at night.

We are now on memorable ground. Here much precious blood was shed, and now, in the silence and solitude of a very dark and rainy night — the family asleep, and nothing heard but the rain and the Hudson, gently murmuring along, I am writing in the very house, and my table stands, on the very spot in the room, where General Fraser breathed his last, on the 8th of October, 1777.

He was mortally wounded in the last of the two desperate battles fought on the neighboring heights, and in the midst of the conflict, was brought to this house by the soldiers. Before me lies one of the bullets, shot on that occasion; they are often found, in ploughing the battle field.

Blood is asserted, by the people of the house, to have been visible here, on the floor, till a very recent period.

General Fraser was high in command, in the British army, and was almost idolized by them; they had the utmost confidence in his skill and valor, and that the Americans entertained a similar opinion of him, is sufficiently evinced by the following anecdote, related to me at Ballston Springs, in 1797, by the Hon. Richard Brent, then a member of congress, from Virginia, who derived the fact from General Morgan's own mouth.

In the battle of October the seventh, the last pitched battle, that was fought between the two armies, General Fraser, mounted on an iron gray horse, was very conspicuous. He was all activity, courage, and vigilance, riding from one part of his division to another, and animating the troops by his example. Wherever he was present, every thing prospered, and, when confusion appeared in any part of the line, order and energy were restored by his arrival.

Colonel Morgan, with his Virginia riflemen, was immediately opposed to Fraser's division of the army.

It had been concerted, before the commencement of the battle, that while the New Hampshire and the New York troops attacked the British left, Colonel Morgan, with his regiment of Virginia riflemen, should make a circuit so as to come upon the British right, and attack them there. In this attempt, he was favored by a woody hill, to the foot of which the British right extended. When the attack commenced on the British left, "true to his purpose, Morgan at this critical moment, poured down like a torrent from the hill, and attacked the right of the enemy in front and flank." The right wing soon made a movement to support the left, which was assailed with increased violence, and while executing this movement, General Fraser received his mortal wound.

In the midst of this sanguinary battle, Colonel Morgan took a few of his best riflemen aside; men in whose fidelity, and fatal precision of aim, he could repose the most perfect confidence, and said to them: "That gallant officer is General Fraser; I admire and respect him, *but it is necessary that he should die* — take your stations in that wood and do your duty." Within a few moments General Fraser fell, mortally wounded.

How far, such personal designation is justifiable, has often been questioned, but those who vindicate war at all, contend, that to shoot a distinguished officer, and thus to accelerate the conclusion of a bloody battle, operates to save lives, and that it is, *morally*, no worse, to kill an illustrious, than an obscure individual; a Fraser, than a common soldier; a Nelson, than a common sailor. But, there is something very revolting to humane feelings, in a mode of warfare, which converts its ordinary chances into a species of military execution. Such instances, were, however, frequent, during the campaign of General Burgoyne; and his aid-de-camp, Sir Francis Clark, and many other British officers, were victims of American marksmanship.

*   *   *   *

Retiring at a late hour to my bed, it will be easily perceived, that the tender and heroic ideas, associated with this memorable house, would strongly possess my mind. The night was mantled in black clouds, and impenetrable darkness; the rain, increasing, descended in torents, upon the roof of this humble mansion; the water, urged from the heights, poured with loud and incessant rumbling, through a neighboring aqueduct; and the Hudson, as if conscious that blood had once stained its waters, and its banks, rolled along with sullen murmurs; the distinguished persons, who forty-two years since, occupied this tenement — the agonized females — the terrified, imploring children — and the gallant chiefs, in all the grandeur of heroic suffering and death, were vividly present to my mind — all the realities of the night, and the sublime and tender images of the past, conspired to give my faculties too much activity for sleep, and I will not deny that the dawning light was grateful to my eyes!

The Battle Ground.

The rain having ceased, I was on horseback at early dawn with a veteran guide to conduct me to the battle ground. Although he was seventy-five years old, he did not detain me a moment; in consequence of an appointment the evening before, he was waiting my arrival at his house, a mile below our inn, and, declining any aid, he mounted a tall horse from the ground. His name was Ezra Buel,[1] a native of Lebanon, in Connecticut, which place he left in his youth, and was settled here, at the time of General Burgoyne's invasion. He acted, through the whole time, as a guide to the American army, and was one of three who were constantly employed in that service. His duty led him to be always foremost, and in the post of danger; and he was, therefore, admirably qualified for my purpose.

The two great battles which decided the fate of Burgoyne's army, were fought, the first on the 19th of

---

[1] Called *colloquially*, in the neighborhood, *Major Buel*, a rank which he never had in the army, but which was *facetiously* assigned him, while in the service, by his brother guides. He is much respected as a worthy man — 1820.

Major Buel, I believe, still lives. I saw him at Ballston Springs, in July, 1823, still active and useful, although almost fourscore; he was then acting as crier of a state court at that time in session at Ballston.— March, 1824.

Appendix. 389

September, and the last, on the 7th of October, on Bemis's heights, and very nearly on the same ground, which is about two miles west of the river.

The river, is in this region, bordered for many miles, by a continued meadow, of no great breadth; upon this meadow, there was then, as there is now, a good road, close to the river, and parallel to it. Upon this road, marched the heavy artillery and baggage, constituting the left wing of the British army, while the elite, forming the right wing, and composed of light troops, was kept constantly in advance, on the heights which bound the meadows.

The American army was south and west of the British, its right wing on the river, and its left resting on the heights. We passed over a part of their camp a little below Stillwater.[1]

A great part of the battle ground was occupied by lofty forest trees, principally pine, with here and there, a few cleared fields, of which the most conspicuous in these sanguinary scenes, was called Freeman's farm, and is so-called in General Burgoyne's plans. Such is

---

[1] In May, 1821, I again visited these battle grounds, and availed myself of that oppertunity, in company with my faithful old guide, Major Buel, to explore the camp of General Gates. It is situated about three miles below Smith's tavern, (the house where General Fraser died), and is easily approached by a cross road, which turns up the heights from the great river road. It is not more than half a mile from the river to the camp. I found it an interesting place, and would recommend it to travelers to visit this spot, as they will thus obtain a perfectly clear idea of the relative position of the hostile armies, and of the route pursued by the Americans when they marched out to battle. The outlines of the camp

nearly the present situation of these heights, only there is more cleared land ; the *gigantic* trees have been principally felled, but a considerable number remain as witnesses to posterity ; they still show the wounds, made in their trunks and branches, by the missiles of contending armies ; their roots still penetrate the soil, that was made fruitful by the blood of the brave, and their

are still distinctly visible, being marked by the lines of defence, which were thrown up on the occasion, and which, although depressed by time, will long be conspicuous, if they are not levelled by the plough. My guide pointed out the ground occupied by the different corps of the army. Col. Morgan, with the Virginia riflemen, was in advance, on the right, that is, nearest the river ; *the advance*, was the post always coveted by this incomparable corps, and surely none could claim it with more propriety. There was much danger that the enemy would attempt to storm the camp of the Americans, and had they been successful in either of the great battles (Sept. 19, and Oct. 7), they would, without doubt, have attacked the camp.

The most interesting object that I saw in this camp, was the house which was Gen. Gates's head quarters. I am afraid that the traveler may not long find this memorable house, for it was much dilapidated — a part of the roof had fallen in, and the winds whistled through the naked timbers. One room was, however, tenantable, and was occupied by a cooper and his family. From the style of the pannel work and finishing of this room, the house appears to have been, in its day, one of the better sort — the pannels were large and handsome, and the door was still ornamented with brass handles. Here Sir Francis Clark, aid-de-camp to Gen. Burgoyne, being mortally wounded and taken prisoner, languished and died. Gen. Wilkinson has recorded some interesting passages of his last moments, particularly his animated discussions with Gen. Gates on the merits of the contest. The recollection of the fate of this brave but unfortunate officer will always be associated with this building, while a single timber of it remains.

sombre foliage still murmurs with the breeze, which once sighed, as it bore the departing spirit along.[1]

My veteran guide, warmed by my curiosity, and recalling the feelings of his prime, led me, with amazing rapidity, and promptitude, over fences and ditches — through water and mire — through ravines and defiles — through thick forests, and open fields — and up and down very steep hills; in short, through many places, where, alone, I would not have ventured; but, it would have been shameful for me not to follow where a man of seventy-five would lead, and to hesitate to explore *in peace*, the ground, which the defenders of their country, and their foes, once trod in steps of blood.

On our way to Freeman's farm, we traced the line of the British encampment, still marked by a breast work of logs, now rotten, but retaining their forms; they were, at the time, covered with earth, and the bar-

---

My guide conducted me from the American camp along the summit of the heights, by the same route, which was pursued by our gallant countrymen, when they advanced to meet their formidable foe, and I had the satisfaction of treading the same ground which they trod, in the silence and solemnity of impending conflict.

In pursuing this route, the traveler, if accompanied by an intelligent guide, will have a very interesting opportunity of marking the exact places where the advanced guards and front lines of the contending armies met. In this manner we advanced quite to Freeman's farm, the great scene of slaughter, and thence descended again to the centre of the British encampment on the plains.

[1] There is a barn now standing near Freeman's farm, one of the beams of which contains a six-pound ball. It was imbedded in the tree out of which the timber was cut; and the builder considerately left the ball in as a memento.— *W. L. S.*

rier between contending armies, is now a fence, to mark the peaceful divisions of agriculture. This breast work, I suppose to be a part of the line of encampment, occupied by General Burgoyne, after the battle of the 19th of September, and which was stormed on the evening of the 7th of October.

The old man showed me the exact spot, where an accidental skirmish, between advanced parties of the two armies, soon brought on the general and bloody battle of September 19.

This was on Freeman's farm, a field which was then cleared, although surrounded by forest. The British picket here occupied a small house,[1] when a part of Col. Morgan's corps fell in with, and immediately drove them from it, leaving the house almost "encircled with their dead." The pursuing party, immediately, and very unexpectedly, fell in with the British line, and were in part captured, and the rest dispersed.

This incident occurred at half-past twelve o'clock;[2] there was an intermission till one, when the action was sharply renewed; but it did not become general, till three, from which time it raged with unabated fury, till night.

*   *   *   *

General Burgoyne states that there was scarcely ever an interval of a minute in the smoke, when some British

---

[1] Major Forbes, of the British army, states, that the American picket occupied the house; both facts might have been true at different periods of the affair.

[2] An evident error, see text.— *W. L. S.*

officer was not shot by the American riflemen, posted in the trees, in the rear and on the flank of their own line. A shot which was meant for General Burgoyne, severely wounded Captain Green, an aid-de-camp of General Phillips: the mistake was owing to the captain's having a richly laced furniture to his saddle, which caused the marksman to mistake him for the general.

Such was the ardor of the Americans, that, as General Wilkinson states, the wounded men, after having their wounds dressed, in many instances, returned again into the battle.

The battle of the seventh of October was fought on the same ground, but was not so stationary; it commenced farther to the right, and extended, in its various periods, over more surface, eventually occupying not. only Freeman's farm, but it was urged by the Americans, to the very camp of the enemy, which, towards night, was most impetuously stormed, and in part carried.

The interval between the nineteenth of September, and the seventh of October, was one of great anxiety to both armies; " not a night passed," says General Burgoyne, " without firing, and sometimes concerted attacks upon our pickets; no foraging party could be made without great detachments to cover it; it was the plan of the enemy to harass the army, by constant alarms, and their superiority of numbers enabled them to attempt it, without fatigue to themselves. By being habituated to fire, our soldiers became indifferent to it, and were capable of eating or sleeping when it was very near them ; but I do not believe either officer or soldier ever slept during that interval, without his clothes, or that any general officer, or commander of a regiment, passed a single night, without being upon his legs, occasionally, at different hours, and constantly, an hour before day light."

The battle of the seventh was brought on by a movement of General Burgoyne, who caused one thousand five hundred men, with ten pieces of artillery, to march towards the left of the American army for the purpose of discovering whether it was possible to force a passage; or in case a retreat of the royal army should become indispensable, to dislodge the Americans from their intrenchments, and also to cover a foraging excursion, which had now become pressingly necessary.[1] It was about the middle of the afternoon, that the British were observed advancing, and the Americans, with small arms, lost no time in attacking the British grenadiers and artillery, although under a tremendous fire from the latter; the battle soon extended along the whole line: Colonel Morgan, at the same moment, attacked, with his riflemen, on the right wing; Colonel Ackland, the commander of the grenadiers, fell, wounded; the grenadiers were defeated, and most of the artillery taken, after great slaughter.

---

[1] Also an error. "The foraging party," says Gen. Riedesel, "was made the day previous to the battle of the 7th." The gathering of forage while the army were forming for battle was merely an incident. Hence the confusion which has arisen on this subject.— *W. L. S.*

At the end of a most sanguinary contest, of less than one hour, the discomfiture and retreat of the British became general, and they had scarcely regained their camp, before the lines were stormed with the greatest fury, and part of Lord Balcarras's camp, was for a short time in our possession.

* * * *

I was on the ground where the grenadiers, and where the artillery were stationed. "Here, upon this hill" (said my hoary guide), " on the very spot where we now stand, the dead men lay, thicker than you ever saw sheaves on a fruitful harvest field." " Were they British, or Americans?" " Both," he replied, " but principally British." I suppose that it is of this ground, that General Wilkinson remarks, "it presented a scene of complicated horror and exultation. In the square space of twelve or fifteen yards, lay eighteen grenadiers in the agony of death; and three officers, propped up against stumps of trees, two of them mortally wounded, bleeding, and almost speechless."

My guide, proceeding with his narrative, said: "There stood a British field piece, which had been twice taken, and retaken, and finally remained in our possession: I was on the ground; and said to an American colonel, who came up at the moment, ' Colonel, we have taken this piece, and now we want you to *swear it true to America ;*' so the colonel swore it true, and we turned it around, and fired upon the British, with their own cannon, and with their own ammunition, still remaining unconsumed in their own boxes."

I was solicitous to see the exact spot where General Fraser received his mortal wound. My old guide knew it perfectly well, and pointed it out to me. It is in a meadow, just on the right of the road, after passing a blacksmith's shop, and going south a few rods. The blacksmith's shop, is on a road, which runs parallel to the Hudson — it stands elevated, and overlooks Freeman's farm.

I saw various places, where the dead were interred; a rivulet, or creek, passes through the battle ground, and still washes out from its banks, the bones of the slain. This rivulet is often mentioned in the accounts of these battles, and the deep ravine through which it passes; on our return, we followed this ravine, and rivulet, through the greater part of their course, till they united with the Hudson.

Farm houses are dispersed, here and there, over the field of battle, and the people often find, even now, gun-barrels and bayonets, cannon balls, grape shot, bullets, and human bones. Of the three last, I took from one of these people, some painful specimens; — some of the bullets were battered and misshaped, evincing that they had come into collision with opposing obstacles.

Entire skeletons are occasionally found; a man told me, that in ploughing, during the late summer, he turned one up; and it was not covered more than three inches with earth; it lay on its side, and the arms were in the form of a bow; it was, probably, some solitary victim, that never was buried. Such are the memorials still existing, of these great military events; great,

Appendix. 397

not so much on account of the numbers of the actors, as from the momentous interests at stake, and from the magnanimous efforts to which they gave origin.

I would not envy that man his state of feeling, who could visit such fields of battle without emotion, or who (being an American), could fail to indulge admiration and affection, for the soldiers and martyrs of liberty, and respect for the valor of their enemies.

General Fraser's Grave.

Having taken my guide home to breakfast, we made use of his knowledge of the country, to identify with certainty, the place of General Fraser's interment.

General Burgoyne mentions two redoubts, that were

THE ENGLISH ENCAMPMENT THE DAY AFTER THE BATTLE OF
THE 7TH FROM THE DRAWING MADE BY SIR FRANCIS CLERKE.

thrown up, on the hills behind his hospital; they are both still very distinct, and in one of these, which is called the Great redoubt, by the officers of General Burgoyne's army, General Fraser was buried. It is true, it has been disputed, which is the redoubt in question, but our guide stated to us, that within his knowledge, a British sergeant, three or four years after the surrender of Burgoyne's army, came, and pointed out the grave. We went to the spot; it is within the redoubt, on the top of the hill, nearest to the house, where the general died, and corresponds with the plate in *Anbury's Travels*, taken from an original drawing, made by Sir Francis Clarke, aid-de-camp to General Burgoyne, and with the statement of the general in his defence, as well as with the account of Madam Reidesel.

The place of the interment, was formerly designated, by a little fence, surrounding the grave. I was here in 1797, twenty-two years ago; the grave was then distinctly visible.

*   *   *   *

On the present occasion, I did not visit the British fortified camp.[1] When I was here in 1797, I examined

---

[1] In May, 1821, I again visited this fortified camp, and found it as perfect as it was when I saw it nearly twenty-three years before, and almost every particular stated in the text was strictly applicable to it. It is about a mile from the river, and was certainly chosen with great good judgment, and had the American army attempted to take it by storm, it would evidently have cost them very dear. While at Ballston Springs during the late summer, some gentlemen of our party made an excursion to this place, and I learned from them, with extreme regret, that the plow was passing over the fortified camp of General Burgoyne, and that its fine parapet would soon be levelled, so that scarcely a trace of it would remain.

Appendix. 399

it particularly. It was then in perfect preservation (I speak of the encampment of the *British* troops, upon the hill, near the ·Fish kil), the parapet was high, and covered with grass and shrubs, and the platforms of earth, to support the field pieces, were still in good condition. No devastation, of any consequence, had been committed, except by the credulous, who had made numerous excavations in the breast works, and various parts of the encampment, for the purpose of discovering the money, which the officers were supposed to have buried, and abandoned. It is scarcely necessary to add, that they never found any money, for private property was made sacred by the convention, and even the public military chest was not disturbed: the British retained every shilling that it contained. Under such circumstances, to have buried their money, would have been almost as great a folly, as the subsequent search for it. This infatuation, has not, however, gone by, even to this hour, and still, every year, new pits are excavated by the insatiable money diggers.[1]

---

[1] This appears to be a very common popular delusion; in many places on the Hudson, and about the lakes, where armies had lain, or moved, we found money pits dug; and in one place, they told us, that a man bought of a poor widow, the right of digging in her ground for the hidden treasure.

Were Professor Silliman alive now (1877), he would find a stock company organized and in active operation for the purpose of digging on the lower Hudson for the treasures of Captain Kidd.— *W. L. S.*

The Field of Surrender.

We arrived at this interesting spot, in a very fine morning; the sun shone with great splendor, upon the flowing Hudson, and upon the beautiful heights, and the luxuriant meadows, now smiling in rich verdure, and exhibiting images of tranquility and loveliness, very opposite to the horrors of war, which were once witnessed here.

THE FISH KIL, NOW FISH CREEK.

The Fish kil, swollen by abundant rains (as it was on the morning of October 10th, 1777, when General Burgoyne passed it with his artillery), now poured a turbid torrent along its narrow channel, and roaring down the declivity of the hills, hastened to mingle its waters with those of the Hudson.

*   *   *   *

Appendix. 401

We passed the ruins of General Schuyler's house, which are still conspicuous, and hastened to the field where the British troops grounded their arms. Although, in 1797, I paced it over in juvenile enthusiasm,[1] I felt scarcely less interested on the present occasion, and again walked over the whole tract. It is a beautiful meadow, situated at the intersection of the Fish kil, with the Hudson, and north of the former. There is nothing now to distinguish the spot, except the ruins of old Fort Hardy, built during the French wars, and the deeply interesting historical associations which will cause this place to be memorable to the latest generation. Thousands and thousands yet unborn, will visit Saratoga, with feelings of the deepest interest, and it will not be forgotten till Thermopylæ, and Marathon, and Bannockburn and Waterloo, shall cease to be remembered. There it will be said, were the last entrenchments of a proud invading army; on that spot stood their formidable park of artillery — and here, on this now peaceful meadow, they piled their arms! their arms no longer terrible, but now converted into a glorious trophy of victory!

Reflections and Remarks.

I have adverted but little to the sufferings of the American army, because but little, comparatively, is known of what they individually endured. Excepting

---

[1] In company with the Hon. John Elliott, now a senator from Georgia, and John Wynn, Esq., from the same state.

the inevitable casualties of battle, they must have suffered much less than their enemies; for they soon ceased to be the flying, and became the attacking and triumphant party. Colonels Colburn, Adams, Francis, and many other brave officers and men, gave up their lives, as the price of their country's liberty, and very many carried away with them the scars produced by honorable wounds. The bravery of the American army was fully acknowledged by their adversaries.

"At all times," said Lord Balcarras, "when I was opposed to the rebels, they fought with great courage and obstinacy. We were taught by experience, that neither their attacks nor resistance was to be despised." Speaking of the retreat of the Americans, from Ticonderoga, and of their behavior at the battle of Hubberton, Lord Balcarras adds: "Circumstanced as the enemy were, as an army very hard pressed, in their retreat, they certainly behaved with great gallantry;" of the attack on the lines, on the evening of the 7th of October, he says: "The lines were attacked, and with as much fury, as the fire of small arms can admit."

Lord Balcarras had said, that he never knew the Americans to defend their entrenchments, but added: "The reason why they did not defend their entrenchments was, that they always marched out of them and attacked us." Captain Money, in answer to the question, whether on the 19th of September, the Americans disputed the field with obstinacy, answered, "They did, and the fire was much hotter than I ever knew it any where, except at the affair of Fort Anne;" and speaking of the battle of October 7th, and of the moment when the Americans, with nothing but small arms, were marching up to the British artillery, he adds: "I was very much astonished, to hear the shot from the enemy, fly so thick, after our cannonade had lasted a quarter of an hour." General Burgoyne gives it as his opinion, that as rangers, " perhaps there are few better in the world, than the corps of Virginia riflemen which acted under Colonel Morgan." He says, speaking of the battle of September 19th, that, " few actions have been characterized by more obstinacy, in attack or defence. The British bayonet was repeatedly tried ineffectually."

Remarking upon the battle of the 7th of October, he observes: " If there be any persons who continue to doubt that the Americans possess the *quality* and *faculty* of fighting, call it by whatever term they please, they are of a prejudice, that it would be very absurd longer to contend with ;" he says, that in this action the British troops " retreated hard pressed, but in good order," and that " the troops had scarcely entered the camp, when it was stormed with great fury, the enemy rushing to the lines, under a severe fire of grape shot and small arms."

In a private letter, addressed to Lord George Germain, after the surrender, he says: " I should now hold myself unjustifiable, if I did not confide to your lordship, my opinion, upon a near inspection of the rebel troops. The standing corps that I have seen, are disciplined. I do not hazard the term, but apply it to the great fundamental points of military institution, sobriety, subordination, regularity, and courage."

It is very gratifying to every real American to find, that for so great a prize, his countrymen (their enemies themselves being judges), contended so nobly, and that their conduct for bravery, skill and humanity, will stand the scrutiny of all future ages.

From the enemy it becomes us not to withhold the commendation that is justly due; all that skill and valor could effect, they accomplished, and they were overwhelmed at last by complicated distresses, and by very superior numbers, amounting at the time of the surrender, probably, to three for one, although the disparity was much less, in the two great battles.

The vaunting proclamation of General Burgoyne, at the commencement of the campaign; some of his boasting letters, written during the progress of it, and his devastation of private property, reflect no honor on his memory. But, in general, he appears to have been a humane and honorable man, a scholar and a gentleman, a brave soldier and an able commander. Some of his sentiments have a higher moral tone than is common with men of his profession, and have probably procured for him more respect, than all his battles. Speaking of the battle of the 7th, he says: "In the course of the action, a shot had passed through my hat, and another had torn my waistcoat. I should be sorry to be thought, at any time, insensible to the protecting hand of Providence; but I ever, more particularly considered (and I hope not superstitiously) a soldier's hair breadth escapes as incentives to duty, *a marked renewal of the trust of being*, for the purposes of a public station; and under that reflection, to lose our fortitude, by giving way to our affections; to be divested by any possible self-emotion from meeting a present exigency, with our best faculties, were at once dishonor and impiety."

Thus have I adverted, I hope not with too much particularity, to some of the leading circumstances of the greatest military event which has ever occurred in America; but compared with the whole extent and diversity of that campaign, the above notices, however extended, are few and brief. I confess, I have reviewed them with a very deep interest, and have been willing to hear some of the distinguished actors speak in their own language. Should the notice of these great events tend, in any instance, to quench the odious fires of party, and to rekindle those of genuine patriotism — should it revive in any one, a veneration for the virtues of those men who faced death, in every form, regardless of their own lives, and bent only on securing to posterity, the precious blessings, which we now enjoy; and above all, should we thus be led to cherish a higher sense of gratitude to Heaven, for our unexampled privileges, and to use them more temperately and wisely, the time occupied in this sketch, will not have been spent in vain. History presents no struggle for liberty which has in it more of the moral sublime than that of the American Revolution. It has been, of late years, too much forgotten, in the sharp contentions of party, and he who endeavors to withdraw the public mind from those debasing conflicts, and to fix it on the grandeur of that great epoch — which, magnificent in itself, begins now, *to wear the solemn livery of antiquity, as it is viewed through the deepening twilight of half a century*, certainly performs a meritorious service, and can scarcely need a justification. The generation that sustained the conflict, is now almost passed away; a few hoary heads remain, seamed with honorable scars — a few *experienced* guides can still attend us to the fields of carnage, and point out the places where they and their companions fought and bled, and where sleep the bones of the slain. But these men will soon be gone; tradition and history, will, however, continue to recite their deeds, and the latest generations will be taught to venerate the defenders of our liberties — to visit the battle-grounds, which were moistened with their blood, and to thank the mighty God of battles, that the arduous conflict terminated in the entire establishment of the liberties of this country.

No. XV.

Sergeant Lamb's Account of his Journey through the Woods from Fort Miller to Ticonderoga, to expedite Supplies for Burgoyne's Army.[1]

During our continuance at Fort Miller, the writer of this memoir was selected by his officers to return alone to Ticonderoga, for the purpose of taking back some of our baggage which had been left there. Going unac-

---

[1] From a *Memoir of His own Life*, by R. Lamb, formerly a sergeant in the Royal Welsh Fusileers, author of a *Journal of Occurrences during the late American War*, Dublin, 1811. For the opportunity of copying from this rare work, the author is indebted to the unfailing courtesy of Mr. Lyman C. Draper, of Madison, Wisconsin.

Appendix. 407

companied on such a solitary route was dreary and dangerous; but yet the selection of one from numbers, seemed to render the man chosen on the occasion, a depositary of peculiar confidence. He therefore undertook the duty imposed, not only without repining, but with alacrity. A small detachment if sent, could not pass unnoticed or safe by such a route through the woods, a distance of twenty miles;[1] and a sufficient force could not be spared on the occasion. The sending of a single soldier appeared therefore the most advisable plan; and it was ordered by General Burgoyne, that he should, after arriving at Ticonderoga, follow the royal army with the baggage escorted by the recruits, and as many of the convalescents remaining at that post as could march with it. Pursuant to this arrangement, he prepared himself, taking twenty rounds of ball cartridge, and some provisions.

About noon he set out, and at four in the afternoon reached our former encampment, Fort Edward, where he stopped awhile to refresh. Thence he proceeded with as much expedition as he could make to Fort Henry on Lake George.[2] Almost eleven o'clock

---

[1] Lamb refers to the distance from Fort Miller to Fort George, where he would take water-carriage, and not of course, to the distance from Fort Miller to Ticonderoga.

[2] Meaning *Fort George* Fort Wm. Henry was then in ruins. Much confusion seems always to have arisen regarding these two forts. The French on Montcalm's expedition against Fort William Henry in 1757, (built by Sir William Johnson in 1755) spoke of going against Fort George — though this fort, which consisted of only a single bastion, was not built until several years after by Amherst.— *W. L. S.*

at night, becoming very weary, he laid him down to sleep a little in a thick part of a wood. Although the day was hot, the night dews soon awakened him shivering with cold, having rested but about two hours; then resuming his march for four or five miles he saw a light on his left, and directed his course toward it. Having gained the place, he was saluted by a man at the door of his house who informed him that a soldier's wife had been just taken in from the woods, where she was found by one of his family, in the pains of child-birth. Being admitted into this hospitable dwelling, the owner of which was one of the Society of Friends, or people called Quakers, he recognized the wife of a sergeant of his own company. The woman was delivered of a fine girl soon after; and having requested her friendly host to allow her to stop until his return from Ticonderoga, at which time he would be able to take her to the army in one of his wagons, he set out on his lonely route again. Previous to his leaving her, she informed him that she had determined to brave the dangers of the woods, in order to come up with her husband; that she had crossed Lake George, and was seized with the sickness of labor in the forest, where she must have perished, had she not been providentially discovered by the kind-hearted people under whose roof she then was. It is worthy of remark that the author not long since in this city (Dublin), with great pleasure, saw the female, who was born as he before related, in the wilderness, near Lake George. She had been married to a man serving in the band of a militia regiment, and the meeting with

Appendix. 409

her revived in his mind the lively emotions of distressful and difficult scenes, which, although long passed, can never be forgotten by him.[1] At Fort George, he was provided with a boat to take him across (*sic*) the lake to Ticonderoga.

Lake George is situate southwest of Lake Champlain, and its bed lies about 100 feet higher. Its waters are beautifully clear, composing a sheet thirty-six miles long, and from one to seven wide. It embosoms more than two hundred islands, affording nothing for the most part but a ground of barren rocks covered with heath, and a few cedar and spruce trees. On each side it is skirted by prodigious mountains. The lake abounds with fish, and some of the best kind, such as the black or Oswego bass, also large speckled trout.[2] It was called Lake Sacrament by the Canadians, who, in former times, were at the pains to procure its water for sacramental uses in their churches.[3]

---

[1] Lamb furnishes the story of this woman's heroism two or three pages forward.

[2] This will be quite a revelation to fishermen of the present day — since it is generally supposed not only that the name *Oswego bass* is a modern one, but that the bass are a comparatively recent inhabitant of Lake George.— *W.L.S.*

[3] The writer here, in common with Cooper, falls into a very common error. The French missionary, Father Jogues, named it *St. Sacrament*, not on account of the purity of its waters, but because he arrived at the lake upon one of the festival days of that name.[1] The early Roman catholic discoverers, says the late Rev. Mr. Van Rensselaer, "frequently connect

---

[1] "Ils arriverant, la veille du S. Sacrament, au bout du lac qué est joint au grand lac de Champlain, Les Iroquois le nomment *Andiatarocte*, comme qui discit *la ou le lac se ferme*. Le Pere le nomma le lac du S. Sacrament."— *Relations*, 1645-6.

There are two island nearly in the centre of it; in one of which, called Diamond island, two companies of the 47th were stationed, commanded by Captain Aubrey, for the purpose of forwarding prisoners over the lakes. These islands were, anterior to this time, said to swarm with rattle-snakes; so much so, that people would not venture to land on them. A bateau in sailing near Diamond island having upset, the people in it gained the shore, but climbed the trees for fear of the snakes, until they got an opportunity of a vessel passing to leave it. Some hogs, however, which had been carried in the upset boat remaining on the island to which they swam, were sometime afterward followed by the owners, who, to recover them, ventured ashore. They found the swine exceedingly fat, and, to their surprise, met but very few of the rattle-snakes which before had been so plenty. A hog being killed on the spot, made a good meal for the people. It was discovered by its stomach that the hog fed upon the rattle-snakes, and had nearly cleared the island of such noxious tenantry.

The wild hog in the woods and the Indian himself are known to feed on snakes as a delicacy.[1] * * * *

---

the discovery of places with the festival name on the calendar." Mr. Cooper, in his *Last of the Mohicans* suggests the name of Horicon for this lake. This, though quite poetical, is merely fanciful, as indeed he claims, and has not the merit of historical truth. The ancient Iroquois name of the lake is *Andiatarocte* — "there the lake shuts itself."— *W. L. S.*

[1] "The Indians," says Farmer Hector St. John, "cut off the head, skin the body and cook it as we do eels, and its flesh is extremely sweet and white."

Appendix. 411

There are but two serpents whose bites or stings prove mortal, viz: the pilot or the copper-head, and the rattle snake. For the bite or venom of the former, it is said that no remedy or cure is yet discovered. It is called *pilot* from its being the first in coming from its state of torpidity in the spring, and its name of *copper-head* is taken from the copper colored spots of its head. The black snake is a good deal innoucous, and is remarkable only for its agility, beauty, and its art or instinct of enticing birds or insects to approach it. I have heard only of one person who was stung by a copper-head. He quickly swelled in a most dreadful manner; a multitude of spots of different hues on different parts of his body, alternately appeared and vanished; his eyes were filled with madness and rage; he fixed them on all present with the most vindictive looks; he thrust out his tongue as the snakes do; he hissed through his teeth with inconceivable strength, and became an object of terror to all by-standers. To the lividness of a corpse, he united the desperate force of a maniac; they hardly were able to keep him fast, so as to guard themselves from his attacks; when, in the space of two hours, death relieved the poor individual from his struggles, and the spectators from their apprehensions. The venom of the rattle-snake does not operate so soon, and hence there is more time to procure medical relief. There are several antidotes with which almost every family is provided against the poison of it. It is very inactive, and unless pursued or vexed, perfectly inoffensive. * *

The author having arrived and completed his business

at Ticonderoga, he accompanied the baggage over Lake George, attended by a number of seamen sent to work the *bateaux* on the Hudson river. On his returning he called on the good Quaker who lodged the sick wife of his fellow soldier; but to his astonishment was told that, on the morrow after he left her there in child-birth, she set out to meet her husband against the wishes and repeated entreaties of the whole family, who were anxious to detain her until his return. She could not be pursuaded to stop, but set out on foot with her new born infant, and arrived safe with her husband, whom she had followed with such fond solicitude. She thus gave an instance of the strength of female attachment and fortitude, which shows that the exertions of the sex are often calculated to call forth our cordial admiration.

In a short time the author had the gratification of conducting the stores and baggage for which he had been despatched, in safety to the army, and to receive the thanks of his officers, for the manner in which he executed the orders confided to him. By this conveyance the forces obtained a month's provisions, and a bridge of boats being constructed upon the Hudson, on the 13th or 14th September, 1777, the royal army crossed it, and encamped on Saratoga plain.[1]

---

[1] Lamb returned to England — having witnessed the surrender at Yorktown — in 1783, where he was affectionately received by an aged mother and a few kind relatives. "He then," the memoir concludes, "had to take counsel about a line of living to earn a subsistence; such is generally the result of a military life. He chose to become a school-master; an arduous occupation, which has enabled him for upwards of twenty-six

Appendix. 413

No. XVI.

BURLESQUE BALLADS ON BURGOYNE'S EXPEDITION.[1]

THE FATE OF JOHN BURGOYNE.

When Jack the king's commander
Was going to his duty,
Through all the crowd he smiled and bow'd
To every blooming beauty.

The city rung with feats he'd done
In Portugal and Flanders,
And all the town thought he'd be crown'd
The first of Alexanders.

To Hampton Court he first repairs
To kiss great George's hand, sirs;
Then to harangue on state affairs
Before he left the land, sirs.

The Lower House sat mute as mouse
To hear his grand oration;
And all the peers, with loudest cheers,
Proclaimed him to the nation.

---

years, to provide for, and educate a growing family, the source of satisfaction and solicitude. He was discharged without the pension [1] usually given for past services, and being frequently advised by his friends to apply for it, in 1809 (twenty-five years after receiving his discharge) he memorialed His Royal Highness, the Duke of York, and was graciously favored by an immediate compliance with the prayer of his petition. He submits the memorial and its answer, in gratitude to the illustrious individual, who so promptly condescended to notice it as he did."

[1] These ballads are from Griswold's *Curiosities of American Literature*, and other sources.

[1] Occasioned by a mere technicality and red tape. See his *Journal of the American War*, page 435.

Then off he went to Canada,
   Next to Ticonderoga,
And quitting those away he goes
   Straightway to Saratoga.

With great parade his march he made
   To gain his wished for station,
While far and wide his minions hied
   To spread his Proclamation.

To such as staid he offers made
   Of " *pardon* on *submission* ;
But savage bands should waste the lands
   Of all in opposition."

But ah, the cruel fates of war !
   This boasted son of Britain,
When mounting his triumphal car
   With sudden fear was smitten.

The sons of Freedom gathered round,
   His hostile bands confounded,
And when they'd fain have turned their back
   They found themselves surrounded !

In vain they fought, in vain they fled,
   Their chief, humane and tender,
To save the rest soon thought it best
   His forces to surrender.

Brave St. Clair, when he first retired
   Knew what the fates portended ;
And Arnold and heroic Gates
   His conduct have defended.

Thus may America's brave sons
   With honor be rewarded,
And the fate of all her foes
   The same as here recorded.

Appendix.

THE NORTH CAMPAIGN.

Come unto me, ye heroes,
   Whose hearts are true and bold,
Who value more your honor
   Than others do their gold;
Give ear unto my story,
   And I the truth will tell
Concerning many a soldier
   Who for his country fell.

Burgoyne, the king's commander,
   From Canada set sail
With full eight thousand reg'lars,
   He thought he could not fail;
With Indians and Canadians,
   And his cursed tory crew,
On board his fleet of shipping
   He up the Champlain flew.

Before Ticonderoga,
   The first day of July,
Appear'd his ships and army,
   And we did them espy.
Their motions we observed
   Full well both night and day,
And our brave boys prepared
   To have a bloody fray.·

Our garrison they viewed them,
   As straight their troops did land,
And when St. Clair, our chieftain,
   The fact did understand
That they the Mount Defiance
   Were bent to fortify,
He found we must surrender,
   Or else prepare to die.

The fifth day of July, then,
   He order'd a retreat,

And when next morn we started,
　　Burgoyne thought we were beat.
And closely he pursued us,
　　Till when near Hubbardton,
Our rear guards were defeated,
　　He thought the country won.

And when it was told in Congress,
　　That we our forts had left,
To Albany retreated,
　　Of all the North bereft,
Brave General Gates they sent us,
　　Our fortunes to retrieve,
And him with shouts of gladness
　　The army did receive.

Where first the Mohawk's waters
　　Do in the sunshine play,
For Herkimer's brave soldiers
　　Sellinger[1] ambush'd lay:
And them he there defeated,
　　But soon he had his due,
And scared[2] by Brooks and Arnold
　　He to the North withdrew.

To take the stores and cattle
　　That we had gathered then,
Burgoyne sent a detachment
　　Of fifteen hundred men;
By Baum they were commanded,
　　To Bennington they went;
To plunder and to murder
　　Was fully their intent.

---

[1] St. Leger.

[2] A man employed by the British as a spy, was taken by Arnold, and at the suggestion of Colonel Brooks sent back to St. Leger with such deceptive accounts of the strength of the Americans as induced them to retreat towards Montreal.

But little did they know then,
  With whom they had to deal;
It was not quite so easy
  Our stores and stock to steal;
Bold Stark would give them only
  A portion of his *lead* :
With half his crew ere sunset
  Baum lay among the dead.

The nineteenth of September,
  The morning cool and clear,
Brave Gates rode through our army,
  Each soldier's heart to cheer :
"Burgoyne," he cried, "advances,
  But we will never fly;
No — rather than surrender,
  We'll fight him till we die."

The news was quickly brought us,
  The enemy was near,
And all along our lines then,
  There was no sign of fear;
It was above Stillwater
  We met at noon that day,
And every one expected
  To see a bloody fray.

Six hours the battle lasted,
  Each heart was true as gold,
The British fought like lions,
  And we like Yankees bold ;
The leaves with blood were crimson,
  And then brave Gates did cry —
" 'Tis diamond now cut diamond!
  We'll beat them, boys, or die."

The darkness soon approaching,
  It forced us to retreat
Into our lines till morning,
  Which made them think us beat;

But ere the sun was risen,
    They saw before their eyes,
Us ready to engage them,
    Which did them much surprise.

Of fighting they seem'd weary,
    Therefore to work they go
Their thousand dead to bury,
    And breastworks up to throw:
With grape and bombs intending
    Our army to destroy,
Or from our works our forces
    By stratagem decoy.

The seventh day of October
    The British tried again,
Shells from their cannon throwing
    Which fell on us like rain,
To drive us from our stations
    That they might thus retreat;
For now Burgoyne saw plainly
    He never us could beat.

But vain was his endeavor
    Our men to terrify;
Though death was all around us,
    Not one of us would fly.
But when an hour we'd fought them,
    And they began to yield,
Along our lines the cry ran,
    "The *next* blow wins the field."

Great God who won their battles
    Whose cause is just and true,
Inspired our bold commander
    The course he should pursue.
He order'd Arnold forward,
    And Brooks to follow on;
The enemy were routed,
    Our liberty was won!

Then, burning all their luggage,
    They fled with haste and fear,
Burgoyne with all his forces
    To Saratogue did steer;
And Gates our brave commander,
    Soon after him did hie,
Resolving he would take them
    Or in the effort die.

As we came nigh the village,
    We overtook the foe;
They'd burned each house to ashes,
    Like all where'er they go.
The seventeenth of October,
    They did capitulate;
Burgoyne and his proud army
    Did we our pris'ners make.

Now here's a health to Arnold,
    And our commander Gates;
To Lincoln and to Washington,
    Whom ev'ry tory hates;
Likewise unto our Congress,
    God grant it long to reign,
Our Country, Right and Justice
    For ever to maintain.

Now finish'd is my story,
    My song is at an end;
The freedom we're enjoying
    We're ready to defend;
For while our cause is righteous,
    Heaven nerves the soldier's arm,
And vain is their endeavor
    Who strive to do us harm.

BURGOYNE'S ADVANCE AND FALL.

An extract from *America Independent.*

BY PHILIP FRENEAU.[1]

Led on by lust of lucre and renown,
Burgoyne came marching with his thousands down;
High were his thoughts, and furious his career,
Puff'd with self-confidence, and pride severe,
Swoln with the idea of his future deeds,
On to ruin each advantage leads.
Before his hosts his heaviest curses flew,
And conquer'd worlds rose hourly to his view:
His wrath, like Jove's, could bear with no control,
His words bespoke the mischief in his soul;
To fight was not this miscreant's only trade,
He shin'd in writing, and his wit display'd.
To awe the more with titles of command
He told of *forts he rul'd* in Scottish land;
Queen's *colonel* as he was he did not know
That thorns and *thistles*, mix'd with honors, grow;
In Britain's senate though he held a place,
All did not save him from one long disgrace.
One stroke of fortune that convinc'd them all
That we could conquer, and *lieutenants* fall.
Foe to the rights of man, proud plunderer, say
Had conquest crown'd thee on that mighty day
When you to GATES, with sorrow, rage and shame
Resign'd your conquests, honors, arms, and fame,
When at his feet Britannia's wreaths you threw,
And the sun sicken'd at a sight so new;
Had you been victor — what a waste of woe!
What souls had vanish'd to where souls do go!
What dire distress had mark'd your fatal way,

---

[1] Philip Freneau — the poet of the Revolution, was a native of New Jersey. A volume of his poems published in Philadelphia in 1786, abounds in patriotic sentiments and allusions to various events of the war. He died in his native state at the advanced age of eighty years.

What deaths on deaths disgrace that dismal day!
Can laurels flourish in a soil of blood,
Or on those laurels can fair honors bud?
Curs'd be that wretch who murder makes his trade,
Curs'd be all arms that e'er ambition made!
What murdering tory now relieves your grief
Or plans new conquests for his favorite chief;
Designs still dark employ that ruffian race,
Beasts of your choosing, and our own disgrace.
So vile a crew the world ne'er saw before,
And grant, ye pitying heavens, it may no more.
If ghosts from hell infest our poison'd air,
Those ghosts have enter'd these base bodies here,
Murder and blood is still their dear delight—
Scream round their roots ye ravens of the night!
Whene'er they wed, may demons, and despair,
And grief, and woe, and blackest night be there;
Fiends leagu'd from hell, the nuptial lamp display,
Swift to perdition light them on their way.
Round the wide world their devilish squadrons chase,
To find no realm that grants one resting place.
Far to the north, on Scotland's utmost end
An isle there lies, the haunt of every fiend,
There screeching owls, and screaming vultures rest,
And not a tree adorns its barren breast!
No shepherds there attend their bleating flocks,
But wither'd witches rove among the rocks :
Shrouded in ice, the blasted mountains show
Their cloven heads, to fright the seas below;
The lamp of heaven in his diurnal race
Here scarcely deigns to unveil his radiant face;
Or if one day he circling treads the sky
He views this island with an angry eye;
Or ambient fogs their broad, moist wings expand,
Damp his bright ray, and cloud the infernal land;
The blackening wind incessant storms prolong,
Dull as their night, and dreary as my song;

When stormy winds with rain refuse to blow,
Then from the dark sky drives the unpitying snow;
When drifting snow from iron clouds forbear
Then down the hailstones rattle through the air.
No peace no rest, the elements bestow,
But seas forever rage, and storms forever blow.
Here, miscreants, here with loyal hearts retire,
Here pitch your tents, and kindle *here* your fire;
Here desert nature will her stings display,
And fiercest hunger on your vitals prey,
And with yourselves let *John Burgoyne* retire
To reign the monarch, whom your hearts admire.

THE CAPTURE AT SARATOGA.[1]

Here followeth the direful fate,
Of Burgoyne and his army great,
Who so proudly did display
The terrors of despotic sway.
His power and pride and many threats
Have been brought low by fort'nate Gates,
To bend to the United States.

British prisoners by convention, - -	2442
Foreigners by contravention, - - -	2198
Tories sent across the lake, - - -	1100
Burgoyne and his suite in state, - - -	12
Sick and wounded, bruised and pounded, Ne'er so much before confounded,	528
Prisoners of war before convention - -	400
Deserters come with kind intention. - -	300
They lost at Bennington's great battle, Where Stark's glorious arms did rattle,	1220
Killed in September and October, -	600
Ta'en by brave Brown, some drunk, some sober,	413
Slain by high-famed Herkerman, On both flanks, on rear and van,	300

---

[1] From a contemporary magazine.

Indians, settlers, butchers, drovers,
Enough to crowd large plains all over
And those whom grim health did prevent
From fighting against our continent;
And also those who stole away,
Lest they down their arms should lay,
Abhorring that obnoxious day;

} 4413

The whole make fourteen thousand men,
Who may not with us fight again,

} 14000

    This is a pretty just account
    Of Burgoyne's legions' whole amount,
    Who came across the northern lakes
    To desolate our happy states.
    Their brass cannon we have got all,
    Fifty-six — both great and small:
    And ten thousand stand of arms,
    To prevent all future harms:
    Stores and implements complete,
    Of workmanship exceeding neat;
    Covered wagons in great plenty,
    And proper harness, no ways scanty.
    Among our prisoners there are
    Six generals of fame most rare;
    Six members of their parliament
    Reluctantly they seem content:
    Three British lords, and Lord Balcarras
    Who came our country free to harass.
    Two baronets of high extraction
    Were sorely wounded in the action.

THE BATTLE OF BENNINGTON, AUGUST 16, 1777.

BY REV. THOMAS P. RODMAN.

    Up through a cloudy sky, the sun
      Was buffeting his way
    On such a morn as ushers in
      A sultry August day.

Hot was the air — and hotter yet,
  Men's thought within them grew ;
They Britons, Hessians, Tories, saw,
  They saw their homesteads too !

They thought of all their country's wrongs ;
  They thought of noble lives,
Poured out in battle with their foes ; —
  They thought upon their wives,
Their children and their aged sires,
  Their firesides, churches, God !
And these deep thoughts made hallowed ground
  Each foot of soil they trod.

Their leader was a veteran man —
  A man of earnest will ; —
His very presence was a host ;
  He'd fought at Bunker's hill !
A living monument he stood,
  Of stirring deeds of fame ;
Of deeds that shed a fadeless light,
  Of his own deathless name !

Of Charlestown's flames, of Warren's blood,
  His presence told the tale ;
It made each patriot's heart beat quick,
  Though lip and cheek grew pale ;
It spoke of Princeton, Morristown ; —
  Told Trenton's thrilling story ;
It lit futurity with hope,
  And on the past shed glory.

Who were those men ? their leader, who ?
  Where stood they on that morn ?
The men were northern yeomanry,
  Brave men as e'er were born ;
Who, in the reaper's merry row,
  Or warrior's rank could stand ;
Right worthy such a noble troop —
  John Stark led on the band.

Walloomsac wanders by the spot
  Where *they*, that morning, stood;
Then rolled the war cloud o'er the stream,
  The waves were tinged with blood;
And the near hills that dark cloud girt,
  And fires like lightning flashed;
And shrieks and groans, like howling blasts,
  Rose as the bayonets clashed.

The night before, the Yankee host
  Came gathering from afar,
And in each belted bosom glowed
  The spirit of the war!
All full of fight, through rainy storm,
  Night cloudy, starless, dark —
They came and gathered as they came,
  Around the valiant Stark!

There was a Berkshire parson — he
  And all his flock were there,
And like true *churchmen* militant,
  The arm of flesh made bare.
Out spoke the Dominie, and said: —
  " For battle have we come,
These many times: and after this,
  We mean to stay at home,

" If now we come in vain" — Said Stark:
  " What! would you go to-night,
To battle it with yonder troops?
  God send us morning light,
And we will give you work enough;
  Let but the morning come,
And if ye hear no voice of war,
  Go back and stay at home."

The morning came — there stood the foe; —
  Stark eyed them as they stood;
Few words he spoke — 'twas not a time
  For moralizing mood;

"See there, the *enemy*, my boys —
   Now, strong in valor's might,
Beat them, or Betty[1] Stark will sleep
   In widowhood to-night!"

Each soldier there had left at home,
   A sweetheart, wife or mother;
A blooming sister, or perchance,
   A fair haired, blue eyed brother;
Each from a fireside came, and thoughts
   These simple words awoke,
That nerved up every warrior's arm,
   And guided every stroke.

Fireside and woman — mighty words!
   How wond'rous is the spell
They work upon the manly heart,
   Who knoweth not full well?
And then the *women* of this land,
   That never land hath known
A truer, nobler hearted race,
   Each Yankee boy must own.

Brief eloquence was Stark's — not vain;
   Scarce uttered he the words,
When burst the musket's rattling peal;
   Out leaped the flashing swords.
And when brave Stark in after time,
   Told the proud tale of wonder,
He said "the battle din was one
   Continual clap of thunder."

Two hours they strove, when victory crowned
   The valiant Yankee boys;
Nought but the memory of the dead
   Bedimmed their glorious joys!

---

[1] General Stark's wife's name was *Elizabeth Page*.

Aye — there's the rub; the hour of strife,
Though follow years of fame,
Is still in mournful memory linked
With some death-hallowed name.

The cypress with the laurel twines —
The Pæan sounds a knell —
The trophied column marks the spot
Where friends and brothers fell!
Fame's mantle, a funeral pall
Seems to the grief dimmed eye;
For ever where the bravest fall,
The best beloved die!

TO THE RELICS OF MY BRITISH GRENADIER.

BY B. W. B. CANNING.

I have in my possession a portion of the skeleton of a British officer of the grenadiers, who was killed in the battle of Oct. 5th, 1777, which was accidentally exhumed in the spring of 1852. The skull has a perforation through the right temple, and the bullet that made it was found inside. A portion of his uniform coat bears the color and texture of the cloth and two heavily gold plated buttons, after a burial of seventy-five years.

Strange bivouac, old Grenadier,
Thou in my quiet study here,
    Hast found at last;
While I, who life's campaign began
When thou for forty years hadst done,
    Patrol the past.

O had your hollow skull a brain,
Your bony mouth a tongue again,
    I know full well
In *why's* and *when's* and *how's* you'd find
A Yankee of the bluest kind
    Your sentinel.

I *guess* for many an hour we'd join
In talk about Sir John Burgoyne,
    And the "whole boodle,"

Who 'gan their game of brag in June,
But on one bright October noon
Laid pride and arms down to the tune
    Of Yankee Doodle.

Just as old Dido ached of old
To be by brave Æneas told
    Quantus Achilles —
Quales" — but I can't write it all —
So I am prurient to recall
How once our fathers pounded small
    King George's follies.

I long for more about that day
When Rebels met in grim array
    The Regulars :
When trumpet clang and plunging shot
And shouting made the battle hot
    About their ears.

When Dearborn, Poor, and Patterson,
And Cilley, Brooks and Livingston,
    With hearts of steel,
Met Phillips, Fraser, Hamilton,
Rolling the tide of slaughter on,
    And made them reel.

When Morgan and his riflemen
" Bearded the lion in his den,"
    And signed his name;
While Arnold — battle's thunderbolt —
Flashed, like a comet on a colt,
    About the plain —

I'd ask what gallant Frazer said,
When bullet from the tree top sped,
    Its work had done :
How stout old earl Balcarras tore,
When Yankees " true to Freedom swore "
    His twelve pound gun.

Appendix.

How many inches on that day
The visage of Burgoyne, I pray,
    A lengthening went?
Didst hear him say — as once before —
That with ten thousand men — no more —
He'd conquering walk from shore to shore
    The continent?

But I forget, old Grenadier,
You never lived yourself, to hear
    What others said :
A luckless missile found you out,
And, killing instantly no doubt,
    It bored your head.

For seventy-five long years, old brave,
You occupied your shallow grave —
    No gun to stir;
At length by plough and not by drum
Disturbed your huge wreck has become
    My prisoner.

And now I'll keep you guarding there
All of your coat the mould could spare,
    And darkling worm ;
With the gashed ball by which you died,
And buttons, too, that lit with pride
    Your uniform.

To those infused with martial leaven,
Of Bemis's Heights in '77
    You'll tell for long :
Aye — and perchance some bard may troll
From out that ragged bullet hole,
    Another song.

THE BURIAL OF GEN. FRASER.

Read before the Annual Meeting of the Saratoga Monument Association, 1874, by E. W. B. Canning, Esq.

On Saratoga's crimsoned field,
   When battle's volleyed roar was done,
Mild autumn's mellow light revealed
   The glories of the setting sun.
On furrow, fence and tree that bear
   The iron marks of battling men,
The radiance burneth calm and fair,
   As tho' earth aye had sinless been.
The gory sods, all scathed and scarred,
   And piled in trenched mounds declare
That mutual foeman, fallen, marred,
   Have found a final bivouac there.
And list! from yonder bulwarked height
   The faint-heard martial signals come:
For those who keep the watch to-night
   Are gathering at the evening drum.

So, Saratoga, lay thy field
   When freedom, 'mid the shock of steel,
Made Britain's rampant lion yield,
   And crushed his terrors 'neath her heel.
Proudly the freeman points to thee,
   And speaks thy unforgotten name;
While on her page bright history
   For children's children writes thy fame.

As the last sunbeam kissed the trees
   That sighed amid its dying glow,
Borne softly on the evening breeze
   Floated the soldier's note of woe.
From out the Briton's guarded lines,
   With wailing fife and muffled drum,
While gleaming gold with scarlet shines,
   A band of mourning warriors come.
With arms reversed, all sad and slow,

And measured tread of martial men,
Forth on their lengthened path they go,
But not to wake the strife again.
No plunging haste of battles there,
   No serried ranks or bristling lines ;
No furious coursers headlong bear
   Their riders where the death flash shines.
The pennon is the soldiers' pall,
   The battery for the bier is changed,
And plumes of nodding sable all
   On chieftains' brows are round it ranged.
The noblest leader of the host
   They carry to his dreamless sleep ;
The heart of British hope is lost,
   And vain the tears that Britons weep.
Thine arm of valor, proud Burgoyne,
   Is paralyzed for ever now ;
While sorrow-stricken comrades join
   Fondly to wreathe dead Fraser's brow.

On yonder hill that skirts the plain,
   A lone redoubt with haste upraised,
O'erlooks around the trampled grain,
   Where oft the dying hero gazed.
"Bury me there at set of sun,"
   (His latest words of ebbing life)
"'Tis mine to see no triumph won,
   Or mingle with the final strife.
If gloom awaits our path of fame,
   I die before the ill befalls ;
These ears shall tingle not with shame,
   Nor longer list when glory calls.
At set of sun, in yon redoubt,
   Lay me to rest as rest the brave."
The flickering lamp of life went out,
   And strangers' land must yield a grave.

Slowly in mournful march they wend
   Their upward pathway to the tomb ;

Unwittingly the foemen send
  Their shots around amid the gloom.
They reach the height, commit their trust,
  And reverent all uncovered stand;
While booming shots updash the dust
  In clouds about the listening band.
Robed and with dignity serene,
  The man of God reads calmly on;
No terror marks his quiet mien,
  As hoarse responds the distant gun.
"Earth to earth and dust to dust:
  Thus the solemn accents fall;
Each receives her precious trust,
  Evening saddens over all.
Pile the mound; no living form
  Nobler soul enshrines than he,
Now bequeathed the darkling worm —
  Pride of Albion's chivalry!
All is done: there wait for thee,
  Fallen chief, no more alarms;
But thy peers anon must see
  Hapless "field of grounded arms."

  *   *   *   *

Years have trolled their changes by;
  Harvests oft have robed the plain;
And the leafy honors high
  Sigh no more above the slain.
Sons of sires who in the black,
  Doleful days of '77
Rolled the tide of battle back,
  Seeking hope and strength in Heaven,
Wondering tread the storied ground,
  And with glowing accents tell
How their fathers victory found,
  And the spot where Fraser fell.
Gallant chieftain, nobler song
  Ought to speak thy honored name;
But our sons remembering long,
  Worthier tribute pay thy fame!

THE PROGRESS OF SIR JACK BRAG.

Said Burgoyne to his men, as they pass'd in review,
  Tullalo, tullalo, tullalo, boys!
These rebels their course very quickly will rue,
And fly as the leaves 'fore the autumn tempest flew,
  When *him who is your leader* they know, boys!
  They with *men* have now to deal,
  And we soon will make them feel,
  Tullalo, tullalo, tullalo, boys!
That a loyal Briton's arm and a loyal Briton's steel
  Can put to flight a rebel as quick as other foe, boys!
  Tullalo, tullalo, tullalo —
  Tullalo, tullalo, tullalo-o-o-o, boys!

As to Sa-ra-tog' he came, thinking how to *jo* the game,
  Tullalo, tullalo, tullalo, boys!
He began to fear the grubs, in the branches of his fame,
He began to have the *trembles* lest a flash should be the flame,
  For which he had agreed his perfume to forego, boys!
  No lack of skill, but fates,
  Shall make us yield to Gates,
  Tullalo, tullalo, tullalo, boys!
The devil may have leagued, as you know, with the States!
But we never will be beat by any mortal foe, boys!
  Tullalo, tullalo, tullalo —
  Tullallo, tullalo, tullalo-o-o-o boys.

No. XVII.

DESCRIPTION OF TICONDEROGA AND THE FORTS SOUTH OF IT IN 1777.[1]

I.—FORT CARILLON.

In this are eight eighteen-pounder guns in double fortified works. It is surrounded on the north side by palisades in front of, and surrounding which is an abatis. Between this fort and the old French redoubt a new log-house (block house) has been built.

II.—THE OLD FRENCH REDOUBT.

This is about two hundred rods east of the fort, and is mounted with six cannons, four of which are nine-pounders and two twelve-pounders. This redoubt has been repaired (its old shape being preserved), and is also surrounded by an abatis.

III.—THE OLD FRENCH LINES.

These have lately been somewhat repaired, but are not mounted. The palisades have also not been repaired.

IV.—THE FIVE REDOUBTS NEAR THE SHORE.

These are situated in a northeasterly direction from the fort at the foot of a hill. They have not been repaired.

N.B.—On the 13th of May, the news reached us, that the rebels were about repairing, and placing can-

---

[1] From the *Military Journal of Major Gen. Riedesel.*

Appendix. 435

nons upon them, but as yet, it is unknown of what calibre they are to be. It has been said, however, that they may be two eighteen-pounders and a few twelve-pounders that are expected about October.

All these redoubts, as well as the lines, are poorly manned.

V.—FORT (MOUNT) INDEPENDENCE.

(*a.*) North of the mountain is a strong abatis where twelve cannons are posted; one of which is a thirty-two-pounder, and the rest are eighteen and twelve-pounders. All of the works are surrounded by a strong abatis.

(*b.*) One hundred yards from the works are smaller fortifications, in which three eighteen-pounders and three twenty-four-pounders are placed.

(*c.*) South of these works are barracks and palisades; and in front of them is another abatis. In the rear of the former are eight nine-pounders. Besides these, there are twelve more nine and twelve-pounders, designed for the defense of the barracks. These, however, are not yet mounted.

N.B.—According to late news, twenty cannons have been taken to a battery, in a northerly direction, at the foot of the fort, with a view of commanding the lake. These are twelve and eighteen-pounders.

(*d.*) There are a few cannons on the half-moon battery, which defend *en barbette*.

(*e.*) There are about one hundred iron cannons on the ships near Carillon; but there are no mortars whatever. These iron cannons are mostly old ones.

Particulars.

The number of troops, at present in Carillon and near Mount Independence, does not exceed 1,300 men; but reënforcements amounting to fifteen regiments, are hourly expected. There is an abundance of provisions. No preparations have been made to build new ships. The vessels of the enemy consist of a rowing vessel, an old sloop, and two two-masters. The troops from New England arrive daily in front of No. 4.

N.B.— Intelligence, as late as May 13th, states, that there are at Ticonderoga (including the laborers) 2,800 men. Their chief business at that time consisted in cantoning and in constructing a bridge, the foundation of which was laid in the winter by the rebels. This foundation consists of between forty and fifty sunken boxes, filled with stones, and laid at a distance of fifty feet from each other. It is thought, that this bridge cannot be finished even in two months, from the 14th of May. It is to serve as a connection between Mount Independence and Fort Carillon, and is to cover the retreat in case one of those posts should be captured. The turnpikes are north of the bridge, but the ships south, in order to defend it. Close behind this bridge is another and smaller one, which is only five feet in width. It is designed for pedestrians, and is between the store houses and Mount Independence.

The rebels have lately received 150 tons of powder. This has been the whole supply the entire winter. They have also received four four-pounders, which

Appendix. 437

were made at Cambridge, near Boston. A great supply of muskets has, likewise, arrived from the West India islands. A French engineer officer has lately reached the rebel army, and was appointed engineer-in-chief.[1]

Fort Skenesborough.

The garrison here consists of about eighty men. No preparations, whatever, have been made at this post for ship-building. There are barracks here, surrounded by palisades, in which provisions, and a large quantity of war material are stored.

Fort Anne.

Is garrisoned by about thirty men, and has a barrack with palisades.

Fort George.[2]

1st. The citadel has only recently been repaired and provided with two nine-pounders. It contains, also, twelve cannons, which are not yet mounted. Barracks for 1,000 men lie twenty yards east of it.

2d. Close to the shore is a large magazine in which there is an abundance of provisions.

3d. To the west of this magazine, where Fort William Henry formerly stood, is the large hospital, a building of great dimensions, and used for the sick from Fort Carrillon. This is said to be surrounded by palisades,

---

[1] Kosciusko, the Pole?— *Translator.*

[2] Fort *Edward* in the original; but, as the well informed reader will see, this is probably a typographical error, as Fort George, at the head of Lake George, is of course the fort here described.— *Translator.*

and to have a small redoubt on the hill south of it.[1] A strong guard is posted here every night. The rebels at Fort George are very busy in cutting down trees and carrying them to the shore to be used in the construction of six strong vessels on the lake. A so-called Commodore Wynkoop, is said to be still in command at this post; only one regiment, it is further said, remains here during summer; but as yet there are only 400 men there. There is also considerable scarcity in ammunition.

No. XVIII.

The Saratoga Monument Association.

The Saratoga Monument Association was incorporated by act of the legislature of the state of New York, passed April 19th, 1859, Chap. 498, Laws of 1859. The first section of this act reads as follows:

"Sec. I. George Strover, William Wilcox and their associates, shall be a body corporate and politic, by the name and style of the Saratoga Monument Association, for the purpose of taking and holding sufficient real and personal property to erect on such spot in town of Saratoga, and as near the place where Burgoyne surrendered the British army, as a majority of the trustees hereinafter named shall deem practicable, a monument commemorative of the battle which ended in Burgoyne's surrender, on the seventeenth of October, seventeen hundred and seventy-seven."

---

[1] The remains of this redoubt, which are still to be seen, bears the name of Fort Gage.— *Translator*.

Appendix. 439

Section four of the act named the first Board of Trustees, but it was amended April 30th, 1873, as follows:

" Sec. IV. The First Board of Trustees shall consist of Hamilton Fish and William L. Stone of the city of New York; Horatio Seymour of Utica; Benson J. Lossing of Poughkeepsie; Asa C. Tefft of Fort Edward; John A. Corey of Saratoga Springs, and Charles H. Payne of Saratoga."

Since the passage of this act, Corey has died, and Mr. Fish has resigned, and John V. L. Pruyn of Albany, Daniel A. Bullard of Schuylerville, and E. W. B. Caning of New York city have been elected trustees. The appropriation toward the erection of the Saratoga monument by the N. Y. legislature of 1874 (Laws of 1874, Chap. 323, page 387) was made in the following form:

" Whenever it shall be made satisfactorily to appear to the comptroller of the state that the Saratoga Monument Association has fixed and determined upon a plan for a monument, to be erected at Schuylerville, Saratoga Co., in commemoration of the battle of Saratoga, and that it will not cost to exceed five hundred thousand, nor less than two hundred thousand dollars, to erect and complete such monument upon such plan, and that the association has received and paid over to the treasurer from private subscriptions and donations, made by the United States or state governments of states, at least a sufficient sum with the amount hereby specified to complete said monument upon such plans, then the state of New York will pay and contribute by appropriation of the public moneys, the sum of $50,000 to aid in the construction of such monument, and the faith of the state is hereby pledged to such purpose upon such conditions. The plans and estimates of the cost of said monument aforesaid, shall be submitted to and approved by the governor and the comptroller of this state, and the comptroller of this state is hereby made the treasurer of said Monument Association. The plans so fixed and adopted as aforesaid, shall not thereafter be changed without the consent of the governor and comptroller, nor so as to increase the cost of said monument.

Officers of the Saratoga Monument Association.

President, HORATIO SEYMOUR, Utica, N. Y.
Vice-Pres., J. V. L. PRUYN, Albany, N. Y.
Vice-Pres., JAMES M. MARVIN, Sar. Springs, N. Y.
Secretary, WM. L. STONE, New York City.
Cor. Sec'y, ED. W. B. CANNING, Stockbridge, Mass.
Treasurer, DANIEL A. BULLARD, Schuylerville, N. Y.

STANDING COMMITTEES.

Committee on Design.

WILLIAM L. STONE, CHARLES H. PAYN,
E. W. B. CANNING, JAMES M. MARVIN,
LEROY MOWRY.

Committee on Location.

ASA C. TEFFT, CHARLES H. PAYN,
E. F. BULLARD.

Building Committee.

CHARLES H. PAYN, LEROY MOWRY,
ASA C. TEFFT, WILLIAM L. STONE.

Appendix.

Executive Committee.

LEROY MOWRY,   CHARLES H. PAYN,
JAMES M. MARVIN,   DANIEL A. BULLARD.

Advisory Committee.

EDWARD F. BULLARD,   Saratoga Springs,
P. C. FORD,   Schuylerville, N. Y.
B. W. THROCKMORTON,   New York City.
OSCAR FRISBIE,   "   "   "

The following affidavits were made by two of the oldest inhabitants of Schuylerville for the use of the Senate Committee having the Saratoga monument under consideration; as they throw light on the surrender ground they are here given:[1]

---

[1] In speaking of these two persons, Mrs. Walworth, in her entertaining and valuable Guide Book to the battle ground, says:

"I have had the pleasure of conversing with these old men, and can bear witness to the clearness and readiness of their memory.

"Mr. Clements is exceedingly interesting, and a man of some attainments. He has been a civil engineer, and told me that he had surveyed the first lots that were laid out in Schuylerville, Philip Schuyler, grandson of the general, and Mr. Beadle, who afterwards laid out the village of West Troy, carrying the chain. Mr. Clements also said he had made the survey that settled the disputed line between the towns of Northumberland and Saratoga, and a curious incident enabled him to verify his work. He found the old survey mark in a log of yellow pine (known to be very durable) under ground, and corresponding with his own lines.

"Mr. McCreedy is one of four generations who have fought in the various wars of the country. His father and grandfather were in the battles of Saratoga; he fought in the battle of Plattsburgh in the war of 1812, and his son took an active part in the late war. His wife, who is near his own age, and has lived with him sixty years, is a very bright old lady. She gives a vivid account of a fourth of July celebration that took place at

STATE OF NEW YORK, } ss.
County of Saratoga.

Albert Clements, being duly sworn, deposes and says: I reside in the town of Saratoga, in said county, in the vicinity of the village of Schuylerville, and have resided there since the year 1789 — am now ninety-five years of age. I came to this town from Dutchess county. Abraham Marshall was residing here then on the farm now occupied by his grandson, William Marshall. I heard him (Abraham) say that he witnessed the surrender of Burgoyne's army; that the British army marched down below the gravel hill located on the west side of the river road, south of Fish creek, and Burgoyne there surrendered his sword. I have frequently heard soldiers who were in Gates's army tell the following incident: After the retreat of the British army from Stillwater towards Schuylerville, the American army pursued them as far as a hill on the south bank of Fish creek, nearly opposite the village of Victory, and there erected a battery, and fired their guns towards the point on the north side of the creek, where Burgoyne happened to be at the table eating, and a ball came on the table and knocked off a leg of mutton.

I remember, when I was a boy, of seeing breastworks extending as much as a quarter of a mile in length along

---

Schuylerville fifty-five years ago, when the veterans of the Revolution had a banquet spread for them on the plain before Fort Hardy, where the British stacked their arms. She says the old men were very spry on that day, and that there was then assembled the largest crowd of people ever gathered at Schuylerville."

Appendix. 443

the hill where Prospect Hill cemetery now is located, in the direction of the road just west of the cemetery. I assisted in tearing them down. They were made of pine logs and earth. I ploughed up a cartridge box containing about sixty musket balls.

I remember the old Dutch Church, which stood on the south side of the road now running from the river road to Victory; I frequently attended meeting there. It was a wooden structure, heavy timbers and clap-boarded.

There were no other buildings on the south side of the creek except General Schuyler's mansion, and only two on the north side at that time.

I visited General Schuyler's mansion when he was there; I saw him signing deeds or leases.

ALBERT CLEMENTS.

Sworn to before me April 13th, 1877.

S. WELLS, *Notary Public*.

STATE OF NEW YORK, } ss.
Saratoga County.

William H. McCreedy, being duly sworn, deposes and says: I am eighty-six years of age; now reside in the village of Schuylerville, in said county, and have there resided for over sixty years past. I remember of hearing my father and grandfather, who were both in Gates's army, say: that they witnessed Burgoyne's surrender; that the terms of the surrender were signed under the Elm tree now standing on the east side of Broad street, in Schuylerville, between the feed store of Simon Sheldon and the blacksmith's shop adjoining on the south; and that the British army marched down the river road just below Gravel hill, south of Fish creek, and surrendered.

I remember seeing breastworks, extending north and south, on the river flats between the village and the river. I dug up five cannon balls there some fifty years ago. I visited old General Schuyler at his mansion several times. I dined there on one occasion; and after finishing my meal, the old general asked me if I had eaten enough. I answered that I had eaten all that I wanted, and he replied: "If you have, knock out your teeth."

My grandfather, Charles McCreedy, and father, James McCreedy, were both in the engagements fought at Bemis's heights, September 19th, and October 7th, 1777. They told me that General Gates's headquarters were south of the old Dutch Church, and were present at the surrender; and that the old turnpike road was about where the canal now is.

WILLIAM H. McCREEDY.

Sworn before me, April 13th, 1877.

S. WELLS, *Notary Public.*

Appendix. 445

No. XIX.

The principal authorities consulted in the preparation of this volume — many of them, on this subject, intrinsically valueless — are, besides the Reidesel and Brunswick Journals, the following:

GEN. WILKINSON's *Memoirs*, Philadelphia, 1816.
LAMB's *Journal of Occurrences during the late American War, to the year 1783*; by R. Lamb, sergeant in the Royal Welsh Fusileers, Dublin, 1809.
ANBURY's *Letters*, London, 1791.
ALLEN's *Biographical Dictionary*.
MACAULEY's *History of New York*.
BARBER's *Historical Collections*.
STEDMAN's *History of the American War*.
HOLDEN's *History of the Town of Queensbury*.
FONBLANQUE's *Life of Gen. Burgoyne*, London, 1876.
SILLIMAN's *Tour*.
DWIGHT's *Travels*.
CARRINGTON's *Battles of America*; by Henry B. Carrington, Bvt. Brig. General, U. S. A., and Professor of Military Science at Wabash University. A. L. Barnes & Co., New York, 1876.
STONE's *Life of Brant* (Thayendanegea).
BANCROFT's *History of the United States*, vol. IX.
IRVING's *Life of Washington*.
RAMSAY's *History of the Revolution*.
SPARKS's *American Biography*.
LOSSING s *Field Book of the Revolution*.
GARDEN's *American Revolution*.
THATCHER's *Military Journal*.
MARSHALL's *Washington*.
DWIGHT's *Summer Tours*.
Visit to the Battle Ground in 1789; by Mrs. Theodore Dwight.
BOTTA's *History of the War of the Independence of the United States*.
TRUMBULL's *Reminiscences of his own Times*.
J. WATTS DEPEYSTER's *Justice to Schuyler*.

446   *Campaign of General John Burgoyne.*

The History of the War in America between Great Britain and her Colonies, from its Commencement to the End of the Year 1778, Dublin, 1779. Chapters XIV, XV, pp. 270-315, especially 281, 284-5, 291, 295-6, 310, etc.

CHARLES SMITH's *American War*, New York, 1797.

CREASY's *Fifteen Decisive Battles of the World, from Marathon to Waterloo*, 15th Ed., 1866, chap. XIII — Saratoga particularly Note 1, page 467-8.

CHARLES NEILSON's *Original, compiled and corrected Account of Burgoyne's Campaign*, etc., etc., Albany; printed by J. Munsell, 1844.

JAMES GRAHAM's *Life of Gen. Daniel Morgan*, etc., etc., New York. Derby & Jackson, 119 Nassau street, 1856.

JOHN ANDREWS's *History of the War with America, France*, etc., London, 1786. II, Chapter XXVIII, 388, 389, 390, 392, 394, 395, 402, 407, 408, 410.

WILLIAM DUNLAP's *History of New York, for Schools*, vol. II, p. 169. New York, 1837.

KAPP's *Life of Steuben*, page 343.

American Military Biography, 2d Ed., page 171.

DAWSON's *Battles of the United States*, I, 289.

ROBERT TOMES' (M. D.) *Battles of America*, Virtue & Co., New York. Part III, pages 480-1, 486-9; 500-1, 509, etc.. 516, etc. Part IV, Chapter LXXXIII, Camden, S. C.

History of Livingston County, N. Y., Lockwood L. Doty (Gates's Insubordination), page 156.

LOSSING's *Life of Schuyler*. (New York Society Library.)

P. STANSBURY's *Pedestrian Tour in North America, prepared in the Autumn of* 1821 (relating to the Battle fields of Saratoga); 12mo., New York, 1822. (N. Y. H. S.)

GORDON's *Gazetteer*.

SPAFFORD's *Gazetteer*.

HOLMES's *Annals*.

LAMB's *Journal of Occurrences in America*, Dublin, 1809.

Memoirs of his own Life, by R. Lamb, Dublin, 1811.

Remembrancer of Public Events, 1775-83, London, 1784.

BELKNAP's *New Hampshire*.

CAMPBELL's *Tryon County*.

Appendix.

WATSON's *Men and Times of the Revolution.*
DUNLAP's *History of New York.*
Brunswick Magazine, No. XI.
WAKEFIELD's *Letters from America,* 1819.
SIMMS's *Trappers of New York.*
Life of Morgan Lewis, in JENKINS's *Lives of the Governors of New York.*
Sketch of Charles de Langlade, in vol. VII *of Wisconsin Historical Collections.*
GREEN's *German Element in the War of American Independence.*
TILGHMAN's *Journal.*
MOORE's *Diary of the American Revolution.*
DE COSTA's *Lake George.*
Life of Peter Van Schaick.
WILSON's *Life of Jane McCrea.*
Travels in America in 1795 of the Duke de la Rochefoucauld-Liancourt.
The Gates Papers in the New York Historical Society.
NILES's *Register.*
BOTTA's *American Revolution.*
Gentleman's Magazine.
Remarks on Gen. Burgoyne's State of the Expedition. London, J. Wilkie, 1780.
Letter to Lieut. Gen. Burgoyne, on his Letter to his Constituents. London: T. Becket, 1779.
A Reply to Lieut. Gen. Burgoyne's Letter to his Constituents. London: J. Wilkie, 1779.
BURGOYNE's *State of the Expedition from Canada,* as laid before the House of Commons, by Lieut. Gen. Burgoyne, and verified by evidence; with a collection of authentic documents, and an addition of many circumstances which were prevented from appearing before the House. London: J. Almon, 1780.
A Supplement to the State of the Expedition from Canada, containing Gen. Burgoyne's Orders, respecting the principal Movements and Operations of the Army to the raising of the Siege of Ticonderoga.
A Letter to Lieut. Gen. Burgoyne, occasioned by a second edition of his *State of the Expedition from Canada.* London: G. Kearsley, 1780.
Orderly Book of Lieut. Gen. John Burgoyne, from his entry into the State of New York until his Surrender at Saratoga, 16th Oct., 1777. From

the original manuscript deposited at Washington's Headquarters, Newburgh, N. Y., map, portraits, and fac-simile. Edited by E. B. O'Callaghan, 1860, in Munsell's Historical Series.

D. WILSON's *Life of Jane McCrea*, with an account of Burgoyne's Expedition in 1777. By D. Wilson, New York, 1853.

An Enquiry into, and Remarks upon the Conduct of Lieut. Gen: Burgoyne. The plan of operation for the campaign of 1777, the instructions from the secre·ary of state, and the circumstances that led to the loss of the northern army. London : J. Matthews, 1780.

Essay on Modern Martyrs, with a letter to Gen. Burgoyne London : Payne, 1780.

Dramatic and Poetical Works of the late Lieut. Gen. John Burgoyne; to which is prefixed memoirs of the author, embellished with copper plates. London : C. Whittingham, 1808.

The Substance of Gen. Burgoyne's Speeches, on Mr. Vyner's Motion, on the 26th of May; and upon Mr. Hartley's Motion, on the 28th of May, 1778. With an appendix, containing Gen. Washington's letter to Gen. Burgoyne, etc. London : J. Almon, 1778.

A Brief Examination of the Plan and Conduct of the Northern Expedition in America in 1777. And of the surrender of the army under the command of Lieut. Gen. Burgoyne. London, 1779.

A Letter from Lieut. Gen. Burgoyne to his Constituents, upon his late Resignation; with the correspondence between the secretaries of war and him, relative to his return to America. London : J. Almon, 1779.

Travels in North America, by the MARQUIS DE CHASTELLUX, London, 1787.

INDEX.

Abercrombie's defeat, 14; wagons captured, 360.
Ackland, major John Dyke, 11, 323; described, 83; accident to, 83; wounded, 58, 60; killed, 86, 331; his position in the march, 44; his grenadiers, 275.
Ackland, Lady Harriet, 75, 83, 333, 335; visits American camp, 84; insane, 86; married Brudenell, 86; account of, 331; died, 332.
Adams, col., killed, 402.
Albany, tories executed at, 243.
Allen, capt., 175.
Allen, Ethan, proposals for exchange of, 336.
Allen, Rev., anecdote of, 232.
Ambuscade near Fort Stanwix, 177.
American army at Ticonderoga, 14; lacked force to man the defences, 15; number of, 110, 114; sufferings of, 401; shouting heard in, 54; riflemen, their execution, 10.
Ancrom, major, 200.
Andiatarocte island, 410.
Anstruther, lt. col., 44, 48, 343.
Armstrong, major, defames Arnold, 68.
Arnent, ensign, 175.
Arnold, 16; volunteer to Fort Stanwix, 272; sent to relieve Gansevoort, 208; his ruse, 211; pursues St. Leger, 218; at head of Continentals, 63, 65; his conduct in battle, 67, 68, 325;

Arnold, engages whole British force, 46; his horse killed, 66, 375; wounded, 66; joined Gates, 40; points out Fraser to Morgan, 325; to be provided against, 284; dismissed by Gates, 371; altercation with Balcarras, 371.
Artillery captured, 46; horse employed, 276; N. Y. brass, 25.
Anburey, Thomas, 11, 350, 360, 410; his Travels, 398; on deportment of the captors, 117.

Bacon, Wm. J., dedication to, 3.
Badlam, major, 175.
Baggage trains loaded up for retreat, 70.
Bailey, ensign, 175.
Bailey, gen., 376.
Balcarras, major, 10; attacked, 61, 63; his camp taken, 398; his narrow escape, 14; his position in the march, 54; his testimony, 402; his grenadiers, 275.
Ball, lieut., 175.
Ballads of Burgoyne's expedition, 413.
Ballston, loyalist insurrection in, 144.
Barker, Peter, 328.
Barker's tavern, 315.
Barn containing six pound ball, 391.
Barner, Major, 33.
Bartlett, Dr. John, 307, 309.
Bateaux captured, 90, 93; their location, 38.
Batten kil, battery at 98; design of retreat to, 56; encampment at, 237;

Batten kil, occupied by the Americans, 88; passed, 376; route to Arlington, 278; view on, 378.
Battle ground described, 370.
Battle of 19th Sept., 45, 49; 7th October, 57.
Battle of Saratoga, one of the fifteen decisive battles, 132.
Baum, Col., 129; detached, 232; sent to Bennington, 29, 30; ruse practiced upon, 31; his instructions, 277; failure of, its effect, 173; skirmish of, 299; wounded, 32; house in which he died, 34.
Baxter boys, suspected, 272.
Beadle, laid out West Troy, 441.
Belknap's New Hampshire, 42.
Bellinger, Lieut. Col., 189, 199; Samuel, killed, 189.
Bemis's heights, attack threatened, 321; Gates occupies, 39; not the battle field, 70, 71.
Bennington, battle of, 232; narrative of, 286, 291; expedition, failure of, 35.
Berkshire incident, 301; volunteers, anecdote of, 242.
Bird, lieut., his diary, 154.
Blauvelt, major, killed, 198.
Bleecker, capt., 175.
Blockhouses built, 261.
Bloodgood, S. D. W., 245.
Bloody pond, 236.
Bogardus, lieut., 175.
Boston, British marched to, 116.
Bottles, found at headquarters, 53.
Bouck, Wm. C., 251.
Bowman, Jacob, killed, 189.
Braddock, his defeat planned by Langlade, 11.
Bradley, commodore, 158.
Brant, Joseph, 169; at ambruscade, 177; leader of St. Leger's Indians, 153; Life of, 139.
Brass cannons captured, 35; their vicissitudes, 35; note.
Brattleboro, expedition to, 279.

Breadbeg, John, wounded, 186.
Brent Richard, 385.
Breymann, lieut. col., 10, 13; sent to aid Baum, 32; retreats by night, 33; reinforcements of, 233; his command, 276; his position in the march, 44.
Breymann's hill, 64; breastwork, 64; entrenchments still to be seen, 52.
Breymann, killed, 65, 375.
Bridge, of St. Luke, 298; scouting party at, 299; at Saratoga falls, 37; boats, 412; of boats cut loose, 320.
Brisbin, James, 358.
British army, its superiority, 10; invested Ticonderoga, 13; how disposed at Crown point, 13; occupy Ticonderoga, 18; crossed the Hudson, 37; its entrenchments, remains of, 37; strength of force, 38; order of march, 44; forward movement signalled, 45; route of army, 45; artillery captured, 46; loss of first battle, 49, 50; reconnoissance brings on battle of 7th Oct., 57; seized with dismay at fall of Fraser, 62; retreat of, 62, 72; provisions short, 72; retreat begun, 72, 74; discovered under arms, 90; trap sprung upon, 92; distressed state of the army, 93, 96; completely invested, 98; capitulates, 110; retained as prisoners, 112; piled their arms, 115, 121; took up its march to Boston, 116; standards captured, 194; provisions captured, 238; advanced pickets captured, 245; force of, 276; in line of battle, 322; incident of, 346; his account of the attack on Diamond island, 349; Indian allies, 358; to join Howe, 359; at Crown point, 359;

Index. 451

British army, Langlade's savages at Skenesboro, 360; force of Canadians, 360; stack their arms, 378; camp ground, 382; forded the creek, 383; encamped at Saratoga plain, 412; retreat, cry of, 70.
British treasure, search for, 399; camp, preservation of, 399.
Brooks, col., suggests sending Hon-Yost to St. Leger, 416.
Brookes's regiment, 374; led by Arnold, 375.
Brookes, lieut. gov., 64.
Bronkahorse, killed, 275.
Brown, col. John, attacks Ticonderoga, 346, 347, 348, 349, 352.
Brudenell, chaplain, 77, 85, 86; marries Harriet Ackland, 332.
Brunswick Dragoons described, 30; reduced in numbers, 16; Journal, 37; troops, flank defense, 64.
Brunswickers, parting volley, 66; captured 35; under Riedesel, 20.
Bryan, Alexander, scout, 40, 353.
Buck shot used by Americans, 57.
Buel, major Ezra, 384, 388, 389.
Bullard, Daniel A., 440, 441.
Bullard, Edward F. 441; his address, 370, 377.
Burgoyne, the disasters of his campaign ascribed to his blunders, 9; dissatisfied with his subordinate position under Carleton, 10; his plan for success, 9; his horse in Portugal, 10; arrived in Quebec, 10; sailed up Champlain, 11; encamped at Bouquet, 11; joined by Indians, 11; life of by Fonblanque, 11; his axiom, that the army must not retreat, 12; arrived at Ticonderga, 14; pursues the Americans by water, 23; at Skenesborough, 24; claims victory at Fort Anne, 27; arrives at, 29; obstacles to his progress, 29;

Burgoyne, incipient step to his defeat, 31; arrives at Fort Edward, 36; arrives at Saratoga, 37; selects Schuyler's house as head quarters, 37; his scouting party, 42; ignorant of the American movements, 43; his order of march, 44; rec'd letter from Clinton, 51; his headquarters after the 19th Sept., 53; his strength reduced, 54; rations cut down, 55; calls council of war, 56; orders retreat, 61; his retreat how delayed, 71; mistake in retreat, 80; camp equipage captured, 82; permits lady Ackland to visit American camp, 84; at Schuyler's mansion, 86; his mistress, 87; accused by Mad. Riedesel of burning Schuyler's mansion, 88; said by Lamb to have been accidental, 88; opens road to Fort Edward, 89; responds to appeal of Mad. Riedesel, 96; proposes expedients to his officers, 97; orders retreat, 98; calls council of officers, 99; humanity of, 99; declines to sign the treaty, 109; signs articles, 110; introduced to Gates, 117, 118; his approbation of Gates's conduct to the captives, 122; delivers his sword, 122; testifies to Schuyler's magnanimity, 124; his former reputation, 125; at Tagus, 125; a sybarite, 126; attributes his failure to the administration, 126; Fonblanque's memoir of, 126; coldly received in England, 128; vindicates himself, 128; author of comedies, 128; dies, 128; cut of surrender of sword, 135; intelligence from St. Leger, 172; gets supplies from Fort George, 172; expedition to Bennington planned, 173;

Burgoyne, anecdotes of his campaign, 225; inhabitants flee before his approach, 225; his force in the expedition, 257; Fonblanque's memoir, 276; his instructions to Baum, 278; plunder to be made, 280; dragoons to be mounted, 283; Warner expected to retreat, 284; prisoners to be made, 285; boastful, 288; his head quarters, 315, 325; entertained by Schuyler, 318; retreat ordered and countermanded, 321; his reliance on Fraser, 326; vindicates his policy, 347; letter to Gates respecting Harriet Ackland, 333, 336; do respecting burning Schuyler's house, 337; his relations with Langlade, 358; duped by Schuyler, 342; his estimate of Indian aid, 361; attempt to justify his defeat, 363; complains of Canadian aid, 364; error in regard to his origin, 367; meets Gates, 379; proclamation, vaunting, 404; clothing perforated, 404; his Itinerary, 11; retreat, 11,12.
Burgoyne's hill, 64.
Butler, col., 140, 177; John, 169; messenger to the fort, 200.
Butler, Walter N., captured, 208; imprisoned in Albany, 209; condemned, 213.
Butler's ruse, 182.

Camden, battle of, 131; Gates at battle of, 69.
Canada, Burgoyne's communication with cut off, 55; conquest of, 152; by English, 152, 153.
Canadian horses purchased, 30; provincials, 64, 65.
Canadians captured, 378; desert Burgoyne, 99; reason of, 99; in the army, 360; their position, 44.

Canajoharie, 197.
Canning, E. W. B., 427, 439, 440; his narrative, 301
Cannon taken and retaken, 59; sworn in, 395.
Carillon, troops in, 436.
Carleton, sir Guy, superseded, 9.
Cartridge box plowed up, 443.
Cassassenny, Indian castle, 140.
Castleton, retreat to, 17, 19, 23.
Cayugas join the British, 191.
Chase, ensign, 175.
Chemung, battle of, 192.
Chestertown; ancient cabin, 99.
Chimney point, 12.
Claus, col. Daniel, 140.
Cilley, col., 59
Clerke, Sir F., wounded, 53; died, 63, 69, 390; his drawing of the camp, 397, 398; James, 44; killed, 276.
Clements, Albert, 441; testimony of the surrender, 442.
Clinton, gov. George, 258.
Clinton, Sir Henry, 37, 51; guarded, 44; news from, 108; ascends the Hudson. 222.
Cochran, col., garrisons Fort Edward, 89; col., 251; died, 254.
Cohoes Falls, 42.
Colburn, col., killed, 402.
Connecticut river, expedition to, 279.
Continentals in action, 47; where placed, 321.
Conyne, lieut, 175.
Coon, Mrs. Hannah, 232; escaped, 234; again captured, 235.
Copper head snake venomous, 411.
Corey, John A., 134.
Cornwallis's pursuit of Greene, 42.
Council of war called, 56.
Coveville (Dovogat), British at, 41, 45.
Cow boys, 213, 237.
Cox, col., killed, 180; regiment of, 174, 176.

Creasy sir Edward, 132.
Crouse, Robert, killed, 189.
Crown point occupied, 12; described, 12.
Culloden, battle of, 75.

Davis, capt. John, 180, killed, 188.
Dayton, col., 151.
Dearborne, major Henry, 372.
De Fermoy, fatal act of, 18, 35, 60, 85.
De Peyster, Captain, 358; J. Watts, 18.
Delancey, Edward, 99.
Dennison, ensign, 175.
De Ridder's crossing, 257.
Desertion encouraged, 113.
Diamond island, 346, 349, 352, 410; fight at, 346.
Diefendorf, lieut., 175.
Dillenback, capt., 185; killed, 189.
Donop, colonel, 76.
Douglass, lieut., killed, 15.
Dovogat, halt at in retreat, 80; name defined, 41, 42, 45.
Dragoons, form the van, 13; to be compact, 281, 282.
Draper, Lyman C., 368, 406.
Drayton, col., 158.
Duncan, major, at Oswego, 152, 153.
Dunham, capt. Hezekiah, 264, 357.
Duplesse, captain, 76.
Dwight, president, 164, 176; Theodore, 72, 286.
Dygert, John, killed, 189.

Edgerton, Eleazur, his feat, 299, 300.
Eisenlord, major John, killed, 189.
Eells, Nathaniel, 271.
Elmore, col., 158.
Embarkation suspended, 113.
Ensign, Ezekiel, 240; store of, 72.
Errata, 12.

Farmer costume, 246

Farms settled by Germans, 99
Faxon, Charles H., 99.
Fellows, general, 80, 82; his batteries, 94.
Ferdinand, prince, 11.
Fields, T. W., 5.
First New York regiment, 25.
Fish creek, 315, 400; forded, 8; location of surrender, 118; British encamp at, 37; horses captured at, 256; see Fish kil.
Fish, Hamilton, 134, 439.
Fish kil, same as Fish creek.
Fitch, Andrew, 380.
Fitch, Asa, 41.
Flag, American, first unfurled, 135; how made, 168.
Floating bridge, 18.
Fonblanque, his life of Burgoyne, 11, 88, 126, 332.
Fonda, Jellis, 169.
Foraging parties sent out, 55, 394.
Forbes, major, 392.
Forces of Americans, 110, 114.
Ford, P. C., 141.
Fort Anne, British army at, 29; garrison of, 437; carrying place, 340; retreat to, 23, 54; testimony of Capt. Money, and Burgoyne, 402.
Fort Carillon, 13.
Fort Clinton captured by St. Luc, 160.
Fort Dayton, 174; Willet arrived at, 207.
Fort Edward abandoned, 36; Col. Warner at, 236; defended, 377; garrisoned, 89; held by Starke, 92, 93; Lamb at, 407; retreat to, 24; retreat from, 231; settled by Col. Lydius, 338; why named, 341, 343, 344.
Fort George, 82, 336; garrison of 437; N. Y., artillery at, 25; condition of, 28.
Fort Hardy, 316, 339, 401; account of, 115.

Fort Independence, 13; fired, 18.
Fort Lawrence, 257.
Fort Miller, 33, 85, 341; journey from, 406.
Fort Nicholson, 339.
Fort St. Frederick, 12; built, 12.
Fort Schuyler described, 159; wretched condition of, 160; see Fort Stanwix.
Fort Stanwix, 344 (same as Fort Schuyler); ambush near, 177; carrying place, 197; invested, 158, 167; siege of, 271; stars and stripes first unfurled at, 135; flag presented 135.
Fort Vaudreuil, 13.
Fort Wm. Henry, in ruins, 407.
Forts, description of, 434.
Fowling pieces in common use, 246.
Fox, capt. Christopher, wounded, 189.
Francis, colonel, brings off the rear guard at Ticonderoga, 19; killed, 20, 402.
Fraser, English brigadier, 11, 12; of house of Lovatt, 76; at head of army, 322; his fall, 325; removal of remains, 328; occupies Fort Miller, 37; his brigade, 276; his position in the march, 44; pursues retreating army, 20; wounded, 57, 61; shot by Tim. Murphy, 249; where he fell, 396; his fall witnessed, 373; doubts of, 374; borne off the field, 72; makes his will, 74, 75; funeral 77, 78; his request for burial, 75; house in which he died, 385; site of his death, 318.
Fraser's grave, location of, 78; his skill in retreat, 79; view of, 397.
Freeman's farm, 64; battle of, 71; route of army to, 45, 46; wooded, 323; battle, 324.
French lines, 434; redoubt, 434.
Freneau, Philip, 420.

Frey, major, captive, 199; attempt to kill by his own brother, 187; wounded, 189.
Friends, hospitality of, 408.
Friends' lake, 99.
Frisbie, Oscar, 441.
Frontenac landed at Oswego, 152.
Furnival's regiment, 372, 376.

Gall, German brigadier, 11.
Gansevoort, Gen., 135; declines to surrender, 200, 202, 204; gen., 158; letter to Schuyler, 160, 163; his speech, 165; his force, 168; papers, 151, 157, 159, 164; visits Albany, 219; addresses his fellow soldiers, 220; promoted, 221.
Gardenier, capt. Jacob, 183; Wm., 183, 185; wounded, 189; lieut., Samuel, wounded, 189.
Garneau, quoted, 360, 364.
Gates, correspondence with Burgoyne, 335; deserts de Kalb, 69; supersedes Schuyler, 39; his head quarters, 40; his head quarters threatened, 71, 321; his marquee, its location, 378; magnanimity of towards captives, 117, 121; orders cessation of arms, 101; entertains British generals, 121; his head quarters, 122; neglectful, 130; died, 131; characteristics of, 131 omits to acknowledge important services, 356; incapacity of, 128, 131; disrespectful to Washington, 130; unfavorable conduct of, 68; his controversy with Clerke, 69.
George IV, his ecstacy at the capture of Ticonderoga, 19.
Germaine, George, 11, 19, 363, 403; his neglect to forward orders to Howe, 126, 127.
German chasseurs, 71; colors saved, 116; deserter's cabin, 99; flats, 174, 197; loyalists, 144;

Index.   455

German, troops, how distributed, 276; their employment, 277; women in the army, 255.
Germans cross the Hudson, 40; decline to desert, 113; desert Burgoyne, 99; sustain brunt of action, 61.
Glen's falls, 343; Am., camp at, 92.
Glover, gen., 90, 370; his brigade, 63.
Goodale, gen., 90.
Grandy, Mrs., 232, 235.
Grant, maj., killed, 23.
Graves, capt., killed, 189.
Great Carrying place, 340.
Great redoubt, 51; attacked, 63.
Green, Charles, 269.
Gregg, captain and his dog, 163, 164.
Grenadiers, attack with bayonets, 323.
Groat, lieut., missing, 189.

Hagget, lieut., mortally wounded, 15.
Hair, lieut., 155.
Hale, col. Nathan, vindicated, 22.
Hale, hon. Robert S., 22,
Hamilton, English brigadier, 11; his brigade, 87, 276; his position in the march, 44.
Han-Yerry, anecdote of, 269.
Hardin, col., 135.
Harnage, wounded, 49.
Haskin's place, 99.
Hay, judge, 303.
Helmer, Adam, 174.
Helmer, capt. Frederic, 189.
Herkimer, gen., 145, 146; issues proclamation, 148; summons military, 174; accused of cowardice, 176; ambushed, 177; wounded, 179; line of battle badly formed, 192; died, 196, 198; his origin, 197; monument ordered to, 198; not erected, 199.
Harvey, general, 276; lieut., heroism of, 48.

Hesse-Hanau regiment, 42, 254.
Hessian forces, 275; burial ground, 380.
Hessians, accompanied by tamed animals, 254; characteristics of, 254; posted at Bennington, 286; total defeat of, 290; compelled to retreat, 374; over estimated, 64.
Hill, lieut. col., 24, 26.
Hon-Yost, see Schuyler.
Hoosac river, village on, 298.
Horses purchased in Canada, 30.
Hospital burrying place, 38.
Howe, reasons of his failure, 126, 127.
Hubbardton, army remains at, 20; battle of, 21, 23, 402.
Hubbardton, retreat to, 19.
Hudson stream, 345.
Hunt, lieut. col., killed, 189.

Indians, alarmed by Hon-Yost, 214; captured, 368; desert Burgoyne, 36, 99; reasons of, 99; friendly, 159, 165; hostile, 161; gigantic, 255; join British at Skenesboro, 360; join Burgoyne, 11; led by St. Luc and Langlade, 11; restrained, 361; their line of march, 153; their position, 44; to invade Fort Schuyler, 140; vengeance threatened, 205; killed at Oriskany, 191, 195.
Iron chain, 14.
Irwine, George, 350.

Jackson, col., 64.
Jay, John, letter to Gov. Morris, 142.
Jemison, Mary, 191, 192.
Jogues, Father, 409.
Johnson, capt., 175.
Johnson, col. John, 140, 169, 117; his regiment, 193; spoil of his camp, 194; companies, 374.
Johnson, Sir William, 36.

Johnstown, Catholic tories, 144.
Jones, capt., killed, 49; surgeon, wounded, 94, 316.

Kalb, de, deserted by Gates, 69.
Kalm, criticise Am. forts, 343.
Killed, how buried, 66,
Kingston, colonel, adjt. gen., 10; sent to propose cessation of arms, 100; blindfolded, 100.
Kirkland, Rev., his report, 216,
Kleprattle, major Enos, killed, 189.
Klock, regiment of 174.
Kosciusko, engineer, 40, 437; battle ground selected by, 370.
Kroonpunt, 12.

Lake George, 344; its altitude, 409; Oswego bass in, 409; portage, 14; outlet, 15.
Lake Sacrament, 409.
Lakes, entrance to, 152.
Lamb, 73; claims the burning of Schuyler mansion to have been accidental, 88; his adventure, 412; serjeant, statement of, 333; serjt., his trip for provisions, 38, 406; col. serjt. R., 18; his account of the action at Ft. Anne. 26, 27.
Lamb's Memoirs, 43.
Lansing, Mrs. Abram, 135,
Lansing house, 377.
Lansing's saw mill, 37.
Larned, his position, 370; in battle of 7th Oct., 58, 64, 96.
Leggett's house, 52.
Lewis, col. Morgan. 307, 309, 310.
Lewis, ensign, 175.
Lewis, qr. master-gen., 70.
Lincoln, major-gen., 347; his position, 370, 371; surprised Ticonderoga, 54; wounded, 71, 376.
Liquor and rations, 56.
Little White creek, 298.
Livingston, col., 67.

Langlade, Charles, 11; planned the defeat of Braddock, 11, 358, 368.
London Universal Magazine, 193,
Long, colonel, 17; his retreat, 23. 24, 26.
Lord, lieut., 347.
Lossing, Benson, J., 131, 134, 439; his Field Book of the Revolution, 125.
Loudon's ferry, 39.
Lovelass, executed, 268, 356, 357; how buried, 357.
Loyalist insurrection in Ballston, 144.
Lydius, Catherine, born, 338.
Lydius, John Henry, 338.
Lyman, gen. Phineas, 339.
Lynd, lt. col., 44.

Madison, corporal, 163.
Magee, ensign, 175.
Manchester pass, 278; retreat to, 24.
Marquizee, engineer, 162,
Marvin, James M., 440, 441.
Mattoon, gen. Ebenezer, 62, 368; his letter to Schuyler describing the battle, 369; birth place, 380.
McClenner, lieut., 175.
McCrea, Jane, 29, 227, 302, 338.
McCreedy, Mr., 441.
McDale, his feat, 244.
McDonald, Johnstown tory, 144; killed, 184.
McLane, 372.
McNiel, wounded, 258.
Mellon, lt. col., 167, 200.
Messessaugues, 155.
Mill creek, depot of provisions at, 238,
Miller, Adam, 176, 184.
Mohawk river and falls, 345.
Mohawks destroy Crown point, 12; inimical, 149; join the British, 36; their sufferings, 192; pursued by Oneidas, 192.

Money, captain, 69; heads an Indian party, 26; testimony of, 402; wounded, 63.
Montcalm defeats Abercrombie, 14.
Montgomery, capt., 27.
Monument suggested. 133, 327; association organized, 134; seal of, 135.
Morgan, 61, 319, 386; attacks the whole British force, 46; his position, 321, 323; his appearance, 119; in action of 7th Oct., 58; posts riflemen, 370, 372; surprised, 90; his corps brought on the battle. 3 92, 394.
Morrison Norman, 304.
Mosely, col., arrived, 376, 377.
Mount Defiance, 14; cannon conveyed to, 17; taken, 348.
Mount Hope, 14; described, 15.
Mount Independence, 435, 436.
Mowery, Leroy, 440, 441.
Murphy, Timothy, 62; shot Fraser, 249; his prowess, 250; anecdote of, 250, 251.
Muskets not common, 294.

Neilson and Benson, scouts, 258; feat of, 240; his success against the tories, 228; killed and scalped, 230.
Neilson's account of the battle field, 69; of the action of Fort Anne, 27; Neilson's barn, attack on, 56.
New England aroused, 320.
New Hampshire regiment, feat of marching, 42.
Niagara fort, fall of, 152.
Nixon, gen., his position, 370; captures a picket and bateaux, 90; ordered to attack, 91.
Non combatants captured, 268.

Ogden, Miss Caroline, 251.
Oneida Indians, friendly, 149.
Oneidas pursued Mohawks, 192.
Onondaga country invaded, 152.

Onondagas join the British, 192.
Oriskany, 174; creek, 175 269; battle ground, 177; defeat of provincials not confirmed, 186; number killed, 187.
Oswegatchie, tories at, 140.
Oswego, bass in Lake George, 409; occupied by armies, 152; St. Leger at, 150.
Ottawas expected, 11; their bravery, 11.
Otter creek, 279.

Page, Elizabeth, Stark's wife, 426.
Palatine tories, 145.
Palmer, Judge Beriah, 123.
Palmer, lieut., 304; killed, 305, 313.
Paris, col., 176; murdered, 186.
Parker, John M., 356.
Parliamentary history, 124.
Partridge, Dr. Oliver, 302.
Patterson's brigade, 63, 90.
Payn, Charles H., 440, 441.
Peters's corps, 278, 281.
Petersham, aid, 44, 276; adj't gen., 96.
Petrie, Dr., 196; lieut., killed, 189.
Pettingill, Samuel, killed, 188.
Phillips, maj. general, a distinguished artillery officer, 10, 13; ascends Mt. Defiance, 17; at Fort Anne, 26; on the retreat, 87; retained in captivity, 113; his command, 276; his artillery, 276; his position in the march, 44; lieut., wounded and died, 50.
Place d'armes, 54.
Point a la Cheveleure, 12.
Poor, gen., in battle of the 7th Oct., 58.
Potato diggers captured, 55.
Potts, Dr., 336.
Powell, brig. gen., 347.
Prisoners taken, 66.
Proctor defeated, 35.

Prospect hill cemetery, 443.
Provisions secreted, 239.
Pruyn, John V. L., 439, 440.
Putnam, Israel, 340; saves powder magazine, 341.
Putnam's creek, 12, 13.

Quackenboss, Abraham D., 273.
Quaker springs, 45.
Queen Anne's war, 338.

Rations of British cut down, 56.
Rations of liquors, 56.
Rattlesnake venomous, 411.
Reconnoissance in force, 56.
Redman, John, 66.
Relics of the battle, 316.
Remembrance, 205, 212.
Richards, J. W, his narrative, 300.
Riedesel, Madame, 43, 72; her services to the wounded, 94; retreats to a cellar, 94; engraving of house and cellar, 95; divides her provisions with the starving, 96; her appearance in American camp, 119; meets Gen. Schuyler, 120; her house attacked, 315; at Fort Edward, 343; describes death of Fraser, 74; admired, 82; her fortitude, 87.
Riedesel, maj. gen., his experience, 10; drilled his troops in Canada, 10; encamped on Crown point, 12, 13; opposed to the expedition of Baum, 30; at Dovogat, 42; his command, 45; saves the army from route, 47; location of the hospital, 52; leads van of British retreat, 79; condemns the order to halt in retreat, 80; offers to cover the retreat, 87; proposes retreat, 98; retained by congress in captivity, 113; addresses his troops on the surrender, 115; saves German colors, 116; his command, 276;

Riedesel, his dragoons to be mounted, 278; occupies Fort Miller, 342; buried bateaux in the fort, 342; quartered at Fort Amherst, 342; pronunciation of name, 370; his house, relic of, 377; his memoirs translated, 5; portrait of, 81.
Rochefaucauld-Liancourt, 381.
Rockingham, 279.
Rodman, Thomas P., 423.
Roff, Johannis, 166 (see Roof).
Rogers, Abraham Yates, residence of, 37.
Rogers's house, 57.
Roman Catholic Scotch tories, 144.
Rome, Fort Stanwix, 197.
Roof, col. John, 196, 197.
Roof's village (Canajoharie,) 197.
Royal Greens, 154.
Royal George flag ship, 13.

Sabbath day forbid, 302.
Sabbath day point, fight at, 230; point why so named, 230.
Sammons, Frederick, scout, 190.
Sammons, lieut Jacob, 183, 188.
Saratoga, battle of, 71; trophies of, 114; British army encamped at, 37, 412; monument association, incorporated, 438; state appropriation, 439; officers of, 440.
Scalp point, 12.
Schoharie disaffection, 145; militia at Fort Edward, 146.
Schroon lake scouts, 258.
Schuyler, gen., 159; at Fort Edward, 24; at Fort Anne, 28; obstructs the roads, 29; sends relief to Gansevoort, 208; prejudices against, 143; superseded, 39, 128; his influence on the army, 129; effect of his supersedure, 317; fortitude of, 271; his courtesy to Mad. Riedesel, 120; mansion in Albany, 124; entertains British officers, 123;

Index. 459

Schuyler, value of his property destroyed, 123; Hon Yost, his death, 218; his brother discharged, 218; Hon Yost, his ruse, 212, 213, 214; deserts St. Leger, 218; Philip, 441.
Schuyler's evidence, 48.
Schuyler, John, 381.
Schuyler's house, its location, 38; burnt, 333; ruins of, 401; mansion rebuilt in 15 days, 88; burning said to be accidental, 88; mills, 317.
Schuylerville, British encamp at, 37; large gathering at, 442.
Scout, A. Bryan, 354, 356.
Seal of Monument Association, 135.
Second engagement, where begun, 71.
Seeber, capt. Henry, 175, 176.
Seeber, capt. Jacob, 180, 189.
Seeber, lieut. Wm., 189.
Seeley, Joseph, 262.
Senecas at Fort Stanwix, 191; killed, 192;
Sergeant's wife, adventure of, 85, 408.
Settlers below Fort Edward, character of, 36.
Seven years' war, 79.
Sexagenary, 245.
Seymour, Horatio, 134, 439, 440.
Sheldon, Simon, 443.
Shelly, sergt., 27.
Sherwood, captain, 278, 281.
Shirley, gen., 152.
Shoemaker, Mr., tory, 208.
Shrimpton, capt., 20.
Sickness in American army, 322.
Silliman's travels, 346, 384.
Singleton, lieut., captured, 195.
Skeleton of British grenadier, 396, 427.
Skene, col., 282; major, 29; misleads Baum, 32, 33; brilliant success of, 173; commanded at Bennington, 286; road cut for, 28.

Skenesborough, 11; British take, 24; retreat to, 17; garrison, of, 437; Indians arrived at, 360.
Smith's house, 53, 72.
Snakes of Diamond island, 410.
Snell, Jacob, killed, 189.
Sorel river, 15.
Southerland, gen., 80.
Sparr, ensign attacked, 161.
Specht, German brigadier, 11; attacked, 61; captured, 65; his regiment, remarkable, 42, 254.
Spencer, Thomas, half breed, 140; his speech, 141, 149.
Spike, Daniel, 357.
Sprouts of the Mohawk, 39.
Stafford, narrative of, 286.
Stansbury, Peter, 328.
Stark, anecdotes of, 232; brilliant success of, 173; commanded at Bennington, 286; cuts off Baum, 31; holds Fort Edward, 92; presides at court martial, 268, 357; Molly, 426.
St. Clair in command at Ticonderoga, 13; evacuates, 17, 18.
Steese, Caty, wounded, 166.
Stevens, col., 16.
Stillwater, battle so called, 71.
St. Leger, 129; to make a diversion on the Mohawk, 9; repulse of, 128; expedition of described, 139; began his march upon Fort Schuyler, 151; force of his army, 153; paper captured, 154; his letter to Bird, 157; encouraged murders, 164; his arrival before Fort Schuyler, 168; his rank, 168; summons the fort, 169, 170; communicates with Burgoyne, 172; advance of, 173; ambushes Herkimer, 177; his statement of the battle, 187; his papers captured, 194; suggests capitulation, 200; his humanity, 201; armistice proposed, 203;

St. Leger, renews summons, 204; appeals to Tryon county, 205; pardon promised to his adherents, 210; raises the siege, 211; sends for Hon Yost Schuyler, 214; commences his retreat, 217; plundered by his own Indians, 217; retreated by the way of Oneida lake, 217; report to Burgoyne, 217; capture of his escritoire and papers, 219; hastened back to Oswego and thence to Montreal, 219; fell back on Oswego, 342; spy sent back to, 416; advance of, 173.

St. Luc, chevalier, 11; influence with Indians, 360, 362, 364, 368.

St. Luke's bridge, 298.

Stockwell, lieut., 175, 271; leaves the fort, 206, 207.

Stone, col. Wm. L., 63.

Stone, Wm. L., 439, 440.

Stoner, Nicholas, trapper, 67.

Street, Alfred B., 134,

Strover, George, 88, 268, 431.

Strover, John, 356, 357.

Sugar-loaf hill, 14, 16; road cut to, 17.

Surrender, treaty of proposed, 99; articles of, 102-107; conduct of troops in piling their arms, 115; terms signed, 443; view of field of, 400.

Swart, Dirk, 271.

Swartwout, capt., 178.

Sword's house, 42, 43, 44, 45.

Tarleton, his march, 42.

Tayler house, 53, 72.

Taylor, Capt., 348.

Teasse, Mrs., her narrative, 309.

Teff, A. C., 439.

Ten Broeck, gen., 61.

Terms of capitulation, 110; not complied with by congress, 112.

Thames, victory of the, 35.

Thanksgiving sermon on the surrender, 129.

Throckmorton, B. W., 441.

Ticonderoga, 12, 13; attack on, 54; evacuated, 17; garrison of, 276, 346; to fall, 140; retreat from, 402; why abandoned, 342.

Timmerman, Jacob, 187.

Tories captured and executed at Albany, 243; in Col. Johnson's force, 140.

Townshend, Dr., 69.

Tory account of the Bennington affair, 291.

Tracy, Mrs. John, 125.

Treaty of surrender decided upon, 99–107.

Tree marking spot of Fraser's fall, 57.

Troops of Gates at time of treaty, 110.

Trophies of Saratoga, 114.

Trumbull, Col. John, 16.

Tryon county appealed to, 205; alarm in, 139; disaffection in, 142, 146.

Twiss examines, Sugar-loaf hill, 16.

Tyrrell, killed, 67.

Uncle, Mohawks so called, 149.

Union village, 235.

Van Benschoten, capt., 175.

Van Courtlandt, Pierre, 146.

Vandenburgh's, E., 230.

Van Rensselaer, Robert, 144.

Van Rensselaer, col. Henry, 24, 25.

Van Rensselaers, their influence in the war, 25.

Van Schaick, col., 146.

Van Schaick's island, 39; reason for fortifying, 39; bridge, 298.

Van Sluyck killed, 180, 189.

Van Vechten, Dirk, 231.

Van Vechten's cove, 41.

Varick, Richard, 124.

Victory, village of, 442.

Virginia riflemen, valor of, 403.
Visscher, regiment of, 174, 178, 179; the killed in, 188.

Wagons and carriages to be captured, 280.
Wallace, lieut. William, 67.
Walloomsac river, 299.
Walradt, Henry, 189.
Walter, George, 176.
Walworth, Mrs. Ellen Hardin, 135, 441.
Warner, col. Seth in command of rear guard, 19; characterized, 20; at Fort Edward, 236; wounded, 236; expected to retreat, 284; calls out militia, 286.
Watts, captain, 154.
Watts, maj., 177, 182; wounded, 189, 190.
Wayne, 16.
Welch, Alonzo, reburies British remains, 38.
Wesson's regiment, 146.
West-Chester cow boys, 213.
West Troy, laid out, 441.
Weston, col., 208.
Wheat field foraged upon, 57.
White, judge, 269.
Whitehall, retreat to, 17.
Whitehall turnpike, 356.
Whitestown, 174.

Wilbur's basin, 43, 72, 77.
Wilcox, William, 438.
Wilkinson, 59, 85, 91, 128, 130; reconnoitres British position, 57; corrected, 399, 370; describes Mt. Hope, 15;· on Arnold, 68; his memoirs, 20.
Willard's mountain, 77, 376.
Willett, col. Marinus, 159, 175, 200; declines to surrender, 202; popular, 206; leaves the fort, 206; his sortie, 193; judge advocate, 209; sword voted to, 195; adventure, 271.
Williams, col. Otho, his march, 42.
Williams, major, 44, 63.
Willsborough, Burgoyne at, 11.
Wolves, cry of on battle field, 55.
Women in the army, 248; strip the dead, 66, 248.
Wood creek, 155; obstructed, 29, 156, 340; American flotilla overtaken at, 23.
Woodruff, Samuel, his narrative, 63, 186, 192, 314, 327; removes Arnold, 68.
Wyandot Panther, 306, 309.

Yankee Doodle adopted as a national hymn, 379.
Yorktown, surrender of, 133.
Younglove, Dr. Moses, 186, 189.

www.ingramcontent.com/pod-product-compliance
Lightning Source LLC
Chambersburg PA
CBHW051847300426
44117CB00006B/294